YEMEN ENDURES

GINNY HILL

Yemen Endures

Civil War, Saudi Adventurism and the Future of Arabia

OXFORD
UNIVERSITY PRESS

OXFORD
UNIVERSITY PRESS

Oxford University Press is a department of the
University of Oxford. It furthers the University's objective
of excellence in research, scholarship, and education
by publishing worldwide.

Oxford   New York

Auckland   Cape Town   Dar es Salaam   Hong Kong   Karachi
Kuala Lumpur   Madrid   Melbourne   Mexico City   Nairobi
New Delhi   Shanghai   Taipei   Toronto

With offices in

Argentina   Austria   Brazil   Chile   Czech Republic   France   Greece
Guatemala   Hungary   Italy   Japan   Poland   Portugal   Singapore
South Korea   Switzerland   Thailand   Turkey   Ukraine   Vietnam

Oxford is a registered trade mark of Oxford University Press
in the UK and certain other countries.

Published in the United States of America by
Oxford University Press
198 Madison Avenue, New York, NY 10016

Library of Congress Cataloging-in-Publication Data is available
Ginny Hill.
Yemen Endures: Civil War, Saudi Adventurism and the Future of Arabia.
ISBN: 9780190842369

Printed in the United Kingdom by Bell and Bain Ltd, Glasgow

In memory of Chris Boucek and Ibrahim Mothana

CONTENTS

CONTENTS

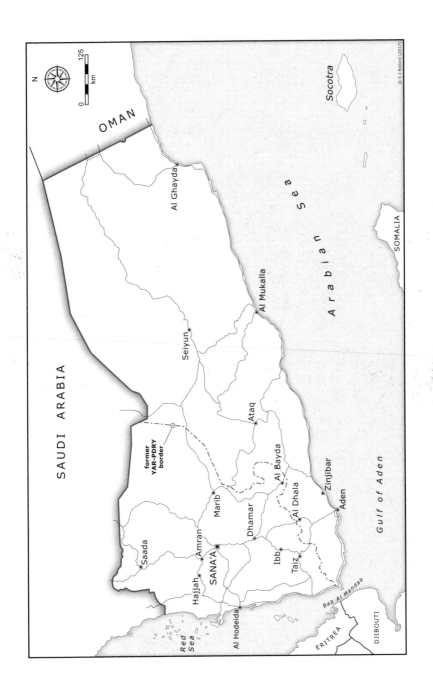

SAUDI ARABIA

OMAN

N

0 125
km

Red Sea

Saada

Hajjah

Amran

SANA'A

Al Hodeida

Marib

Dhamar

Ibb

Taiz

former
YAR-PDRY
border

Al Bayda

Al Dhala

Zinjibar

Aden

Seiyun

Al Ghayda

Al Mukalla

Ataq

Arabian Sea

Socotra

SOMALIA

Gulf of Aden

Bab Al Mandab

ERITREA

DJIBOUTI

© S J Ballard (2017)

PREFACE

Truth is elusive in Yemen. A child plays in a street in the mountain capital, Sana'a. He runs along wearing oversize plastic sandals, shouting to his older brothers to slow down. 'Stop!' he cries. An afternoon crowd of male qat-chewers idly observe the young boys, slumped in the dust, their backs resting against a breeze-block wall. The men's cheeks bulge, skin stretched taut. Tiny green fragments of masticated qat leaves spatter their lips.

Today, as every day, spectators sit knees akimbo, watching Allah's street show. Each man hitches his ankle-length white robe around the top of his shins. Fingers twitch inside a flimsy plastic bag, nestled in the robe's hammock folds, plucking and stripping fresh qat leaves from their stalks. If I approach the men with my notebook and ask them to describe the scene they just witnessed, one will say: 'I saw the boy! He had plastic sandals on his feet.' Another will disagree: 'He was barefoot and there was dirt on his face.' A third, older man thinks the little boy had the look of a djinn about him.[1]

This is how it is with the truth in Yemen. There are many versions of the same moment, and each of them is somehow valid. Eyewitnesses are universally inconsistent, but in Yemen the truth is especially fluid. It is often elaborate, sometimes unbelievable and always many-layered. Above all, Yemen is a world of relationships, not institutions, and each version of events that is revealed to you depends on the speaker's assessment of your connections and suspected affiliations. You may be tested with deliberate misinformation many times over before you are rewarded with genuine opinions. People may take weeks, or months, to allow their deeper truths to emerge.

PREFACE

For more than three decades, during the long-running presidency of Ali Abdullah Saleh, Yemenis learned to function in a system of power that thrived on speculation, denial and false allegations. Saleh's decision-making was highly personalized and chaotic, and he deliberately fostered confusion. Saleh's wily political tactics were so baffling and erratic that even ministers and members of parliament didn't always entirely understand how things got done—and those who did were reluctant to admit it. Senior officials survived by restricting themselves to their own immediate sphere of influence, which meant that few people had a reliable grasp of the links between events or the motivations of prominent figures.

Even after Saleh's demotion from the presidency in 2011 and the elevation of his deputy Abdu Rabbu Mansour Hadi in 2012, ministers remained nominally in charge but the edifice of government retained an air of illusion. Civil servants occasionally performed the functions expected of a state bureaucracy, but power was not effectively structured through formal institutions. Indeed, much of Saleh's informal power base endured. Since the outbreak of civil war in March 2015, Hadi's flight from Yemen to Saudi Arabia, and the start of the Saudi-led air campaign in Yemen, the culture of feint and slander continues to be stoked by factional politics and a highly partisan media. As a result, what Yemenis claim is happening in their country is often extremely confusing, but sometimes much more interesting than what might really be going on.

Yemenis are acutely sensitive to this tapestry of truth, but it takes time for foreigners to adjust to the subtle triggers in play.[2] Fortunately, Yemenis sit still in one place most afternoons, chewing qat and looking to talk. Conventional economic activity grinds to a halt in time for midday prayers but afterwards, at qat chews, business carries on by other means. Marriage bargains, commercial deals and political alliances become possible when all parties unwrap their qat bundles and sit down to chew. (Qat is a drug with its own rituals. It is classified as a Class A narcotic by the US Drug Enforcement Agency, and US diplomats in Sana'a have long been forbidden to chew. The British government didn't classify qat until 2013, or ban it until 2014, accounting both for the presence of British diplomats at qat sessions in Sana'a and the sale of qat on the Edgware Road in London in the preceding years.)

PREFACE

Even in 2015, despite the privations of war, the qat market proved to be highly resilient.

When I arrived in Yemen for the first time in 2006, 'Do you like qat?' was often the second question—after 'Where are you from?'—that fell from the lips of my taxi drivers. If my driver was chewing when he asked me, bubbles of green saliva would froth and pop in the creases at the edges of his mouth. If my answer was 'yes', I risked the gift of a qat twig, plucked from the driver's lap and thrust towards me in the back seat of his Toyota Cressida. The fresh leaves of the *Catha edulis* plant produce an amphetamine with the dubious side-effects of constipation, impotence, insomnia and depression. They taste and smell like munching a garden shrub, but refusing to chew is like declining a Friday night drink with work colleagues in a British pub—refusal evokes disappointment and suspicion; it inhibits social bonding.

I went to a qat chew at least once a week when I was living in Yemen. In the first hour after lunch, guests are usually restless and the discussion is scattered. Here and there, a topic of conversation wells up and bursts. I might start an exploratory thread of conversation with my neighbour, but soon we are both distracted by an argument in the far corner. Gradually, as a group, we settle down, masticating and ruminating. Qat makes us all content and reflective. We are following one single conversation now, speaking in turns. I have a slimy wodge of qat leaves crammed into my left cheek and I'm holding a qat posy in both my hands. As the afternoon wears on, I strain harder to hear what people are saying, because clear speech is distorted by hamster cheeks packed with qat.

Long, barefoot afternoons lounging on cushions among new friends in an airless, smoke-filled room can induce powerful feelings of confidence and intimacy, but unless you're among a group of close confidants you must tread carefully with your comments and remember that the qat parley is—above all—about putting in a good performance. Qat itself distorts the discussion. So, when the qat party breaks at the end of the afternoon and men peel away in the plum-coloured twilight, it's the poetry of each man's proclamation that distinguishes the moment. The speaker's apparent sincerity of feeling, his goodwill and intent—these are the things that matter, not the accuracy of what he has said.

PREFACE

To understand Yemen, you need to be able to hold multiple realities in mind simultaneously, and accept that things are not always quite what they seem. Yemen has suffered from this because most experienced foreign journalists don't stay very long in Sana'a. During Saleh's presidency, they were in and out in a flash: a few weeks to write a colour piece after the latest terrorist attack, and a predictable feature about qat. With a few notable exceptions, Western newspapers relied on rookie freelancers, who were already living in Sana'a when the 'Arab Spring' protests started, to cover the 2011 uprising. Iona Craig, Tom Finn and Laura Kasinof were among those who braved bullets, grenades and water cannon to tell their stories, rising more than admirably to the challenge. Since 2015, journalists reporting in Yemen face even greater challenges.

When I moved to Sana'a as a freelance reporter in 2006, Yemen was a low-value news country, and I was the only Western correspondent working more or less full-time for British and American media. I spent a great deal of time pitching stories to news editors, who were largely indifferent to the intricacies of Yemeni politics. I stayed for a year, and I returned in 2008 to write a briefing paper for the British think tank Chatham House, highlighting the extent of elite corruption and flagging up early signs of infighting within Saleh's regime.[3]

In January 2010, I set up the Chatham House Yemen Forum, a global policy consortium, marking my transition from freelance journalist to analyst and policy advisor. Chatham House opens its doors to diplomats, academics, politicians and activists, and facilitates discussions between a range of groups and stakeholders. For four years my job was to talk to all sides, understand the internal logic of each stance and chart the interplay between these different positions. It meant building trust with factions that were diametrically opposed to one another, and maintaining enough independence to move between them—in one incident in late 2011, passing between Saleh's palace and the camp of a rival military general in the space of an hour (p.227–234).

In 2013, I stood down from my position at Chatham House, and started work as an independent consultant, providing support to policymaking in fragile and conflict-affected environments. The following year, the United Nations Security Council authorised sanctions against three named individuals in Yemen, including Ali Abdullah Saleh; six months later, the Security Council added Ahmed Ali Abdullah Saleh and Abdulmalik al-Houthi to the UN sanctions list. In April 2015, I joined the United Nations Panel of Experts on Yemen, advising the Security Council on implementation of the sanctions measures, comprising an asset freeze and a travel ban. I served in this consultancy post, as armed groups expert, until March 2016.[4]

I conducted several hundred interviews during my research for this book, which spans my career as a journalist (2006–2009) as well as my time as a Chatham House analyst (2010–2013) and an independent consultant (2014–2017); however, it reflects my personal opinions.[5] Although I have made considerable efforts to verify my sources' claims, I cannot be certain that I have eliminated all errors of perception on my part, nor on theirs. As a result, what follows should be treated as informed comment; at the very least, it reveals my sources' perceptions of the chief protagonists, of each other, and themselves at the time at which we spoke, and this in itself offers an insight of sort into Yemeni politics.

Most of the interviews took place in person in Yemen, Saudi Arabia, the USA and the UK, but I spoke to a number of sources by Skype, WhatsApp or telephone. More than a hundred people were unwilling to speak on the record, so I have allocated a unique reference number to each of these sources in the footnotes.[6] In most cases I have also indicated when and where these interviews took place.

Thanks are due to all sources who agreed to be quoted and to everyone who read and commented on the text, including Louisa Loveluck, who helped with fact-checking. The success of the Chatham House Yemen Forum lay in the strength of its network, and this book has benefited from extensive discussions with the forum's many contributors and supporters, including good friends and close associates in Yemen. In addition, I owe generous thanks to former colleagues at Chatham House—in the Middle East and North Africa programme, and beyond—who worked with me on the Yemen Forum, but especially warm thanks are due to Kate Nevens, Léonie Northedge, Peter Salisbury and Rob Lowe.

On a personal note, I'm grateful to Louise Lee Jones for suggesting that I go to Yemen in the first place, to Shunmay Yeung for giving me a friendly shove and to Catherine Goodman for being the first link in the

PREFACE

chain. Frank Gardner and Rachel Reid both gave me early encourage-
ment. Friends and family did their best to keep me rooted when I came
back home to London and patiently saw me through the most restless
stages. M.B. Thoren kept me going at what I thought was the very end,
and Meryl Evans helped me to cross the finishing line.

INTRODUCTION

When I first arrived in Yemen in 2006, this hybrid state—part dicta-torship, part democracy—stood at a crossroads. Could its leader, President Ali Abdullah Saleh, steer the country towards a more stable and prosperous future, or would he and his rivals plunder the failing economy and fight amongst themselves? This book records the choices they made, and it is written as a contemporary history.

Yemen Endures documents corruption, revolution, civil war and tragic, squandered potential. It charts Saleh's presidency, as well as the 'Arab Spring' protests that led to him losing office. It explains how Saleh went on to form an expedient alliance with an armed group, the Houthis, whom he had previously persecuted while he still held power. It records the circumstances that prompted Saudi Arabia to start an air campaign against Saleh and the Houthis in March 2015, which in parallel with fighting between rival domestic groups and according to United Nations estimates had killed at least 10,000 civilians nearly two years later.[1] It also exposes significant failures in Western foreign policy.

Yemen Endures introduces the reader to a complex political culture and offers a series of face-to-face character portraits, rendering regime play-ers, rebels and activists in their own words. To the uninitiated, Yemen is certainly confusing and unpredictable—a state of affairs perpetuated by the absence of reliable hard facts, the quixotic influence of qat and a prevalence of AK-47s. Even to the initiated (and to Yemenis themselves), there are moments when it feels that mayhem is close to the surface.

Yet society and politics are undoubtedly governed by an underlying logic, which regulates and constrains Yemen's occasionally chaotic ten-

1

dencies. Under Saleh's protracted leadership, competing tribal, regional, religious and political interests agreed to hold themselves in check by a tacit acceptance of balance. This implicit system of power-sharing bound itself together through a dense network of personal relationships, which—in effect—formed the foundation of the regime. Access to, or exclusion from, this system was defined by marriage, military stipends, business contracts and political pay-offs. Personal interests trumped the authority of formal institutions in almost every instance.

For thirty-three years, Saleh played this system with relative ease. He co-opted his rivals and set them against each other, with an uncanny instinct for the degree of stress and strain that the system could withstand. He also exploited outside interests to his own advantage, confident that foreign emissaries could never match his intimate grasp of patronage dynamics. However, during the first decade of the twenty-first century, the underlying balance began to slip out of kilter. Saleh's efforts to reapportion military and economic benefits to the advantage of his eldest son, Ahmed Ali, threatened the fundamental basis of the elite power-sharing agreement.

In essence, Saleh governed by sharing the proceeds of crude oil sales, often using informal—rather than formal—channels. However, in 2002, Yemen hit peak oil, and from that point on—despite rising global oil prices—Saleh's patronage network became inherently unsustainable. At the same time, while elite rivals squabbled over their relative distribution of favours, increasing numbers of Yemeni citizens began to lose faith in the system altogether. During the 2000s, the three main groups posing an explicit security challenge to Saleh's regime—al-Qaeda, southern separatists and the Houthi rebels—all developed powerful messages about political exclusion and social justice.

By 2011, on the eve of the 'Arab Spring' uprising, it seemed there were hardly any resources left for ordinary Yemenis to share among themselves. After three decades of sustained looting of state assets, Yemen sat at the wrong end of almost every human development league table, keeping company with many countries in sub-Saharan Africa. Development indicators offered a miserable litany of hunger, child stunting and women dying in childbirth. Children and young people under the age of twenty-five made up three-quarters of the population, but youth unemployment was sky-high and the country's economic prospects offered no comfort. Parliamentary politics—paralysed by corruption and factional interests—had become rotten, dysfunctional and unresponsive.

In January 2011, a group of university students marched on the streets of the capital, Sana'a—inspired by a successful revolt in Zine el Abidine Ben Ali's Tunisia—aiming to stake a claim in their country's future. Within a month, hundreds of thousands of women and men were gathering peacefully at symbolic 'Change Square' sites in cities across the country to demand Saleh's downfall, and an end to corruption. Initially, the protesters spoke with one clear voice: they wanted a legitimate government, which was capable of striking a new balance between the regime and state, and between the state and society. As time went on, the protest movement itself fell prey to the politics of balance.

This book tells the dramatic story of the 2011 uprising, and charts the course of diplomatic negotiations that led to Saleh's resignation from power. It exposes a ruthless and vicious power struggle inside Saleh's regime, which predated the popular uprising, then gradually hijacked it, and remains unresolved. It argues that failure to broker a viable power-sharing agreement—firstly within the old regime, and secondly between established and emerging power centres—rather than formal state failure, sabotaged the political transition process. And yet it also reveals the extent to which widespread self-interest and profiteering continue to stifle the country's future potential, despite the transition of power from Saleh to his former deputy, Abdu Rabbu Mansour Hadi in February 2012.[2]

For several years in the immediate aftermath of the 'Arab Spring' uprising, diplomats spoke of Yemen's controlled transition as a rare success story. Compared to events in Syria, Libya and Egypt, Yemen appeared to be relatively stable. However, in 2014, the Houthis—who belong to a unique Shia sect, the Zaydis—marched out of the northern mountains, overran the capital, Sana'a, and forced Hadi to flee the country. Saudi Arabia's decision to intervene by launching air strikes in March 2015, on the basis that Iran was backing the Houthis, has implications for the internal politics of both Yemen and Saudi, as well as Riyadh's future relations with Sana'a, Aden, and Tehran.

This book sets the problem of weak, unstable government in the historical context of long-term state formation. It starts by exploring the tentative construction of authority under the historic Zaydi Shi'i Imamate, a theocratic system of government that dominated the northern highlands for a thousand years (Chapter 1). It charts intensified pressure for modern statehood during the twentieth century, set in motion by the demise of the Ottoman Empire, the growth of Arab nationalism and the collapse of British colonialism. In 1962, Egyptian-backed revolutionaries deposed the incumbent Imam in Sana'a and established a military republic, supposedly embarking on the twin processes of modernization and state-building. Instead, this Cold War power-shift birthed a behemoth of mafia-style corruption when mid-ranking army commander Ali Abdullah Saleh came to power in the late 1970s (Chapter 2).

Saleh dominated national life for more than three decades—first as leader of the Yemen Arab Republic (North Yemen) and then, after a 1990 merger with the People's Democratic Republic of Yemen (South Yemen), as head of the unified republic. In a country with an innovative record of killing off its heads of state, Saleh's longevity is a remarkable feat. His promotion in 1978 followed a coordinated double murder in which assassins killed the presidents of North Yemen and South Yemen within 48 hours. (This leitmotif of Yemeni history is still playing itself out. Saleh himself narrowly escaped slaughter during the 2011 uprising, and assassination attempts on senior politicians are rife in modern Yemen.)

Initially, Saleh survived by encircling himself with kinsmen from his own Sanhan clan and appointing close relatives to key positions at the top of the army. He shared hard power among the northern tribes, through recruitment into the lower ranks of the military, and turned a blind eye towards the graft and wheeler-dealing of division commanders. This ad hoc system adapted to unification with South Yemen in 1990 and political competition, of sorts, following the establishment of parliamentary democracy in the early 1990s (Chapter 3). However, senior commanders continued to bypass the Ministry of Defence and report directly to Saleh, effectively creating standing armies, supplied by obliging arms dealers, under the control of future rivals for the presidency (Chapter 4).

By the end of the 2000s, Yemen's military procurement system had created a spectrum of warlords, operating in close proximity to international black markets. Somalia's civil war provided a lucrative local opportunity for Yemen's arms dealers, but weapons trading

INTRODUCTION

formed only one part of an integrated illicit trading network that shifted people, guns and subsidized diesel across the busy international shipping lanes of the Gulf of Aden, which were also beset by Somali piracy (Chapter 5). According to one 2008 estimate, half of Yemen's subsidized fuel was leaked to Saleh's inner circle and then smuggled out of the country, to be sold at a profit for market prices in the neighbouring states of Africa and the Gulf. In that same year, subsidized diesel was costing the government around $3.5 billion, nearly half the national budget.

By 2008, Yemen's Western donors were pushing hard for economic reforms, in an attempt to mitigate the worst effects of falling oil production (Chapter 6). Saleh had licensed a small group of technocrats who were close to his son, Ahmed Ali, to pursue the donors' desired reforms. Donors often came away from their encounters with these ambitious young men believing that their best hope lay in supporting Ahmed Ali's future succession. This implicit link between reform and succession politicized the reform agenda along factional lines and paralysed the relevant government ministries. Meanwhile, Saleh demonstrated a shrewd ability to agree to the bare minimum that the donors requested, while turning the situation to his family's advantage.

Yemenis and Saudi nationals of Yemeni origin had played a critical role in the early development of al-Qaeda (Chapter 7). In the immediate aftermath of 9/11, Saleh positioned himself as a US ally and authorized a short-lived, erratic crackdown. However, donors feared that terrorism would flourish in the event of Yemen's economic collapse, and following a 2006 jail-break in Sana'a in which more than twenty terrorist suspects and convicts escaped, the tempo of terrorist activity began to increase. In January 2009, the leaders of al-Qaeda's branches in Yemen and Saudi Arabia announced the creation of a single entity, al-Qaeda in the Arabian Peninsula (AQAP), and proclaimed the overthrow of the Saudi royal family as a central aim. By the end of that year, AQAP had tried and failed to assassinate a prominent Saudi prince and botched an attempt to detonate a bomb on a Northwest Airlines flight in the skies over Detroit.

During the course of the following year, the White House came to view AQAP as al-Qaeda's most dangerous global franchise—in part, thanks to the charisma and popular appeal of a bilingual US-born Yemeni cleric, Anwar al-Awlaki. Awlaki, whose link to AQAP—initially, at least—appeared to be tenuous, was nevertheless blamed for inciting 'lone wolf' terrorist attacks in the West (Chapter 8). His prolific English-language web output meant he was little known among Yemenis themselves, but his physical presence in Yemen influenced US counterterrorism policy, which in turn weighted US officials' attitudes to change and risk in Yemeni politics. In 2010, the Pentagon struck a deal with Saleh to increase military aid in return for Saleh's permission to pursue an aggressive shadow war, and put Awlaki's name on a controversial 'kill list'.

For the best part of a decade, the Pentagon had channelled military aid, equipment and training to bespoke security and intelligence units under the command of Saleh's son Ahmed Ali and Ahmed's cousins. The decision to boost military aid to these boutique units on the eve of the 'Arab Spring' left the Pentagon with all their eggs in one basket—effectively, supporting a single family faction—at a point when popular opposition was growing: southern separatists (Chapter 9) and the Houthi rebels in Saada (Chapter 10) were already in open revolt. At the same time, internal regime tensions were becoming increasingly acrimonious, and regime players were themselves preoccupied by the prospect of a future confrontation.

On Friday 18 March 2011, a bloody rooftop salvo directed at Sana'a's Change Square provided the pretext for Saleh's regime to divide (Chapter 11). More than fifty people were killed and one hundred injured when plain-clothes snipers opened fire on protesters kneeling in the streets for midday prayers. Saleh's most powerful general, Ali Mohsin al-Ahmar, swiftly declared his support for the uprising—along with sympathetic ambassadors, tribal chiefs and cabinet ministers—and stationed his troops at the perimeter of Change Square. If senior US officials stopped short of publicly calling for Saleh to go, at first, they privately felt he was becoming more of a liability than an asset. Washington backed a controlled transition, sponsored by Saudi Arabia and the Gulf states, to ease Saleh out of office in return for a guarantee of immunity from prosecution.

During spring and summer, as diplomats contrived to engineer Saleh's resignation, Yemen's popular uprising morphed from a struggle between the regime and the street into a battle between competing regime factions (Chapter 12). The rivals' bitter and visceral sense of entitlement was visibly exposed when violence disfigured the streets of Sana'a in May and again in September; proxy battles flared outside the capital throughout the year. In November, Saleh—badly burned and wounded after surviving a bomb blast inside his palace mosque in June—finally bowed to international pressure and agreed to stand down. He was cornered by the prospect of UN Security Council sanctions and a travel ban, and constrained by his generals' assessment that there was no hope for an outright military victory.

Three months later, in February 2012, Abdu Rabbu Mansour Hadi stood for election as a consensus candidate in a one-man ballot, under the terms of the Gulf-backed transition deal (Chapter 13). Hadi accepted an enthusiastic public mandate to serve as a two-year caretaker president, becoming the first southerner to hold power in Sana'a. However, two years after Hadi's election, the substructure of Saleh's regime remained intact—albeit weaker and divided—and initially, at least, it seemed that the transition had simply shifted the political advantage from one elite faction to another. In part, Hadi owed his position to the support of the international community, and continued to rely heavily on foreign endorsement.

As a priority, Hadi embarked on a military restructuring plan (Chapter 14) designed to break apart the fiefdoms of Saleh's generals, in parallel with an ambitious national dialogue programme. However, security conditions were gradually deteriorating, as the transition process stalled. In February 2014, Hadi's term had to be extended to allow for the drafting of a new constitution, a constitutional referendum, and elections to be completed. Meanwhile, the Houthis—who had been suspicious of transition politics from the outset—were moving south from Saada towards Sana'a. In September, they overran the capital, occupied government buildings, and forced Hadi to appoint a new cabinet. When Hadi approved a federal model in January 2015, which the Houthis were unwilling to accept, they kidnapped Hadi's chief of staff, and placed Hadi himself under house arrest. They formed a new executive body and issued a new constitution, for good measure.

Saudi Arabia expressed alarm that Iran was backing the Houthis, but the precise nature of that relationship still proves hard to define. In fact, the Houthis were in cahoots with Saleh. In February 2015, when Hadi managed to escape from house arrest in Sana'a, the Houthis pursued him south to Aden, along with army units loyal to Saleh. Hadi fled first to Oman and then to Riyadh, where he requested help to defend the 'legitimate' government of Yemen. The Saudis started an air campaign at the end of March with Western support (Chapter 15), expecting to fight a quick war. However, two years later, with thousands dead and many more thousands wounded, and the economy in ruins, Saleh and the Houthis are still in control of Sana'a. In the south, vigilante armed groups—including AQAP, separatist militias, and a local franchise of the Islamic State of Iraq and the Levant (ISIL, also known as Da'esh)—are competing to exploit the breakdown of Hadi's authority.

Yemen Endures argues that Saleh's ousting from formal power in 2012 offered an historic opportunity to bolster Yemen's weak institutions and move towards the formation of a transparent, accountable civil state. However, the international community's decision to extend an immunity agreement to Saleh, and to leave the old elites in place, ensured that the 'open moment' created by the youth-led street protests was certain to be squandered. In addition, Hadi's personal failings contributed to the unravelling of the transition project. Five years' later, in 2017, it seemed reasonable to assert that each of the West's primary foreign policy objectives—reducing the threat from terrorism, promoting good governance and improving the country's development indicators—had conclusively failed.

Even before the current conflict, the poorest country in the Middle East struggled with shrinking oil resources, falling water tables and widespread hunger. By March 2017, the United Nations Office for the Coordination of Humanitarian Affairs estimated that 19 million Yemenis—around two thirds of the population—required some form of humanitarian assistance, and seven million people did not know where they would find their next meal.[3] The failure of international mediation suggests that Yemen's wars look set to continue—possibly for many years to come; meanwhile the tasks of reconciliation and reconstruction already appear formidable. The outcome of this latest power struggle between rival groups within Yemen, and between Yemen and its Gulf neighbours, will affect the structure of the state and the future of Arabia.

1

THE LAST IMAM

THE 1962 REVOLUTION IN THE YEMEN ARAB REPUBLIC

The notion of Yemen—as an amorphous place, without clear boundaries or precise definition—predates the formation of Western nation states by more than a thousand years. During the Roman-era incense trade, which enriched the prosperous south-western tip of the Arabian peninsula, Arabs were already referring to a geographical entity known as Yemen, but it was 'not a world of settled frontiers, nor yet of state power in the modern form'.[1] This awkward, sharp-angled wedge of a country did not agree its desert border with Saudi Arabia until the dawn of the twenty-first century.

The notion of Yemen also predates the seventh-century birth of Islam. The *hadeeth*—a posthumous compendium of the most reliable and worthy sayings attributed to the Prophet Mohammed, compiled by the ninth-century Islamic scholar, Muhammed ibn Ismail al-Bukhari—records the Prophet's praise and admiration for the people of Yemen. Al-Bukhari quoted Mohammed as saying: 'Belief is Yemeni and wisdom is Yemeni. Pride and haughtiness are the qualities of the owners of camels, while calmness and solemnity are found among the owners of sheep.'[2]

The Prophet's link between temperament and topography divided the Bedouin nomads on the desert plains of what is now Saudi Arabia from the shepherds and arable farmers in the fertile highlands at the southern tip of the peninsula. Yemen's mountain pastures, cropped with sorghum, onions and coffee, still catch the seasonal rains on shallow staggered terraces that layer the steep hillsides like sculptured millefeuille pastry. Clusters of stone tower houses, built of creamy rough-hewn bricks, teeter on the pinnacles like vertical extensions of the cliffs. Half-moon windows fashioned with tiny mosaics of coloured glass wink and twinkle when the lights come on at nightfall, like the patterned rainbow ends of many kaleidoscopes.

The Arabic word for 'right' is *yimeen*, and al-Bukhari noted that Yemen was so called 'because it is situated to the right of the *Ka'ba'*, the square stone block located at the centre of the Great Mosque in Mecca'.[3] Since al-Bukhari's day, Yemen's northern highlands have been settled by Zaydis, a distinct branch of the Shi'i movement within Islam. Followers take their name from Zayd ibn Ali, a direct descendant of the Prophet Mohammed, through Mohammed's daughter Fatima and her husband Ali. The Zaydis' designation of Zayd ibn Ali as their eponymous Imam sets them apart from Twelver Shi'ism, the dominant branch of Shi'i Islam, found in Iran, Iraq, Lebanon, Bahrain and Kuwait.[4] Zaydi Shi'as are reputedly closer to the Sunni school of jurisprudence than any other branch of Shi'i Islam.

Scions of Fatima and Ali, through their two sons Hassan and Hussein, are known as *sayyid*, and being *sayyid* is an essential precondition for consideration as the Zaydi Imam.[5] (The word 'imam' means spiritual and temporal ruler in an Islamic state, as well as cleric.) The 'crux of Zaydism' rests on legitimacy through this line of descent.[6] However, true claims to the Zaidi Imamate do not rely exclusively on the blood-line; rather—in theory—they also rest on the principle of *khuruj* or 'coming out' against oppression, during periods of poor governance or control by unjust authority.[7] Despite these defining principles, Yemen's Imamate displayed several periods of hereditary succession, and the Qasimi dynasty, whose members held the highlands from the seventeenth century to the early nineteenth century, was characterized by semi-institutionalized succession.[8] Anthropologist Paul Dresch's definitive English-language account of Yemeni history credits the Qasimi dynasty with creating the first significant image of political order in the north, arguing that the shape of the state 'lingered in people's imagination' long after the Qasimi dynasty foundered over rival claims to power.[9] However, the extent of Qasimi authority fluctuated over time, and was complicated by the presence on the Arabian Peninsula of the Ottoman Turks.[10]

At the turn of the twentieth century, another father–son succession sequence again weakened the traditional principle of *khuruj*. In 1904, Imam Yahya inherited power from his father, in what would extend to seven decades of family rule.[11] Yahya was alert to encroaching regional and international pressure making its presence felt at the periphery of his sphere of control, but he was torn between his reluctance to surrender supreme personal authority and the apparent need to establish a modern, functioning bureaucracy.[12] He began the tentative construction of the architecture of a modern state, but his ambivalence gave rise to a reform movement that generated its own momentum, which eventually ended in the annihilation of the Imamate.[13]

During World War I, Imam Yahya steered a skilful course between hostile imperial powers. He maintained nominal loyalty to his Turkish overlords, saw out the conflict without direct entanglement and exploited the opportunities that arose when the Ottoman Empire was dismantled by the 1920 Treaty of Sèvres.[14] Immediately after the armistice, Yemen's Imam was the only Arab ruler neither under Western control nor on a Western payroll.[15] Yahya went on to create a prototype army on the Turkish model and set out to expand his power base, conquering, co-opting and carving out a domain that 'claimed a place of its own on the world map'.[16] In the process, Yahya pursued a divide-and-rule strategy to play rival sheikhs and tribes against each other, and, in so doing, the 'rudiments of state power emerged'.[17] The extent of Yahya's rhetorical claim as the rightful ruler of all Yemen ran south to Aden port, which had been under British control since 1839, but the Imam never formally claimed Aden, nor ventured to disturb Britain's immediate sphere of influence around the port, despite stirring up trouble among tribes in Aden's hinterland. The British were sufficiently worried about the Imam's hostile intentions to send T.E. Lawrence to Sana'a in 1921. According to Lawrence biographer Michael Korda, Yahya 'wished to extract the highest price possible for pledging his loyalty to Britain' and promising not to attack Aden, but Lawrence judged that 'Aden could probably defend itself, if necessary'. Lawrence offered the Imam a Ford motor car as a gesture of peace and retreated to Aden, to revise his working manuscript of *Seven Pillars of Wisdom*.[18]

To the north, Abdulaziz Ibn Saud was pursuing a parallel process of conquest and consolidation, also set in train by the departure of the Turks. In 1932, he announced the creation of the Kingdom of Saudi Arabia and declared himself potentate. A dispute between Yahya and Ibn Saud over the buffer territory of 'Asir flared into confrontation in 1933, when Saudi forces 'marched on the disputed areas of the Sa'udi-Yemeni borders',[19] allegedly with British financial support and military equipment.[20] Yahya sued for peace at the Treaty of Ta'if in May 1934,[21] and agreed to a settlement of disputed regions that allowed Ibn Saud to acquire 'Asir.[22] However, the two failed to reach a final agreement on the exact demarcation line between their rival spheres of influence.[23]

Three months earlier, at the Treaty of Sana'a, Yahya had agreed an administrative division with the British that roughly accorded to the former Anglo-Turkish boundary. Yahya's Imamate now had more clearly defined parameters to the north and south, and the extent of the state was becoming clearer, but the shift to modern governance and efficient bureaucracy 'required expertise, which lay elsewhere'.[24] Decisions remained in the Imam's hands, corruption was rife and Yahya continued the traditional practice of taking hostages to enforce compliance from prominent families. In 1934, Yahya signed his treaties with the British and the Saudis as 'His Majesty Imam Yahya Muhammad Hamid al-Din, King of Yemen', imitating the modern, international form of address newly appropriated by other Arab monarchs. The Yemeni Imam still had to be *sayyid*, but anachronistic Zaydi notions of righteousness were supplanted by obedience to a dynastic order that foretold the drive towards a more contemporary form of authority.[25]

Yahya was tolerant of Sunni Shafai observance prevalent in the southern areas of his domain, but there was still resentment of Zaydi—in particular, *sayyid*—domination among Shafais living in the border zone close to the Sunni Shafai-majority British protectorate.[26] Zaydis and Shafais alike breathed life into a growing reform movement, and self-appointed reading groups emerged as 'circles of dissent [...] and markers of a widespread mood'.[27] Prominent reformers placed great emphasis on education and learning as a route to progress. Among them, Ahmed Numan criticized Yemen's lack of trained professionals. 'It is not possible to find a doctor [...] there are no experts in agriculture [...] and no industries,' he lamented.[28]

Numan helped to establish a modern school in the highland city of Taiz before moving to Cairo, where he forged links with the Muslim Brotherhood, in partnership with Yemeni poet Muhammad al-Zubayri. Al-Zubayri was temporarily jailed when he returned to Yemen in 1941, along with numerous other young reformers who aroused the Imam's suspicions.[29] Towards the close of World War II, Numan and Zubayri fled beyond the Imam's control to join the hotbed of Arab nationalism in Aden.[30] Intellectual life in Aden was more diverse than in Sana'a, and for modernizers and Yemeni nationalists living in Aden but looking north the Imam's kingdom appeared backward and oppressive.[31]

Changes set in motion by World War II were to intensify the pressure for modern statehood, and a plot hatched in Aden at the end of the conflict would eventually prove decisive. But for the time being Aden lay beyond Yahya's legitimate reach, and from the onset of the conflict his attention was diverted by the question of wartime alliances. Both the British and the Italians could see the strategic importance of the Imam's territory as a platform for protecting their competing colonial interests across the Red Sea and in the Horn of Africa, as well as providing a wider foothold in the region. Yahya knew Italy's Benito Mussolini wanted to use his kingdom as a base for airstrikes, and although the Imam's traditional antipathy towards the British in Aden seemed set to favour Rome, he was wary of commitment to a single nation that could embroil his tiny fiefdom in a messy imperial conflict.[32]

The British Colonial Office dispatched writer and explorer Freya Stark, reporting to the regional intelligence services headquarters in Cairo, to infiltrate the Imam's domain. Stark was tasked with assessing the extent of Italian influence over the Imam, discovering the existing nature of Italian military assistance to Yemen and gauging the Imam's personal loyalties in the matter of European affiliations.[33] Stark's previous expeditions to Syria, Iraq and Iran had earned professional respect and attention, but the bold lady traveller had already created scandal in the British colony in Aden by requiring an emergency medical evacuation during her first attempted exploration of Hadramaut in 1934 and conducting a brazen flirtation with the twice-married French tycoon Antonin Besse, who ran a regional trading empire from the port.[34] On Christmas Day in 1934, the couple snatched a few reckless, romantic moonlit hours lying on cushions in a cosy boat and sailing round Aden's volcano, Jebel Shamsan, with only their Somali captain as a witness, while Besse's adult daughter stayed at home to host the dancing and the dwindling hours of a dinner party.[35] (Besse's Scottish wife was away, travelling.)[36]

Stark's wartime return to Yemen began in November 1939 with a boat trip down the Suez Canal from Cairo to Aden, where she rented two rooms overlooking a harbour that was crowded with British war-ships.[37] While plotting the details of her imminent northern foray, Stark penned pro-British Arabic-language radio broadcasts dotted with flourishes of Wordsworth's poetry.[38] She arrived in the Red Sea port of Hodeida in February 1940, with a movie projector and three propa-ganda films hidden in her luggage, telling Yemeni customs officials that she was travelling with a portable commode.[39] During two months in Sana'a, Stark befriended the foreign minister's wife and screened her footage of British fighter planes, grazing sheep and rose-covered English cottages to the 'entire royal harem'.[40]

Stark was initially excluded from an audience with male members of the Imam's court, and complained of the need to 'wear down every-body's prejudice by the mere delicacy of behaviour', but gradually gained the trust of Yemeni officials; and towards the end of her stay she was rewarded with the Imam's presence at one of her evening screen-ings.[41] Her surveillance reports on Italian arms shipments and the condition of Yemeni troops proved invaluable to British military plan-ners and intelligence analysts. A year after Stark bade farewell to Sana'a, Imam Yahya sent more than 1,000 lb of fine Mocha coffee to the British governor in Aden. The camel train bearing down on Government House carrying the Imam's gesture of friendship created consternation among British officials, as there was no room to store all the coffee bags. The coffee was eventually sent to London to help the war effort, and Yahya's gift was generously interpreted, by one corre-spondent at least, to mean the Imam was at last on Britain's side.[42] Yemen in fact stayed neutral during the war, most likely because of Italy's premature defeat in Abyssinia in 1941.[43]

* * *

Yemeni Arabs sporting turbans and black and green cloaks had joined a London conference at St James's Palace in 1939 to debate the

Palestine question.[44] However, as World War II drew to a close, Yemen stood on the sidelines during the burst of Arab nationalism that gave rise to the creation of the Arab League. In 1944, Yahya sent observers rather than full delegates to an Alexandria conference to discuss the formation of a pan-Arab body, and there were no Yemeni signatures on the resolution calling for unified educational, financial, commercial, legal and foreign policies by all Arab nations.[45] Yemen was absent again in February 1945, when Arab delegates assembled in Cairo to draw up a constitution for a federation of all Arab lands, and a month later the Yemeni representative attending the foundation ceremony of the Arab League was rendered mute on the matter of political issues at the Imam's command.[46]

In contrast, Yemen lined up among early joiners at the United Nations, bringing total membership of the new organization to fifty-seven member states in 1947.[47] A few months later, the UN General Assembly voted 33 to 13 to partition Palestine into two states, and Yemen was among six Arab delegations—along with Iraq, Syria, Lebanon, Egypt and Saudi Arabia—that rose and stalked out of the Assembly chamber when the result of the vote was announced. One Syrian delegate complained that the UN charter was already dead. 'Not of a natural death,' clarified the Syrian Arab. 'It was murdered.'[48]

Yahya had once again managed to preserve his country's independence in the postwar carve-up, and although Yemen retained its reputation for aloof isolation, the Imam watched with avaricious interest as American oil exploration transformed the fortunes of the young state of Saudi Arabia. In the early 1930s, Standard Oil of California (Socal) won its first oil concession from the Saudi king, and a few years later, when Socal's drillers struck oil, the king's first royalty check topped $1.5 million.[49] Exploration stalled during the war, but in 1948, the renamed Arab American Company (Aramco) discovered the eastern Ghawar field, which is still classified as the largest conventional oil deposit in the world.[50] The Ghawar find accentuated growing US strategic interest in the Arabian Peninsula, encouraged by Ibn Saud's condition that oil exploration companies working inside the new kingdom must be wholly American and not include Europeans, particularly the British, whom he supposedly distrusted because of their colonial interests.[51]

15

Aramco cemented its dominant position in US–Saudi commercial relations in 1950, when the firm's gross production of crude oil increased to 548,000 barrels of oil a day—more than Yemen was to achieve at the height of its own oil production half a century later.[52] The USA and Saudi Arabia's deepening commercial dependence on each other was accompanied by high-level contact between the two countries' leaders. On Valentine's Day in 1945, Ibn Saud and Franklin D. Roosevelt met for the first and only time on-board the USS *Quincy*, anchored north of the Suez Canal, as the US President made his way home from the wartime Yalta Conference with the Soviet Union's Joseph Stalin and Britain's Winston Churchill.[53] The Saudi delegation came aboard with a gift of eight sheep and, having found an affinity with his floating host, the limping King came away with one of Roosevelt's spare wheelchairs.[54] Later that year, Saudi Arabia and the USA drew up the Dhahran Air Field Agreement, permitting the USA to build an airbase near Dhahran, a small Aramco company town on the Persian Gulf.[55]

Yahya was once reported to have said that he and his people would 'rather eat grass than allow foreigners to enter the country', but in 1946, eyeing lucrative developments to the north, Yahya summoned the US consul in Aden to establish regular diplomatic relations between Yemen and the USA.[56] Harlan B. Clark, from Brookfield, Ohio, drove to Sana'a in a jeep to meet Yemen's foreign minister.[57] Clark's trip to Sana'a was swiftly followed by a visit from Colonel William Eddy, US Minister to Saudi Arabia,[58] and a year later, a new American oil consortium began seeking State Department support to win exploration concessions in Yemen. Yahya sent one of his fourteen sons, Abdullah, to visit Phillips Petroleum Company, which dominated the new conglomerate, in Oklahoma. Abdullah returned home without granting any formal concessions, but consortium bosses waited with anticipation for the approval of the prince's father.[59]

Assassins killed Imam Yahya a few months later, in January 1948. The plotters, based in Aden, also hoped to slay Yahya's most likely successor, his son, Ahmed, but the plan backfired. Initial reports of the half-cocked coup were confused, and an Arab League delegation from Cairo, dispatched to investigate affairs in Yemen, got no further than Riyadh.[60] One acerbic American observer speculated that 'Yemen might rush into the 19th century from the 13th'—still a century behind the rest of the world—as a result of the murder, but hopes that Yahya's replacement would substantially advance the cause of progress were misplaced.[61]

The Yemeni authors of a secret Sacred National Charter, drawn up in Aden at the end of the war, had named a member of another prominent *sayyid* family, Abdullah Ahmed al-Wazir, as their chosen replacement, to govern 'on the lines now followed by the most advanced nations of the civilized world'.[62] Ahmed, however, suspected that his father was murdered with British connivance, and everything in the Imam's court now 'turned on personal intrigue'.[63] Ahmed brought the life of Abdullah Ahmed al-Wazir to an abrupt and early close, executed his suspected conspirators, jailed hundreds more, allowed the tribes to ransack Sana'a and decamped from Sana'a to the royal palace at Taiz.

British diplomats saw Yahya's successor as a figure of ridicule.[64] Political officer Harold Ingrams described Ahmed as a short, fat man with bulging eyes and forked beard, dressed in flowered satin. 'He seemed the Bluebeard of my youth come to life,' Ingrams wrote in 1941.[65] The new Imam was said to live in a state of morphine dependency and expectation of imminent divine judgement.[66] He was subject to recurrent 'mystical crises during which he lost touch with the world, absorbing himself in fasting and prayer', according to a French doctor practising in Yemen.[67] *Time* magazine suggested that if Ahmed 'failed to inspire one of Edward Lear's famous limericks, it was only because Lear never heard of him'.[68]

In affairs of state, Ahmed revealed himself as a micromanager who clung to every trifle of power,[69] and, with reformers in chains and shackles, it seemed that development had stalled in the north.[70] However, formal slavery was substantially reduced during Ahmed's rule, and within a few years of the coup, many prisoners were released as a result of family connections.[71] The liberal poet Zubayri had escaped to Cairo in 1948, and during the 1950s he was broadcasting on Egypt's Voice of the Arabs.[72] Transistor radios offered efficient means for communicating Arab nationalist sentiments throughout the region. 'There is no doubt that northern tribesmen whom urbanites later mocked for ignorance were listening regularly to Cairo by the mid-1950s,' Dresch observes.[73]

Numan had joined Zubayri in Cairo, and now they both put their names to a pamphlet, 'The Demands of the People'. Their reformist tract was first published in Aden, where northern exiles were thriving among the trade union movement rooted amid the urban proletariat.[74] 'Poverty has driven hundreds of thousands abroad. The rulers of the country have been evil, false and ignorant,' the text declared. In 1950, widespread drought had led to starvation throughout the north, and in one year alone it was rumoured that 30,000 pilgrims to Mecca failed to come home. Economically, the country was rotting.[75]

Ahmed had flirted with talk of reform before becoming Imam, but once in power his attitude was contradictory and he was unwilling to change government practice.[76] Although he sought investment and strategic advice from outsiders, the proud rhetoric of independence tied his hands, and he seemed unable to exploit the shifting postwar parameters to his own benefit.[77] Instead, Ahmed opted for short-term tactics. 'Having factions around him, provided he remained in charge, was integral to the way he ran his court and indeed his country.'[78]

* * *

Cold War politics were rapidly changing the contours of global diplomacy. On Yemen's northern borders, Ibn Saud was transforming himself into Islam's pre-eminent leader as custodian of the two holy shrines at Mecca and Medina. US President Harry S. Truman had recognized Islam's potent antidote to Moscow's godless manifesto—the Saudis 'hate the Bolsheviks', Truman noted, curtly, in 1947[79]—and supported Ibn Saud's appropriation of religious authority as part of America's anti-Soviet agenda.[80] Truman committed political, military and economic support to his allies, and in the postwar years Washington reached a series of military agreements with Riyadh that strengthened the link between the two capitals.[81] These implicit deals traded oil export and security guarantees in return for Saudi acquiescence to US interests in the region.

Truman's inheritor Dwight D. Eisenhower moved the relationship on a step further when he afforded the private sector greater scope to represent America's interests in Riyadh, and effectively gave Aramco a corporate stake in the process of Saudi state-building.[82] Aramco's partnership with the US Ford Foundation provided technical assistance to

Ibn Saud to restructure his political bureaucracy, and Aramco even ran its own intelligence networks, which surpassed the capacities of the US government.[83] Aramco hired Osama bin Laden's father, a migrant from Yemen's eastern desert province of Hadramaut, as a bricklayer at Dhahran. Mohammed bin Laden became a direct beneficiary of the 1950s corporate makeover of Saudi Arabia, which eventually propelled him all the way to the position of royal builder, with contracts to renovate the Prophet's mosque at Medina and the Grand Mosque at Mecca.[84] When the Saudi royal family confronted the prospect of bankruptcy incurred by their extravagant spending habits, Mohammed bin Laden allegedly stumped up emergency cash to meet the national payroll and to service the interest payments on the national debt.[85]

Meanwhile, Egypt's new firebrand president, Gamal Abdul Nasser, viewed elite self-interest in Saudi Arabia with anger and disdain. Nasser had risen to power after a 1952 military coup that deposed Egypt's puppet king, and now he roundly excoriated reactionary Arab monarchs and Western-leaning regimes for fraudulence and depravity.[86] Cairo became a powerful centre of anti-colonial propaganda, as Nasser—self-appointed 'spokesman for all the Arabs'—railed against Britain, France and their regional allies.[87] The Saudis, alert to a pincer movement combining Nasser's evocative pan-Arabism with burgeoning Socialist influence, began to position themselves as guardians of Islam. They supplied money and arms to supporters of Egypt's leading Islamist dissident, Sayyid Qutb, and offered refuge to the fleeing members of the persecuted Muslim Brotherhood.[88]

Nasser's 1956 decision to nationalize the Suez Canal 'in the name of the people' and to occupy the offices of the Suez Canal Company, owned and run by the British and French, was interpreted by many Arabs as a defiant bid for self-respect and regional leadership.[89] When Britain, France and Israel were forced to climb down from their short-lived reactionary military offensive and the Suez Canal reopened in April 1957, 'every Arab knew that [Nasser] had fought in their name'.[90] Nasser's influence on young Yemeni men, who came of age at the height of Nasser's rhetorical call for Arab dignity, would last a lifetime.[91] At the start of the twenty-first century, a retired Yemeni bureaucrat living in Sana'a confessed that he had only cried twice in his life. 'The first time was when Nasser died and the second time when my brother died,' he told me, with evident sincerity.

The Eisenhower Doctrine, formulated as a response to Nasser's audacity in Suez, attempted to counter declining European prestige in the Middle East with American pragmatism.[92] In 1957, US Ambassador James Prioleau Richards spent eight weeks visiting thirteen countries, seeking to draw them into a cash-for-compliance alliance.[93] Eleven of Richard's hosts offered their explicit or tacit approval, while only Yemen and Sudan rejected his diplomatic embrace.[94] An editorial in the *New York Times* registered approval for Richard's whirlwind diplomacy, arguing that widespread acceptance of the plan had converted it from a 'unilateral American declaration [...] into a multilateral alignment which [...] rests on a common policy of defense against Communism'.[95] Richards' mission was intended to isolate Nasser from many of his neighbours and 'set up a shield between the Middle East and Russia', but it had the knock-on consequence of driving Egypt and Syria to establish the United Arab Republic (UAR) in 1958, which Yemen joined later the same year to form the United Arab States (UAS), as a calculated affront to the British.[96]

Meanwhile, Cold War strategic interests were pushing the Americans to make inroads into the Imam's domain, literally building a highway from the coffee port of Mocha to Sana'a. Competition for influence and resources provoked rivalry, not only between capitalism and communism but also between Russia and China, and while the Russians were building Hodeida port, the Chinese were constructing the road from Hodeida to Sana'a.[97] In the aftermath of the Suez debacle, the humiliated British were determined to maintain control of Aden; and 'on this tiny foothold rested questions of global strategy'.[98] By the mid-1950s, the population of the British colony was around 140,000, including Yemenis from the north and migrants from the British Empire and beyond.[99] Aden was reputed to be 'the most politically sophisticated territory in Arabia',[100] and the busiest port in the world after New York.[101]

Ahmed's emissary to the outer world was his son, Crown Prince Mohammed al-Badr, who flew to London in 1957 for discussions on the Aden–Yemen border.[102] He also negotiated arms deals with the Russians and the Egyptians,[103] who sent shipments to Yemen in 1956 and 1957—the latter at Salif, where 'Egyptian officers directed the unloading of T-34 tanks, piston-engine trainer planes, anti-aircraft guns, military vehicles and small arms'.[104] Two years later, when his ailing father travelled to Italy for a rest cure, the Crown prince took temporary charge of the kingdom. Al-Badr gave several speeches that seemed to promise reform, but they only served to encourage reformers' false hopes of transformation. Ahmed soon returned, and another vengeful round of executions followed.[105] Egyptian contempt for the Imam's failure to keep his quaint and farcical court in order was gradually becoming plain, and Nasser's envoy in Sana'a began to boast of running affairs in the capital.[106] Bad blood was rising between the two leaders and, in 1961, Ahmed penned a poem in classical Arabic condemning Nasser's pan-Arab socialism. 'The poem evidently loses something in translation,' wrote one American journalist, 'but its point is clear enough: "The Koran says, do not nationalize other people's property. Let us return to Islamic laws and let us have union on our own terms."'[107]

Syria had already broken away from the UAS tripartite pan-Arab experiment four months earlier, and now Nasser kicked out Yemen, branding Ahmed a reactionary, along with Jordan's King Hussein and Saudi Arabia's King Saud, who had succeeded Ibn Saud in 1953. Nasser accused this reactionary sovereign triumvirate of fostering conditions that were an affront to the law of justice and the law of God. 'Political freedom is nonsense without freedom from feudalism and capitalism [...] They accuse me of conspiring to topple their regimes. If I were really to conspire, I'd finish them in two months,' he told an audience at Port Said in December 1961.[108]

It was to take Nasser seven months longer than he estimated to witness the first steps towards the demise of the thousand-year-old institution of Yemen's Imamate. Ahmed died in his sleep in September 1962, before Nasser's intrigue could get the better of him, and posthumous reports of his decline were fantastic and salacious. 'He was a man of enormous appetite: he would do away with an entire roast lamb at a single sitting and then gulp down a pound of honey as a between-meals snack,' claimed *Time* magazine.[109] Ahmed was reported to have suffered from at least five diseases in various stages of development, including rheumatism and heart trouble.[110] Descriptions of the ageing Imam's palaces, filled with unworkable plumbing, gilt furniture, fading carpets and hundreds of stopped clocks, seemed as fitting for children's nursery tales as the history books.[111]

* * *

Among his first decisions as Yemen's new leader, Crown Prince Mohammed al-Badr—now Imam, by appointment of Sana'a's *ulema*[112]—took measures to appease the liberals.[113] He announced a programme of reform, abolishing some restrictive economic laws and releasing political prisoners, but he was 'personally and politically incapable of containing the contradictions inside Yemeni society'.[114] A successful September coup that followed hard on the heels of al-Badr's succession was to prove decisive both for Yemen and the increasingly tense alignment of regional powers. The unexpected creation of the new Yemen Arab Republic (YAR) controversially split the Arab world in two, forcing US President John F. Kennedy to rewrite his Middle East policy and driving Saudi Arabia further into the arms of American weapons dealers.

The new Imam 'knew his immediate opponents were in the army and took measures to win their loyalty'.[115] He raised their pay, and promoted Colonel Abdullah al-Sallal, 'a known nationalist', to command his bodyguard. Al-Badr had only been in power for a few days when Sallal parked his tanks in the palace yard, on 26 September, and blasted the building with artillery.[116] Sana'a radio reported al-Badr's demise, but he had escaped the shelling and slipped away.[117] Contemporary reports claimed the fugitive Imam had either dressed in woman's clothes or donned a common soldier's tunic to evade detection by Sallal's jubilant forces.[118]

Tribesmen wearing brass-trimmed bandoleers, native levies armed with Napoleon-era muskets and new army recruits in crumpled khaki uniforms now patrolled the capital of North Yemen.[119] When US reporter George de Carvalho interviewed Sallal at home in Sana'a, the Iraqi-trained commander justified his revolution on the grounds that the Imams had been corrupt and archaic. 'I'm fighting against hunger, sickness and ignorance in Yemen. That is my goal, and you can label it anything you want to. I want a constitution within a year or two, and elections within five years.'[120] The new president of Yemen sat 'shoeless on a mattress, surrounded by fellow officers, adding an occasional cigarette butt to the litter of orange peels on the mosaic floor [...] "In Baghdad," he says, "I was dazzled by all the wonderful things that did not exist in Yemen. If I viewed Baghdad as progress, you can understand what Yemen is like [...] Western diplomats should help us—for them, Yemen must be the worst post in the world."'[121] Egypt, in fact, was playing a decisive role. During his father's reign, al-Badr had forged ties with Nasser, but Nasser chose to back Sallal.[122] If the boastful claim by Nasser's envoy that he ran Sana'a indirectly was true before the coup, Egypt was directly in control now.[123] Egyptian soldiers arrived in the first few days after the coup—and Colonel Anwar Sadat, who would replace Nasser as Egypt's president in 1970, was among them.[124] By early 1963, 'there were probably 15,000 in Yemen; six months later there were double that—and in every Yemeni office, as offices were set up, was an Egyptian adviser without whom nothing was allowed to happen'.[125] In Sana'a 'a police state emerged'[126] and a state of emergency was declared.[127] In 1963, political associations were banned,[128] and Yemen's reformers and liberals were silenced. Public discussion was 'suppressed and politics at state level, much as under the Imams, disappeared into plot and counter-plot'.[129]

Meanwhile, the Imam mounted a fight-back from the Zaydi heartlands in the northern mountains. Although the 'older pretensions of the Imamate had long gone',[130] al-Badr now drew on inherent Zaydi loyalties to confront the threat posed by Sallal's republican troops, who were backed by a foreign army.[131] (Sallal himself was a Zaydi, but not a *sayyid*.)[132] The extent of the Imam's territory spread south to the outskirts of Sana'a, and south-east through the tribes in Marib, Amran and al-Jawf. At a November 1962 press conference, with sixteen journalists huddled on mats in a camel-skin tent, al-Badr claimed to command 20,000 tribesmen, and predicted that he would be back on the throne in a few weeks.[133] A year later, de Carvalho made it from Sana'a to the Royalist sector, where he reported that al-Badr 'roves constantly along the northwest front in a Dodge wagon and never sleeps more than two nights in the same place'. The ousted thirty-six-year-old Imam complained of betrayal, telling de Carvalho: 'Nasser's biggest single target in Yemen is me [...] We were brothers, but when I refused to become his stooge, he used Sallal against me.'[134] Still smarting from their defeat at Nasser's hands in Suez and determined to protect their continuing interests in Aden, the UK ran a clandestine effort to support the Imam's 'ragtag' army.[135] Arabic-speaking British and French mercenaries were recruited and commanded by retired Special Air Service officer Colonel Jim Johnson, who took leave of absence from his job as a Lloyd's underwriter to plan the operation. An initial £5,000 cheque was paid through the bank account of a London hotel, where one of Johnson's associates was chairman of the board, and, as early as November 1962, a small British party was noticed just north of Sana'a.[136] Johnson arranged for supplies to be dropped inside the conflict zone by a variety of aircraft.[137]

King Saud and King Hussein of Jordan, mindful of Nasser's previous threat to topple them both along with the Imam, pledged men, money and munitions to overthrow Sallal. Distinctions between Hashemite and *sayyid*, Sunni and Zaydi were overlooked in the common hatred of Nasser.[138] In November 1962, when Saudi Arabia reported bombing raids by Egyptian planes inside the kingdom, Washington found itself in a bind over the question of diplomatic recognition for Sallal's new government.[139] President Kennedy initially withheld endorsement for Sallal out of deference to Saudi Arabia but, as Moscow and Peking continued to supply aid to Sana'a, the USA became increasingly anxious about losing influence.[140]

Reports that Egyptian planes had violated Saudi airspace coincided with the resolution of the Cuban Missile Crisis, and Kennedy soon became preoccupied with the policy questions that arose as a result of Yemen's 26 September revolution. Robert Komer, Kennedy's Middle East point man at the National Security Council, recalled that President Kennedy had a tendency to absorb himself in matters that captured his personal interest 'Like Yemen. My God! If there was ever a backward corner of the Arabian Peninsula, Yemen is it!'[141] Kennedy, who was rumoured to give excellent briefings on Yemen, wanted to use the unfolding crisis to spur reform in Saudi Arabia, by demonstrating the perils of the Imams' apathy and conservatism.[142]

Progress in Riyadh had stalled with the 1953 succession of King Saud, who was profligate, reckless and politically clumsy.[143] Saud set a new benchmark for wasteful extravagance, 'creating a new Saudi stereotype almost single-handedly as he rode through the sandy streets throwing money into the air', and allowing a parasitic network of royal relatives to exploit their proximity to the throne for personal advantage.[144] Saud's younger half-brother, Crown Prince Faisal, displayed a singular appetite for reform and shrewd judgement and, from 1958, won an intermittent mandate to impose restraints as prime minister, but internal tensions within the House of Saud were building.[145]

Kennedy and his advisors wanted to prevent Saudi preoccupation with Yemen diverting 'attention and resources' from the tenuous process of internal reform.[146] The State Department even warned that 'major Saudi military participation seems likely to lead to violent repercussion at home, very possibly even the demise of the Royal Family'.[147]

More broadly, Kennedy wanted to pull back from the discredited Eisenhower Doctrine to redefine US policy in the Middle East.[148] Kennedy was convinced that drawing Egypt into America's embrace, replacing Eisenhower's isolation with conditional parameters for engagement, would prove more effective at countering Russian influence in Cairo, while provoking leverage for reform in Saudi. The liberal Kennedy was personally sympathetic to figures within his own administration who made the case for promoting progressive nationalism as a tactical method of diffusing pro-Communist discontent and social unrest.[149] The new mindset led to increased US aid spending in Egypt, despite Nasser's militant anti-monarchist rhetoric, while the Saudi allocation was simultaneously slashed. Kennedy was 'turning America's anti-Communism policy on its head'.[150]

When Prince Faisal arrived in Washington nine days after Yemen's provocative coup, he discovered that Kennedy was unwilling to offer arms packages or military hardware, as Eisenhower might have done. Instead, the zealous US President pressed his Saudi guest on the urgent need for domestic reform and, urged by Kennedy to give rein to his own technocratic inclinations, Faisal issued a ten-point reform manifesto on his return home.[151] Faisal's 'basic law for government' included the pledge to abolish slavery, which was swiftly enacted, but most of the other provisions—such as decentralization and a stronger judiciary—remained works in progress.[152]

In December 1962, Kennedy finally recognized the new Yemeni government, and a month later American officials convened a secret meeting between Saudi Arabia and Egypt to discuss an armistice in Yemen.[153] Kennedy 'tried his utmost to help Nasser extricate himself from Yemen', and the two men conducted a frank and personal exchange of letters over the course of several years.[154] Despite this, Egypt continued its air offensive against Saudi targets, and Prince Faisal warned American diplomats: 'I cannot sit much longer with my arms folded while Nasser attacks not only my neighbor Yemen but also my

own country.'[155] When it finally dawned that Nasser was not respond-
ing to American pressure, Kennedy dramatically switched course. In
1963, he approved Operation Hard Surface, which involved the
deployment of eight F-100D fighter aircraft and one transport-type
command support aircraft to patrol the Saudi–Yemen border.

Operation Hard Surface demonstrated America's overriding commitment to preserving Saudi Arabia's territorial integrity and marked
a retreat from concerted US efforts to sponsor a serious reform agenda
in Saudi Arabia.[156] The initial White House stance towards Egypt
reflected a desire to appeal to Nasser's potential for moderation, but
critics of Kennedy's tentative Middle East policy were not appeased.[157]
London's *Daily Telegraph* fulminated: 'Nowhere have the blunders of
President Kennedy's policy-makers been worse exposed than in Yemen
[…] Cairo has become the Communist back-door into Arabia. What
has resulted from American recognition of the Yemen Republic is a
little Cuba on the Red Sea.'[158]

* * *

Meanwhile, the conflict in Yemen 'spluttered on like a defective
fuse'.[159] Journalist George de Carvalho, still embedded with the
Imam's troops, observed:

> The incredible fact is that the Egyptians are losing in Yemen. Ragged, bare-
> foot Yemeni tribesmen, armed only with ancient rifles and faith in Allah,
> are kicking hell out of Nasser's elite troops despite their overpowering
> Soviet equipment, overwhelmingly superior firepower, and unchallenged
> airpower […] [The conflict seemed a] battle between the 10th century and
> the 20th […] 'We captured 14 field radios,' sighed Prince Abdullah Ibn
> Hassan, 25, a cousin of the Imam. 'But none of my men know how to use
> them.' Nor can they use captured tanks or trucks, since none of the tribes-
> men know how to drive […] Says Prince Abdullah: 'All my men need is
> bread and bullets […] We bow only to God.'[160]

Several European observers were to draw similar conclusions. At the
end of 1962, the International Committee of the Red Cross sent a
two-man delegation to Royalist territory to explore the possibility of
establishing a medical mission.[161] After meeting Prince Faisal in Jeddah,
Dr Guido Pidermann and Dr Jean-Maurice Rubli flew to the Royalists'
rear base at Najran, in southern Saudi Arabia. The Saudi welcoming

party, serving coffee on carpets spread in the desert, was almost immediately disrupted by an Egyptian MiG attack, which sent the two Swiss
scrambling for cover. Dr Pidermann, who was shot in the foot, found
himself operating *en plein air* on one of the welcoming dignitaries. The
following day, the base came under aerial attack three more times.

Despite Dr Pidermann's injury, the ICRC delegation ventured deep
into Royalist territory, covering great distances on mule tracks and
footpaths. Within Yemen, the pair could move only at night because of
superior Egyptian air power. Their encounter with the Imam occurred
'somewhere in the Yemeni mountains': they were not able to be more
precise. The ICRC delegates noted that Saudi Arabia and Jordan were
providing substantial help to al-Badr. 'We have observed planes from
the national aerial company of Saudi Arabia—and marked as this—
transporting arms and munitions to Najran. We don't know if they
were destined for the Saudi border troops or the Yemeni troops.' They
added: 'Spicy detail: all the pilots were Americans.'

Dr Pidermann and Dr Rubli learned that Royalist troops controlled
the countryside and the mountains, while Republican forces held
Hodeida airport, Sana'a airport, Saada city and all the main axes of
communications. 'It's difficult to say how long this war will last,' wrote
the two doctors. '[This is] an example where a modern army with an
aviation which absolutely controls the air is defeated by primitive warriors, armed almost exclusively with old fashioned guns and knives.'

The two Swiss medics proposed immediate and practical measures
to provide treatment for Yemeni refugees and wounded combatants.
Neither Saudi Arabia's Prince Faisal nor Yemen's deposed Imam were
acquainted with Red Cross principles or the mandate of the ICRC, but,
after extensive discussions, the Swiss doctors convinced their Arab
hosts to sign the Geneva Conventions as a precondition for their cooperation with the intended medical mission. The first page of the doctors' report to their Geneva manager recorded allegations that
Egyptian napalm bombs were damaging civilian health, as well as
destroying herds and crops.

A parallel ICRC delegation visiting Republican Sana'a early in 1963
encountered frustrating idiosyncrasies that consistently dogged the
early Swiss missions.[162] Sallal had agreed to sign a declaration approving the principles of the Geneva Conventions and the Red Cross, but

the final text was not exactly as the doctors hoped or expected. Similarly, the Swiss succeeded in obtain Sallal's permission to receive a list of prisoners of war, but unfortunately 'due to negligence or bad will of subordinates, this list is reduced to three names only. And we had to struggle to get this meagre result,' wrote Roger du Pasquier, the Swiss mission chief.

A promised inspection of the Republicans' Saudi prisoners of war also proved tantalizingly insubstantial. Every time the delegates arrived at the house where the prisoners were supposedly held, they were told that both the director of the establishment and his prisoners were absent. Yemeni guards informed their Swiss visitors that the captive Saudis were being held on word of honour and allowed to roam free during the day, with the obligation of presenting themselves at night to the police. 'Although we asked again and again to meet them, we haven't been able to meet any of the beneficiaries of this liberal regime,' du Pasquier noted sourly.

A follow-up mission to Republican Yemen, from March to May 1963, left du Pasquier's replacement in a state of despair.[163] 'Work in Yemen is not easy,' wrote Dr Jürg Baer. '[I have] difficulty obtaining reliable information because everything, even the numbers of victims, the wounded etc—all the information that ICRC delegates must ask and must know for his own tasks are military secrets'. On one occasion, the commander of Egyptian forces in Sana'a told an incredulous Dr Baer that he held no prisoners of war because all his captives had decided to take up weapons to fight against their former paymasters. 'I can believe that many changed their minds but I think not all of them did,' Dr Baer retorted. 'I guess that at least a few among them did not change their mind and you are obliged to keep them in prison.'[164] The Egyptian General promised the disbelieving Swiss that he would check the situation with his Yemeni counterparts. He returned after five or six minutes, saying: 'They have no prisoners of war either. Sorry, I can't help. I think this is a unique situation and probably the first case in the history of the Red Cross.' 'So do I think,' replied Dr Baer, with bitter irony. He subsequently learned that the Republicans were holding several hundred prisoners of war in Sana'a.

Unfamiliar with Yemen's culture, indignant at the blatant abuse of official privilege and humiliated by accusations of spying, the fastidious

Swiss doctor eventually wrote to his Geneva bosses confessing that he was not up to the challenges that Yemen posed.[165] '[I] never know if an answer is correct or not [and] this aggravates the work enormously [...] The probability that there are hundreds of prisoners of war is a fact that [I] cannot prove [and it] is openly denied by the authorities.' Dr Baer complained that Yemeni officers and bureaucrats would only accept the Geneva Conventions as long as they were useful to their own cause.[166] 'I am lost,' he added. 'I can't understand what's going on.' He concluded that an Arabic speaker would have more success in winkling information out of his Yemeni counterparts, adding: 'Maybe I made some mistakes (but I don't know which ones).'

Dr Baer was relieved from his post in May, just as Egypt's use of poison gas was hitting the front pages of Western newspapers. Richard Beeston from the *Daily Telegraph* filed a report on 8 July detailing 'tragic proof' from the mountain village of al-Kawma, where seven people had already died and twenty-five were facing a lingering death from the effects of the gas attack.[167] Beeston met coughing villagers with deep open wounds from gas blisters and a woman who had been blinded by rubbing her eyes with her contaminated fingers. 'The village headman told me that when the bomb fell it gave off a cloud of brown smoke and had a "dirty smell [...] Soon after, people began coughing up blood. Some bled from the nose."'

Beeston was shown the remains of the gas bomb, which consisted of two circular bands of metal about 2 ft across. 'Into each were screwed fifteen canisters about the size of a car's carburettor.' He speculated it was too sophisticated for Egyptian manufacturers and was likely to have been made in Russia or Czechoslovakia. When Beeston returned to Saudi Arabia, he took the remains of the bomb with him on the back of a mule and presented it to Prince Faisal, who sent it to the UN for examination.[168]

According to Beeston, there had been at least three or four other poison gas attacks during the previous month. He wrote: 'President Nasser can now claim the distinction of being the first person to employ chemical warfare since Mussolini used mustard gas on Ethiopian tribesmen during the thirties. The use of gas is in defiance of the Geneva Conventions.' Egypt had signed the Geneva Protocol for the Prohibition of Poisonous Gases and Bacteriological Methods of

Warfare in 1925, and ratified the better-known Geneva Conventions in 1952. A *Daily Telegraph* editorial, accompanying Beeston's report, called for British diplomatic intervention to compensate for the shortcomings of a short-lived, ineffective UN mission:

> [T]he United Nations in its motorised transport has no means of visiting the remoter areas. And probably no desire to do so. It is in the Yemen to act as undertaker to the monarchy [...] Britain today could from its Aden base patrol the Yemen skies in the name of humanity. But such a role, compatible with British traditional friendship for Arab peoples, could follow only on a United Nations inquiry. Britain owes it to her moral as well as political sense to demand such an inquiry.[169]

A former British military intelligence officer with a proven record of trying to undermine Communist governments was already on the ground at the same time as Beeston, conducting what amounted to a covert investigation. Neil McLean spent the whole of July in Royalist Yemen, passing through many bombed-out villages, and saw for himself the effects of napalm and high explosives. McLean, now Member of Parliament for Inverness, was moonlighting as a military adviser to the Imam and had lobbied the British government to deny recognition to Sallal.[170] McLean's summary of the visit, written in August 1963, estimated that one in three villages in the area that he visited had been bombed. He saw many fragments of high-explosive bombs and noticed that on many of the fragments there was Russian lettering. 'When I passed through the villages of Al Kowma [...] Al Ashash, Al Darb, Jaraishi and Hassan Bini Awair [...] I saw that chemical bombs had also been used in addition to the normal napalm and high explosives.'

In a 'secret' report on his visit to Al Kowma village, roughly six weeks after the bombs fell, he described an 'unusual, unpleasant and pungent smell.[171] It smelt to me rather like a sweet sour musty chloroform mixed with a strong sour odour of geranium plant.' The village children still had scars and sores, the adults had coughs and weakened sight, and the cows' udders were covered in scabs. Six young children had died after vomiting blood, and, of the rest, their flesh was 'falling off' when they scratched themselves. McLean noted that the number of human fatalities was comparatively small because the inhabitants of many of the villages had left their homes and taken refuge in neighbouring caves:

The heaviest casualties take place when the village market places are bombed on market days. In a raid on the 1st July at Ahum, near Wusha in north-west Yemen, I was told by some of those who had been present that well over 100 people had been killed and many wounded.

McLean's accompanying sketch of an alleged poison gas bomb, in the possession of the ICRC's archives, matched that described in Beeston's *Daily Telegraph* article as well as the photos published alongside Beeston's article.[172] A House of Commons seal occupies the top left-hand corner of the paper on which McLean drew his diagram of the bomb, but there is no indication to whom he sent the report. McLean concluded that an independent commission with technical experts should deploy to the Royalist areas to investigate the use of explosives, napalm and gas bombs on the civilian population by the Egyptian and Republican air forces. 'The International Red Cross are, in my opinion, under an obligation to do this anyway on humane grounds and also to send medical teams to deal with the casualties,' he concluded.

The Imam was also pressing the ICRC to send a commission to report on the bombings, but it was another two years before the organization issued internal guidance to their representatives on the ground. In July 1963, Dr Marcoli, an ICRC delegate in Jeddah, wrote to Geneva that he would like details on the gas affair because the proportions that it was taking were enormous. 'All the eyes of all the nations are watching our behaviour here and I personally, Marcoli, tell you that this gas affair, knowing the dimensions has taken, is too big for my diplomatic training and preparation, which is almost non-existent.' He added: 'Personally, I am in good physical and moral health—the heat is hell, but I stand it. But the other burning heat of high diplomacy and high politics is much less bearable.'[173]

A month later, Geneva requested further information from the British Red Cross, aware that a British government minister had made a statement in the House of Commons saying that investigations had 'so far shown no evidence of the use of any gas other than a form of tear gas.'[174] (McLean's written account was not completed until after the Commons statement.) The British Red Cross dispatched a transcript of the debate, but it was another five months before McLean sent his report to Geneva, postmarked 24 January 1964, with a handwritten cover note on House of Commons paper, saying: 'Herewith some notes on the bombing of Yemeni villages, with apologies for delay.'[175]

Meanwhile, the ICRC's competency was still unclear to those working for them in the conflict zone, with one delegate writing: 'Can you tell us what we are allowed to do? We haven't found anywhere instructions forbidding us or telling us to intervene in such cases. In doubt, we have abstained.'[176] Finally, in February 1965, staff in Geneva sent a telegram to the Sana'a delegate, stating: 'We remind you that according to general and permanent instructions, the role of an ICRC delegate doesn't consist of investigation upon complaints relating to violations of human rights, but to practically assist the victims. Thank you for abstaining from verifying the information demanded of you.'[177]

According to Richard Beeston, senior Red Cross officials were aware that the Egyptians were using chemical weapons, but they kept quiet about it until the final months of the war. 'I think the Red Cross was concerned that they would be turfed out of Sana'a and it would disrupt their medical operations, if they accused Egypt of using chemical weapons,' Beeston told me, during an interview in London in 2009. 'They held their tongue until their own convoy was bombed by Egyptian planes in 1967, but when their statement finally came, it was overshadowed by the Six Days War.'[178]

2

VICTOR'S PEACE

THE END OF THE COLD WAR, UNIFICATION
AND THE 1994 CIVIL WAR

By 1965, a slim, straight-backed Swiss man, André Rochat, was running the ICRC mission in Royalist territory, organizing the exchange and repatriation of prisoners of war.[1] There were around 60,000 Egyptian troops in Yemen, but despite their 'claim to defend the republic, they scarcely controlled more beyond Sana'a than the Turks had sixty years before'.[2] Soviet-made Ilyushin bombers continued to destroy Royalist villages, and even in Republican-held areas Yemenis were growing increasingly resentful of the Egyptian presence. The conflict generated an estimated 20,000 Yemeni casualties.[3] Hundreds of singing war orphans paraded the streets of Sana'a each morning.[4]

From the outset, the Egyptian army fought an asymmetrical war in difficult terrain that was compounded by their lack of topographical data.[5] Egyptian field commanders complained they were running a war without maps, and Egyptian intelligence chief Salah Nasr admitted that information on Yemen was non-existent.[6] The high fatality rate among Egyptian soldiers, combined with the notorious brutality inflicted on prisoners of war captured by Yemen's Royalist insurgents, created rising discontent in the Egyptian military.[7] In 1966, 20 senior officers were arrested on charges of plotting a coup against Nasser.[8] By contrast, the Royalists had no need to pursue a quick win. They simply had to stave off defeat and sap Nasser's forces of credibility and resources.[9]

Egypt's use of chemical weapons was often attributed to an army that was desperate to stem its own heavy losses. However, repeated attempts to broker peace deals between Egypt and Saudi Arabia came to nothing, and despite negotiating a cease-fire with Faisal in 1965, Nasser continued to play 'his own game in the Middle East with Russian marbles'.[10] In 1966, when the British indicated their forthcoming withdrawal from Aden, Nasser ordered Egyptian forces to consolidate their positions in Yemen, intent on waiting the British out.[11] 'If anyone thinks we have become tired,' Nasser vowed, 'let me say that we are a struggling nation, a fighting nation, a patient nation. We can stay in Yemen for one, two, three, four or even five years.'[12]

Meanwhile, Egyptian interests repeatedly stoked internal politics in Yemen, and attempts to 'pursue independent Yemeni positions [...] were all frustrated by Egyptian policy'.[13] Sallal faced recurrent cabinet resignations and growing unrest in his incompetent government, which was increasingly dependent on Cairo. When reformer-poet Muhammad al-Zubayri was murdered in April 1965, Sallal was forced to appoint Ahmed Numan as prime minister, in order to appease the tribes.[14] Sallal then spent the best part of a year in Egypt, while Numan explored the prospect of a peace deal between the Royalists and the northern tribes.[15]

On Sallal's return to Yemen, in August 1966, the presidential council retaliated by leaving for Cairo in protest. Egyptian military police escorted the Yemeni delegation to military hospitals for 'medical treatment', creating a situation where 'in effect the whole Yemeni government was detained by Egypt'.[16] Sallal proclaimed a new pro-Egyptian administration in Sana'a, and critics of Egyptian influence were 'shot by firing squad'.[17] Anti-Egyptian sentiment was growing so strong that Sallal was forced to rely on Nasser's men for personal protection, and emissaries dispatched with bundles of cash to buy the loyalty of dissident tribes were 'murdered and the money returned'.[18]

Saudi Arabia continued to supply the Royalists by parachute drops and camel caravans, crossing from the border towns of Najran and Jizan. However, it was Israeli aggression that decided the outcome of Yemen's revolution and sealed the demise of the Imamate. Israeli Prime

Minister Levi Eshkol's six-day assault against the combined armed forces of Egypt, Jordan and Syria in June 1967 signalled the end for Egypt's presence in Arabia. When Nasser met Faisal at a conference of Arab heads of state in Khartoum at the end of August, he agreed to withdraw from Sana'a. For Nasser, 'it was the beginning of the end'.[19] By October, Yemen's roads were crowded with Egyptian convoys headed for the coast, and even Sallal's Egyptian political advisers were preparing to return home.[20]

Five years after the first shots were fired outside the Imam's palace, Yemen's revolution culminated in a 70-day siege, with Royalist forces encircling Sana'a at the end of November. For more than two months, Royalists cut off all roads to the capital,[21] while a coalition of volunteers rallied to defend the republic, supplied with Russian weapons delivered by regular airlifts.[22] Sallal's departure for Iraq in November triggered a bloodless coup that installed a governing council in Sana'a, and by February 1968, the volunteers had reversed the siege and the council claimed victory for the republic.[23] The Saudis had agreed to ease their support for the Royalists as part of the Khartoum deal with Nasser—although they threatened to reverse that position because of Soviet involvement—but the Royalist campaign collapsed when they divided into squabbling groups before they could seize the capital.[24]

With the outcome of the revolution decided, Riyadh came to an agreement that recognized the new (northern) Yemen Arab Republic (YAR), in return for the creation of a consultative council that brought together many of Yemen's feuding tribes.[25] However, the Saudis remained anxious about the consequences of Britain's withdrawal from Aden, which occurred in parallel with the Sana'a siege. The People's Republic of South Yemen, which had replaced the defunct colonial structure, was now controlled by Marxists calling for the overthrow of traditional Arab regimes, and Soviet and Cuban advisors and trainers began trickling in.[26] During the 1980s, King Fahd is said to have admonished Conservative officials for the British decision to quit the colony. 'You brought Communism to the holy land of Arabia and we will not let you forget it!' the Saudi royal complained, during one routine meeting in Riyadh.27[27] It was, however, a Labour prime minister, Harold Wilson, who took the decision to disengage from Aden, as Britain's colonial era fizzled out and London wrestled with a domestic 'economic crisis that led to a devaluation of sterling in 1967'.[28] The 'wind of change' was already blowing through British colonies in Africa, and Yemeni nationalists took note. In addition, Republicans in North Yemen were encouraging the growth of nationalist groups in the south,[29] while Egypt provided 'military and political support' to launch a struggle against the British.[30] Rhetoric from Egypt and Sana'a spoke of extending the revolution to the Federation of South Arabia, a cluster of Britain's tribal protectorates, and 'overthrowing colonialism'.[31]

The uprising against the British started in Radfan on 14 October 1963, close to the border with the YAR.[32] In December, an attempt to kill the governor of Aden, Sir Kennedy Trevaskis, led to the imposition of a state of emergency.[33] British administrators had denied migrant workers in Aden the right to vote and were refusing to negotiate with the labour union. In October 1964, union leaders called for an election boycott, and later that year, the National Liberation Front (NLF) 'began eliminating the Aden Special Branch'.[34] In 1965, Sir Arthur Charles, the British speaker of the Aden Legislative Council, was shot and killed as he was leaving his tennis club at sundown.[35] The imperial power opted to downsize in the face of urban labour politics and grenade attacks, but British control over the colony unravelled further still during 1966. Rather than discontent being defused by the announcement of their intended departure, revolutionary violence intensified, and casualties soared from fewer than one hundred a year to over one thousand between 1964 and 1967.[36]

The prospect of an impending transfer of power stoked tensions between two rival leftist factions, the NLF and the Front for the Liberation of Occupied South Yemen (FLOSY). FLOSY and the NLF 'murdered each other in growing numbers' as well as continuing their revolutionary struggle against the departing colonial power.[37] As the countdown to independence disintegrated into a bloody spectacle, the British retreated 'behind wire and sandbags'.[38] This downward spiral of violence brought the scheduled departure forward by just over a month.[39] The British initially rejected the ICRC's offer to activate a humanitarian mission, but Rochat flew to Aden and persuaded the authorities to allow him to apply the Geneva Conventions to prisoners of war and political prisoners.[40] The last British troops were airlifted to an assault ship on 29 November 1967, leaving South Yemen to determine its own fate, just weeks before the decisive siege of Sana'a.[41] FLOSY, which was backed by Egypt, had been left exposed as Nasser's grip began to unravel in the north,[42] and among Rochat's last acts he negotiated a deal to evacuate FLOSY political prisoners to asylum in Cairo.[43]

The NLF swiftly took control of Aden, declaring the first and only Marxist state in the Arab world, and 'identifying itself with revolutionary socialist struggle'.[44] South Yemen became a single, formal political entity, unifying Aden port with the tribal hinterlands for the first time. Tribal disputes were suspended by decree in January 1968, and tribalism 'collapsed from within'.[45] In North Yemen, a series of shaky postwar governments gradually consolidated the achievements of a parallel revolution—in which a blacksmith's son had replaced a *sayyid* dynasty—but tribalism remained firmly intact. Yemen as a whole was still divided by the lingering imprint of two former imperial powers, Britain and the Ottoman Turks, who had defined their competing spheres of influence half a century earlier.[46] Dresch remarks: 'Perhaps strangest of all is how naturally the country divided.'[47]

* * *

Saudi Arabia emerged from the Six Days' War substantially stronger.[48] Nasser was discredited and Egypt, now on the Saudi payroll, was no longer playing a dominant regional role. Across the Arab world, Islamic revivalism was emerging as a nascent force to challenge the ascendance of secular Arab nationalism. In Riyadh, Faisal (now king) was drawing on his religious credentials to promote Islam as a 'constituent part' of Saudi foreign policy, with the assent of the CIA and the State Department.[49] During the 1970s, Saudi-sponsored Islam became 'a weapon against leftist and subversive Arab nationalist ideologies that threatened not only the Saudi state but also Western interests in the Arab world'.[50]

If Egypt's aggressive involvement in Yemen's civil war had provided a shock to Saudi Arabia's territorial integrity, it had also exposed the weakness of the Kingdom's internal security arrangements. On 7 June 1967, two days after the start of Eshkol's lightning offensive, anti-American protestors gathered outside the US consulate and Aramco offices in Saudi Arabia's Eastern Province. There were not enough troops to discourage the demonstrators, partly because of extensive

deployments to the front with Republican Yemen. By the time reinforcements were dispatched from Riyadh, the protestors had turned
into a rampaging mob and Aramco was preparing to evacuate its
American employees.[51]

President Lyndon B. Johnson—who succeeded Kennedy after the
1963 assassination—had never shared his predecessor's predilection for
reform in the Middle East, and he now 'positioned American military
support squarely behind Saudi Arabia'.[52] At a bilateral meeting in
Washington, Johnson reportedly assured Faisal: 'As long as I am in
office, I will not permit your country to be gobbled up by the
Communists.'[53] Under Kennedy's premiership, arms sales to Saudi
Arabia had doubled, but Kennedy largely authorized military sales to
equip US-led training missions with Saudi forces.[54] The spending trend
increased exponentially after 1964, while Saudi procurement patterns
also changed dramatically.[55]

In the midst of the Yemeni civil war, in response to Nasser's repeated
cross-border aerial bombardments, Riyadh had requested improved air
defence systems. In 1965, the Saudi Ministry of Defence had signed a
$15 million order for four C-130 transport planes. Later that same
year, the Saudis had ordered equipment worth $300 million from the
British, including supersonic fighter jets, as well as Hawk missiles in an
additional $125 million deal with the USA. These weapons were not
delivered until after the Six Days' War, but it was the experience of
territorial violation during the Yemen civil war—not the threat from
Israel—that began the shift in Saudi's arms purchasing pattern.[56] Saudi
Defence Minister Prince Sultan, who oversaw the 1965 arms deals,
was praised by the US Ambassador for his 'activist, dynamic' handling
of the defence portfolio.[57]

Throughout the civil war, contemporary accounts speak of 'Yemen',
'Egypt' and 'Saudi Arabia' as parties to the conflict, but Saudi Arabia's
border with North Yemen was still largely undefined and North Yemen
had, until the year before the war, been federated with Egypt in the
UAR. For the duration of the conflict, the territory constituting modern Yemen was divided into more than three blocs: Nasser's republic,
the Imam's Royalist rump, and the crown colony in Aden and the surrounding tribal protectorates. Even after the conflict, Saudi Arabia's
influence extended to state and non-state actors in North Yemen and

South Yemen, while the two neighbouring governments each tried to build a new state apparatus 'in a period dominated by Gulf and Saudi oil wealth'. Both Yemens 'lived in the shadow of the Saudi state'.[58]

In North Yemen, the 1970s saw wobbly progress towards consolidation of the new republic. The status of the *sayyid* class had been irrevocably altered as a result of the revolution, and Zaydi tribesmen—in particular, Zaydi tribesmen from the Hashid tribal confederation[59]—were playing a more prominent role in government and national politics.[60] Postwar reconciliation between Sana'a and Riyadh led to a $20 million Saudi grant to the governing presidential council led by Abdulrahmin al-Iryani, a 'cautious "Liberal"' from a non-*sayyid* family of judges who retained the 'manners of the old regime'.[61] Saudi cash infusions to the government in Sana'a were repeated thereafter, and many Yemeni sheikhs received their own Saudi stipends, establishing the basis of extensive and durable cross-border patronage networks that would last for more than four decades.

The 1970s were a decade of turbulent and treacherous politics in Sana'a, with an element of tragic farce thrown in for good measure. Saudi Arabia's influence put successive governments 'in a perpetual state of instability', as recipients of Saudi money tried 'to use their relative strength vis-à-vis the state to exert greater concessions, more access to state funds or leverage over rival communities'.[62] There was widespread gossiping about the 'influence of a foreign country',[63] and prime ministers 'changed frequently, supposedly under Saudi pressure'.[64] Prime Minister Hasan al-Amri resigned in 1971, after crossed wires at a telephone exchange created a misunderstanding that enraged the premier and ended in the execution of a local photographer.[65] Al-Amri's disgrace briefly boosted al-Iryani—Yemen's first civilian head of state—whose political career lasted until 1974, when he 'learned of a plot to oust him' and opted for 'permanent exile' in Syria.[66]

Al-Iryani's replacement, Colonel Ibrahim al-Hamdi, initially enjoyed the backing of the tribes as well as the progressives, and he 'spoke in persuasive terms of progress'.[67] He was the 'first of Yemen's leaders to master mass politics',[68] but his attempt to curb the influence of tribal leaders 'earned him powerful enemies, particularly because they had previously formed part of al-Hamdi's support base'.[69] Initially careful not to cross the Saudis, al-Hamdi eventually alienated them, too, by 'making peaceful overtures towards south Yemen' and holding talks with southern President Salim Rubayyi Ali (who was also known as 'Salmayn').[70] In addition to Saudi fears about the creeping influence of socialism, Riyadh objected to the idea of a united, populous Yemen.[71] In October, assassins murdered al-Hamdi and his brother at home in Sana'a, shortly before further unity talks with Aden.[72]

South Yemen was now formally called the People's Democratic Republic of Yemen (PDRY), and the new constitution deliberately pitted the PDRY 'against its more populous neighbour, calling for the liberation of "society from backward tribalism"'.[73] After the British withdrawal from Aden, the NLF had taken over a state that 'barely existed and an economy that had collapsed'.[74] The new PDRY leadership nationalized the economy, including several foreign-owned companies,[75] and introduced state-led development policies.[76] Land was confiscated from traditional power brokers who had cooperated with the British, and these sultans and sheikhs—many of whom had fled to Saudi Arabia at the time of the British withdrawal and the subsequent NLF takeover—were tried as 'lackeys of the imperialists'.[77]

Few NLF leaders 'had received a higher education and none had experience of government', and divisions over the pace of Socialist economic reforms quickly emerged between 'right' and 'radical left' factions.[78] Policy differences also hinged on the 'level of commitment to and strategies for promoting unity' with North Yemen,[79] regional alliances in foreign affairs and 'the relative weight to be given to the Soviet bloc'.[80] Salmayn had gained a favourable impression of Chairman Mao's Cultural Revolution during a visit to China, and he was 'often labelled a Maoist',[81] while rival power broker and NLF party leader Abd al-Fattah Ismail 'favoured a centralized party on the Russian model'.[82] Salmayn's conciliatory overtures to al-Hamdi, who had tried to encourage Aden to adopt a pragmatic position with Saudi Arabia, also provoked consternation among Ismail's pro-Soviet faction.[83]

In North Yemen, the Saudis were backing President Ahmed al-Ghashmi with generous sums of cash, but al-Ghashmi lacked a 'firm grip on politics', and within a year of his appointment he fell prey to a convoluted southern plot.[84] In June 1978, al-Ghashmi was killed by a briefcase bomb, delivered to Sana'a by Salmayn's emissary, who al-Ghashmi supposedly assumed was bringing cash or anticipated documents. In waiving the search of the emissary's briefcase, al-Ghashmi unwittingly allowed himself to become 'collateral damage in a war being waged among the leadership of the south'.[85] Whether it was Salmayn himself—or his traitorous colleagues—who had sent the bomb, Salmayn stood accused of bringing the PDRY into disrepute, and rivals moved swiftly to challenge his authority.[86] An emergency all-night session of the Politburo saw Salmayn pitted against Ismail and his allies.[87] Fighting between the two factions started at dawn, but Salmayn was swiftly detained, tried by a revolutionary court and executed by firing squad.[88] Within 48 hours, the presidents of both North Yemen and South Yemen had been eliminated.[89]

A month later, mid-ranking army commander Ali Abdullah Saleh came to power as president in Sana'a. Saleh, who had built his military power base through a controlling stake in the army's trade in bootleg alcohol, epitomized the 'self-made man' who emerged in the aftermath of Yemen's 1962 revolution.[90] An early portrait of the young premier that once hung in the lobby of the Bilquis Hotel in Marib showed a handsome Arab leader, staring into the future with resolution and confidence. He sported a brown suit, a trim moustache and a neat Yemeni variation of an Afro haircut. Saleh came to define the experience of an entire generation of Yemenis—at home and abroad. Khalid, a Briton born to Yemeni parents in the 1970s, remembers watching Saleh's inauguration on television as a child growing up in Birmingham. 'I never imagined that he would still be president when I moved to Yemen as a parent myself,' he told me three decades later.[91]

Saleh's elevation to the premiership came during a 'period of ideological malleability, Saudi intrigue and war profiteering'.[92] Neither Yemenis, nor American spies stationed in Sana'a, seemed to hold out much hope that the new president would last long in the job. The CIA boss ran a tab on Saleh's survival, and gave good odds that the new appointee would not survive more than a few months.[93] Many Sana'a observers viewed the untested president as 'uneducated, naïve and vulnerable to manipulation because of his lack of domestic support', but Saleh quickly demonstrated that he was prepared to take numerous risks to stay in office and adroitly handled two early threats to his authority.[94] Within a year, he had forestalled an attempted coup by a group of leftists—who, defeated, fled to Aden—and halted a border war with the PDRY.

Fundamental ideological differences between North Yemen and the PDRY were stoked by the fact that both[95] states were harbouring their neighbour's exiled opposition movements.[96] After the British withdrawal from Aden and the NLF's power grab, FLOSY had taken refuge in the north—'a key source of friction between the two countries'[97]—while Saleh's new regime was vulnerable to a group of pro-unity Marxist sympathizers 'operating by the name of the National Democratic Front (NDF) that found a safe haven in the south'.[98] In January 1979, 'war broke out between the Yemens, and the Southerners took a number of towns beyond the border'.[99] Saleh displayed an early example of his trademark pragmatism by pursuing negotiations with the NDF leadership,[100] and the dispute was brought under control within a matter of months, with Syria, Iraq, Kuwait and Saudi Arabia all helping to mediate a ceasefire.[101]

During 1979, a series of unexpected regional upheavals intensified US and Saudi perceptions of risk in the Middle East, affecting the way that Washington and Riyadh framed policy towards Sana'a and Aden. In January, a popular uprising in Iran forced the shah, Mohammed Reza, into exile.[102] The Iranian Revolution increased Saudi fears of encirclement by hostile regimes, and generated anxiety that the House of Saud—an oil-rich monarchy allied with Washington—would suffer a similar fate. Later that year, in November, the Saudi royal family confronted an open challenge to their authority, when a radical cleric and his armed supporters besieged the Great Mosque in Mecca, decrying elite corruption and Western influence.[103] Saudi authorities repressed the siege at Mecca after two weeks, but before the year was out the Soviet army invaded Afghanistan, triggering a decade-long war between the USSR and American proxies, with covert Western and Saudi support to the *mujahideen*.

The 1979 border war between Sana'a and Aden erupted at the start of this turbulent year, reinforcing fears that the USSR—emboldened by the fall of the Shah, Washington's ally—would support PDRY subversion in North Yemen. US President Jimmy Carter moved quickly to signal his support for Saudi Arabia by promising to deliver $300 million of American arms to Saleh, including 12 F-5 jet fighters, if the Saudis agreed to foot the bill.[104] Such was Carter's urgency to reassure the Saudis that he invoked an emergency loophole in the Arms Export

Control Act, permitting US officials to bypass the need to secure the approval of Congress.[105] American aircraft were soon shuttling in and out of Sana'a, bringing tanks and anti-tank missiles. In addition, US officials announced their plans to send several hundred military trainers to Sana'a,[106] and North Yemen was briefly said to belong to 'the American camp'.[107]

Saleh publicly welcomed Carter's arms deliveries, promising to 'exert all our efforts' to block the threat of Communist expansion. If some Yemeni cabinet ministers found it unpalatable to 'look like a client of the Americans' when Washington had just negotiated a peace treaty between Egypt and Israel, following the 1978 Camp David Accords, Saleh himself was willing to adopt a more audacious stance.[108] In addition to US military assistance, Saleh brazenly announced that US business investment was necessary to insure stability in Yemen. 'We believe that the fundamental basis of security and stability, both international and domestically, is social and economic development in a democratic atmosphere, in which everyone feels he is master of his own destiny,' he told the *New York Times*.[109]

Later that year, however, Saleh opened up parallel 'channels of trade with the Soviet Union that permitted the YAR to import hundreds of millions of dollars' worth of military equipment and thus replace the much smaller "aid" package that the US offered through Saudi Arabia'.[110] Yemen officials groused that the US package was not generous enough and delivery arrangements were too slow, but one contemporary US observer, *New York Times* columnist William Safire, acknowledged that Saleh was deftly playing both superpowers against the Saudis.[111] Safire noted: 'Instead of finding and backing a reliable ally in Yemen against a militant Communist threat, we and our Saudi friends have been maneuvered into dumping weaponry into the hands of a canny chieftain.'[112] Saleh was preoccupied by Aden's superior firepower, and his ability to negotiate weapons deals with rival foreign suppliers played an important part in strengthening his regime after 'its very shaky first two years'.[113] In 1979, he made the first moves in what would become an enduring pattern of trying—but not always succeeding—to position himself for maximum advantage between the USA, Russia and Saudi Arabia, and later with other regional allies such as Saddam Hussein's Iraq.[114]

Carter's decision to route US military aid to North Yemen through Saudi Arabia created the impression that the Americans were closely aligned with Saudi self-interest in Sana'a.[115] In Riyadh, the pattern of escalating US arms transfers to Saudi Arabia set in motion during Yemen's civil war continued throughout the 1970s. By the middle of the decade, Saudi Arabia's foreign military sales agreements were worth more than $5 billion, and defence contracts were pouring into US companies.[116] In 1978, the Carter administration supported a Saudi request for 60 F-15 planes, in a three-way supply package including Israel and Egypt.[117] When President Reagan succeeded Carter in 1980, he faced an outstanding Saudi request to buy AWACS, an all-weather surveillance and command-and-control plane. The State Department justified the AWACS deal on the grounds that Riyadh and Washington shared regional strategic interests, citing, among other threats, the ongoing Soviet presence in South Yemen.[118]

In South Yemen, the wheels of factional politics continued turning throughout the 1980s.[119] In the aftermath of al-Ghashmi's assassination, Ismail had come to power as president, and he retained his control over the NLF, now known as the Yemeni Socialist Party (YSP), as secretary general. (The US State Department and the CIA assumed that Ismail's aides had planted the bomb that killed al-Ghashmi, and they were disturbed by the prospect of further radicalization in South Yemen as a result of Ismail's ascendancy.)[120] During his presidency, Ismail signed a twenty-year friendship treaty with Moscow, granted the USSR rights to a naval base in Aden and openly endorsed the Soviet invasion of Afghanistan.[121] However, Ismail was a northerner by birth, 'albeit a long-time resident of Aden'.[122] In addition, he was doctrinaire, his policies did not produce the investment and assistance needed to lift the PDRY out of poverty, and 'few appear to have trusted him'.[123] In 1980, he was ousted by Prime Minister Ali Nasser Mohammed, who was 'a much more popular politician'.[124]

Ismail was sent into exile in Moscow, with a medal and the title of honorary chairman of the YSP.[125] Ali Nasser Mohammed retained his previous position as prime minister, while acquiring the two posts that Ismail had just vacated: PDRY president and YSP secretary general.[126] Unlike his two predecessors, Ali Nasser used his profile as president to appeal to the wider public, speaking in 'simple and direct language' about necessary improvements to living standards.[127] His core support came from technocrats and civil servants, but, over time, he was perceived as favouring his home area of Abyan and adjacent Shabwah at the expense of other areas.[128] However, Ali Nasser's pragmatic efforts to improve relations with Saudi Arabia, Oman and North Yemen appeared to win valuable support in Moscow, where the Kremlin was now attempting to reach out to the Gulf monarchies and moderate Arab states.[129]

Ismail eventually returned from exile and began agitating for Ali Nasser to be demoted, while simultaneously trying to regain his own standing within the Socialist Party.[130] Ismail condemned Ali Nasser's efforts to pursue closer ties with Saleh, and criticized 'his personal excesses, consumerism, corruption, and alleged betrayal of the socialist revolution'.[131] During the mid-1980s, the PDRY faced a 'balance of payments crisis [...] and "factional" disputes sharpened', with each side stockpiling arms and buying weapons from abroad, fearing that the other side would move first.[132] In 1985, as a concession to his critics, Ali Nasser handed the post of prime minister to Haidar al-Attas from the eastern desert province of Hadramaut, but accusations of patronage based on tribal and family links remained acute and the plotting continued.[133] By the beginning of 1986, 'it had become a matter of who would fire the first shot'.[134]

On 13 January 1986, two men opened fire at a meeting of the Politburo at its pastel green headquarters in Aden, slaughtering the vice-president, the defence minister and several other senior politicians in a 'gangland-style massacre'.[135] Ismail managed to escape, but he was killed by rocket fire later that day, in widespread streetfighting.[136]

During the next two weeks, competing factions—both pledging allegiance to Moscow—deployed tanks, rockets and naval gunboats in the struggle to eliminate each other.[137] Prime Minister al-Attas was abroad when the clashes began; the Kremlin summoned him to Moscow, where he issued appeals to stop the bloodshed via the state press agency, TASS; but the fighting in Aden continued unabated.[138] Thousands died in house-to-house battles,[139] and when the fighting finally subsided, it was Hadrami politicians who dominated the new government.[140] Among them was Ali Salim al-Beidh, who became general secretary of the Socialist Party, and Haidar al-Attas, who switched his portfolio from prime minister to president.[141] Yassin Saeed Noman, an 'able technocrat' from Lahj, replaced al-Attas as prime minister. Meanwhile, Ali Nasser took refuge in North Yemen with several thousand followers, whom the Gulf states agreed to fund on the condition that 'they did not make trouble';[142] nevertheless, the new leadership in Aden saw him as 'a constant menace'.[143]

Together, al-Beidh, al-Attas and Noman strove to rebuild the country's economy but neither the PDRY nor the YSP ever recovered from the damage caused by the 1986 conflict.[144] Russia maintained ties with Aden, but the Soviet system itself was changing,[145] and there was a 'subtle downgrading of relations' with the PDRY.[146] Mikhail Gorbachev had been appointed general secretary of the Communist Party of the Soviet Union in 1985 and his 'famous address to the Party Congress, on "openness" and "reform" (*glasnost* and *perestroika*) came six weeks after the Aden fighting'.[147] Within four years of Ali Nasser's unsuccessful coup, Soviet forces had withdrawn from Afghanistan, revolutionary uprisings had toppled Moscow's allies in Central and Eastern Europe, and the fall of the Berlin Wall had paved the way for the unification of East and West Germany.

The 'Russian empire was dissolving', Moscow could no longer afford to support countries of 'marginal interest' and the PDRY was 'virtually bankrupt'.[148] After the 1986 power struggle in the Politburo, many southerners had concluded that the country 'could no longer carry on under a socialist leadership and unity was seen as a viable way forward'.[149] Sana'a and Aden had flirted with the prospect of unification for nearly two decades, but the PDRY leadership had mostly viewed unity as a precursor to Socialist revolution in the north, and on this basis Saleh had resisted. Now, with the Socialists weakened and the PDRY humiliated, support for unity began to gather momentum.[150] In November 1989, Saleh and al-Beidh met in Aden to discuss the details of a proposed merger, announcing plans for a nationwide referendum a year later.[151] After just six months, on 22 May 1990, Saleh assumed the title of president of the United Republic of Yemen, and al-Beidh became his vice-president.[152] The promised referendum never happened.

* * *

Unity entailed the merger of two neighbouring states that had followed distinctly different trajectories for much of the twentieth century. One was a conservative, tribal society, while the other had endured colonialism and Marxism, and their 'respective leaderships had historically been at odds'.[153] Unity, however, was immensely popular, and viewed by many in both populations as a 'panacea for the ills of the two societies'.[154] Preparations for integration were rushed, and disputes over the new constitutional framework were resolved in a cursory fashion when al-Beidh agreed to abandon the southerners' preferred model of federalism during a car ride that he took with Saleh in Aden.[155]

By 1990, northerners outnumbered southerners by roughly four to one, but Saleh waived his demographic advantage by putting the two countries on an even footing during the initial two-year transition period, at the end of which all citizens over the age of eighteen would have the right to vote.[156] Al-Attas became prime minister and southerners occupied half the posts in the transitional cabinet.[157] The two governments made plans to merge their tax authorities, airlines, news agencies and broadcasting organizations, but both sets of armed forces remained 'intact and operating on a parallel basis'.[158]

Before unification, the economies of both Yemens had been heavily dependent on aid and loans, as well as remittances from migrant labour.[159] Improving Yemenis' standard of living should have been an early priority for the new administration, but when Saddam Hussein ordered the Iraqi army to invade Kuwait in 1990, Yemen had the 'great misfortune to be on the UN Security Council—the only Arab state among fifteen members'.[160] Yemen abstained from the Security Council vote condemning the invasion, but Saleh openly criticized Saudi Arabia for inviting American-led forces into the kingdom as part of Operation Desert Storm.

Provoked by Saudi Arabia's swift and punitive deportation of thousands of Yemeni workers, Saleh then accused the Saudi foreign minister, Prince Saud al-Faisal, of trying to scuttle Yemeni unification by bribing PDRY officials to abandon the deal, just a few weeks before the scheduled merger. The Saudis 'are completely terrified by our freedom and democracy in Yemen', Saleh claimed.[161] Saleh's antagonistic stance riled the Saudis and the Americans, as well as the Kuwaitis and other Gulf monarchs. International development assistance was slashed and nearly a million Yemeni workers were expelled from the Gulf, leading to a crash in remittances that ran into billions of dollars.[162] Labour unrest and demonstrations against rising living prices spread nationwide in the years that followed unification.[163]

Geologists had discovered oil in the border zone between the two Yemens during the 1980s, but large-scale commercial extraction was delayed until after unification.[164] If the prospect of oil riches had played a part in pulling the two governments together on the eve of unification,[165] once unity was achieved, 'oil-related commerce fell largely into Northern hands' and the southerners began to feel cheated out of their rightful share of the profits.[166] Tensions over the allocation of oil resources mirrored southern suspicions regarding distribution of political power. The YSP remained intact after unification but its appeal was limited in the north,[167] where Saleh's ruling party, the General People's Congress (GPC), dominated political life. The YSP also faced competition from a new political party, Islah (the Yemeni Congregation for Reform), founded by Sheikh Abdullah al-Ahmar, paramount sheikh of the Hashid tribal confederation and Saleh's essential mediator with the northern tribes.

Islah—by virtue of Sheikh Abdullah's stewardship—was often associated with northern tribal interests. In addition, it represented political Islam.[168] The YSP leadership grew increasingly perturbed by Islah's creeping influence, aware that the party leadership was making a conspicuous effort to appeal to those who were troubled by the problem of poverty in the south.[169] Ideological tensions were compounded by a new wave of land disputes, triggered by the homecoming of traditional tribal leaders, who returned from exile to 'claim back land confiscated by the PDRY, or to reassert their influence'.[170] At the same time, the Yemeni *mujahideen* were also returning home from Afghanistan, following the Soviet retreat from Kabul. Throughout the 1980s, the Yemeni *mujahideen* had been encouraged and financed by tribal, clerical and military power brokers in Sana'a; now, they were hostile to Saleh's power-sharing arrangement with the Socialists. When the YSP leadership fell prey to an assassination campaign in the early 1990s, northern politicians blamed southern vendettas, but the Socialists themselves accused the Islamists and 'increasingly, the president's security apparatus'.[171]

In this atmosphere of intense distrust, parliamentary elections marking the end of the initial two-year transition period, scheduled for 1992, were postponed until 1993.[172] In the final poll, the GPC took the majority share of the vote with 123 seats, while Islah came second with 62 seats and the YSP trailed behind with 56.[173] All three parties agreed to form a coalition government, with al-Attas as prime minister and Sheikh Abdullah al-Ahmar as speaker of parliament.[174] However, the YSP's weak performance meant it ended up with only one seat on the five-member presidential council, effectively demoting al-Beidh.[175] Angry and humiliated, he withdrew to Aden and then to Hadramaut, complaining that Saleh had not honoured the terms of the unity agreement.[176] In agreeing to unification on Saleh's terms, al-Beidh had gambled and lost, in the face of strong opposition from his YSP colleagues, who had preferred a federal model. 'From the outside, the YSP seemed to burst at the seams. It appeared to be fragmenting as members contradicted each other in public statements and slowly lost their composure.'[177]

In February 1994, Saleh and al-Beidh were invited to Amman to smooth over their differences, where they signed the Document of Pledge and Accord in front of King Hussein. However, it was 'clear from their body language that it would not be implemented: King Hussein had to force the two Alis to shake hands in front of television cameras'.[178] A full-scale military offensive started two months later, and Saleh's troops swiftly proved they had the initiative. In May, al-Beidh proclaimed the creation of a new entity, the Democratic Republic of Yemen, as an independent state with its capital at Aden, and he named Haidar al-Attas as his prime minister.[179] Saleh dismissed al-Beidh's allies from the cabinet and tightened his 'military stranglehold on Aden',[180] which fell to northern forces in July when it was 'sacked by the army and militias from Islah'.[181]

The two-month civil war in 1994 'destroyed much of the buoyancy surrounding the idea of unity and, by extension, democratization'.[182] The UN dispatched Lakhdar Brahimi, one-time Algerian freedom fighter turned diplomat and peacemaker, to mediate the fall-out from the conflict, but the southerners' status never fully recovered.[183] The paradox of unification lay in the fact that both the northern and southern political elites seemed to believe that unification would solidify their respective authority.[184] However, within four years of unification, the 'remnants of the PDRY regime' were destroyed and many of the YSP leaders were forced into exile,[185] while Saleh's military victory allowed him to impose a victor's peace. After the war, there were 'endless cases of those with good connections seizing property' in the south, and the 'effect was felt by Southerners to be a Northern invasion'.[186]

By the early years of the new millennium, ubiquitous portraits plastered over shopfronts and city walls underscored the sense of Saleh as the godfather of the unified republic. His official website boasted: 'He is the founder of modern state of Yemen based on democratic basis, political pluralism and freedom of the press.'[187] Yet unemployment stood at 35 per cent, more than a third of the population was living in poverty and half the population was illiterate.[188] Yemen was second only to Sudan among Arab countries in the scale of its hunger count,[189] it had one of the lowest rates of water availability rates in the world and Yemeni women consistently came last in the World Economic Forum's Global Gender Gap Index.[190] The Fund for Peace placed Yemen as the country eighth most at risk of disintegration in its 2005 Failed States Index. Southerners were not alone in waiting for Yemen's as yet unfulfilled promise of democracy and prosperity to come to fruition.

3

AN ILLUSORY STATE

PARLIAMENTARY POLITICS AND PRESIDENTIAL PATRONAGE

'If you want me to govern like Jacques Chirac, give me the French people'

Statement attributed to Yemeni president
Ali Abdullah Saleh

MPs' bodyguards crammed the juice kiosk across the street from Yemen's parliament building, while the morning *majlis*—or council— was in session. Idle retainers sat cheerful and chatting in grubby plastic chairs, their AK-47s stacked amid the dangling strings of oranges and mangoes. The proprietor had plastered the walls of his stall with posters of Ali Abdullah Saleh and Sheikh Abdullah al-Ahmar, tribal chief and speaker of parliament. At midday, when MPs emerged from the debating chamber, the militiamen were already on their feet. Waiting drivers threw the ignition in their Toyota Land Cruisers, engines turning over, ready to race with a flourish down 26 September Street and carry their sheikhs away to lunch.

Yemen's head of state, senior officials, ministers, politicians and judges are exempt, in effect, from needing a licence to carry firearms, but Yemeni dignitaries rarely bear weapons themselves.[1] Instead, the presence of armed bodyguards communicates status, and the employment of armed retainers constitutes a standard feature of Yemeni political life.[2] In 2006, MPs were estimated to employ more than a thousand armed escorts, providing men in their constituency families with jobs in return for loyalty, influence and security.[3] A year later, after heavy pressure from local civil society organizations and Yemen's Western donors, MPs passed a decree banning guns from being carried openly in the capital. With the ban in force, retainers waiting across the street from parliament simply stashed their Kalashnikovs discreetly out of sight inside their bosses' Land Cruisers.

During Saleh's presidency, Yemen's House of Representatives—al-majlis al-nawab—functioned as a status parade and a sophisticated nexus of patronage. Influential sheikhs were often selected as MPs because they carried the votes of their community, and their social dominance enabled them to eliminate potential rivals. As a result, the electoral system reinforced personality-based power politics, securing resources for sheikhs to distribute throughout their constituencies and reinforcing their authority at the local level as agents of Saleh's regime. Legal regulations stipulated that MPs must be literate, but these rules were not enforced, and one third of Yemen's 301 MPs were estimated to be fully or partially illiterate.[4]

Despite its relative poverty, Yemen was the first country on the Arabian Peninsula to 'declare itself a participatory parliamentary democracy' based on universal suffrage.[5] The unique circumstances of unification in 1990 generated a pragmatic internal argument for parliamentary democracy to reconcile the Socialist south, Islamic clerics and the northern tribes. However, Yemen's organic democracy experiment ran against the grain in Washington, where officials in the Clinton administration were mindful of the potential for Yemen's putative political pluralism to destabilize the country's neighbours. After the first parliamentary elections, in 1993, a visiting US dignitary sounded a cautionary note in Sana'a: 'I don't think you should look on what you do here as a model for anyone else to follow.' Deputy Assistant Secretary of State David Mack suggested Kuwait's more controlled, limited-participation poll as a more suitable precedent for Yemen.[6]

Yemen's rush to establish democracy during the early 1990s brought the vote to a poorly prepared, conservative tribal society. The parallel shift towards commercial extraction of oil allowed Saleh to establish a quick-fix patronage structure that distorted party politics, leaving the system vulnerable to manipulation. Ready oil money encouraged the sense of heady optimism that followed unification, but it blinded Yemen's leaders to the need for sound economic planning. Instead of empowering technocrats and equipping state institutions with the authority and resources to govern effectively, Saleh opted for unsustainable cash-based methods of control that allowed him to bypass the painstaking process of state-building. The distribution of oil rents enabled the president to establish and manage a shifting patronage structure, governing tribal sheikhs through a system of direct subsidies.[7]

Within Ali Abdullah Saleh's patronage system, friction between the state and the tribes was highly pronounced. 'Yemen is the only place in the Arab world where the tribe is still intact and the state is merely first among equals,' explained one Western diplomat.[8] The tribes knew that the best way to get something from the patronage network was to foment a crisis and ask the regime to resolve it. If tribesmen blocked a road, blew up an oil pipeline or kidnapped a foreign tourist, the president's representatives would show up with cash and cars to settle the problem. Hyundai four-wheel drives, retailing in Sana'a for $30,000, were standard sweeteners. 'The mentality is "what's in it for me", not "what's good for my country"', complained one jaded oil industry executive.[9]

By the mid-2000s, Yemen's oil sector provided 90 per cent of export earnings and 75 per cent of government revenue, but the World Bank predicted that state revenues from oil sales would fall to zero within the next decade.[10] Yemen's two main oilfields are Marib and Masila: in Marib, the towers of the processing plant rise from the endless cadmium orange sands like a gleaming steel-pipe Shangri-La. From here, light crude flows west to the Red Sea, while oil from Masila runs south to the al-Shihr terminal on the Gulf of Aden. While it existed in sufficient quantities, oil pumping out of these desert cathedrals helped to create the illusion of a Yemeni state, but oil production passed its peak in 2002. By the end of the decade, the extraction trend at both these two mature fields had turned downwards and daily output had nearly halved.[11]

The 2009 Arab Human Development Report sourly remarked that Yemen had failed to break its vicious cycle of population growth, environmental degradation and natural resource depletion during the 'short window of opportunity' while the going was good. Yemen, it warned, was rapidly running out of time.[12] Transparency International described corruption as endemic and worsening, with a corrosive effect on government ministries and traditional social structures.[13] Corruption was simultaneously acting as the glue that kept everything in place while robbing the country of longer-term choices. 'Corruption is both a product of the power structure and the power structure itself,' said one Yemeni economist.[14] 'Stopping corruption is impossible because it's the lifeline of the patronage network.'

At $930, Yemen's GDP per capita in the mid-2000s was woefully low, but the beneficiaries of Saleh's patronage networks had come to harbour inflated expectations of what the system would provide.[15] 'Everybody's survival depends on patronage and almost all political activity revolves around deciding who to pay off and who to stab in the back,' said one observer.[16] 'While the political class is caught up in maintaining these alliances, they seem incapable of creating a long-term strategic vision. That's no way to run a country but they could just about get away with it, if they had decent reserves of oil.' Instead, as it gradually dawned on people that there was less and less to go round, so there was a greater incentive to pilfer and steal, and more and more competition between the key beneficiaries.

By 2006, the pattern of tribal extortion had become such a self-perpetuating cycle that sheikhs who negotiated directly with the president were often more powerful than senior members of the government. Ministers went to cabinet meetings only to listen, and even then, they heard only what the president wanted them to know. 'Saleh deliberately avoids showing all his cards to the ministers, in case they get their own ideas,' said one international observer.[17] As a result, ministers had no authority to take their own decisions, and they were afraid to act without first getting a green light from the president's office. Promoted to high office, Yemeni ministers were expected to practise 'big-man' politics, but many swiftly found themselves holding a poisoned chalice.

Political power was highly personalized, and informal structures often produced much swifter and more effective results than the formal bureaucracy. As a reporter, I quickly learned to rely on a well-placed presidential aide, rather than Ministry of Information officials, to get results. During one short-tempered exchange with a ministry official, I revealed that my contact in the president's entourage had already told me it was OK to have the permission I needed. The ministry apparatchik exploded with fury. 'I am the official in charge of you!' he shouted, banging one fist on the desk. Whenever I was caught between official and unofficial structures, it was nearly always my informal contacts who opened the door for me.

As head of state, Saleh straddled both formal and informal power structures. Granting access to state resources as well as cash, he balanced different interests within a complex nexus of rival factions that relied directly on his personal authority, like iron filings pulling towards a magnet. 'Saleh rules through proxies, using the TAPE B formula to control traditional and emerging social forces. That's T for the tribes, A for the army, P for political parties, E for extremists and B for the business families,' said one Yemeni political analyst, who often helped me to navigate the country's political complexities:[18]

> Ours is a pluralistic society with diverse sources of power, but we are not pluralistic in Western party political terms, and it's a mistake to think that power lies in the political parties. Even the main opposition party negotiates directly with Saleh, because they know that authority lies with the president himself. They try to act like a proper opposition party but it's often just for appearance's sake.

Saleh consciously cloaked his authority in the language of democracy, while simultaneously trying to prevent genuine competition. In a political environment with such weak democratic structures, opposition groups could end up strengthening the regimes they sought to weaken, by indulging in 'elite, lobby-style politics'.[19] At the same time, many opposition figures understood that aggressive political activity was likely to leave them marginalized, prevented from having any impact at all. In the years before the 2011 uprisings, many of Yemen's opposition figures had come to accept that they must make serious concessions in order to be able to operate. This stemmed, in part, from Saleh's inconsistent and unpredictable use of incentives and threats, which acted as a 'control spectrum' that affected dissenters' calculations. If a relatively minor incident had the potential to trigger a disproportionate response, then any form of dissent was likely to be undertaken with greater caution.[20]

Saleh's Yemen was often portrayed as a weak but nascent democracy, but 'I don't think that's an accurate way of viewing the power structure,' said one European analyst:[21]

Political parties don't exist in order to govern, although there is an extensive party system. Parliamentarians don't exist in order to pass effective legislation, although there are regular elections. And civil society doesn't really exist to hold the government to account, although there's an extensive network of NGOs and a relatively free media [...] The General People's Congress is not a ruling party in the normal sense because not all members of the decision-making elite are members of the party and not all members of the party have access to the levers of power. The opposition parties are not opposition parties in the normal sense because they harbour powerful factions who are creatures of presidential patronage. Parliament acts as a convenient forum where people can let off steam, which allows the regime to monitor political discontent as an early warning mechanism.

One former Yemeni minister put it rather more succinctly. 'Our parliament primarily serves the purposes of the elite,' he told me. 'This is a common Arab political manoeuvre. You throw up a structure that actually fulfils the opposite purpose to the one that seems to be intended. In Yemen, our elite is now utterly dependent on a system that threatens to undermine the whole country.'[22] In the former minister's view, Yemen's looming economic crisis, forced by diminishing oil production, was eroding Saleh's revenue base, with profound implications for national stability. Patronage, not parliamentary representation, had held the country together, and as the tide of patronage began to recede, it was gradually exposing the shipwreck of Yemeni democracy. 'Yemen has never been a real state in the modern sense but it has, nevertheless, performed some basic functions. The most important thing now is to stop these limited functions from failing,' he said.

* * *

High-level corruption was an open secret in the closing years of Ali Abdullah Saleh's regime, but even his political opponents tended to err on the side of the status quo, before the regional uprisings in 2011. Many Yemenis, especially among the older generations, believed that the likely consequence of change would be civil chaos. These fears, both real and imagined, reduced expectations of progress.[23] In addition, concerns that Saleh's removal would create a power vacuum or that genuine reform might unleash forces that would 'undermine, destabilise, marginalise, destroy or kill the politically relevant actors' were ever-present.[24] With more than half the population born after unification, the great majority of Yemenis were too young to remember any alternative to Saleh, and many supporters of the status quo were worried that a new president would attempt to replicate Saleh's model, but without Saleh's previous experience.

This ambivalence was played out during the 2006 presidential elections. Saleh had initially announced that he would step down, allowing someone else to contest the ballot. The news was hailed among pro-democracy advocates as proof that parliamentary politics was reaching maturity, However, nine months ahead of the scheduled vote, Saleh reversed his position by accepting the ruling party's nomination as presidential candidate. He later confirmed this at a stage-managed rally in Sana'a.[25] I had arrived in Yemen just a few weeks before the nomination rally and was caught unawares on the day of the announcement, trapped in gridlocked traffic alongside Saleh's jubilant supporters heading home after hearing his acceptance speech. My photos of the traffic jam depict an impromptu carnival parade of battered mini-buses, crammed with young men hoisting flags that displayed a rearing horse, the ruling party's mascot.

The opposition parties—now clustered together in a coalition known as the Joint Meeting Parties (JMP)—responded to Saleh's U-turn by raising their game and setting aside their considerable differences to field a single compromise candidate, Faisal bin Shamlan. It was the first time Saleh had faced a credible challenger.[26] Bin Shamlan, a septuagenarian economist, had resigned from his post as oil minister in a previous power-sharing government in protest over corruption, allowing him to speak with credibility on the need for reform. Meanwhile, personalities and grandiose promises dominated the campaign, leaving little room for detailed policy discussion. One presidential manifesto glibly pledged to 'fix all of Yemen's problems'.

Campaign posters went up immediately and multiplied prolifically, their progeny freshly tacked to the brickwork. In Bilad al-Rous, just ten miles from Saleh's own village, the ruling party's support was so strong that there was no visible sign of support for any of Saleh's presidential rivals. Hafez al-Bukari, director of the Yemen Polling Centre, dismissed the notion that apparently spontaneous displays of election iconography reflected voters' genuine political convictions, and warned that people were simply protecting themselves. He also explained that many Yemenis held the mistaken belief that the opposition was running against the state, rather than a rival party. 'Many people simply can't differentiate between the current ruling party and the government. The GPC is the dominant party, both in terms of resources and control of media coverage. And after decades of the status quo, people think that all benefits arising from the state are actually coming from the president himself.'

One afternoon, I heard the sound of a band marching at the end of my street in old Sana'a. I grabbed my camera and notebook and ran downstairs, buttoning a *balto* (the traditional all-encompassing black cloak) over my clothes and tucking my headscarf in place at the garden gate. I could hear stallions' hooves on the cobbles and the sound of neighing horses. It sounded as if there was a powerful crowd chanting, pushing through the narrow lanes of the souk, full of purpose and excitement—but I stepped into an empty street. A rustbucket was parked in front of the local grocery shop, run by a man who was rumoured to be a PSO agent. The bodywork of the empty car was plastered with posters of Saleh, and a hundred perfectly trimmed moustaches bristled back at me from the bonnet. A loudspeaker, strapped to the roof of the car, broadcast patriotic music in support of the ruling party.

Across the country, thousands of people turned out to hear the presidential candidates speak at mass rallies in every major city in Yemen.[27] The media reported all the signs of a vital and popular election campaign in full swing, but there was something deceptive about both the rallies and the media coverage. 'We're not ready for a peaceful transition of power,' said Yemeni journalist Nasser Arrabyee:

> The opposition parties have chosen their candidate very carefully, because they need someone capable of nudging the boundaries peacefully and moving the goalposts gradually. They aren't serious in confronting Saleh because they understand that now is not the time. If they mounted a successful challenge, it would lead to violence. That's why they've picked Faisal bin Shamlan, who's an independent man from Hadramaut, rather than a candidate from the powerful Hashid or Bakil tribal confederations.

Shortly before the ballot, Sheikh Abdullah al-Ahmar—paramount sheikh of Hashid, speaker of parliament and leader of Islah—announced that he would vote for Saleh on the grounds that it was better to support 'the devil you know.'[28] However, he added: 'I don't think the election results will be fair, because all the state's resources are in the hands of President Saleh.' Sheikh Abdullah's personal endorsement of the president showed that his own position at the centre of the regime trumped his leadership role as head of Islah, illustrating the unique logic of patronage that was holding the Yemeni state together. Bin Shamlan soldiered on without Sheikh Abdullah's support, like a retired man who has been pulled out of his comfortable armchair to run the village cricket club until a permanent replacement can be recruited.

It was Sheikh Abdullah's son, Hamid, who seemed to possess the fire in his belly that bin Shamlan lacked. When Hamid addressed the crowd at bin Shamlan's campaign finale rally in Sana'a, he was bearded, turbaned and guarded by sandalled lackeys with spare rounds of ammunition looped into their belts. Hamid was billed as bin Shamlan's warm-up act, but in reality bin Shamlan was breaking ground for Hamid, so he could lay the foundations and build his own house in time for the next round of presidential elections, scheduled to take place in 2013. Not enough supporters turned out to fill all the seats in the stadium, drawing complaints that police were preventing people from reaching the event, but the crowd was adamant that their man would bring about the changes that Yemen needed. 'I'm voting for bin Shamlan because he'll eradicate the corruption that dominates our government and institutions,' said one man. 'Authority has been in the hands of one family for too long,' said another.

Half a million people were said to gather at Saleh's final rally a few days later, held at a traditional parade ground close to the main presidential palace, many of them bussed in by the party machine from surrounding villages. The displays of traditional dancing and horsemanship made bin Shamlan's jamboree look like shaky amateur dramatics. The sheer number of people massing in front of the grandstand generated a febrile intensity that was amplified by the absence of video screens to relay the proceedings to the swelling crowd. Only those spectators standing directly behind the concrete crash barriers in front of the grandstand could see the entertainments, and no one occupying these prime positions wanted to give up their spot. Police reinforcements were sent in to hold back the horde but they couldn't stop the building frenzy as hundreds of people pressed forward for a better view. Dozens of limp bodies were hauled over the barriers and dragged away from the crowd, unconscious.

When the president's convoy finally appeared, Saleh emerged from an air-conditioned fuel-injection chariot, flanked by an expensively tailored entourage, and took his place on the VIP grandstand in front of a bank of microphones. The candidate's speech was tantalizingly short, and as he approached the climax of his monologue, his aides released a batch of white doves. In their initial confusion, the birds flew straight into the stadium rafters before fluttering over the crowd. Saleh waited for the first moment of applause before he turned and dashed towards the rear exit of the tiered grandstand. The crowd surged after him, and the police fell back as hundreds of people swarmed over the crash barriers and onto the grandstand. Diplomats and journalists stumbled and fell in the aisles, running for the same door that the president had taken, but the exit was closed. Consternation began to spread, as the realization dawned on people that they might be trapped. It wasn't until the president was safely clear that his guards reopened the doors, and others around him were able to flee the elated crowd.

Election day was a public holiday and the city was quiet, as many in Sana'a had returned to their villages to vote. A campaign was in full swing to persuade men to leave their guns at home to prevent the bloodshed that had blighted Yemen's previous elections. At the polling stations, women were siphoned into separate rooms and told to remove their veils so female election officials could check the photos on their identity cards. By mid-afternoon in Sana'a, crowds of men who had already voted sat munching qat, each with a single purple ink-stained finger, as they watched the latecomers arriving at their local polling stations. In old Sana'a, a teacher who had just voted for bin Shamlan said:

> The GPC is paying money for people to vote for Saleh and they're putting pressure on government employees like me. Everyone in the army and the civil service will vote for the GPC or they won't get their salaries. Of course I'm worried about my job and I expect problems in the future if they find out how I've voted but I'm not afraid because sometimes you reach a point where you want to speak the truth.

Bin Shamlan ended up with 22 per cent of the vote, while Saleh won a comfortable 77 per cent mandate for another seven-year term. 'The result is bound to be rigged,' one sceptical Western diplomat had muttered during the election campaign,[29] while journalist Nasser Arrabyee predicted: 'Saleh will win by hook or by crook.' Even with a rigged result, these results represented progress of sorts in a region where most elected heads of state considered it an embarrassment to romp home with anything less than 90 per cent, and European Union election observers judged the poll to be an 'open and genuine contest'.

Opposition parties protested, claiming fraud, but at least one Western official supposedly counselled them to accept the result; and the opposition coalition eventually released a statement to the effect that they wanted 'to avoid a clash or a confrontation with the authorities which [might] derail the process of change that has begun'.[30] A new crescent moon was sighted three days after polling, the mullahs declared Ramadan, and all controversy and contention was forgotten for the duration of the fasting month.

In the early days of Ramadan, a contact at the Ministry of Information summoned me to his office at short notice. I was expecting yet another meeting to negotiate a filming permit I needed, but a political security agent greeted me at the main entrance to the building. She confiscated my mobile phone and gestured towards a hired bus, parked in the ministry courtyard. As I clambered on board, I realized I was the last person to take my seat. Thirty male Yemeni journalists automatically reorganized themselves in pairs and threes so, as the only woman, I could sit alone. I prompted a similar reshuffle every time I used the public minibuses that flew around the streets of Yemen's capital, Sana'a, charging 20 riyals for a hop-on, hop-off journey.[31] The engine started, and we rumbled past a handful of armed guards at the ministry gate, driving into the slow-grinding traffic inching its way around Liberation Square in the centre of Sana'a. Strong afternoon sun glazed the bus windows, and we all had dry mouths and empty stomachs. Juice bars lining the square would stay closed until dusk, but ragged crowds were forming and re-forming around several newspaper kiosks that dotted the central concrete reservation of Liberation Square. Henna-dyed horses with lurid tassels dangling from their leather saddles stood waiting for pleasure riders to pose for photos.

By now, I had gathered that we were heading for the president's city centre residence, just a few minutes away from the parliament building.

As we passed the turning to the palace, our bus sailed past a platoon of soldiers into a military cordon, and drew to a halt outside the gates of the compound. Snipers on one knee, proposal-style, watched our movements from the palace roof as we filed off the bus. It was my first visit to the president's residence and I stared at the neat green lawns, tidy flowerbeds and unpitted asphalt in disbelief. The world on the other side of the palace walls bore no resemblance to this image of prosperity and orderly management.

In the shade of the palace building, the Sana'a press pack mingled with hundreds of murmuring dignitaries, stroking beards and rubbing shoulders. I was the only foreigner invited to witness Yemen's political elite as they waited to congratulate their long-time president, Ali Abdullah Saleh, for his recent re-election to serve another seven years in power. At 5 p.m., we were given the signal to shuffle forward, taking our place in a tidy queue to shake hands with the leader in front of the television cameras. Step by step, we filtered slowly from a surging rabble into disciplined single file and climbed the steps to the red carpet where the president stood, glad-handing his guests. The reception room was a hothouse and our host's skin gleamed in the heat of the camera spotlights. When I approached the premier, he gripped my hand firmly. '*Men?*' he said. Who are you? A translator hurried forward, as Saleh's hand enclosed my fingers.[32] 'I'm a British journalist,' I answered in Arabic.

The president stood stocky and proud, in a black shirt and black suit, and I caught a glimpse of startling charm, but I towered over my inquisitor by a good few inches. As Saleh released my hand, I stalked away from the television cameras, returning to the garden. The afternoon heat was fading fast, and sheikhs, ministers and politicians sat in cross-legged circles on the grass waiting for *iftar*—the meal that follows the Ramadan fast. The men were clad in Arabian robes, military uniforms and smart Western suits, with a smattering of sandals and moustaches.

The only other female guests were unveiled and in their fifties. They were complaining of the weight on their feet. Palace staff found us a private room, inside the palace, where the three female officials removed their shoes and stretched their stockinged toes, relieved to be sitting down. On the table in front of us, Saleh's staff arranged bottles of chilled water and plates of sticky dates and hot samosas, covered in cling film. 'How do you find Ramadan?' one of the women asked me. 'It teaches patience,' I replied.

After several minutes of small talk, we heard a commotion in the corridor. The president passed our room, his retinue moving with him. When he caught sight of us, he stopped and came to the door, speaking first to his lady colleagues. Then he turned to me and asked if I had a good impression of Yemeni women. 'I've met lots of talented and assertive Yemeni women, but it's a pity that there's only one woman in parliament,' I ventured. 'A woman was running Yemen long before there was a woman running your country,' Saleh retorted, turning on his heels. He was referring to Bilquis, who Yemenis claim as their pre-Islamic queen, but I never had a chance to find out whether he meant Boudicca, Elizabeth I, Queen Victoria, Elizabeth II or Margaret Thatcher.

When dusk finally fell, the imam's raucous broadcast from the president's private mosque shattered our tangible anticipation. In the garden, the men surged forwards towards benches of food in a wave of collective relief. In our ladies' waiting room, we pulled back the cling film from the plastic trays of dates and samosas and sank our teeth into sugar and grease. I had eaten lunch at home, but these were the first morsels that the my companions had consumed since dawn, despite the heat, mountain altitude and full day's programme of official duties. Prayers followed their brief snack, as the sky darkened. In our makeshift harem, the women officials took their turn to give thanks in the corner. Once everyone had finished praying, we were ready for dinner.

From the high ceilings of the presidential banqueting hall, five glass chandeliers the size of small municipal roundabouts dangled over forty round tables laid with white linen. Attended by a crowd of earnest migrant waiters, we consumed baked fish, mounds of rice and boiled lamb joints, fried prawns and pasta. Seated at the top table and partially obscured from view by an extravagant fruit platter, Saleh talked to Prime Minister Abdul Qader Bajammal as both men ate their food. Around us, the room remained in constant motion—a bobbing, flowing, Brownian motion of garrulous generals, mullahs and MPs. 'I love to cook,' said the woman seated on my right, spooning her *cherfout*, a signature Yemeni yoghurt dish, layered with absorbent bread and flavoured with bitter herbs, into her mouth. 'But I don't have time these days. I'm too busy.' As a prominent public official, she had surrendered her traditional housekeeping role.

After twenty minutes, just as I was sampling sweet biscuits dripping with splendid Yemeni honey, the president stood up and walked out, trailing fleet-footed aides. This rapid departure of power from the room prompted an instant exodus of notables into the Sana'a night. Only an excited mob remained, knitting themselves into a small frenzy around the leader's vacant table as they rushed to consume his unwanted food. A lean troop of soldiers had been watching the feast with envy, stomachs empty from the day's fast. Now, their restraint broke. Officers patrolled the room with apples shining in their hands, faces smiling and jolly. Their uniformed men swarmed on the generous remains, shoulder-slung Kalashnikovs pointing skywards as they bent over half-empty plates to consume the sumptuous leftover food with their bare fingers.

* * *

'Political reform in Yemen has stalled. The country has reached an impasse in the transition to democracy,' said a despondent homeward-bound election observer in an airport departure lounge a week after Saleh's *iftar* reception at the palace. She had arrived in Yemen with high expectations for the 2006 presidential election campaign, but now she was utterly deflated. 'I'm pinning my hopes on the idea that promises made during the election campaign are going to generate some momentum, because Yemen simply cannot afford to remain unchanged.' When European Union monitors published their full and final report on the elections a few months later, they listed unfair use of state resources, the exclusion of women from participation at all levels, clear bias in the state media, detention of opposition supporters and concerns that the counting process lacked credibility.

The campaign had indeed provoked a national debate about corruption, but, in the event, it appeared that the election raised people's expectations of change without successfully pressuring Saleh to deliver. A few months after the ballot, Rageh Badi, editor of the weekly newspaper *Al-Sahwa*, voice of the Islah party, warned me that Yemenis were in danger of losing faith in the electoral process altogether:

> Poverty is growing, and people want confidence that better things will come. There is no one to hold Saleh to account except the people because

the Yemeni constitution gives absolute authority to the president. Saleh has the power to appoint the cabinet, the *shoura*, the higher judiciary, the provincial governors and the high command of the armed forces.[33] We are pushing for constitutional amendments to reduce the authority of the president and boost effective parliamentary mechanisms for bringing the executive to account, but we can't force constitutional change, because we don't have a majority.

In a fourth-floor strip-lit office in a dingy cinder-block building in Sana'a, *Al-Sahwa*'s male staff wandered about in their socks or bare feet. In contrast to the frenetic GPC apparatchiks, Islah men carried themselves with civility and an air of self-restraint. They wore neat suits but seemed poor cousins to the well-dressed GPC spin-doctors who had tasted the fruits of the West on junkets abroad with Saleh, and seemed to want more. It was a fitting irony, then, that Islah was appealing to the EU as a referee in its squabble with the GPC over constitutional reform. 'The final EU monitors' report is accurate and unbiased, that is why the ruling party is quibbling about it,' Rageh explained, before lamenting Islah's relative impotence in relation to the influence of international donors. 'America and the European donors are much more effective than us in exerting pressure on Saleh. The government listens to foreign powers because it pays off, but there's no pay-off in listening to opposition voices.'

At that time, Islah had the fastest-growing membership of any political party in Yemen and an active women's section, and it was 'increasingly using democratic rhetoric' to legitimize its position.[34] However, Islah's representation in parliament had fallen during the two decades since unification, reflecting the growing institutional dominance of the president's ruling party, Islah's slower learning curve as the weaker force within an emerging political framework and the constraints of patronage-based politics.[35] During parliamentary elections in 2003, Islah's campaign strategies began to demonstrate growing sophistication and the party secured significant gains in urban areas, but it had yet to field its own presidential election candidate.[36]

Saleh himself had condemned Islah as 'the forces of darkness', but Yemen's main opposition party was better described as 'a pragmatic, relatively moderate Islamist party'. The key to understanding the party's role within the national political framework was to appreciate the factionalized and highly centralized nature of Saleh's system of patronage. Islah was 'a party of the establishment centre', and the type of politics in which Islah's leaders took part was a 'style of patronage and connections rather than of ideology or of activists as vanguards of the masses'.[37] Rather than leading an Islamist confrontation with the state, Islah instead 'played a mediating role between the state and the country's more conservative religious elements'.[38]

Islah harboured both moderate and hardline Islamists, including bombastic firebrand preacher Sheikh Abd al-Majid al-Zindani. A former advisor to the ministry for education, al-Zindani had helped to conscript Yemen's *mujahideen* for the Arab campaign against the Red Army in Afghanistan during the 1980s.[39] With his brightly hennaed beard and pillbox skullcap, al-Zindani stood as a poster child for Western anxieties about Islamist rabble-rousers, and in 2004, he was placed on the US Treasury list of 'specially designated global terrorists' for his alleged role in providing financial support to al-Qaeda operations; al-Zindani denied the accusation, while Saleh made a public statement on Yemeni television to vouch for his good character.[40]

Al-Zindani's prominent position within Islah contributed to Western suspicion about the party's true agenda, but he articulated popular anti-American sentiment and represented an important piece in the political jigsaw that Saleh had to assemble. 'Zindani is massive!' grinned one of Sana'a's teenage taxi drivers, promptly shoving a cassette of the Qur'an into his stereo when asked for his opinion of the cleric.[41] However, al-Zindani's profile began to wane after the 2006 elections, and his demotion from leadership of Islah's Shoura Council the following year represented an 'indication of the rising power of the moderates within the party'.[42]

Sheikh Abdullah al-Ahmar had established the Islah party in 1990 with 'considerable financial backing' from Saudi Arabia,[43] and he led it—as both sponsor and container—for the best part of two decades. His immediate family held five seats in parliament, representing a small power bloc in their own right. (The YSP only held seven seats.)[44] After his death from cancer in 2007, Sheikh Abdullah's power portfolio splintered among his sons, with the eldest, Sadek, succeeding his father as paramount sheikh of Hashid.[45] Hamid continued to bankroll the party, but Islah's vice-chairman, Mohammed al-Yadoumi, was promoted to fill the chairman's vacancy.[46] The role of speaker of parliament passed out of family control, but the position of deputy speaker was awarded to another of Sheikh Abdullah's sons, Himyar. Sheikh Abdullah's alliance with Saleh had formed a 'cornerstone of the political status quo for nearly three decades',[47] but in the years following his passing both Islah—and Hamid—began to play an increasingly assertive and independent role, setting the scene for a future showdown over parliamentary patronage and the politics of balance.

4

GIRAFFE ARMY

AK-47S, ARMS-DEALERS AND WARLORDS

'Yemen's leader needs the tribes in one hand and the army in the other'

Western diplomat, Sana'a, 2007

Our shooting party was in high spirits. We had broken off from a long afternoon visiting my Yemeni friends' relatives in the central highland provinces. The family saloon—a rickety old jalopy—climbed a scree track on the lip of a dam, struggling for traction. Every jolt produced a burst of noise and hilarity. We were all giddy with the thrill of transgression, initially happy to escape from Sana'a for the weekend and now, briefly, guiltily, eluding our parochial duties with relatives down in the valley.

My Yemeni escorts were second-generation migrants to the capital—urban sophisticates whose wealth and connections had emboldened them to defy many of the values and conventions with which they had been raised. Their identity was still rooted in tribal soil, but they could now see far beyond the customs and expectations of their grandparents. Although they treated their elderly relatives with impressive deference, my presence in the midst of the village folk gave this homecoming visit the flavor of a theme-park ride. Village residents handled me with caution, like an expensive contraband product that could get everyone into trouble if something went wrong.

69

My friends wanted to teach me how to fire an assault rifle as part of the authentic Yemeni experience, and they drove me up the flank of a nearby mountain to a spot that was used for target practice. A young man called Ahmed was waiting on the ridge to meet us, and he stepped forward as we pulled off the track and threw open the car doors. A US green-card holder, home for the summer, Ahmed had been shooting and chewing qat all afternoon. The whites of his eyes had turned scarlet. He laughed at my ankle-length black robes and the blonde hair escaping from my headscarf, then he handed me a well-worn Kalashnikov. 'Look along the sights and aim across the water to that hillside. You won't hit anyone.' The men ranged around me, excited, and bubbling with advice. Someone stood back, taking photos with a digital camera. 'Is this right? Am I holding it right?' I asked. 'Yes,' said Ahmed. 'But keep your upper body in contact with the weapon when you pull the trigger.'

I stood on a narrow plateau at the head of a dammed lake, looking at a flat expanse of milky stewed tea—the water muddied by particles of soil and dust. It was the last hour of daylight, and the dun-coloured rocks had lost their daytime glow, but the air was still warm. In the greying twilight, I could just make out a track on the far slope, running between scrubby bushes, but the features on the hill were indistinct. I laid the index finger of my right hand lightly against the trigger and my left-hand grip on the gun was steady, but my courage failed me. I was reluctant to shoot when I couldn't see clearly as far as the weapon's range. I brought the rifle down from my shoulder, weighing its steel frame in both hands for a few heavy seconds. Ahmed, who had probably learned to shoot before he could write, was irritated by my hesitation and suddenly impatient. 'Let's go,' he said. 'We're running out of qat.'

Kalashnikov assault rifles are the most widespread military weapons in the world and they have become an integral part of the social fabric in Yemen.[1] Shock-and-awe journalists often cite the popular figure of fifty million small arms in circulation in Yemen but in the mid-2000s six to nine million was accepted as the most realistic estimate. Just 1.5 million of these weapons were thought to be in the hands of the state, and demand was rising in line with population growth.[2]

The revised estimate of six to nine million weapons still placed Yemen among the world's most heavily armed societies, with roughly forty weapons for every hundred people. Comparative gun ownership levels in the USA were more than twice as high,[3] but AK-47s—the firearm of choice for insurgents, pirates and organised criminals[4]—conveyed a disconcerting image to US citizens who might not think twice about owning the latest model from Smith & Wesson, the NASDAQ-listed US handgun manufacturer.[5]

The worldwide profusion of AK-47s can be traced to 1947, when the Russian-made assault rifle first entered active service.[6] General Mikhail Timofeyevich Kalashnikov, injured in battle during World War II, designed a simple, robust weapon with minimal working parts in order to better equip the Russian army. Moscow went on to ship millions of Kalashnikov weapons to clients and allies throughout the Cold War, many of which were funnelled into illicit global markets dealing in small arms.[7] As Soviet designs were not subject to patent restrictions, they gave rise to numerous copycat variations.[8]

In Yemen's case, Russian-made AK-47s were dispatched to Aden throughout the lifespan of the PDRY. Vast stockpiles remained nominally under the control of the southern army when it was loosely integrated with the YAR military, following unification in 1990. Four years later, Saleh chose to rely on Islamists and northern tribes to prosecute his civil war against the south, and, as payment in lieu, militiamen were allowed to loot the accumulated surplus of the former southern army.[9] During the ensuing years, small arms became part and parcel of Yemen's political and social order, especially in the north, and gun ownership helped to maintain informal systems of community justice that compensated for the absence of a strong, consistent state.

For Western visitors, the sheer visibility of privately owned firepower in Yemen can be intimidating. In 2006, before parliament imposed a ban on carrying weapons in the capital, I went to meet a powerful sheikh and member of parliament who ran a company that serviced the oil industry. Clusters of armed militiamen were squatting on the pavement outside his office building, framing the doorway to the lift lobby, like characters in a contemporary Arab version of Bruegel's early modern portraits of Dutch mercantilism.

Yemenis' evident pride in bearing weapons is bound up with notions of manhood, and fathers teach their sons an unwritten code based on honour, generosity, courage, self-control and autonomy.[10] In my translator's family home, a haven of professional prosperity and tranquility on the outskirts of Sana'a, I sat and watched while Mohammed and his brothers loaded their Kalashnikovs in the living room. Their twinkle-eyed mother was baking bread downstairs in the basement, and their teenage sisters, who were cooking lunch in the kitchen, came to stand at the door and watch us, smiling indulgently.

Visiting Saudi men who want to look the part while travelling in Yemen can even rent Kalashnikovs for display purposes at the Yemeni border.[11] A Saudi businessman once admitted to me it was possible to hire an entire armed entourage 'just to feel important', he said, chuckling.[12] He plucked a figure out of the air, quoting 20 men for $1,000 for a week, but implied that the variable price depended on negotiation with local sheikhs or officials in the Yemeni police force.

Yemen's gun-toting culture might offer a titillating diversion for adventurous Saudi tourists, but weapons in Yemen are assets and a form of currency in themselves.[13] 'Guns for men are like gold for the ladies,' said Ali, as we drove to a market town south of Sana'a. I was travelling with staff members of Dar al-Salaam—House of Peace—a prototype civil society organization campaigning to end tribal violence in Yemen. 'Men will go without food to arm themselves,' Ali added, inverting the first two bands of Maslow's hierarchy of needs.

There were eight of us squeezed into a Land Cruiser—five staff members, me, a Canadian journalist and Dar al-Salaam President Abdulrahman al-Marwani. The boss and his team were dressed in their best suits, each one proudly sporting a corporate badge in his jacket lapel that showed the black silhouette of an assault rifle with a red line through it, like a no smoking sign. A spare wheel cover, bolted to the back of the Land Cruiser, displayed the same logo.

Abdulrahman hadn't arranged travel permits for his two foreign charges—me and the Canadian, Glyn—to leave the capital. Instead, he charmed his way through a succession of checkpoints, handing out posters, badges and pens to the scrawny jejune soldiers who came to tap on the driver's window. The irony of preaching non-violence to men who relied on the military to support themselves and their families was overlooked. Instead, there were shy smiles all round, and they waved our car through quickly and courteously.

Abdulrahman's charisma was utterly infectious. He was tactile, generous and affectionate, constantly grasping the shoulders and elbows of friends and colleagues who stood within arm's length. His handsome, animated face transmitted delight and humour. He already had two wives and several children of his own, but he was amassing a surrogate family of male orphans who revered him as a peacemaker and a father figure.

Nineteen-year-old Ahmed was Dar al-Salaam's youngest, newest volunteer. Ahmed's father had recently been killed in a revenge cycle that had already slain several dozen of his relatives, stemming from a land dispute that started before he was born. When Ahmed arrived at Dar al-Salaam's offices, asking for help, the campaigner convinced the boy to join the organization and act as an interlocutor. Gradually, Ahmed persuaded his relatives to allow Abdulrahman to mediate. On the day of our outing to Dhamar, Ahmed was going home in a suit. We dropped him at a crossing on the main road, and left him standing in a knot of goats. Abdulrahman gave him a bear hug and a kiss on the cheek before we drove on to Dhamar and the gun souk.

It was midday when we picked our way over the rubble at the edge of the market and walked in single file through a network of covered alleys that led to the gun shops. A shaded circle of lock-ups, built with concrete breeze blocks and metal shutters, faced a sunny patch of hardened earth. The mood among the vendors was languid, verging on listless. It was the final half hour before lunch, and pint-sized boys were playing at their fathers' feet, but the gentle banter dried up as we walked in. Incredulous eyes bulged on the faces that turned towards us, and the atmosphere stiffened noticeably.

Abdulrahman sprang into action, clasping hands and working a small crowd that gathered round him. He dished out Dar al-Salaam badges like sweets—but, once again, the irony of arms traders wearing 'no weapons' lapel buttons was entirely lost. With Abdulrahman distracting most people's attention, Glyn and I set quickly to work, asking questions and documenting the visible stock. We counted roughly twenty lock-ups in this section of the souk, selling assault rifles, handguns and bullets. Boutique stores such as these were rumoured to be display fronts for heavier weaponry—rocket launchers and anti-aircraft missiles—that could be viewed and purchased by private appointment.[14]

One-eyed Abdullah was among those who accepted Abdulrahman's token gift, and pinned it to an unbuttoned red blazer, which fell open over his enormous girth. Abdullah said his family had been selling weapons for 150 years. Stout and paunchy, his grey hair was topped off by a red and white mashadda head-dress. He had papered the walls of his cubby-hole store with a quotation from the Qur'an, a picture of Saleh and a poster of the late Palestinian spiritual figurehead Sheikh Yassin, assassinated several years earlier in an Israeli missile strike.

Abdullah had mounted a selection of new and used hand-guns in front of a poster of the Dome of the Rock in al-Aqsa Mosque in the holy city of al-Quds (Jerusalem). Thirty pistols and twenty Kalashnikov derivatives were hanging on homemade nail hooks. Among his selection of second-hand weapons, he showed me models from Hungary, a Colt AR-15— 'property of the US government'—and a wooden-handled German rifle that he told me was fifty years old. Abdullah also stocked box-fresh Chinese assault rifles and brand-new Chinese pistols. Bullets stacked in flimsy cardboard boxes were priced at four for a dollar.[15]

Abdullah was busy explaining that Yemeni soldiers came to the souk to hawk guns and munitions, to supplement their salaries, but, as we were chatting, the temper among neighbouring traders began to quicken and shift like a spring wind. Glyn and I had both taken our cameras out and this was judged to be a provocation. The vendors were uneasy about our presence and unsure of our motives. We had disturbed the hornets in their nest and they surrounded us, shouting.

It was the hour of empty stomachs and craving for qat, and everyone was becoming fractious. Abdulrahman hustled us away, guiding us back through the warren of streets to his waiting Land Cruiser. We drove straight to the house of a local sheikh, where Abdulrahman led midday prayers, barefoot on the carpet in the *mafraj* (a reception room for entertaining guests). At lunchtime, we crammed into an adjacent unfurnished guest room, where the carpet was covered with plastic. I squatted on the floor, surrounded by two dozen retainers, picking mutton off the bones with the fingers of my right hand. The sheikh and his retainers had propped their AK-47s outside the door, like umbrellas on a rainy day at a gentlemen's club in London's Pall Mall.

A long mediation session followed lunch—tense and drawn out. A tentative peace deal based on a livestock bargain had broken down and a rolling feud, prompted by a land dispute between two local tribes, had recently reignited. The week before our arrival, a member of the rival tribe had tried to shoot the sheikh who now sat in front of us, wedging qat leaves in his mouth and complaining that the police were turning a blind eye. 'Either they will bring me the man who tried to shoot me or my own militia will kill him,' he warned. 'It's shameful if I can't defend myself. This situation is humiliating me.' The sheikh was grandstanding, and Abdulrahman was playing for time, promising to lobby senior officials in Sana'a on the sheikh's behalf. 'The authorities are aware of this case now and we are doing what we can to raise your concern. You are a well-known sheikh, and you have a duty to be patient and wise. I beg you not to retaliate until our procedures come to a conclusion,' implored Abdulrahman.

On the drive home, Abdulrahman explained that guns are often held in trust by an agreed mediator until revenge killings are resolved. He spoke of tribal values regulating rural life and lamented the state of the criminal justice system. 'There is no confidence in our judges here and no confidence that anyone will implement a verdict. People prefer to take matters into their own hands.' His assistant, Ali, said that tribal quarrels almost exclusively grew out of petty disputes. 'It's mainly land issues, but sometimes we end up dealing with love crimes and the violation of marriage contracts.'

Ali and Abdulrahman described a sorry story of bloodshed filling the vacuum created by the absence of strong government,[16] but, as with many things in Yemen, there was a subtle, confusing counter-current running through the problem of tribal violence. At times, it seemed, laws made in Sana'a were regarded as irrelevant and ineffective by the tribes, but at other times, ministers' intrusive and inconsistent attempts to enforce their authority over rural communities were perceived as a threat and were generating tension.[17] It was clear, however, that local officials would not intervene in intertribal conflicts unless they received explicit orders from Sana'a. At the highest level, managing the tribal balance was a political decision and, therefore, constituted the president's business.[18]

* * *

A few years ago, a Western official reportedly sought an audience with Saleh to discuss Yemen's many and various arms trade violations, and flagged up the role of several powerful, well-connected arms traders. In particular, the diplomat complained about the actions of one notorious businessman, a close ally of Saleh's. 'Oh, you want me to talk to him?' asked Saleh, sardonically, picking up the telephone. 'Well, he happens to be here at the palace already. Let's ask him to come and say hello.'[19] (Although this anecdote has the ring of an urban myth, it effectively illustrates a perceived relationship.)

Saleh's ally was one of several dominant arms brokers belonging to a nonpareil network of business and commercial interests that sat cheek by jowl with his regime. Acting as conduits between Saleh's military commanders and international arms wholesalers and retailers, he and his fellow dealers worked like spiders, spinning a web of 'hard power' that held Yemen's elite in place. They functioned as a lethal oligopoly, supplying a family-dominated oligarchy that owed its continuing position to its stranglehold over the state security apparatus.

Yemen does not legally produce small arms, so almost all weapons for military and private use are imported, mainly from the former Soviet satellite states in Eastern Europe.[20] The arms procurement structure authorized by Saleh revealed a great deal about the nature of Yemen's 'state' institutions under his presidency. 'The army does have a central purchasing department and army officials are at least nominally responsible for negotiating supply contracts but all rules in Yemen are made to be broken,' one Yemeni source told me.[21]

Formally, the Ministry of Defence procured Yemen's military equipment through a centrally authorized channel, but, informally, division leaders also had the right to negotiate their own independent arms deals[22]—effectively creating standing armies that sat inside the state structure. Army commanders could usually, but not always, be relied upon to act consistently with the collective, private interests of the regime, if not the public interest invested in the state, and this distinction between the regime and the state was a crucial one. The commanders themselves reported directly to Saleh 'outside the normal channels of the Ministry of Defense and without constitutional mandate', and they acted as the 'final authority in nearly every aspect of regional governance'.[23]

Yemen's supreme military commanders belonged to the President's Sanhan clan, which rose rapidly to prominence after Saleh was appointed to the top job in 1978. A minor subgroup within the larger Hashid confederation, Sanhan had historically supplied soldiers for the

Imam's army, and gained visibility after the revolution with the growth of the Republican military, from the mid-1960s onwards.[24] Saleh himself had risen to the presidency through the army, and swiftly moved to buttress his position as president by appointing close relatives to key roles. His brother, Mohammed Abdullah Saleh, became chief of the Central Security Forces (CSF), while his half-brothers, Ali Saleh al-Ahmar and Mohammed Saleh al-Ahmar were posted to strategic command positions.[25] A third figure—a Sanhan kinsman but not a blood relative—also joined the ranks of Saleh's trusted senior officers. His name was Ali Mohsin al-Ahmar. (Ali Mohsin is not related to Sheikh Abdullah al-Ahmar.)

In the ensuing three decades, Ali Mohsin grew into a figure of mythic proportions in the minds of Yemen's metropolitan gossipers and *mafraj* political philosophers. Once a direct rival for Saleh's crown, and believed to have stirred enormous discord in the years preceding the 2011 uprising, Ali Mohsin was both one of Saleh's closest allies and one of his most dangerous rivals. As commander of the First Armoured Division, Ali Mohsin was widely recognized as a controlling power broker at the very heart of the regime, and almost without exception he was mentioned in hushed and furtive tones. Before 2011, his photograph rarely appeared in the media and he had no public persona. An outline of his position at the heart of Yemen's power nexus could be pieced together only through speculation, rumour and second-hand information.

Ali Mohsin's attributed role reflected a shadow image of the cult of personality that surrounded Saleh himself. According to *mafraj* mythology, Ali Mohsin and Ali Abdullah Saleh had agreed an informal power-sharing deal before Saleh stepped up to the plate in 1978. Ali Mohsin would become de facto president if Saleh were killed, or died suddenly, but Saleh was anointed as the one who would step forward first.[26] The covenant was formed at a time of rapid turnover among Yemen's leaders, and agreed by the wider group of Sanhan commanders as a guarantee to protect their collective interests; but Saleh went on to surprise everyone—and perhaps not least himself—by hanging on to power and seeing out the century as head of state.

Throughout the 1980s and 1990s, conventional wisdom pivoted on the assumption that Ali Mohsin was the most likely successor to replace

Saleh in the event of the incumbent's sudden death. However, in 2003, Saleh began to restructure the Republican Guard and demoted some of Ali Mohsin's allies, as he began building a power base for his eldest son, Ahmed Ali, then in his early thirties. In 2005, US officials estimated that Ali Mohsin still controlled more than half of Yemen's 'military resources and assets',[27] but during the next few years, Saleh deliberately eroded Ali Mohsin's command-level support. By the end of the 2000s, Yemen's political class thought that Ali Mohsin was probably getting too old to harbour serious ambitions for the top job, but they perceived him as a future kingmaker.[28]

Ali Mohsin's animosity towards Ahmed Ali was well known within political circles. His anger at Saleh's attempt to tip the balance of military support in Ahmed's favour mirrored Sheikh Abdullah's resentment at Saleh's attempt to lay the ground for a managed political transition to his eldest son at some point in the future. The young pretender, Staff Colonel Ahmed Ali Abdullah Saleh, commanded his own divisions of the Republican Guard and the Special Forces.[29] Ahmed's Facebook album, accessed in 2009, revealed a small boy wearing an outsize *jambiya* (a dagger with a curved blade), sitting by his father's side at what seemed to be a tribal-style convention. He had his father's deep brown eyes and imitated his father's composed camera-ready stare. As an adult, he was pictured striding side by side with Jordan's King Abdullah at an arms fair.

In the years before the 2011 uprising, if you asked politely at the newspaper kiosks in Sana'a's central Liberation Square, you could get your hands on back copies of Ahmed's glossy eighty-page *Republican Guard* magazine, offering crosswords, whimsical editorials and articles on military strategy. The September 2004 issue contained features on modern Russian torpedoes, the art of military leadership and the role of the intelligence services in peace and war. In a previous issue, an editorial titled 'Typical Reader' meditated on the achievements of US presidents and intellectuals, such as Rosfelt (sic), Amirson (sic) and Henri Thoro (sic). Ahmed's editorial stated: 'If I want to evaluate someone, I will ask him: "How many books have you read and what have you read?".' Ahmed observed that for Rosfelt (Roosevelt), books were the 'light that leads to civilisation' and for Thoro (Thoreau), books were the 'world's future stored'.

Saleh and Ali Mohsin had both forged their careers in the crucible of revolution and unification, but Ahmed's literary pretensions suggested that his had been a softer political and military initiation. Ahmed's mother had died in a car crash when he was just a young boy, and it was said that he was close to his eldest sister, Bilquis, who went on to marry her cousin, Yahya. For Yahya's part, it was said that he had reluctantly succeeded his own father, Mohammed Abdullah Saleh, as the CSF chief of staff. However, Yahya refused to sit at his late father's desk, doing business on a brown leather sofa suite in the corner of the office instead, as I learned when I met him at the CSF headquarters in Sana'a in 2007.

Yahya was softly spoken and oddly shy. He seemed embarrassed by his shaky English, but it was certainly good enough for us to talk without a translator. In addition to his responsibility for the CSF, Yahya also supervised an elite US-trained counter-terrorism unit (CTU), which recruited a clutch of young Yemeni women from the military police, whom I wanted to meet. Yahya told me that male terrorists often disguised themselves as women in order to evade detection and arrest, so the women on the CTU followed their male colleagues on house raids. 'Yemen's strict social code means that female suspects cannot be touched by the men on the unit,' he said.[30] A rigorous training programme had taught the women on his unit how to enter a house by force, drive a military vehicle and shoot.

The women's locker rooms were tucked away in the corner of the CSF headquarters, in a compound housing the CTU barracks. Each woman on the unit travelled to work in the morning wearing a veil and full-length black robes, but switched to heavy black boots and fatigues that were specially designed to cater to Islamic principles of modesty. Their spokeswoman pulled back her long-sleeved, loose-fitting camouflage jacket to show me a pistol strapped to her belt. Yahya's girls wore hijab under their regulation berets to conceal their hair, but unlike most Yemeni women, who covered their faces but allowed strangers to see their eyes, these girls bared their faces and hid their irises behind mirrored lenses.

After forty minutes chatting about their families and their working lives, there was a knock at the door, and a male soldier relayed the message that Yahya was waiting outside to talk to me. Parked in front of the door to the women's quarters stood a Humvee-style car and an empty school bus. The asphalt was bristling with moustaches and rifles, ringing both the vehicles. I boarded the bus, as directed, and found Yahya sitting alone in an aisle seat, apparently for the sole purpose of talking to me in private. 'Do you like them?' he asked me. I sat down across the aisle from him, amused by this impromptu debrief. Yahya's manner was reserved, and he seemed genuinely curious to gauge my response. He was visibly pleased when I related praise from a senior US diplomat who had briefed me before my visit to the CTU compound. 'It's one of our favourite security institutions to work with because it's new and there is no corruption,' the American had told me. 'They are forward-looking and proactive. They're willing to try new approaches and tactics. And they are growing gradually, as they develop additional capacity.'

Yahya hopped off the bus, jumped into his Humvee and disappeared in a squeal of burning rubber. His brother, Tariq, whom I met a year later, was much more guarded, and refused even to reveal his identity. Stocky and cocky, with a shaven head, Tariq just smiled and laughed when I asked who he was, but later I discovered that he commanded the president's personal security unit. Yahya's other brother, Ammar, ran the US-funded National Security Bureau (NSB) as de facto chief.[31] Together, Yahya, Tariq, Ammar and Ahmed represented a new generation of Sanhan military commanders who expected to carry their fathers' legacies into the future. This incestuous configuration bore close resemblance to another mid-ranking army clan, the Tikritis, who bestrode Saddam Hussein's Iraq. One European development consultant working in Yemen astutely concluded that the US government was partnered 'with a family, not a nation'.[32]

* * *

US military advisers training Yahya's CTU rented a cavernous newbuild villa in the sprawling Hadda district, on Sana'a's affluent southern outskirts. Landlords and property owners in this part of town went in for high walls and anonymity. The combination of conspicuous wealth and foreign tenancies created a permissive air of exemption that rubbed off on some of the neighbouring Yemenis. The adjacent house was standing empty: it was rumoured to belong to a Yemeni sheikh who used it solely to throw parties.

The US trainers had turned their hired mansion—fitted with chandeliers and ornate plasterwork cornices—into an outpost of the R&R

department. They had painted a crude black and white 'missing in action' mural on the wall of their basement, installed a home gym, set up a projector screen to serve as a home cinema in one of the bedrooms and positioned a football table by the front door. Their drinks cabinet was stocked to bursting with brand-name imported spirits, not the cheap contraband knock-offs that could be bought surreptitiously in Yemen.

I went with a friend to the Americans' house for dinner one evening, on a night when they were 'locked down'—that is, restricted to their home base on the orders of senior US security personnel because a tribal shoot-out had erupted earlier that day, on a street close to their villa. Tribesmen firing anti-aircraft machine guns mounted on pick-up trucks had driven up and down a busy arterial road all afternoon. Shooting finally ended in the car park of a local hospital, where the two tribes collided as they brought the wounded for treatment. The quarrel allegedly involved a land dispute, but apparently arbitrary incidents such as this one passed for 'white noise' in Sana'a—the atmospherics of a dicey security environment.

Our American hosts supplied us with barbecued steak, rack-grilled over a flame fire in the garden, and Jack Daniels. A *tabouleh* salad for the vegetarians, which the Americans ordered from a nearby restaurant by phone, arrived three hours later than planned, with the apologetic delivery man claiming that the main road was still closed because of the shoot-out and disruption that followed. The dining table was crowded with tattoos, powder-bulked biceps and the faint stain of heartbreak. Many of the guys serving us dinner had picked themselves up after their marriages failed, dusted themselves off and devoted themselves to hunting down evil. 'I don't believe in killing people,' said Buck.[33] 'Killing people ain't no solution to the problems in the world. But if you're gonna do it, I'll show you how to do it right.'

Buck and his housemates had been stationed in several global flashpoints over the last two decades—Colombia, Rwanda, Somalia and Sierra Leone. They had also served in Iraq, and they regarded themselves as conviction careerists, justified in taking on the West's dirty work, while liberals averted their eyes and moaned about human rights abuses. 'We keep you safe, and we're the ones who get our hands bloody. I get tired of people like you complaining,' said Buck, in response to a liberal inquisitor, who helped herself to the Americans' generous rations of red wine as she took them to task for Washington's adventurism in the 'war on terror'.

We headed home after midnight, a procession of women morphing on the moonlit doorstep into black-hooded figures. The Yemeni guards watched us silently as we trooped through their gatehouse to the waiting taxi. I assumed, rightly or wrongly, that the guards felt humiliated by this flagrant violation of the local cultural code, and that their impotence to stop the Americans' offensive social antics underlined the fact that the dollars bolstering the CTU carried more clout with Saleh than the Prophet's words. It was a kind of occupation, a humiliation—and perhaps it was tinged with envy—but, in any case, they could only watch and serve.

The US military footprint in Yemen was and still is extremely light compared with Iraq, Afghanistan and some of the Gulf states. In any other context than Yemen, hosting a dinner party for unmarried women seems so entirely commonplace as to be unbelievable that it could cause offence. In Yemen, however, it amounts to a thoughtless, indulgent and destructive abuse of privilege that Westerners are guilty of all the time. A few months later, when one of our hosts lost a handgun, the US embassy launched an inquiry and the men were shipped out a few days later.

Yemen has received US military aid since the 1970s, although the link was broken briefly in 1991, following Saleh's support for Saddam Hussein's invasion of Kuwait.[34] At that time, US aid was punitively slashed from $42 million to less than $4 million in the space of 12 months.[35] It wasn't until 2001 that US money started sloshing around again, when Congress designated Yemen a 'front-line state' in the war on terror, and US military financing rose from zero to $20 million almost overnight.[36] By 2010, the figure for combined US military and intelligence spending had reached $150 million.[37] Foreigners have been training and equipping the Yemeni army since Imam Yahya established a garrison based on the Turkish model in the early twentieth century, and retained Ottoman trainers.[38] During the Cold War, there were an estimated 2,000 Soviet advisors, 10,000 Soviet military personnel and 400 Cubans in the PDRY,[39] while Saleh's YAR relied on Iraqi security advisors and received military aid from Iraq.[40] In the early years of the twenty-first century, the Yemeni army was still a bride with several foreign suitors, including France, the UK and Jordan. Jordanian military instructors began training Yemeni forces in 2002, under a deal worked out between the Jordanian military and US Special Operations Command.[41]

* * *

Saleh's military employed an estimated 200,000 personnel, including servicemen in the air force and the navy.[42] Military jobs provided a reliable income for vast numbers of young men who would otherwise have struggled to find a career in a country with 40 per cent unemployment. With a grunt's basic monthly salary at just over a hundred dollars, topped up with food rations, military earnings were low both in real terms and relative to civil servants' wages, yet they also served to distribute government funds to a broad cross-section of the population.[43] 'Everyone wants to join the army because the army is money,' said one Yemeni friend. 'Soldiers send their salaries home to their families, so the government is feeding large numbers of people in the countryside through army wages. The army is the employer of last resort.'[44]

The military rank and file came overwhelmingly from non-tribal peasant stock, while tribesmen dominated the upper echelons.[45] The command structure of Saleh's army was deliberately maintained in order to minimize the risk of a coup. Each infantry wing sported a unique livery, and recruits to one particular army division dressed in yellow jumpsuits, camouflaged with brown blotches. They looked like bruised bananas or a skinny, gangly adolescent regiment of Flintstone characters wearing brown helmets; I often wondered how best to describe them. It was a visiting academic who eventually hit the nail on the head, poking fun at the discrepancy between the idea of the army as a formidable national institution and the sometimes farcical reality. 'Zaraffat,' he said, derisively, as we sped past a sentry post together one day in a taxi. Giraffes.

The officer class included a significant number of Sunni Shafis, who were reputed to be better educated than their northern counterparts.[46] The top army leadership was almost exclusively northern, and the super-elite was predominantly Sanhan—a monopoly position that enabled them to profit from 'grand corruption'.[47] At command level, the primary means of extorting state resources for personal gain relied on systemic embezzlement. While there may have been notable exceptions, commanding officers were known to inflate the headcount under their control, then claim salaries and supply quotas for 'ghost soldiers' who neither existed nor reported for duty. Officers allegedly pocketed the cash and sold off weapons, ammunition, food and blankets, vehicles, fuel and tyres, as a way of topping up their paltry take-home pay.[48] In a similar vein, mysterious depot blasts and stockpile fires were thought to conceal the illicit sale of military weapons.[49]

The activities of the Yemen Economic Corporation (YECO) were testament to a second form of systemic manipulation that appeared to profit from vast economies of scale.[50] Originally involved in 'supplying boots and uniforms, bread and canned goods to soldiers', YECO quickly expanded into other fields such as land deals and general imports, until it had a controlling stake in a range of sectors, including farming, retailing, packing and canning, and transport and refrigeration.[51] By the beginning of the 2000s, YECO formed 'the very substance of the military-commercial complex',[52] in which production was 'not the basis of wealth and power' but rather 'personal wealth accrued from control of the import business and of currency transactions linking Yemen to the wider world, and many of those who exercised such control were army officers'.[53]

YECO was supposedly independent of state enterprise, but it owed its commercial dominance—in part—to the authorized seizure of southern resources during the 1994 civil war, when senior northern officers took control over land and government-held businesses throughout the south.[54] The military, either directly or through YECO, continued to claim land for military use and sell it on to private developers. However, the full extent of YECO's activities was unclear.

As one Yemeni commentator said to me: 'YECO is an organization with close ties to the president. It doesn't pay its fair share of taxes, duties, licences or import fees. It's the primary beneficiary of industrial and commercial operations throughout the country and government ministers are essentially complicit because they cannot enforce the law.'[55]

The presence of enmeshed military and commercial interests resting just beneath the surface of the state architecture is familiar from Pakistan, Iran and Nigeria. It's a timeworn model that flourished to a greater or lesser extent throughout the Middle East and Africa during the latter half of the twentieth century. However, the collapse of the Soviet Union at the end of the Cold War and the liberalization of international financial and commodity markets combined to form organized crime's 'big bang'.[56] Criminal elites established illicit super-highways trafficking narcotics, hardwoods, caviar and sex workers throughout Eastern Europe's fledgling post-Soviet states. Their interests extended well beyond Europe, including 'buying and selling arms within the former Soviet Union and exporting them to the world's trouble spots'.[57]

Organized crime in Yemen thrived on a similar franchise, and throughout the 2000s, Yemen was a reliable destination for weapons from Belarus, Russia and Ukraine.[58] Licences to import heavy weapons—known as End User Certificates (EUCs)—were issued by the Ministry of Defence as a guarantee that the buyer was the final recipient of the materials and the purchase was legitimate. However, in Yemen, the allocation of EUCs formed part of the patronage system, with importers and distributors receiving a share of the cut. The president personally oversaw the allocation of EUCs, as they directly affected the balance of hard power within the regime, and ministry officials were often reduced to rubber-stamping deals that were made at the palace.[59]

By the end of the 2000s, Yemen's military procurement system had created a spectrum of hand-picked strongmen, supplied by obliging dealers, who were motivated by their own entrenched financial interests, operating in close proximity to international black markets.[60] 'Ali Mohsin's military power stands beyond the full control of central government,' argued one Yemeni analyst. 'In addition to his formal role as a military commander, he enjoys a private income stream, which gives him some autonomy. The infrastructure for a permanent war economy is already in place.'[61] Yemenis contemplating the prospect of future instability feared that the limited functions of the government would shrink further still, as the elite became increasingly preoccupied by the balance of power between 'the faction […] the clan, the family or even the individual'.[62]

5

ACROSS THE GULF

PIRACY AND PEOPLE-SMUGGLING FROM THE HORN
OF AFRICA

'Commercial imports, mainly from Yemen, remain the most consistent
source of arms, ammunition and military materiel to Somalia'
UN Monitoring Group on the Arms Embargo to Somalia, 2008

Haroun and I are both children of Margaret Thatcher's Britain, born
and raised in the 1970s.[1] When we met in December 2006, we were
both enrolled as students at the same Arabic language institute in Sana'a
but in other ways our lives were following very different trajectories.
Haroun had just been released without charge from a Yemeni jail, but
his reputation was tainted with the unproven but lurid accusation of
gun-running to Somalia. 'I was arrested during Ramadan,' he told me,
sitting in an atrium café inside a shopping centre on Algeria Street. 'I
came out of the mosque with my friends after dawn prayers. Six guys
with Kalashnikovs grabbed us, handcuffed us and shoved us in a Land
Cruiser. At the beginning, I wasn't sure what was happening. I thought
it might be a kidnap attempt.'

Haroun was driven to the main political security prison in Sana'a,
where he spent the last ten nights of Ramadan, the holiest nights of the
year, in solitary confinement. 'I was held below ground but I could hear

8

the call to prayer from the nearest mosque, so I prayed in the dark.'
Haroun said he spent a week in total blackness, and a month in isolation. He counted the tiles that lined his cell, guessing that the tiny
room was just over 5ft wide and 6.5ft long. He had a thin filthy mattress and a bucket. Food came three times a day, but it was 'inedible'.
He said he wore the same clothes for a month.

According to Haroun, security officials interrogated him more than
a dozen times during his imprisonment. The longest inquisition lasted
for twelve hours, and he was blindfolded on each occasion, except the
very last. He said he was tightly handcuffed, beaten and kicked; he was
allowed to observe prayer times during these lengthy interrogations,
but his hands remained cuffed. Towards the end of his incarceration,
guards moved Haroun from his dungeon cubicle to a larger, communal
cell on the ground floor, which he shared with several Yemenis. It was
here that he found some old newspapers, and learned that he was suspected of smuggling weapons to Somalia. He was released a few weeks
later, without any charges filed against him.

With his long beard and his MP3 player loaded with Islamic lectures
and Qur'anic recitation, Haroun fitted the stereotype of many Western-
born converts to Islam, drawn to Yemen's Salafi madrassas. The word
'salaf' means predecessors or early generations, and Salafism is a movement that seeks to return to the simplicity of Islam as practised by the
Prophet and his companions as the guardians of true Islam. Salafis can be
characterized as dogmatic in their emphasis on ritual and their literal
interpretations of the Qur'an. They also denounce innovation added to
Islam in subsequent generations, especially those facets attributed to
foreign cultural influences, and particularly associated with the West.

Many Salafis reject democracy and 'all forms of statist politics'.[2]
However, significant internal divisions separate 'quietist' Salafis, who
are 'apolitical in principle, refusing any party system', from 'activist'
Salafis, who are willing to engage in political competition, and finally
'jihadi' Salafis, who advocate the use of violence against their religious
and political enemies.[3] I was surprised when Haroun agreed to meet
me, because of strict Salafi curbs on contact between men and women,
but he said he was willing to break convention because he wanted to
publicize the abuse that he had suffered at the hands of his Yemeni jail-
ers. 'This experience has only deepened my faith, because Allah willed
it. It is written,' he said.

In 1997, the year of Tony Blair's landslide Labour election victory, Haroun left Britain to work in the Gulf. Haroun told me that he had wanted to live on the Arabian Peninsula, closer to the heart of Islam. He had arrived in Yemen just a few months before our meeting, in summer 2006, with his young family, because he and his wife wanted to raise their children in a more religious environment, and Yemen had an unparalleled reputation for piety among Salafi circles. The couple chose to live in an apartment building, close to al-Iman university in the Sana'a suburbs. Among other residents in living the same building were a group of Western Muslims, some of whom were also caught up in the dawn swoop in which Haroun himself had been arrested.

However, Haroun's group was thought to be associated with a then little-known Yemeni-American cleric called Anwar al-Awlaki, whom the Yemeni security services had arrested several weeks before the October round-up, without much fanfare.[4] Haroun's group was also believed to be linked to a Somali, whose arrival in Yemen during Ramadan of 2006 triggered the dawn swoop in which they were all arrested. The Yemeni raid supposedly shattered a Western surveillance operation to monitor the apartment building where Haroun was living.

Yemeni officials initially claimed that the suspects had confessed to weapons smuggling, fundraising for terrorism and links with Yemen's al-Qaeda terror network. A house search reportedly turned up al-Qaeda documents and thousands of US dollars and euros. Then, suddenly, the authorities seemed to drop the case, and all the Western suspects, including Haroun, were released. Yemeni prosecutors admitted that the group had been freed because there was no evidence to support the charge of an al-Qaeda-backed gun-running conspiracy. Haroun was deported in December 2006, shortly after our meeting, and the trial of the one remaining suspect—the Somali—collapsed when he refused to enter a plea.

* * *

Yemen has been a weapons-trading hub for the Red Sea states and the Horn of Africa since the nineteenth century. Two continents collide where Arabia reaches across the Red Sea to kiss Africa at the Bab al-Mandab. In 1880, the vagrant French poet-photographer Arthur Rimbaud was living in Aden. He negotiated with his Aden employers, the coffee traders Viannay, Bardey et Cie, to establish a franchise in eastern Ethiopia.[5] Once resident in the walled city of Harar, Rimbaud supplemented his coffee-trading income by running guns to Menelik, future emperor of Ethiopia.[6]

Throughout the twentieth century, diverse groups plotted intended advantage by procuring arms through Red Sea trade routes. During World War 1, T.E. Lawrence learned that the Germans planned to ship weapons from Yemen to Abyssinia to begin an uprising in the Horn.[7] During the 1970s and 1980s, the Palestinian Liberation Organization supposedly relied on weapons transferred via Yemen's Red Sea islands. In 1996, Osama bin Laden created a 'naval bridge', shipping weapons between Aden and Port Sudan.[8]

It was the collapse of the USSR and the end of the Cold War that established the lucrative regional arms trade in which Yemen has played a dominant role. Both the PDRY and Siad Barre's Somalia had received money from Moscow, but while the withdrawal of foreign support contributed to Siad Barre's deposition and ushered in two decades of Somali civil war, North and South Yemen agreed to a voluntary merger.[9] Newly unified Yemen, with its stock-pile of PDRY Kalashnikovs and its elastic military procurement structure, was ideally placed to corner the regional arms market, in violation of a UN embargo on the delivery of all weapons and military equipment to war-torn Somalia.[10]

Illicit transfers flourished for a decade, until the revelation came to light that surface-to-air missiles used in the 2002 bombing of the Paradise Hotel in Mombasa, Kenya, and an attempted attack on a flight from Mombasa bound for Israel were shipped through Somalia from Yemen.[11] The following year, the UN established a monitoring group to report on violations of the arms embargo. An early report from the monitoring group noted that the Yemeni government had provided a small amount of military assistance to Somalia's caretaker government, but considered the flow of weapons from two private sources in Yemen to be much more significant:[12]

> First, there are reportedly high-level officials within the Government of Yemen who are willing to provide Yemeni end-user certificates and facilitate the sale and delivery of weapons to officials of the Transitional National Government (Yemeni officials deny this). Secondly, businessmen in Yemen obtain weapons and ammunition from the general population in

Yemen that are then shipped to Somalia, where demand and prices are much higher.

Over the next few years, arms embargo violations took a 'sustained and dramatic upswing', and by 2005, the UN was warning that weapons transfers from neighbouring states were leading to increased militarization in Somalia. The monitoring group determined 'with a reasonable degree of certainty' that Yemen was supplying arms directly to both Somalia's temporary government—now called the Transitional Federal Government (TFG)—as well as opposition groups. The monitoring group noted that the flow of arms to Bakaraaha Arms Market in Mogadishu was 'a good barometer of arms flows into and around Somalia'. The UN declared that a 'very significant quantity of the arms available for sale at Bakaraaha come from Yemen', noting the role of criminal groups and arms-trading networks supplying the market.[13]

The monitoring group also recorded several official arms transfers from the Yemeni government to the TFG, noting that Yemen's Antonov An-26 military aircraft made eight arms deliveries in the first ten days of July 2005. Yemeni officials defended these shipments, saying that thousands of police uniforms, food supplies and personal weapons were delivered at the TFG's request, consistent with Yemen's 'clear policy aimed at restoring stability in Somalia, ending the civil war there and supporting the central government'. In view of the financial burden that the government had undertaken by assisting the TFG to fight against terrorism and 'ensure that no new Taliban emerges in Somalia', Yemen made a gutsy plea for financial compensation from the international community.

During the first six months of 2006, as TFG bureaucrats seemed to be clinging to power by their fingertips in Somalia, the popular Union of Islamic Courts gathered momentum and support. As the Islamic Courts movement evolved from a community-funded sharia court coalition into Somalia's strongest fighting force, a clandestine arms race was taking place, with large cargo planes and fishing dhows making weapons deliveries 'almost on a daily basis'. New recruits and foreign volunteers were training for battle in military training camps, as the Islamic Courts extended the territory under their control.

When the Islamic Courts seized Mogadishu in June, they began by dismantling warlord checkpoints and establishing a taxation system.

Mogadishu residents, tired of endless mayhem, initially welcomed the Islamic Courts' law and order administration, but Somali refugees fleeing to Yemen in late 2006 told stories of Taliban-style oppression.[14] One cinema owner described how the Islamic Courts destroyed his business, while a young woman spoke of her punishment for flirtation and simple courtship. A great number of new male arrivals in Yemen in the closing months of 2006 seemed likely to be warlord militiamen who had lost their retainers, but they were reluctant to speak openly about their former employment.[15]

Somalia's successful Islamist power grab created consternation in Washington, where US Assistant Secretary of State for African Affairs Jendayi Frazer claimed the usurpers were 'controlled by East Africa al-Qaeda cell individuals'. With US troops already deployed in Iraq and Afghanistan, and US military chiefs haunted by the 1993 'Black Hawk Down' debacle in Mogadishu, conventional deployments to Somalia were out of the question. The White House relied on airstrikes against Islamic militants, sent in Special Forces and turned to neighbouring Ethiopia, as a surrogate force and intelligence-sharing ally.[16] Ethiopia swiftly played the patriotic card by claiming the Islamic Courts supported a long-standing secessionist movement in Ethiopia's eastern Ogaden region, home to four million ethnic Somalis; furthermore, Ethiopia likened the Islamic Courts to the Taliban.[17] When Ethiopian troops invaded Somalia on 24 December, the leadership of the Islamic Courts was hounded out of Mogadishu in a matter of days. Washington celebrated January's swift rout, but the TFG, newly installed in the capital, could not survive without Ethiopian military support, and the continuing presence of Ethiopian troops provoked the rump of the Islamic Courts to mount an insurgency challenge to the foreign occupation. The USA initially provided Ethiopia with enough 'aid and comfort' to withstand mounting financial and political pressures to withdraw, but the perception of a US-backed Christian occupation served as a rallying cry for jihadists and further polarized the conflict.[18]

By now, Somalia was 'literally awash with arms', and Somalia's capital was fracturing into rival anarchies.[19] The Islamic Courts' militant wing, Harakat al-Shabaab al-Mujahidiin (Mujahideen Youth Movement), began to transform itself into an effective, autonomous network of terrorist-type cells. Mogadishu insurgents were copying tactics from

Iraq and Afghanistan, using targeted assassinations and car bombs in their assault on Ethiopian troops, Ugandan peacekeepers and the TFG 'puppet' government. Warlords, freelance militia and pirates were arming and rearming, as part of the evolving ecology of Somalia's conflict. Weapons traders, meanwhile, were successfully sidestepping a growing international maritime presence in the Gulf of Aden. Covert arms shipments were common, and weapons were reaching Somalia in larger numbers of smaller vessels or through remote locations along land borders. Somaliland had become a significant entry point for weapons, in addition to the coasts of Puntland and central and south Somalia, and Mogadishu arms traders were travelling via Somaliland in order to reach Yemen to order weapons consignments. Weapons originating in Yemen's private arms markets, as well as Yemeni government stocks, found their way to Somalia.[20]

In the closing weeks of 2008, the monitoring group noted that although the UN arms embargo had been in effect for more than sixteen years, most serviceable weapons and almost all ammunition available in Somalia had been procured since the start of the ban. The expert panel concluded: 'Commercial imports, mainly from Yemen, remain the most consistent source of ammunition and military materiel to Somalia.' They acknowledged that Yemeni curbs on domestic arms sales since June 2008 had reduced the volume of exports to Somalia. However, they noted that weapons from Yemen continued to 'feed Somali retail arms sales and the needs of armed opposition and criminal groups'. They concluded that Yemen's inability 'to stem the flow of weapons across the Gulf of Aden has long been, and is likely to remain, a key obstacle to the restoration of peace and security to Somalia'.[21] Yemeni ministers were quick to plead multiple constraints to curbing the arms trade. They argued that their country's modest resources, its embryonic coastguard and its long coastline created challenges that they could not surmount. Yemeni bureaucrats presented the arms trade as a consequence of poverty among Somali fishermen, who turned to weapons smuggling to make a fast profit. The presence of large numbers of Somali refugees in Yemen facilitated the passage of arms shipments 'without the knowledge of the competent authorities', they argued.[22] They also tried to frame the conflict in Somalia as a 'direct threat to the security and stability' of Yemen, because of the 'large-scale migration of Somalis to Yemen, which has considerable adverse consequences'. Sana'a insiders, however, rejected the official explanation, with one analyst pointing his finger directly at Yemen's own arms dealers.

* * *

Someone had drawn an arrow and written the word 'HEAD' on the lid of the coffin that Djiboutian baggage handlers were stacking upright in the plane's rear galley. The name of the deceased— 'Mohammed'—was inscribed in capitals in shaky marker-pen on the front panel of the plywood box. To travel from Sana'a to northern Somalia, I was flying via Djibouti City, a joint civilian–military use airport shared by the French Foreign Legion and the US Combined Joint Task Force based at Camp Lemonnier. Faded mugshots of suspects in Yemen's 2000 USS *Cole* bombing were still tacked to the wall of the airport's immigration office.

Soft-suited aid workers and Somali women clutching their belongings in plastic bags crowded on to our tiny Daallo Airlines aircraft like shoppers cramming home-bound buses in central London.[23] Headquartered in the UAE and managed by a Dubai World subsidiary, Daallo Airlines was established in 1991 after the demise of Siad Barre's national flag carrier.[24] Although the airline was flying under a cheery free-market slogan—'Connecting Africa to the Global Village'—the plane itself was a Russian-made Cold War relic, a sturdy turbo-prop designed to land on unpaved runways in remote locations.

In the mid-2000s, Bosaso airport on Somalia's north coast handled less than two thousand passengers in a single year, processing roughly the same number of people every month that passed through London's Heathrow every fifteen minutes.[25] On Google Earth, the landing strip at Bosaso looked like a surgeon's scalpel line, a pale white incision running east–west across golden ochre sand flats. As we flew lower and lower on our approach to the beach, our Antonov-AN 24 cast a quickening shadow on the seaside runway. A Mercedes four-wheel drive with blacked-out windows shot towards us across the sand, cutting a diagonal path through dozens of tyre tracks that ran parallel to the tideline. We touched down on compacted sand and the late Mohammed was carefully lifted down in his wooden box.[26]

It was summer 2007, and Bosaso had not yet become a pirate town or a kidnapping zone, but the stage props and actors were already in place for the drama that would follow. A few months after my visit, a French journalist, a Spanish doctor and an Argentine nurse were taken hostage, forcing the tiny clutch of Western NGOs based in the port city to withdraw their foreign staff.[27] Airport militiamen patrolled the sand wielding AK-47s, their eyes shielded from the littoral glare in wrap-around sunglasses. A lone immigration official took my dollars and wrote out my visa longhand on his battered wooden desk. Delicate tendrils of cool air, drifting off the rippling backwash, did little to ruffle the muggy midday heat in the clerk's sweltering office.

All the while, a war was raging in everyone's peripheral vision just a few days' drive away in Mogadishu, and every morning buses and trucks unloaded a fresh civilian exodus in Somalia's most northern port. During two decades of drought, famine and flying bullets in south-central Somalia, tens of thousands of urban nomads had swelled Bosaso's population from 15,000 to 250,000.[28] New arrivals set up flimsy homes with sticks and plastic sheets using their bare hands, while men queued for casual labour on the docks and women sold themselves as service workers to Bosaso's settled residents. Beyond the last line of shanty houses, livestock (camels and goats), which formed the backbone of Bosaso's formal economy, stood corralled on stony ground. Clan traders, appointed by elders from Bosaso's pastoral hinterlands to negotiate the sales of local herds to Saudi Arabia and Yemen, brought their animals to the port for transit. Before the advent of Somali piracy in 2008, the livestock trade accounted for the vast share of northern Somalia's foreign exchange earnings and significant numbers of jobs.[29] The festival of Eid al-Adha was the busiest time of the year, supplying hajj pilgrims in Mecca with thousands of livestock for Islam's ritual annual slaughter.

Houses in Bosaso's low-rise coastal community were painted in a sweetshop palette of butterscotch, peach, pistachio and cornflower blue. Enough local residents were flush with money from diaspora remittances and profits from livestock shipments to drive a visible construction boom, throwing up bricks-and-mortar villas surrounded by 10ft walls. Slim white minarets with angular green rocket-top balconies suggested the influence of Gulf money that people said was trickling in. But there were no advertising hoardings in the congested streets around the port where Somalis changed their money, bought pay-as-you-go mobile phone credit and browsed bootleg cassettes of Eminem and Destiny's Child. Shopkeepers commissioned murals displaying their goods and services, so Bosaso's largely unlettered population knew what was on sale. A tenuous parallel economy thrived inside the shanty city of flapping plastic and sticks, with separate teashops, general stores and a shanty cinema running off a small generator that screened three films a day.

The harbour itself was crawling with snappish, truculent armed guards. Labourers hauled sacks of Indian rice from a docked vessel. Rolls of barbed wire, building materials, stacks of plastic chairs and a fleet of brand-new SUVs stood on the docks. This was the entry point for a supply chain that ran all the way through the Horn. As well as commercial goods, Mogadishu arms dealers and local militia relied heavily on the port and the hinterland road network for weapons transfers.[30] Sources in Yemen and Bosaso told me that arms from Yemen were also flown here on a regular basis. 'A procession of jeeps with blackedout windows heads out to the far side of the air-strip when the planes come in,' said one Somali. A Yemeni friend added, with bitter humour, that small turboprops often flew from Somalia to the southern Yemeni port of Mukalla, supposedly to deliver sheep, because 'we don't like our sheep to get sea-sick. And we pretend it's just a coincidence that there's a cargo plane stuffed with munitions standing on the tarmac at Mukalla but everybody knows how it all works.'[31]

Rumour and speculation grew like bindweed in this shifty, apparently unaccountable place, where the CIA allegedly ran an interrogation house and people claimed that Europe's toxic waste was dumped offshore. During a curt introduction at his central compound, the governor banned me from asking any 'political' questions and told me to stay away from local military sites.[32] On the governor's desk, a silk flower arrangement sat centre stage atop a shabby laminated plastic tablecloth displaying Dubai's skyline. Heavy ragged red curtains blocked the light at the windows and a single lethargic fan was trying to stir the soupy, fetid air inside the room. Armed militiamen sat everywhere, and clinging to them was the heavy smell of stale sweat. Outside in the parking lot, amid piles of sand, a burnt-out car and more militiamen with guns, a young boy washed the dust off visitors' windscreens for a handful of Somali shillings.

Echoing the Yemeni government's argument, the governor explained that his administration, with its few resources, could not effectively patrol Bosaso's extensive, isolated coastline. He complained that the international community had ignored his repeated requests for patrol boats, radios and coastguard training. 'We do our best,' he said, 'but the smugglers are often one step ahead.' A few hours later, a joint interview with a police officer and a smuggling boss produced more illuminating answers. The pair sat side by side in the back of a parked car and finished each other's sentences, as if they were whittled from the same stick. They described the relationship between the local authorities and the smugglers as a game of cat and mouse, with informers in both camps. 'Police informers infiltrate the trafficking network, but the smugglers have allies within the police force, too,' they said, together. They spoke of an intricate brokerage chain for refugees buying transit to Yemen, with competing agents in every town on the main route from Mogadishu to Bosaso.

Mousa, barely twenty, was among those shopping for passage from Bosaso to Yemen. He had been press-ganged into a Mogadishu militia by his clan elders when Ethiopian troops invaded Somalia. In January 2007, there were a hundred men in Mousa's unit, but six months later, when we met, he said he was one of only three survivors. 'If I go back to Mogadishu, a bullet will kill me, so I might as well take the risk at sea,' he reasoned. Mousa was willing to pay $100 to spend several days packed in an overcrowded fishing boat, lured by the promise of automatic refugee status in Yemen or the prospect of travelling further north to Saudi Arabia.[33] He would trust his life to men like Mohammed, a stick thin fisherman-turned-trafficker who claimed to earn $600 a month crewing the smuggling boats.[34]

Mohammed's wage should have been a reasonable sum in Bosaso, but he was agitated and shabbily dressed with sly, nervous eyes. He had spent several years crewing tightly packed fishing dhows, beating his passengers as a crude form of crowd control, and often watching people die of suffocation in the overcrowded hold. He was deadened to his own cruelty, saying, simply: 'If they move, we hit them and if they die, we throw the bodies overboard to lighten our load.' Although Yemen's landing beaches lie only 170 nautical miles from Bosaso, the slow-moving refugee dhows can take days to reach Shabwa province on the southern coast. Boats land close to the former incense port of Qana, currently known as Bir Ali, where thousand-strong camel trains once ran north across the Empty Quarter.[35]

Nowadays, Yemen's Bir Ali is a shabby fishing port with a modest little market. Trucks rumble through on the main coastal road from Mukalla to Aden, and goats roam the petrol station forecourt. Sand drifts pockmark the desolate landscape, interrupting 'an ancient flood of lava' that pours to the sea.[36] Volcanic craters with their sides abruptly shorn away by landslides look like millers' storeroom heaps of powdery cocoa and pale, creamy kamut, collapsing under their own weight. Dolphins play in a quiet inlet in the shadow of Husn al-Ghurab (the Fortress of Crows) and camels range the dunes, running in a wide undulating band for dozens of miles at al-Nushaymah. At dawn and dusk, fishermen's skiffs breach the surf line and later, when the skiffs return, fathers and sons squat on the sand flats, gutting their catch.

During the 2000s, before Yemen's latest bout of war disrupted the pattern of regional migration networks, it was here that Somali smugglers would bring their boats in sight of the coastline and wait until darkness before sailing into shallow water. Night after night, hundreds of weak, exhausted men, women and children were pushed into the sea at gunpoint and forced to swim to the shore. The lucky ones found their sodden belongings floating in the surf, and made their way through the dunes to find transport that would take them to a nearby UNHCR processing centre. The ones who couldn't swim, or whose limbs were too stiff from the journey, were unable to keep themselves afloat. Their bloated corpses came to rest beyond the tidemark, buried by local fishermen in unmarked graves. There were even tales of corpses washed up on Yemen's beaches with their hands tied.

In 2006, I spent a week camping at a rudimentary beach hotel near the landing sites with Swiss camerawoman Marie-Laure Widmer Baggiolini and several armed chaperones from Bir Ali's police force. Each night, one of our chaperones kept guard outside our bamboo lean-to, gripping his Kalashnikov, and during waking hours, he travelled with us in our Land Cruiser. The glittery-eyed Bir Ali police chief, wearing a *futa* (a sarong-style skirt) and sandals, followed behind in a 'technical'—a flatbed pick-up truck with an upright post for mounting a machine gun. In daylight, we swept the sand flats in our two-car convoy, and from time to time we found Somali stragglers, lost and disorientated, who told us that Yemeni soldiers had robbed them of their money. When it got hot, we rigged up some shade, stringing tarpaulin sheets between the roofs of the two cars and lying down in the dirt to sleep. We ate our evening meal on the beach, squatting in the car headlights, before driving the length of the sand flats again in the darkness.

On our last night, a small fleet of boats arrived close to midnight. As we sped down to the sea with our camera rolling, hundreds of barefoot Somalis were already streaming off the beaches. At the water's edge, a group of women searched for their possessions, while two men, each with a plastic bag of clothes at his feet, stood in our headlights to change their sopping shirts. In the dunes, we found two inconsolable teenage boys, cringing and crying at the sight of our camera. An adult man lay prone in a sand drift, with silvery-white sand crystals glittering on his face in a policeman's torchlight. He sat up to drink the water we offered, his mouth foaming. Around us, the footprints of a human herd, all heading in the same direction, studded the dunes.

On the main coastal road, scores of Somalis stood milling around waiting for fate to intervene in their favour. Their stomachs were empty and their clothes were rank and salty, but it would be hours more before they reached UN protection, and medical treatment and food. Adil Mokhtar Mohammed described how they'd been loaded on to the boats in Bosaso 'like animals' and made to squat in rows. 'If you get tired and ask for relief, the crew will hit you,' he said. 'You can't open your bag to reach for food and water because you're not allowed to move. After a while, you're so desperate you think it would be better to throw yourself into the sea.' A French documentary maker, Daniel Grandclément Chaffy, who by coincidence had arrived in the same batch of boats, confessed that he, too, had been so tormented during the sea crossing that he longed to fling himself into water to escape the smugglers' brutality and the refugees' distress.[37]

I spent months interviewing Somali refugees in Yemen, and over time I came to recognize the look of new arrivals. Their eyes were hollow with shock, and for some it took weeks for the trauma to evaporate. It clung to them like the smell of salt water and the memory of swimming through the starlit sea with death all around them.

Seventeen-year-old Abdi Ainta Omar arrived in Yemen in a four-boat flotilla, crewed by nervous sailors who received a mobile phone call telling them that the Yemeni security services had opened fire on boats that were sailing further ahead. When the six-man crew pushed their passengers into deep water, more than two dozen people drowned on Abdi's boat. 'I thought I was going to die, too,' he said, speaking to me months later in a Sana'a café. 'I was clinging to a heavy bag of clothes and the sea was dragging me down. I was swimming past corpses. It would stir even the hardest heart,' he whimpered.

* * *

Yemen first granted automatic refugee status to Somali nationals in 1991, when Siad Barre's government stuttered and collapsed. During the following two decades each one of Mogadishu's erratic power-shifts provoked a fresh cycle of migration to Arabia, pausing only during the annual monsoon season when high winds in the Gulf of Aden made the sea crossing too dangerous. During the late 2000s, the number of Somalis willing to risk the journey more than trebled, rising from 23,000 recorded arrivals during 2006 to 77,800 by 2009. According to the Office of the UN High Commissioner for Refugees (UNHCR), Yemen hosted upwards of 170,000 registered refugees, but Yemeni sources often claimed the true figure of Somalis and Ethiopian migrants in the country was closer to 1 million.[38]

The presence of an impoverished migrant community in Yemen, where unemployment was already running at around 40 per cent, placed visible strain on the increasingly shaky social infrastructure. Fewer than one in ten registered Somalis lived in the sole UN refugee camp, near Aden, and the vast majority of Somalis chose to fend for themselves by washing cars and selling incense. 'We do our best to make our little piece of bread go round,' Foreign Minister Abu Bakr al-Qirbi told me in 2006, before the numbers of new arrivals skyrocketed. The poorest state in the Middle East could barely afford such generosity, nor indefinitely sustain unlimited newcomers, but neither could it revoke its guarantee of sanctuary to Somalis.

During the final years of Saleh's presidency, the price of sea passage kept rising—from $50 to $150—and in addition refugees and migrants could pay up to $150 for their land journey to their departure port in

Africa, and then again to cross the Saudi border. Cash payments were made at the start of the journey in Somalia, but Somali smugglers most likely had reciprocal business links with Yemeni counterparts. Based on the UN's 2009 figure of 77,800 registered arrivals in Yemen, gross annual regional turnover could run to around $20 million—or even higher, given that many migrants choose not to register on arrival in Yemen. With contempt and frustration striking competing undertones in his voice, a senior Western diplomat stationed in Sana'a once told me: 'There are people high up in this country who have been making good money from refugees landing on the beaches, and whether it's people or weapons or goods that they smuggle, there are powerful allies here who have made this possible.'[39]

The refugee trade was the most visible tip of an adaptable, integrated network shifting people and drugs from Africa to Arabia, and bringing guns and cheap diesel back again. Several sources in Yemen speculated that the refugee boats were unlikely to sail home empty once they had dropped their human cargo, and in 2008, the UN monitoring group stated that dhows used to ferry Africans to Yemen were loaded up with 'arms and ammunition on the return journey'.[40] After dozens of research interviews with contacts in Yemen and Somalia, I developed the impression that this lucrative smuggling trade was highly organized, with big deals agreed between brokers in Yemen and Somalia and small-scale delivery operations taking place on the coast—although I never saw any hard evidence to support this. 'Local military officials probably know what's going on and they'll be happy as long as they get a reasonable cut,' said one experienced security source.[41]

Diesel smuggling from Yemen to Africa was a crucial piece in this illegitimate jigsaw, reflecting the differential between subsidized products on sale in Yemen and the market rate in the Horn and the Gulf states, which was several times higher. In 2008, during a global oil-price spike, the World Bank recorded a notable shortage in diesel fuel in Yemen, sparked by 'growing domestic demand (which includes smuggling to neighboring countries)'.[42] One estimate suggested that half of Yemen's subsidized fuel was leaked to leading figures in Yemen and then smuggled out of the country.[43] Narcotics were also floating about in the local mafia mix, with Yemeni newspapers occasionally carrying stories about cannabis seizures in the eastern desert province of Hadramaut.[44] According to one private security source, Somalia had also become a trans-shipment point for heroin from Baluchistan on the Afghanistan–Pakistan border, which then made its way from Somalia via Yemen into Saudi Arabia.[45]

The 2008 spike in Somali piracy—or more precisely 'hostage-taking at sea'[46]—offered another lucrative revenue stream for interlocking business networks stitching Yemen to Somalia, with annual ransom payments running to hundreds of millions of dollars. Almost overnight, Somalia's piracy boom turned Bosaso into 'a place where you can get kidnapped faster than you can wipe the sweat off your brow' and the waters of the Gulf of Aden into 'the most dangerous shipping lanes in the world'.[47] In 2008, the UN monitoring group found that a majority, if not all, of the ports used for weapons shipments in Somalia had also 'harboured groups or individuals held responsible for acts of piracy',[48] adding: 'There appears to be an intersection between piracy and other criminal activities, such as arms trafficking and human trafficking, both of which involve the movement of small craft across the Gulf of Aden.'[49] Early piracy incidents targeted ships sailing close to the boundaries of Yemen's territorial waters, pointing to a tangential Yemeni role in piracy. One maritime security specialist speculated that Somali pirates were making cash payments to buy fuel and hire (or steal) boats from Yemeni fishermen and dhow masters at ports on Yemen's south coast.[50]

By the end of 2008, international naval forces had established a transit corridor between Yemeni and Somali territorial waters in an effort to deter further piracy attacks. The multinational task force patrolling the transit area had a specific counter-piracy mandate, and its members were not tasked with stopping smuggling or enforcing the UN arms embargo to Somalia. In an attempt to improve Yemen's shoreline security, Western donors were funding and training the coastguard, and in general the training scheme was fairly well regarded. However, many Western diplomats recognized that the coastguard could not function properly in the absence of an effective customs framework, while others acknowledged that Yemen's coastguard could not go too far with its counter-smuggling work without impinging on powerful vested interests.

When Yemen's Ministry of Transport started issuing licences for private companies to hire out trained coastguard personnel as armed escorts for ships travelling through Yemeni territorial waters, and charging 'up to $55,000 per ship, per trip',[51] Western diplomats voiced their exasperation. Although Saleh claimed to want to improve Yemen's border controls, with strong encouragement from his Western allies, Yemenis understood that shutting down illicit networks in the Gulf of Aden would stamp out revenue streams for some of the most powerful people in the country. Small-time one-off deals—or the alleged activities of scapegoats like Haroun—paled into insignificance alongside large-scale moneymaking activities inside these shadow networks, which underpinned the power structure of Saleh's Yemen.

6

THE CHICKEN AND THE EGG

ELITE COMPETITION, CORRUPTION AND REFORM

One August night in Sana'a, I was invited to a home screening of *The Secret*—a self-help film that claims to reveal the most powerful law in the universe: the law of attraction.[1] The film presents the keys to prosperity, health and happiness in documentary format, narrating the three principles of 'ask' (know what you want and ask the universe for it), 'believe' (feel and behave as if the object of your desire is on its way) and 'receive' (be open to receiving your gift from the universe). The 92-minute DVD features new-age 'talking heads' explaining how the law of attraction is borne out by popular psychology, quantum physics and theology.

Jalal Omar Yaqoub greeted guests arriving at his in-laws' house in Hadda on the night of the screening with a beautiful toddler sleepily cradled in his arms. The deputy finance minister had installed a DVD projector, screen and canvas gazebo on the fourth-floor roof terrace in preparation for the showing. 'Don't forget to dress warmly or bring something warm to wear since we will be showing the film outdoors,' Jamal's email invitation had warned. Yemen has precious little comfort to offer its own elite in the way of self-conscious privilege, and Jalal's rooftop cinema club soirée was elevated high above dual carriageway traffic that shrieked past just a few blocks away. Empty newbuild villas climbed the barren slopes of neighbouring Jebel Hadda, where high walls and unlit apartments, still awaiting tenants, radiated the promise of privacy and exclusive confinement.

Jalal switched on the projector after dinner, and we settled down in plastic chairs to the sound of a faux-classical overture. A prophetic voice informed us that, throughout history, great leaders of industry, religion and government had used the Secret to their own advantage but kept it hidden from ordinary people. The film's narrator now invited us to participate in a revolutionary social movement by harnessing the law of attraction to encourage the change that we wanted to achieve in our own lives. When the mains power cut out in the middle of the screening, Jalal laughed. 'We must use the power of positive thinking to solve Yemen's electricity problems,' he joked, as he went to check on the backup generator that chugged into life a few moments later.

Suave, handsome and self-effacing, Jalal seemed to embody the secret of success that he had chosen to share with an audience of diplomats, visiting journalists and NGO workers.[2] His impeccable dress sense and designer accessories—Mont Blanc pen, Ray-Ban shades and Bulgari glasses—enhanced the impression of extraordinary good fortune. As a well-connected family man and a capable, dynamic technocrat, he positioned himself squarely at the forefront of the national debate about political and economic reform, and he was forging a reputation as one of the brightest young minds in the civil service. Jalal recognised the need for root-and-branch improvement to Yemen's dysfunctional system of government; but at first, he struggled to gain the attention of senior colleagues. It wasn't until Yemen was cut from a list of countries eligible to join the Millennium Challenge scheme, a Bush administration plan tying aid to governance benchmarks,[3] that Jalal and his reform-minded peers were able to convince their superiors of the merits of complying with Western-backed reforms; Yemen stood to gain millions of dollars in US aid, in return for aggressive anti-corruption efforts. Jalal's coterie pushed hard for presidential endorsement for their reform drive and in 2006, they succeeded in convincing Saleh to steward anti-corruption legislation through parliament. Saleh publicly denounced corruption, replaced himself as head of the Supreme Judicial Council, established the Supreme National Authority for Combating Corruption (SNACC) and instituted 'best practice' for public procurement.

Initially, at least, Jalal's closest allies for reform were confidantes among the donor community, rather than government officials. When his proposals fell on deaf ears inside the civil service, he turned to prominent diplomats for support, and working together, they were able to ratchet up the pressure on Saleh to engage with the necessary reforms. Jalal used his leverage with the donors to create traction for his ideas inside the government, and in return, Western donors were inclined to frame Jalal as a hero. 'It's important to work with people inside the structure because their judgement on timing and sequencing is crucial. They know how to push easier reforms at the beginning and wait for the right time to tackle harder challenges,' said one Western advocate for Jalal's approach.[4]

However, Jalal's hotline to international diplomats, presidential backing and mercurial mobility frequently rankled with the time-serving bureaucrats and creatures of traditional patronage who populated the top ranks of Yemen's civil service. 'He was like a gem that was constantly being polished,' one of his critics said.[5] Jalal resigned from his first junior ministerial job in 2007 after stepping on powerful toes in a turf war at the Ministry of Planning and International Co-operation. 'We expect a lot from a small number of people under pressure and we often forget how risky it is for them as individuals,' said one of his pro-reform Western allies.[6] Jalal was reappointed to a job in the finance ministry, where he drafted a ten-point 'self-help' plan for Yemen that was later endorsed by US Secretary of State Hillary Clinton.[7] With Yemen's oil output in long-term decline, Jalal saw the logic in reforming crude oil sales, and encouraging private sector investment that would create jobs, boost skills and 'grow the pie'. Reporting to the prime minister, Jalal also headed a team that cleaned up the bidding process for monthly crude oil purchases by foreign buyers, cutting the commission of local agents.

Jalal belonged to Ahmed Ali's inner circle, and he traded on the impression that he had Ahmed Ali's personal authority to pursue governance reforms. It was far from clear whether Ahmed Ali had a genuine interest in reform or indeed to what extent Jalal really had Ahmed's mandate to pursue extensive change.[8] Nevertheless, donors often came away from their encounters with Jalal believing that their best hope in encouraging effective reform in Yemen lay in supporting Ahmed Ali's future succession. The reform agenda was already highly politicized—as one Yemeni friend put it: 'The opposition parties try to make you feel that you are living in Mogadishu, while the ruling party wants you to think that you are living in Geneva'—but the link between reform and succession had the knock-on effect of further politicizing the reform agenda along factional lines and paralyzing the relevant government ministries.

In the event, Yemen's renewed attempt to join the Millennium Challenge programme would prove fraught with difficulties, only to be abandoned when Saleh unexpectedly released a prominent terrorist suspect from jail against Washington's wishes. Within a few years of Saleh's public denunciation of corruption, signs of reform momentum were slowing to a halt. Donors continued pushing for specific measures—such as civil service job cuts, ending diesel subsidies and introducing a general sales tax—intended to ease pressure on the state budget. However, Saleh's patronage system was so complex and entrenched that any effective reform was sure to damage powerful interests and risk engendering reprisals.[9] One former minister, who had been involved in a previous attempted round of economic reforms during the 1990s, argued: 'If there's any chance that reform will institutionalize power, transfer it to the state and diminish his personal control, Saleh will withdraw his co-operation from the technocrats.'[10] Increasingly, it seemed that Jalal's efforts were being exploited by Saleh, by giving the donors just enough sense of traction to keep them satisfied that they had found a local 'champion' or 'change agent'.

Saleh's ambivalent engagement with the need for reform did, at least, suggest some belated recognition of the problem with Yemen's oil-dependent economy. In a keynote speech at a Sana'a investors' conference in 2007, Saleh indicated that he was ready to amend Yemen's legal framework in order to encourage inward investment.[11] Yemen's ranking in the World Bank Ease of Doing Business Index shot up twenty-five places in reward for abolishing the minimum capital requirement and launching a one-stop shop for business start-ups.[12] Early headline successes included Dubai Port World's deal to operate the port of Aden and Qatari Diar's mutli-million dollar luxury residential development at Sana'a's Rayyan Hills. However, more enthusiastic investors proved difficult to entice. 'The Saudis don't want to invest any money in here and the rest of the GCC isn't really interested. Outside the energy sector there's very little investment going on,' said one Western diplomat, speaking in 2008.[13]

Jalal had once revealed to me the existence of a new informal group, meeting once a week with the purpose of stimulating investment. He called it 'the committee with no name'. Also on the committee was Salah al-Attar, head of the General Investment Authority, and Faris Sanabani, strategist and communications advisor to the pro-reform group, in his role as presidential advisor and publisher of the *Yemen Observer*, an English-language newspaper mostly read by diplomats and donors. In time, this little guild came to be known as the 'investment committee', recruiting other members who were sympathetic to the cause. To their credit, the committee understood the gravity of Yemen's economic problems and they were attuned to the need to act quickly, but in their urgency to get things done, they marginalized people who stood in their way, even other ministers who were constitutionally responsible for stewarding reforms. They were a tight-knit group—and at times, their patois had more in common with a high-end sales pitch or company PR, rather than the linguistics of government.

As Yemen's security situation gradually deteriorated over the following years, the committee failed to generate sustained, integrated investment on the scale that they expected. Yet, even as the volume of inward investment slowed to a trickle, Saleh demonstrated a shrewd ability to turn the situation to his family's advantage. As I already knew from my visit to Dhamar with mediator Abdulrahman al-Marwani, land disputes were common in Yemen, and the commercial exchange of land could be a highly contested process. In order to minimise the risk that foreign businessmen would find themselves embroiled in tribal feuds, the investment drive was accompanied by the creation of a government-led investment vehicle, Shibam Holding, which was established in 2008 as a state-backed real estate developer with support from the World Bank.[14]

From the outset, Shibam was intended to regulate the acquisition of land for investment and remove other obstacles that had previously deterred potential investors, including local agents' feeding frenzy to promise high-level access. Shibam's CEO and chairman, Saad Sabrah, claimed he was trying to create a 'friction-free environment between the investor and the governmental officials and therefore minimizing any types of corrupt transactions'.[15] Saad worked closely with the General Investment Authority, which presented Shibam as the joint-venture partner of choice for new investment coming into the country, and with the Land Authority, which allocated Shibam a significant proportion of land previously held by YECO and other government institutions.[16] While Shibam's high-level connections may, in some cases, have generated investor confidence and facilitated the acquisition of land, this modernisation project also intensified resentment among Saleh's rivals—in part, simply due to who was involved in the process, and who got the political credit.

Ahmed Ali was among the benefactors of this new system, through his sponsorship of the reform process, including the operations of Shibam Holding and the General Investment Authority. He also chaired the 'committee with no name', later known as the investment committee. Regardless of the founding members' original intentions, their modernization project—both the inward investment drive, and long-term economic reform under the ten-point plan—came to be associated with Saleh's family faction, and the net effect of their efforts was to steal a march on those who could not bring Ahmed Ali's clout to bear when it came to marshalling land and resources. Indeed, the key members of Ahmed Ali's inner circle were increasingly perceived by others as a government-in-waiting—aspiring to power, impatient and ambitious, careful to court international support, and willing to work innovatively, or cut corners, to get what they wanted.

These perceived 'inheritors' could often be found hanging out at fashionable and expensive Western-style restaurants and coffee-shops in Sana'a's Hadda suburb, which were popular with many younger members of Yemen's wealthy elite. Outside the privileged enclave of Hadda, the rest of the country was struggling to scrape enough money together to get by, and was barely equipped to manage normal daily challenges, let alone to cope with rising inflation. One development worker, who had been living in Yemen for years, pinpointed his own personal indicator for gauging how bad the problem of hunger was in rural communities. 'I ask the children when they last had a sweet to eat, and they often tell me it's only once a year, during Ramadan,' he told me.[17]

In 2008, the cost of food on sale in Yemen rose sharply in response to a worldwide price spike, and, in order to cope with higher prices, many Yemeni families sold their livestock, spent less on medicine and water, or began to eat less or eat cheaper food. Some even sold their pre-pubescent daughters into early marriage.[18] The UN World Food Programme hired one development consultant to conduct an assessment on the impact of the price spike. The resulting study, and a parallel appraisal by the UN Development Programme, recorded a sharp increase in the number of people living below food subsistence levels.[19] 'We heard reports of people dissolving qat in tea and feeding it to their kids to suppress their appetite,' the consultant told me.[20] 'We heard several stories of men committing suicide because they couldn't feed their families. I sent field teams into the poorest areas of the country, and those kinds of stories were widespread.'

During that summer, construction workers were putting the finishing touches to Al-Saleh Mosque, a multi-million dollar vanity project that dominated the Sana'a skyline, located close to the president's main palace compound on the outskirts of the city. In August, I was invited to tour the mosque complex a few weeks before the official opening ceremony. A spotless white hard hat was the only item adorning a coat-stand in the corner of the director's office, where an assortment of patient petitioners in dusty sandals sat on brand-new leatherette sofas waiting for the resolution of dilemmas and requests that required the director's sole attention. Hanging about indefinitely was a ritual of access to Yemeni officialdom that I had learned to endure, but on this occasion I was ushered to the head of the queue. From the window by the director's desk, I watched barefoot farmers ploughing the rutted earth with scrawny oxen, in fields surrounding the mosque complex.

Official estimates of the project's cost hovered around $50 million, but rumours were running round town that local businesses had been pressured to donate large lump sums after construction bills began to spiral.[21] When I asked the director to calculate the final tally for total spending on the mosque, he narrowed his eyes and said: 'Not very much.' There was a look on his face that told me not to push him for any further information. When I asked what style would be used for the call for prayer, the tight-lipped director made eye contact with his deputies, which seemed to say: 'What shall I tell her?' I wanted to know if the style of the *adhan* would be Sunni Shafai or Zaydi Shi'a, but the director shook his head, with a nervous smile playing on his lips.

My helpful suggestion—'in the middle?'—provoked awkward laughter from everyone in the room. 'The muezzin was chosen for his beautiful voice,' was the only comment that I managed to extract.

'All the materials are from Yemen and all the labour is Yemeni!' the director had boasted, but hoardings showing an Egyptian contractor's logo were displayed all over the site. During a guided inspection, the director's assistants showed me polished slabs of Omani marble and extravagant Burmese teak doors, carved with eight-point stars. A Turkish wool carpet, patterned with gold and green mandalas, was still being laid across the vast expanse of the prayer hall. A 6-tonne chandelier from the Czech Republic, bearing one of the 99 names of God on each of its lanterns, hung suspended from a roof of American oak. The exterior tiling, at least, suggested the imagination of a Yemeni architect, echoing the gingerbread and white-icing brickwork in Sana'a's old medina.

Yemeni taxi drivers speeding past the mosque gates with me in the back seat regularly complained that President Saleh should have spent the money on something more useful. The pitifully neglected women's hospital just a few hundred yards away stood as an instant rebuke to wasteful expenditure and personal grandeur, but the mosque held a fascination in the public mind and it drew excitable crowds in the opening weeks. It was the largest, most extravagant building in the whole country and, as one of Saleh's aides explained, it was the exception that proved the rule of the president's modesty. 'He's been in power for thirty years and there's not even an airport named after him. You wouldn't find that in most other countries in the region,' the loyal agent said.[22] However, for many of Saleh's critics, including veteran anti-corruption campaigner Dr Saadaldeen Talib, the gap between such ostentatious wealth and the sheer scale of desolation endured by hungry, malnourished Yemenis was a clear indictment of his regime's venality and short-sighted self-interest.

* * *

The young starry-eyed democrat sitting next to Saleh on the president's private plane was euphoric. Dr Saadaldeen Talib had just been elected as a member of Yemen's 1997 parliament, representing the ruling party in a constituency in Hadramaut. Hand-picked by the president from the new intake of MPs to join him on a post-election trip to

Germany, Dr Saad allowed himself to believe that he had a bright future serving his country, the newest democracy in Arabia. 'I was flattered. I thought Saleh saw me as a brilliant young man and a new talent in parliament. I thought he wanted to nurture me.'

Dr Saad told me he was rather taken aback during his cosy in-flight tête-à-tête with the president, when Saleh tried to tap him up for a large donation to help bankroll the political party he had just been elected to represent. According to Dr Saad, the president said: 'Your family owns half of Singapore and half of Egypt, so surely you can afford to be generous.' Saleh appeared to be in thrall to the popular image of entrepreneurial Hadrami trading families, who had travelled beyond Yemen's shores as sailors, peddlers, teachers and preachers to return as businessmen and real estate magnates.[23] Dr Saad replied, as politely as he could: 'No, I'm afraid we just have a few properties.' (Political patronage usually ran the other way, but I understood that Dr Saad intended to ridicule Saleh's cupidity as brazen.)

Dr Saad was thirty-eight when the president blew the lid off his illusions about Yemeni democracy, but he didn't falter in his stride. He secured a place on the parliamentary oil and gas committee and spent the next decade fighting for his ideals in politics. Instead of being a placeman, he became a thorn in Saleh's side—by accident and inclination, rather than design. His combustible character mix of determination, a head for detail and a commitment to democratic principles meant Dr Saad was twice nominated as Yemen's best parliamentarian by a popular Yemeni newspaper before he was deselected by the GPC party hierarchy. A few years later, however, he staged his own political reincarnation as an anti-corruption watchdog.

It was still the rainy season when I visited Dr Saad, just a few days after my visit to Jalal's house. I ran from my taxi through an afternoon squall into his spacious hillside villa in a Sana'a suburb. He sat, Yemeni-style, wrapped in a *futa*, scattering qat stalks on the carpet and puffing on a shisha—like Lewis Carroll's caterpillar[24]—underneath two framed portraits hanging on the wall, one of his father and one of his grandfather. We started off on the wrong foot when I made a clumsy opening gambit by assuming that the narrow-lapel 1960s-style suit that Dr Saad's father was wearing in the painting might indicate Nasserite sympathies. 'Was your father a supporter of Nasser?' I asked. I had overlooked the fact that Nasser's role in Yemen and the wider region appeared very different when viewed from the south. My host's eyes widened with affront and surprise. He belonged to a prominent Hadrami tribe—the Kathiri—and hailed from the ranks of the Kathiri aristocracy. The last Kathiri sultan was overthrown in 1967 when the British withdrew from Aden, and the Kathiri aristocracy were subsequently brutalized by the PDRY's land distribution policies. Dr Saad's family were still nursing a forty-year-old antipathy against the Socialist south and Nasser's Socialist influence, which pushed them into two decades of self-imposed exile.[25] For Dr Saad and his relatives, the collapse of the PDRY in 1990 and the partial restoration of tribal landholdings following unification came as a long overdue blessing.

Dr Saad was living in Egypt at the time of unification:

I came rushing back to Yemen full of hope in 1990. I thought the new freedoms being unleashed were fantastic. We had political freedom, freedom of movement and trading freedoms that were previously unthinkable, and unrivalled in the region. People living in the south were ecstatic. They were happy just to see biscuits and juice on sale in their shops, because they'd only had Russian and Chinese-made stuff for years. We were bursting with confidence. It was our golden moment.

Dr Saad began the process of registering a new company in Dubai, but Yemen's pro-Iraqi stance over the invasion of Kuwait put paid to all his plans. Dr Saad had already obtained a residency permit to live in Dubai, but the UAE authorities now denied residency status to his wife. Everything he'd been progressing towards suddenly halted, so he stayed in Yemen and worked as a consultant to an engineering company with an interest in Aden's shipyards, while the newly unified Yemeni government set about integrating two cadres of civil servants, two diplomatic services and two different sets of expectations. 'The international community's response to Saleh's sympathy for Saddam was a huge setback, but I still believed that Yemen had a bright future as a dynamic, energetic new democracy and our confidence would prevail.'

When civil war broke out in 1994, Dr Saad backed the north against the southern Socialists because of his family's experience under socialism. Not long afterwards, Dr Saad was asked if he wanted to be a GPC candidate in the forthcoming parliamentary elections. 'I was lucky because the Socialist Party had decided to boycott the elections, which left the door wide open for me. I was hopeful and optimistic because I knew there was more oil to be discovered and I was convinced that increased export revenue would help to improve our stability and prosperity.' Dr Saad was successfully elected, then swiftly appointed to the parliamentary oil and gas committee that scrutinized proposed exploration and production contracts before MPs formally approved the deals by act of parliament. 'I was the only one on the committee willing to expose the scandals,' he told me. 'I wanted to be a hero, but it quickly turned bad.'

Dr Saad spent the next few hours recounting the details of two cases from the late 1990s, in which he attempted to bring the committee's attention to apparent procedural violations in the standard processes of granting exploration and production rights to foreign oil companies. In both cases, Dr Saad believed he had uncovered potential evidence that pointed towards high-level corruption, enabling regime insiders to benefit personally at the expense of the state. However, when Dr Saad tried to provoke a discussion about the terms of these new concessions, he told me that he encountered hostility and suspicion, including from his fellow party members. 'They asked me: "Who are you working for? What are your hidden interests?"'

Given the controversy that Dr Saad stirred up in trying to bring these cases to light—in his own words, 'all hell broke loose'—and the highly personalized nature of patronage politics in Saleh's Yemen, retrospective accounts of these two cases inevitably varied. According to Dr Saad, the future beneficiaries of both deals tried to sidestep his opposition and pressured their parliamentary supporters to secure the necessary votes that they needed to validate the two contested agreements. In one notorious incident, Dr Saad claimed he was physically intimidated by senior politicians who were set to chair a decisive vote.

Notwithstanding the specific (and sometimes lurid) allegations and rejoinders involving these two cases, Dr Saad's stories suggested the extent to which regime officials might be willing to interfere with the principle of parliamentary oversight. Dr Saad's experiences also demonstrated the penalties faced by would-be reformers who tried to work through Yemen's weak democratic institutions, especially those who set themselves up as regime critics—as opposed to technocrats like Jalal Yaqoub, and regime insiders, who had chosen to promote change from within; yet they, too, encountered entrenched opposition and ran their own personal risks. If Dr Saad had agreed to play by the informal rules of the game instead, he might have held onto his seat in parliament for years to come but he had crossed 'a red line set by the regime for the use of formal political institutions' in trying to hold the executive to account.[26]

By Dr Saad's own admission, his provocative behavior earned him a 'reputation as a troublemaker' and his obstinacy ultimately cost him his parliamentary career. 'I kept my seat on the oil and gas committee until the parliamentary term finished, and that's when they kicked me out.' He was dismissed from the ruling party on the eve of the 2003 elections. Dr Saad eventually joined a US-backed pro-democracy organisation with offices in Sana'a, where he ran their parliamentary programme and started a lobby group called Yemen Parliamentarians Against Corruption (Yemen PAC).

Dr Saad staged his political comeback a few years later, when Saleh authorized the creation of the new anti-corruption body, SNACC, and he found himself elected to the board with the support of his Yemen PAC allies. As a symbolic gesture, he bought a small Toyota Prado for official committee use instead of the standard-issue Toyota Land Cruiser, and he vowed that he would return it to the committee after five years of service.

SNACC had been up and running for more than a year when I interviewed Dr Saad, and he said he was struggling all the way for the new anti-corruption committee to be effective. He portrayed himself as a 'maverick', working alongside a phalanx of GPC loyalists. 'It doesn't help matters that we can't remove anyone from their post who works above deputy ministerial level,' he said. He recounted an early case, where SNACC looked into a crooked deal and wrote a letter to the prime minister, asking to freeze the agreement. 'They cancelled the deal, but we couldn't do anything about the minister in question because all ministers have constitutional protection. We can only ask parliament to remove a minister at the MPs' discretion. I left the country in protest and told everyone I wouldn't come back until the minister stood down. They removed him in the last reshuffle and that was that.'

He went on:

The US can't push Saleh too far on reform because they believe there's no alternative and Saleh knows that. Only real reform, not a superficial farce, will be the salvage of Yemen. We need large-scale investment from the Gulf but investors need to have confidence in us first, and in the meantime, how much emergency bail-out money will be needed to keep the country afloat? Billions of dollars a year, just to keep the same regime in place. The problem puts us between a rock and a hard place because the reforms that donors are asking—the diesel subsidy reduction and cuts in the civil service—will cause real pain. You can't allow the standard of living to deteriorate so much and then ask Yemenis to endure more hardship. Plus, it's especially hard to convince the people it's in their interests when these decisions are announced by a government surrounded by thieves.

Three years out from the popular uprising, it was rare to encounter such outspoken criticism of Saleh's patronage system. Dr Saad was one of just a few analysts who did not have a direct stake in the existing system, to my knowledge, and was willing to risk articulating the mechanisms of patronage as well as the implications, in such unambiguous language. As a journalist, I found it enormously helpful to speak to men and women like Dr Saad, and yet I was aware that they, too, were sometimes compromised by their own political history as well as their 'outsider' status. Factional politics further complicated these dynamics. (Dr Saad and his Yemen PAC colleagues supported the anti-corruption law in parliament, after negotiating for specific amendments—including the election of SNACC members, instead of appointment by the president—but they stopped short of giving Jalal's reform drive a public endorsement.)

Dr Saad was in full flow:

There are those who say that Yemen has always muddled through, but has this country ever been in such a precarious situation as it is today? The leadership doesn't have the will, skill or capacity to reform the economy to promote diversification and growth. They have created such a tight network of corruption that even they don't know how to unpick it and we can't even absorb the aid money that donors are giving us. We're in the hands of a completely ignorant patrimony that believes in killing the chicken instead of stealing the eggs. At least the new generation understands that they need to keep the chicken alive if they want to keep stealing the eggs, but when the oil runs out there won't be anything left for them to inherit. My sadness is this. In 1990, I had high hopes for democracy, for unification and for our economy. I have invested energy and passion in my country for more than twenty years, but I feel completely disillusioned by Saleh. This country is like a runaway train rushing down the mountain, and at some point it's going to crash.

Dr Saad predicted the trouble would start long before the oil finally runs out:

The moment the government can't pay civil service salaries, that's when things are going to hit the wall. They'll default on payments to people in the south first but it won't be an attempted secession, like it was in 1994. The country will disintegrate, and the centre of gravity in the country will split apart. People will fight over the roads first, in order to control the trading routes and, eventually, there'll be an invasion of Sana'a by the tribes.

Dr Saad had just sent his wife and teenage children abroad, because he wanted his kids to have a good education, but he acknowledged that not everyone in Yemen had that option:

Millions of young Yemenis are cynical about the economy, the injustice and the sour feeling that the country is being robbed. This was one of my strongest motives for accepting a position in SNACC. It was a chance to vindicate myself for being kicked out of parliament. I could say to the elite: 'Here I am, I'm still standing.' And I could tell the Yemeni people: 'Even if they hunt you down, it doesn't mean that you're dead.' But this is the crossroads for me now. The country is collapsing, and I wonder if my work in SNACC has a purpose any more. I have to make a decision. Do I leave Yemen and move abroad with my family, or stay here and fight corruption? I have to think of my children, as well as my own ambitions. What if I challenge an influential person, try to hold him accountable through SNACC and he sends five armed men to my front door?

It was dark by the time our interview drew to a close, and the shift through dusk from first to second evening prayers was already complete. At the doorway, Dr Saad handed me a spiced Hadrami cake as a parting gift. 'I did my PhD thesis on liver transplants. I was supposed to be a doctor. I didn't choose this life, but look what has happened to me,' he said ruefully, as we huddled in the front porch and watched light rain falling on the bonnet of his Toyota Prado, parked in the yard. Dr Saad smiled as he sent me off with his driver, waving goodbye from the door-step in his bare feet.[27]

7

LAYLA AND THE MADMAN

YEMEN'S ROLE IN THE ORIGINS OF AL-QAEDA

'Is it possible, then, to break whole armies with one small grain of sugar?'
Nizami, *The Story of Layla and Majnun (The Madman)*, trans. Rudolf Gelpke

The allure of battlefield jihad flickered in Nasser al-Bahri's heart for the first time while he was still a schoolboy. The thirteen year-old's desire for a heroic destiny stirred while he watched television news footage of Israeli soldiers assaulting Palestinians. 'I wanted to go and kill the Israelis right then,' he told me.[1] Nasser was so incensed by the plight of the Palestinians that he committed to memory the text of the 1917 Balfour Declaration, named after Britain's wartime foreign secretary, who articulated his government's favourable stance towards a Jewish homeland in Palestine. 'I hated Balfour,' said Nasser, during our meeting on the eve of Ramadan, as we sat in a Sana'a restaurant discussing our early impressions of political events and favourite historical figures. 'I liked another one,' he added. His hero was the Ottoman sultan, Abdul Hamid II, who refused to issue a charter allowing the Jews to settle in Palestine while it was still under Ottoman control.

Nasser was born in the late 1960s and grew up in Saudi Arabia, a child of prosperous Yemeni migrants living in the Red Sea port of Jeddah.[2] Nasser hit adolescence in the 1980s, when Jeddah became a national 'transit station' for Saudis travelling to Afghanistan to fight the Soviet troops.[3] Throughout his teens, Nasser enviously observed the *mujahideen* coming and going to and from Afghanistan. One night during Ramadan, eighteen-year-old Nasser introduced himself to an Afghan visitor in his local mosque after evening prayers. When the Afghan invited him to share *iftar* the following day, Nasser had his first chance to talk directly to a jihad leader, who quickened the teenager's interest with heady tales from Afghanistan, but it was still several years before Nasser would have his chance to enlist and fight.

Other Yemenis of the same generation living in Jeddah were exhilarated by the contemporary fervour for jihad. In 1986, the year that Nasser encountered his Afghan interlocutor in the neighbourhood mosque, a former British diplomat visited his old friend from Aden, a sultan from the southern Fahdli tribe, whose family had left the country when the Marxists came to power.[4] The Briton had been on good terms with his Yemeni host during the 1960s, as a tribal leader and father of young boys growing up in Abyan province. Now, one grown-up son, Tariq, supposedly slighted the family's British guest by refusing to welcome him to their new home in Jeddah. 'He came into the house while we were having lunch, but he walked straight past the room where we eating, much to his father's fury and distress. I gathered that he was planning to head off to Afghanistan,' the Briton recalled.

Prominent among the Yemeni community in Jeddah was Mohammed bin Laden's son, Osama, and 'the pipeline to Afghanistan' ran directly through his apartment.[5] Bin Laden 'rapidly emerged as a talented fund-raiser', and the Saudi government supported the national recruitment drive with discounted air tickets for aspiring jihadis.[6] In 1987, the Soviet military announced their phased withdrawal from Afghanistan, but jihadi recruitment continued, with an estimated 6,000 Arabs arriving in Afghanistan over the next six years.[7] Among the rival groups competing to recruit fighters, Osama was the 'golden Saudi goose', who gradually consolidated his dominance with the Saudi government's financial and political backing.[8]

In 1989, Osama came home to Jeddah, believing the 'fable, promoted by the Saudi press, that his Arab legion had brought down the mighty superpower'.[9] Osama had recently authorized the creation of a secret organization called al-Qaeda, which would last for a period of 'open duration' and require *bayat*—a loyalty oath—from its new members.[10] Speaking in the bin Laden family mosque after his homecoming to Jeddah, Osama stopped short of advocating violence against the Americans, who had also financed the struggle against the Soviets.[11] However, Iraq's 1990 invasion of Kuwait changed the regional balance and began bin Laden's shift towards calling for US troops to leave the Arabian Peninsula.[12] As the world adjusted to the post-Cold War order, Osama shifted from favoured Saudi son to global pariah, which saw him stripped of his Saudi citizenship and multimillion-dollar family fortune.[13]

Throughout the 1990s and beyond, several Yemenis raised in Saudi Arabia, including Nasser al-Bahri and Tariq al-Fahdli, were to play critical roles in the development of al-Qaeda and its offshoots in Yemen. Abdul Rahim al-Nashiri, a suspect in the 2000 attack on the USS *Cole* in Aden harbour, and 9/11 hijacker Khaled al-Mihdhar were also ethnic Yemenis raised in Saudi Arabia.[14] So was Abu Hassan, leader of Yemen's proto-terrorist organization, the Aden-Abyan Islamic Army, which tried to bomb US troops in 1992, while they were stationed in Aden en route to Somalia.[15] Another ethnic Yemeni living in Saudi Arabia, known simply as Khallad, was a childhood friend of Osama bin Laden's.[16] Khallad would eventually provide vital evidence that would enable FBI investigators to establish bin Laden's links to the *Cole* bombing and 9/11.

During the early years of the 1990s, Arab jihadis were caught up in a series of new wars, sparked by the collapse of the USSR. Nasser, now in his early twenties, seized his chance to leave Saudi Arabia and prove his worth. He had already cut his teeth in Bosnia, Somalia and Chechnya by the time he walked past the Taliban's two T-55 Soviet tanks stationed outside the walls of Tarnak Farms, bin Laden's dilapidated mud-brick Kandahar home in Afghanistan, in his late twenties.[17] Now that bin Laden was shorn of his family fortune, there was sometimes nothing to eat in the compound other than bread and pomegranate seeds.[18] However, Nasser decided to stay, attracted by bin Laden's anti-American mission and the promise of training for a new asymmetric kind of warfare.[19]

It was 1996, and FBI investigators handling bin Laden's case file were beginning to hear of the term al-Qaeda for the first time, but FBI agent Daniel Coleman 'couldn't even get his superiors to return his phone calls on the matter'.[20] Two years later, when twin bombs exploded outside the US embassies in neighbouring African capitals Nairobi and Dar es Salaam, killing more than 220 people, bin Laden 'was still obscure, even in the upper reaches of the FBI and the term "al-Qaeda" was almost unknown'.[21] However, US investigators who flew to Kenya immediately after the blast took only four days to find 'one of the most important pieces of information the FBI would ever discover, allowing investigators to map the links of the al-Qaeda network all across the globe'.[22] It was a phone number in Yemen.

In a suburban Nairobi hotel, FBI agents found an Arab business traveller with bloodstained bandages on his hands and $800 in his pocket. He claimed he was a Yemeni nut merchant, visiting a bank near the embassy at the time of the blast, but the suspect was in fact a Saudi.[23] Mohammed al-'Owhali had been sitting in the passenger seat of the blast truck and had jumped out just before the explosion. He was supposed to throw a stun grenade into the embassy courtyard, but he failed to get the embassy guards to raise the access barrier, and fled.[24] As FBI interrogators picked his cover story apart, they gained the upper hand psychologically, and when they finally mentioned bin Laden, al-'Owhali volunteered the first telephone number that he'd called after the bombing. It was registered to a house in Sana'a, and they discovered that bin Laden had called the same number before and after the bombing.[25]

In the eyes of US military planners, the link was enough to justify retaliation against bin Laden's perceived interests in Sudan and Afghanistan, including strikes on two camps near to Khost in Afghanistan, but it was almost another year before the FBI placed bin Laden on their 'Most Wanted' list.[26] Bin Laden survived the strikes on Khost because he was in Kabul at the time, but his followers became increasingly worried for their leader's safety.[27] It was then that Nasser's dedication, vigilance and willingness to assume personal risk to protect his mentor earned him the elevation to chief bodyguard. Bin Laden handed Nasser a gun, loaded with two bullets, and gave orders that the protégé, now known as Abu Jandal, must kill his mentor if al-Qaeda's chief was on the brink of being captured. Lawrence Wright, author of *The Looming Tower*, notes that: 'Abu Jandal took care to polish the bullets every night, telling himself: "There are Sheikh Osama's bullets. I pray to God not to let me use them."[28]

If Abu Jandal's character inspired bin Laden's confidence, his Saudi upbringing and his Yemeni origins were also valuable to the nascent organization. To legitimize the campaign against US soldiers stationed in the Arabian Peninsula, bin Laden needed the support of Peninsula Arabs.[29] Both men were born to Yemeni fathers and raised in Jeddah, and there was a decade's age difference between the pair. Bin Laden tasked Abu Jandal with oversight of al-Qaeda's guesthouses in Kabul and Kandahar, where he would meet many of the recruits that were arriving in Afghanistan.[30] Among the trainees that he encountered passing through bin Laden's camps was 9/11 hijacker Mohamed Atta.[31]

Bin Laden was now focused on striking the Americans on their own soil, and he sought educated and technically minded men with English-language skills and experience of living in the West in order to bring his hijack plan to fruition. In late 1999, four friends—Mohamed Atta, Ramzi bin al-Shibh, Marwan al-Shehhi and Ziad Jarrah—arrived in Afghanistan from Hamburg.[32] They were told that 'they had been picked for a secret, undisclosed mission', but only three of the four members of the Hamburg cell were eventually able to enter the USA. American consular officials repeatedly rejected visa applications made by Atta's Yemeni flatmate, Ramzi bin al-Shibh.[33] The 9/11 Commission report notes that visa restrictions for travel to the USA provided Yemeni nationals with 'fewer martyrdom opportunities' and restricted them to planning and support roles.[34] Roughly a fifth of bin Laden's volunteers were thought to be Yemenis, but it was Saudis—with their preferential travel status—who would dominate the hijack roles.[35]

Visa problems also frustrated two Yemeni passport holders—Khallad and Abu Bara—who belonged to a parallel four-man planning cell. In the first few days of 2000, the members of this second cell flew to Malaysia's capital Kuala Lumpur to prepare for an adapted 9/11-style operation that was planned for Asian airspace but later abandoned.[36] Khallad and Abu Bara joined two Saudi boys from Mecca—Nawaf al-Hazmi and Khaled al-Mihdhar, an ethnic Yemeni.[37] Khallad used the same phone number in Yemen that FBI investigators had discovered in the days after the Nairobi embassy attempt, as a 'message board' to arrange the Malaysia meeting.[38] The National Security Agency monitored a conversation that revealed both the meeting and the list of three attendees.[39] The only name to be revealed in full was that of Khaled al-Mihdhar, whose father-in-law owned the house in Sana'a to which the phone was registered.[40]

Bin Laden's former playmate, Khallad, was now a veteran jihadi with a prosthesis, as he had lost his lower right leg in an Afghanistan battle. He was also involved in a plot to target a US vessel in Yemeni waters proposed by another al-Qaeda operative, AbdulRahim al-Nashiri.[41] Bin Laden had approved the maritime terrorism plot in late 1998, provided the money and directed Nashiri to start preparing the operation.[42] Bin Laden sent Khallad to Yemen to help Nashiri obtain explosives for the planned ship bombing, but Khallad was arrested by the Yemeni authorities as a result of mistaken identity. Khallad was released during the summer of 1999 after his father and bin Laden intervened on his behalf.[43]

Khallad later learned that al-Qaeda's leader, 'apparently concerned that the detainee might reveal details of Nashiri's ship operation while under interrogation, had contacted a [Yemeni official] to request Khallad's release'.[44] In a legendary deal that underpinned the mythic narrative of Yemen as a safe haven for terrorism, bin Laden promised not to confront President Saleh's interests if Saleh gave bin Laden's terrorist organization a free hand to plan and organize inside Yemeni borders.[45] Following this so-called 'covenant of security', al-Qaeda aimed its attacks in Yemen at Western targets, but US pressure soon forced Saleh to renege on his part of the deal.

* * *

In January 2000, Nashiri's first attempt to execute his ship-bombing plan failed. Five Yemeni passers-by were the first to discover the evidence when they found a fibreglass fishing skiff partially submerged on a beach in Aden. They stripped the boat of its motor, clumsily dropping it in the sea, and unwittingly began unpacking the explosives in the hatch. While they were tossing the explosive bricks to the shore, the original plotters arrived to rescue their boat. They had intended to strike an American naval destroyer, USS *The Sullivans*, in Aden harbour.[46]

Abu Jandal arrived home in Yemen at about this time, apparently ignorant of Nashiri's maritime terrorist plot. He was now a married man and travelling with his Yemeni wife. The couple had wed a year earlier during

Abu Jandal's courier trip to deliver a dowry payment for bin Laden's own wedding to a teenage Yemeni girl, which was supposedly intended to boost al-Qaeda's recruitment in Yemen.[47] Abu Jandal later told a *Newsweek* reporter that his 2000 homecoming was the 'first time in my life that I had a passport with my real name on it'.[48] However, he was incarcerated in the round-up that followed Nashiri's successful assault on the USS *Cole* in October, and held in solitary confinement.[49]

The *Cole* attack killed seventeen American sailors, who were queuing for lunch in the ship's galley when a dinghy drew up alongside and blew a hole in the hull. The two suicide bombers were supported by a local coordinator, Jamal al-Badawi.[50] A cameraman, Fahd al-Quso, was also tasked with filming the attack to capture footage for propaganda videos, but he overslept and missed the explosion.[51] Al-Qaeda's media committee swiftly issued a propaganda video that included a re-enactment of the attack, which was aired in part on Al Jazeera and passed around by young supporters in Saudi Arabia and Yemen.[52] Al-Qaeda leaders considered the video 'an effective tool in their struggle for pre-eminence among other Islamist and jihadist movements'.[53] The attack on USS *Cole* 'galvanized al-Qaeda's recruitment efforts' and prompted contributors from the Gulf states to turn up at bin Laden's Afghan camps 'carrying Samsonite suitcases filled with petrodollars'.[54]

Before the *Cole* blast, bin Laden had provided a clue about the location of a coming attack by strapping a distinctive Yemeni *jambiya* dagger across his midriff for a video release that warned of imminent violence against US targets.[55] FBI staff working on the bin Laden file instinctively recognized the signs of bin Laden's work in the attack on the *Cole*,[56] but the CIA needed 'not just a guess but a link to someone known to be an al-Qaeda operative'.[57] During the weeks following the attack, the Yemeni authorities found and arrested both Badawi and Quso, who said that Khallad helped direct the *Cole* operation from Afghanistan or Pakistan.[58] Quso admitted that he had delivered $5,000 to Khallad in Bangkok, supposedly so he could buy a new prosthetic leg.[59]

FBI investigator Ali Soufan was not allowed to question the detainees himself, and had to rely on Yemeni officials relaying snippets of information second-hand. However, he remembered the name Khallad from a source in Afghanistan, which provided the 'first real link between the *Cole* bombing and al-Qaeda'.[60] US intelligence agencies had already connected Khallad to previous al-Qaeda terrorist operations, including the 1998 embassy bombings, and now Yemeni officials provided strong evidence of Nashiri's involvement; his links to bin Laden and the 1998 embassy bombings were even better known. However, the USA did not obtain direct evidence about bin Laden's personal involvement in the attacks until Nashiri and Khallad were captured in 2002 and 2003.[61]

Despite this positive step forward, the *Cole* investigation was dogged by allegations of complicity between the Yemeni authorities and the bombers, and complaints that Yemeni officials tried to obstruct the FBI in order to protect senior figures within the regime. Soufan was eventually allowed to interview Quso himself, but 'before the interview began, a colonel in the PSO entered the room and kissed Quso on both cheeks—a sign to everyone that Quso was protected. And indeed, whenever it seemed obvious that Quso was on the verge of making an important disclosure, the Yemeni colonel would insist that the session stop for meals or prayers.'[62] The FBI had a hunch that the bombers 'had been tipped off about the arrival of the *Cole*, and they wanted to expand the investigation to include a member of the president's own family and a colonel in the PSO'.[63]

If criticism of the Yemenis' attitude was valid, rivalry between senior US officials and inter-agency tensions meant the Americans failed to make best use of the information that the Yemenis gave them. The US investigation was dogged by repeated clashes between Ambassador Barbara Bodine, an old hand in the Middle East, and the lead FBI man, John O'Neill, who speculated that Yemen might be the 'most hostile environment the FBI has ever operated in'.[64] Bodine considered O'Neill naive and abrasive, and refused to renew his deployment at the Sana'a embassy.[65] A parallel stand-off between the CIA and the FBI over information-sharing meant that crucial clues that emerged in Yemen during the *Cole* investigation were overlooked. Those clues pointed directly towards the 9/11 plot.

During his interrogation of the *Cole* cameraman, Soufan discovered that Quso had handed $36,000 to Khallad in Bangkok—not $5,000 to buy a new prosthesis, as originally claimed.[66] The FBI 'wondered why money was leaving Yemen when a major operation was about to take place. Could there be another operation under way? Soufan sent Khallad's photo to the CIA asking for information about him and whether there might have been an al-Qaeda meeting in the region', and asking if there was any tie to Khallad.[67] The CIA did not respond to Soufan's clearly stated request, even though they were aware of Khallad's second meeting in Asia—the one in Malaysia.[68]

Before the Malaysia meeting, Saudi spies had already told the CIA that Mecca boys Mihdhar and Hazmi were members of al-Qaeda. Armed with this knowledge, CIA agents had broken into Mihdhar's hotel room in Dubai, en route to Malaysia, photographed his passport and faxed the document back home to their US-based colleagues. 'Inside the passport was the critical information that Mihdhar had a multi-entry American visa, due to expire in April.'[69] Hazmi and Mihdhar arrived in Kuala Lumpur using their Yemeni documents, and travelled on to the USA using their Saudi passports, arriving in Los Angeles on 15 January 2000.[70] A month later, they settled in San Diego and began looking for flight schools.[71]

It was the movements of Hazmi and Mihdhar that 'offered the most realistic hope for American intelligence to uncover the 9/11 conspiracy', but the CIA did not place Mihdhar on the State Department watchlist for suspected terrorists, and the agency did not inform the FBI that the pair was in the country.[72] Lawrence Wright notes: 'If the CIA had responded to Soufan by supplying him with the intelligence he requested, the FBI would have learned of the Malaysia meeting' and of Khallad's connection to Mihdhar and Hazmi. The bureau 'already had the authority to follow the suspects, wiretap their apartment, intercept their communications, clone their computer, investigate their contacts—all the essential steps that might have prevented 9/11'—on the basis of a pre-existing indictment for bin Laden.[73] The 'simple fact of their detention could have derailed the plan'.[74]

In June 2000, Mihdhar flew home to Yemen, just as FBI officers and CIA analysts were gathering in the USA for a hostile and obstructive meeting, where the FBI 'knew that clues to the crimes they were trying to solve were being dangled in front of their eyes'.[75] People started 'yelling at each other', but the CIA would not disclose crucial intelligence to the FBI for fear that their own operations might be compromised in any future criminal trial.[76] From Yemen, Mihdhar applied for another US entry visa, but 'no one was looking for him' when he returned to New York in July 2001.[77] A month later, FBI staff discovered that Mihdhar was in the country, but they still didn't know about his link to Khallad or his connection to al-Qaeda's telephone switchboard in Yemen.[78] In late August, they began a case review that required completion within a month.

Eighteen days later, on 11 September, Mihdhar boarded an American Airlines plane at Washington Dulles airport. Flight 77 crashed into the Pentagon at 9.37 a.m., killing 189 people.[79]

* * *

It was two detainees in Yemeni jails—Quso and Abu Jandal—who enabled the FBI to make the initial connection between al-Qaeda and 9/11. *Cole* investigator Soufan was still in Yemen when the planes hit their targets in New York and Washington. He received a satellite phone call from FBI headquarters on 12 September, telling him that 'Quso is our only lead'.[80] Despite his hunch that something larger was afoot before 9/11, Soufan still knew nothing about the rendezvous in Malaysia.[81] Now, the CIA station chief in Sana'a gave him three surveillance photos and a complete report about the Kuala Lumpur meeting.[82] When Soufan realized the agency had deliberately withheld the information he repeatedly requested, and knew that two of the hijackers had been in the country for more than a year before the attacks, 'he ran into the bathroom and retched'.[83]

Soufan summoned Quso for questioning and showed him the CIA's three surveillance images from Malaysia, but Quso claimed he was unable to help. It wasn't until the CIA gave Soufan a fourth photo from Malaysia, which Soufan also showed to Quso, that he made a positive identification of Khallad. This was the first, crucial link in the chain between al-Qaeda and 9/11, in which a Yemeni witness, implicated in the *Cole* bombing, linked one of bin Laden's known associates to the 9/11 hijackers.[84] Quso also identified Marwan al-Shehhi, one of the 9/11 pilots, saying that the pair had met in a Kandahar guesthouse, run by Abu Jandal.

Abu Jandal was still in Yemeni custody following his detention in the round-up that followed the *Cole* bombing. He now came face to face with Soufan and his American colleagues, and complained to his Yemeni guards about the presence of 'infidels' in his prison cell.[85] 'He took one of the plastic chairs and turned it around, sitting with his arms crossed

and his back to the interrogators.' When the prisoner eventually turned
to face his American inquisitors, he avoided eye contact, but Soufan, a
Muslim, confounded Abu Jandal's expectations of Westerners, and
gradually built a rapport that won him round.

After five days of questioning, Soufan showed Abu Jandal a news
magazine containing photos of the Twin Towers burning, and told
him: 'Bin Laden did this.'[86] A local Yemeni newspaper in the interrogation room carried the headline 'Two Hundred Yemeni Souls Perish
in New York Attack'. Abu Jandal seemed visibly shaken at the scale of
the operation and the estimated number of dead, which, in the
immediate aftermath of the attacks, ran to tens of thousands. Soufan
seized the moment to confront the detainee with a series of new
mugshots, and, using information supplied by Quso about the link
with al-Shehhi, pressed Abu Jandal to disclose the identities of several
men in the photos.

'I know for sure that the people who did this were Qaeda guys,' said
Soufan. He took seven photos out of the book and laid them on the table.
'How do you know?' asked Abu Jandal. 'Who told you?' 'You did,' said
Soufan. 'These are the hijackers. You just identified them.' Abu Jandal
blanched [...] 'I think the Sheikh went crazy,' he said. And then he told
Soufan everything he knew.[87]

Soufan had successfully outwitted Abu Jandal, and bin Laden's former
liegeman briefly lost his emotional composure. 'He knew the 9/11 per-
petrators very well, and he was scared of the consequences of his admission,' Soufan said, reflecting on their encounter during a phone discussion with me a decade later. 'He realized that it was in his best interests
to cooperate and we were able to build on that.' Pentagon military commanders preparing battle plans for Afghanistan were waiting for information about 'the structure of al-Qaeda, the location of hideouts, and the
plans for escape'.[88] Abu Jandal provided 'details that we did not have,'
said Soufan, including information about bin Laden's communication
methods and weaponry stockpiles. Soufan, who appeared before the US
Senate Committee on the Judiciary in 2009 to condemn the use of torture during the questioning of terrorist suspects, claimed his non-violent
interrogation of Abu Jandal between 17 September and 2 October was
'done completely by the book'. 'It was probably one of the most successful interviews that I did during my FBI career,' he told me, during our

interview in 2010, and it yielded a 'treasure trove of highly significant actionable intelligence'.[89]

The successful start of Operation Enduring Freedom in Afghanistan on 7 October raised the question about which other countries, if any, the US military should pursue. General Tommy Franks of US Central Command wondered how action in Afghanistan was connected to 'what might need to be done in Somalia, Yemen or Iraq'.[90] Saleh had learned his lesson from backing Saddam's invasion of Kuwait in 1990, which landed Yemen in diplomatic quarantine for the best part of a decade. In the restive months after 9/11, Saleh made sure that Yemen was seen as an ally, rather than a target for invasion, and tried to salvage his country's image in Washington. He rounded up dozens of terrorist suspects, including bin Laden's father-in-law, but external pressure to adapt to the new diplomatic contours of the 'war on terror' only increased after the bombing of a French oil tanker off Yemen's coast in 2002.[91]

In November 2002, Saleh gave the Americans permission to launch a Predator drone strike, operated remotely by the CIA. The Hellfire missile hit a car in Marib province, killing suspected al-Qaeda leader Qa'id Sinan al-Harithi, four Yemenis said to be members of the Aden Abyan Islamic Army and a Yemeni-American who had allegedly recruited volunteers to attend al-Qaeda training camps.[92] High-level cooperation between Sana'a and Washington was supposed to be a secret, and all hell broke loose in the Yemeni media when it emerged that the USA had acted with Saleh's consent. The backlash exposed Saleh's delicate balancing act between counterpoised domestic and Western visions of legitimacy, and Saleh was 'described as being "highly pissed" at the disclosure'.[93] Two months later, a Yemeni gunman shot dead three US missionaries working in a clinic in the southern highland town of Jibla.

When the USA invaded Iraq in 2003, the Yemeni government took several steps to restrict young men travelling to Syria and Iraq. The controls were imperfect, and significant numbers of Yemenis joined the insurgency against US troops. According to documents found in Sinjar, on Iraq's border with Syria, Yemen was among the top four countries of origin for foreign fighters entering Iraq; Saudi Arabia and Libya took the top two spots, with Syria and Yemen in joint third place.[94] Yemen had previously initiated a unique dialogue project aimed at encouraging jailed al-Qaeda supporters to renounce violence, based around discussion of the Qur'an.[95] Abu Jandal was among the participants in the project, which initially attracted favourable media coverage, but praise faltered in 2005 when it emerged that several former graduates of the programme had joined the Iraqi revolt.

A year later, Yemen's special terrorism court ruled that Yemeni participation in the Iraqi insurgency was perfectly legal. Judge Mohammed al-Baadani acquitted nineteen defendants—fourteen Yemenis and five Saudis—on the grounds that sharia law permitted the armed confrontation of Western occupiers in Muslim countries. Judge al-Baadani scolded the defendants for 'sneaking off to Iraq without the approval of the president or their parents', but he acknowledged the Qur'an's exhortation to jihad as a core religious duty. 'Throwing those men in jail would get rid of 19 bad people, but it would make enemies out of 19 million Yemenis. Which one would America choose?' he asked a *Wall Street Journal* reporter who covered the trial.[96]

* * *

Abu Jandal was released from jail after a presidential pardon, having graduated from the dialogue programme.[97] When we met in 2008, he had retired from active jihad and was driving a taxi in Sana'a. He arrived wearing a neatly pressed shirt and slacks, with two mobile phones strapped to his leather belt. I had already heard about his legendary charisma, and now he persuaded the restaurant staff, who were clearing up after lunch, to let us sit in the garden even though they had stopped serving food and the restaurant was shutting.[98] The kitchens were closed, so Abu Jandal sent the waiters across the road to the shops, handwriting our drinks order on a clean page in his pocket-size flip-top notebook and insisting on giving them his money, even though I had made it clear from the outset that I intended to pay.

The waiters came back with several cans of Mountain Dew and a packet of chocolate biscuits. As we talked, Abu Jandal lined up the curled ring-pulls from our open drink cans, placing them side by side on the tablecloth, and played with delicate wooden tooth-picks, stacked in a small plastic box in the centre of the table. Abu Jandal had slender hands and tapered fingernails, and he cracked his knuckles absent-mindedly. He said he had come straight from an audience with a high-level Yemeni official, and he told me he was thinking of establishing a think-tank that would conduct studies on the legitimate conduct of jihad—presumably, only endorsing participation in violent struggles that were authorized by senior clerics and state officials. Abu Jandal said the new venture had Saleh's personal backing, but he needed funding to get it off the ground. He rejected the suggestion that his new think-tank would endorse violence in Yemen, saying: 'It's Osama bin Laden's word that Yemen should not be a battleground. I know people who would make America dizzy if they came out of their shells, but Yemen is not a legitimate target.'

Two years before my meeting with Abu Jandal, twenty-three terrorist suspects and convicts had escaped from a high-security prison in Sana'a, supposedly by tunnelling their way into the bathroom of a local mosque. At least one security official was rumoured to have received a handsome sum for facilitating the escape. (Among the escapees was USS *Cole* plotter Jamal al-Badawi, who was apprehended the following year and placed under house arrest, after pledging allegiance to Saleh.)[99] The renaissance of Yemeni terrorism that followed the jailbreak was boosted by an influx of cash and manpower from Saudi Arabia, following the kingdom's own crackdown on its own terrorist networks north of the border, as well as the presence of returnees from Iraq.[100] Saleh was often criticized for operating a 'revolving doors' policy that set terrorist suspects free as fast as they were imprisoned, often in response to pressure from powerful sheikhs who pushed for the release of their tribesmen. However, the bathroom escapees now began to attack Yemeni security and intelligence targets in retaliation for their alleged torture and humiliation in captivity.[101]

During 2008, the notion of a new generation began to take root, based on the activities of younger jihadis who rejected the 'tacit nonaggression pact between older members of Al-Qaeda and the government'.[102] The tempo of terrorist activity in Yemen steadily increased as al-Qaeda-inspired groups carried out a low-level bombing campaign against Western targets in Sana'a, including a botched mortar strike on the US embassy. This visible wave of violence added to the impression of renewed danger emanating from Yemen, but Abu Jandal was critical of the plotters' inefficiency and lack of discipline:

> Osama bin Laden has a clear, strategic vision for al-Qaeda but there is no effective leadership in Yemen. Eighteen to twenty-year-olds freshly recruited here have very little military experience and no background in

understanding the faith. You need time to make good fighters, to train them with military skills and to qualify them in religion but the Iraq returnees are naive and reckless. They want to be heroes, and it's all about action and reaction. They're too impulsive.

Yemen's newly reconstituted terrorist networks seemed to be functioning as a cluster of splinter cells, prompting speculation about their command structure, but Abu Jandal was sceptical about their links to al-Qaeda's central leadership. 'The groups now claiming to act in bin Laden's name aren't organized and their activities don't seem to be planned according to any strategy,' he told me. In order to press the point, Abu Jandal invoked the popular tale of Layla and the Madman from classical Arabic literature. The madman was Qais, a heartbroken poet, who roamed the wilderness when his beloved, Layla, was forced to reject his marriage proposal because her father insisted that she wed another suitor. 'Everyone claims that Layla loves him, but her heart belongs to Qais. There is only one Qais and that's Osama bin Laden. It's nearly a decade since I last spoke to Osama and I still miss him very much. If I could, I would go to see him immediately. He influenced me more than my own father.'

Abu Jandal had once occupied a central role in the daily management of al-Qaeda in Afghanistan, where he had regular access to the group's leader. During interrogation by Soufan in the weeks after 9/11, Abu Jandal betrayed bin Laden, compromised his own value system and played a part in dispersing the organization that he had helped to create. When the Yemenis eventually released him from prison, the US military had destroyed al-Qaeda's Afghanistan base using information that Abu Jandal had provided. If he resented the circumstances that had brought about his premature retirement from the battlefield, he didn't say. He did, however, seem to be uncomfortable with the disaggregated nature of twenty-first-century global jihad, where the anger and fury underpinning al-Qaeda's original model had grown beyond one man's personal control. He displayed nostalgia for a golden era, when al-Qaeda was a smaller, more disciplined organization held together by personal loyalty. 'I followed the instruction of good teachers. That's the difference between me and the youth who now oppose me,' he told me. 'The young ones send me death threats and they accuse me of being a spy.'

When we met in summer 2008, Abu Jandal claimed there was disorder among Yemen's jihadi leaders, and he was critical of two prominent figures, Qasim al-Raymi and Nasser al-Wuhayshi, who had also served bin Laden in Afghanistan. 'Al-Raymi is a good fighter but Wuhayshi couldn't lead two chickens and they're both poor commanders. If they were unified, they would be capable of hitting the government hard,' he said. 'I don't exclude links to the international al-Qaeda structure, but they're very weak. Al-Raymi and Wuhayshi don't understand what Osama bin Laden wants.' His parting shot was: 'The battle is huge. It's still under bin Laden's command and I want to tell you it's only just the beginning.'

A few weeks after our meeting, suicide bombers detonated two car bombs at the gates of the US embassy in Sana'a, killing more than two dozen people. It was 'far from clear how much direction Nasir al-Wuhayshi had over the attack',[103] but within four months, he had become emir of a new transnational al-Qaeda affiliate, al-Qaeda in the Arabian Peninsula (AQAP), with al-Raymi serving as his military commander. AQAP's creation was only announced two days after President Barack Obama's January 2009 inauguration. It merged terrorist networks in Yemen and Saudi Arabia, making Yemen the new centre of gravity for terrorist activity in the region. Over the following year, while Abu Jandal squandered his enforced leisure time—no doubt, on a government stipend—Wuhayshi went on to build al-Qaeda's most dangerous global franchise.[104]

8

SHADOW WAR

US CRUISE MISSILES AND DRONES

Al-Qaeda in the Arabian Peninsula (AQAP)'s military commander, Qasim al-Raymi—dressed in a khaki T-shirt, military-style vest and traditional Yemeni mashadda headdress—jabbed his finger in the air as he faced the camera.[1] With pride and indignation, he recounted the rout of the Yemeni army during an attempted military operation against AQAP and their tribal hosts in Marib in July 2009. 'These raids carried out against the tribes of Faith and Wisdom are nothing but an extension of the Crusades against Islam and the Muslims, led by tyrannical America,' al-Raymi declaimed.[2] Speaking over archive footage of advancing tanks, a narrator's voice told the viewer that the main reason for the regime's attack on Marib was 'to break the prestige of the tribes and to disarm them'.[3]

In al-Raymi's eyes, this treachery in Marib was the result of a 'rotten deal' by General David Petraeus, Chief of US Central Command, and Saudi Arabia's deputy interior minister, Prince Mohammed bin Naif.[4] The Americans had chosen to use Yemeni soldiers to 'bear the brunt' of their counterterrorism operations and avoid having to 'spill their own blood', while Mohammed bin Naif had 'bought off the conscience of the Yemeni officials with Saudi riyals'.[5] Al-Raymi claimed that Mohammed bin Naif had 'more authority in the interior ministry in

135

Yemen than in the ministry of his own father', septuagenarian Interior Minister Prince Naif, but he was confident that the 'resolute and firm' inhabitants of 'Mohammed's peninsula' would not be tempted to join elite games played with US and Saudi money. 'The mujahideen, all praise be to Allah, were able to repel the military attack.'

For Princeton scholar and prolific blogger Gregory D. Johnsen, the battle of Marib video was 'the most technologically impressive piece of propaganda' that AQAP had produced to date.[6] Johnsen pointed out that the video featured interviews with several captured soldiers, backing up AQAP's claims 'that it did what it said it did', and noted that AQAP had turned the government's usual PR tactic on its head by displaying its own cache of newly seized weapons, plundered from a military supply truck.[7] Johnsen had previously described al-Raymi as 'the single most dangerous individual in the organization, responsible for masterminding numerous suicide attacks'.[8] Now, he argued that al-Raymi's claim that Yemenis were 'turning to Internet forums to get the real story' about the Marib battle was 'particularly powerful', because it showed that AQAP understood people distrusted government propaganda and was 'attempting to take the moral high road'.[9]

In his online tirade, al-Raymi had singled out Ammar Saleh, de facto head of Yemen's NSB, for ordering the raid on Marib in collusion with the Americans and the Saudis, but he also blamed local tribal leaders for consenting to the assault. 'The biggest shame is for the tribal sheikhs to turn into foot soldiers and slaves of Ali Abdullah Saleh, who is himself a slave to the Saudi riyal and the American dollar,' al-Raymi railed. 'I say to those sheikhs [...] where is the manhood and the magnanimity [...] or did it die with your forefathers and you have buried it with them?'[10] Al-Raymi goaded the tribesmen to abandon their corrupt sheikhs who were complicit with Saleh's regime, deriding them as 'sell-outs'.[11] 'The hardest thing for the mujahideen to bear is injustice,' he added.[12]

Al-Raymi's appeal to the tribes came at a time when the traditional tribal system—the nerve centre of Yemeni politics—was under increasing strain, as a result of a cash shortfall underpinning the system of patronage. Policymakers feared that Yemen's unfolding economic crisis would amount to diminished state control, giving AQAP greater room for manoeuvre. This view was based on the reasoning that Yemen's tribes would continue to offer AQAP safe haven in the event of state collapse, but at least one US official acknowledged that they faced constraints 'as a group without a tribal base in a tribal society'.[13] Australian analyst Sarah Phillips warned that Yemen's tribes were primarily motivated by a 'desire for political autonomy from a central power', and noted that AQAP offered 'little more than a lightning rod for entrenched grievances'.[14] The organization was 'vulnerable to the threat that Yemen's tribes may ultimately find its presence a liability', because AQAP's goal of gaining political control and establishing a caliphate would consign the tribes to a 'subordinate status'.[15]

Nevertheless, throughout 2009, the fear of al-Qaeda's impending revival on the Arabian Peninsula was a constant cause of concern in Western foreign ministries and haunted the thoughts of senior Saudi princes. Riyadh's counterterrorism chief, Prince Mohammed bin Naif, oversaw Saudi Arabia's combined efforts to apprehend, incarcerate and rehabilitate the kingdom's 'most wanted' terrorist suspects, including those who absconded to Yemen. In August 2009, Mohammed bin Naif received a telephone call from Saudi national Abdullah al-Asiri, offering to travel home from his refuge in Yemen's Marib province and turn himself in. Presuming that al-Asiri was repentant, the prince arranged to meet him in person in Jeddah, but al-Asiri arrived carrying a hidden suicide bomb, in the form of pentaerythritol tetranitrate (PETN) explosives packed inside his rectum.[16] Al-Asiri killed himself in the ensuing explosion, but the prince was only lightly injured.

Al-Asiri had targeted Prince Mohammed bin Naif as the public face of the kingdom's counterterrorism campaign and patron of Riyadh's flagship rehabilitation centre for former Guantanamo detainees. The rehab centre boasted a relatively low rate of recidivism among its alumni, but several recent graduates had fled to Yemen following their release.[17] Among them were Said al-Shihri and Mohammed al-'Awfi, who both appeared in AQAP's January 2009 web video, announcing the merger of al-Qaeda's branches in Yemen and Saudi Arabia, and proclaiming the overthrow of the Saudi royal family as a central aim.[18] AQAP's maiden video statement followed two days after Barack Obama's inauguration and was released on the same day—22 January— that President Obama signed an executive order to close the detention facility at Guantanamo Bay, which still housed nearly 100 Yemenis, the largest remaining national population group.

During the Obama administration's first year, US officials explored a range of options to send the Yemenis home, but lack of confidence in Yemen's proposed rehabilitation plans combined with concerns about the country's mounting instability to stall repatriation negotiations. In May 2009, Human Rights Watch noted that Yemen itself had become 'the biggest obstacle' to shutting down the camp—a fact that had more to do with 'the environment to which the men will return than the men themselves'.[19] (However, several detainees did have family links to active terrorists, such as Qasim al-Raymi's brother, Ali.)[20] US officials were keen to dispatch some of the Yemenis to Prince Mohammed bin Naif's rehabilitation centre in Riyadh, but the Saudis proved reluctant from the outset.

State Department Coordinator for Counterterrorism Daniel Benjamin claimed that the Obama administration viewed Yemen as a foreign policy priority right from the start and, in parallel with the Guantanamo review, US officials embarked on a full-scale rethink of Yemen policy.[21] During 2009, a 'steady stream of high-ranking officials' travelled to Yemen for meetings with Saleh, including White House counterterrorism adviser John O. Brennan.[22] In September, Brennan told Saleh he was looking to expand US military action in Yemen, and Saleh offered him 'unfettered access' to Yemeni airspace, coastal waters and land for US counterterrorism operations. In return, Saleh said he could not be criticized if these operations failed. 'I have given you an open door on terrorism, so I am not responsible,' he said.[23]

On 17 December, three months after Brennan's visit to Sana'a, a US submarine positioned in the Gulf of Aden unleashed a BGM-109D Tomahawk laden with cluster munitions.[24] The Tomahawk hit the tiny community of al-Ma'jalah, in Abyan province, killing more than forty people, including many children.[25] When Saleh's government issued a statement claiming responsibility for the strike, Obama called Saleh, reportedly to 'thank him for his cooperation and pledge continuing American support'.[26] The White House had intended to target an AQAP training camp, but a subsequent investigation carried out by Yemen's parliament interviewed the surviving residents of al-Ma'jalah, who denied they had any connection with Al Qaeda.[27]

CSF chief Yahya Saleh ordered his CTU to raid a suspected Qaeda safehouse in Arhab and a 'logistics centre' in Sana'a on the same day as the missile strike in al-Ma'jalah.[28] Five days later, on 22 December, there was a second missile strike, this time in Shabwa province, and on Christmas Eve, another strike in Shabwa.[29] Saleh's government claimed that AQAP's emir, Nasser al-Wuhayshi, and his deputy, Said al-Shihri, had been killed in the third strike, but these assertions were swiftly disproved. December's triple bombardment represented 'Yemen's widest offensive against jihadists in years', and marked the first use of US cruise missiles in Yemen since the 2002 assassination of al-Harithi.[30] Gregory D. Johnsen argued that this latest assault would force AQAP's hand, and the organization would 'have to respond in some manner'.[31]

On Christmas Day, Nigerian student Omar Farouq Abdulmutallab attempted to bomb Northwest Airlines flight 253 in the skies over Detroit. With such a short planning horizon, it seemed unlikely that AQAP had managed to mount this operation solely in response to the strikes in Yemen. However, on 26 December, the media began reporting that Abdulmutallab told US officials he had 'obtained explosive chemicals and a syringe that were sewn into his underwear from a bomb expert in Yemen associated with Al Qaeda'.[32] The PETN explosive in Abdulmutallab's pants was identical to the incendiary material used by Abdullah al-Asiri in his failed attempt to kill Prince Mohammed bin Naif four months earlier.

The revelation that Abdulmutallab trained and obtained explosives on the Arabian Peninsula had global newsmakers frantically typing 'Yemen' into Google. For the tiny group of Western analysts following events in Yemen, the Christmas holidays were suddenly interrupted by mobile phones that started beeping and buzzing, and rang almost continuously throughout the following month. In January, once the festive period was over and visas could be easily obtained, foreign correspondents began to arrive in Sana'a in droves. 'It was like an invasion,' said one Yemeni reporter, who worked as a fixer for a range of global news organizations. Not since the fatal attack on the USS *Cole* in Aden harbour in 2000 had Yemen been subject to such intense international scrutiny.

During the early months of 2010, Washington think-tanks held a flurry of panel discussions and talks on Yemen, as consultants, journalists and policy wonks played catch-up. The crux of the discussion was the renewed risk that Yemen posed as a safe haven for terrorism. Analysts had been crying wolf about Yemen's collapse for years, but 'the wolf is finally at the door. Yemen is teetering and the system is failing,' admitted one US official.[33] Yemen's slow transition from oil-dependency to a post-oil economy presented the challenge of maintaining security and stability with ever fewer resources. The question for US policy-makers and analysts was: how to manage or mitigate that risk?

* * *

Yemeni public opinion is widely hostile to US policy in the Middle East, and Yemen's geographic proximity to Islam's holiest sites raises unique challenges for the West's active pursuit of wanted terrorists. On 10 January, President Obama explicitly ruled out the prospect of putting US combat troops on the ground, focusing instead on the US military's light footprint in the country, and emphasizing the role that military trainers were 'playing in providing support to Yemen's counter-terrorism operations'.[34] Twelve months after signing an executive order to close the detention factility at Guantanamo Bay, Obama announced a moratorium on the transfer of all Yemeni detainees.

US domestic political dynamics and the broad foreign policy parameters were already firmly set, and the administration's focus on AQAP 'grew more intense' after Detroit.[35] At times, the US foreign policy machine seemed like a heavy juggernaut tearing down the highway on a dark, rainy night. Yemen looked like just another bit of slow-moving roadkill that was about to get caught in the wheels. When Fox News ran a web poll in January 2010 asking: 'Should the US engage in Yemen Offensive?' more than half of the respondents clicked 'yes'. One contributor wrote: 'Terrorists are like cockroaches in the kitchen [...] You only get rid of them by spraying the entire house. We either need to accept the fact that we are going to be attacked or accept the fact that we are going to have to take this out on a lot of innocent people to get at the bad ones.'[36]

Advocates of further kinetic action were not confined to the right of the political spectrum. During a week on the think-tank circuit in Washington DC in spring 2010, I lost count of the number of times I heard analysts of all stripes talk about 'killing the bad guys'. To my European ears, these words sounded crude and the logic underpinning them seemed problematic. How to distinguish between the 'good guys' and 'bad guys' in Yemen, for a start, given the regime's previous alliance with extremists, its role in regional organized crime, and continued rumours of links between members of the regime and *takfiri* networks? And what if the new 'bad guys' were Americans? Having played a significant role in the formation and early evolution of al-Qaeda, Yemenis were once again at the centre of a significant and dangerous mutation in the organization's tactics, involving the recruitment of US-born Muslims and converts.

In the weeks after the attempted Detroit attack, the US Senate Foreign Affairs Committee warned that al-Qaeda was targeting 'non-traditional recruits to launch attacks against American targets within the Middle East and beyond'.[37] US officials had amassed 'growing evidence of attempts by Al Qaeda to recruit American residents and citizens in Yemen' and in Somalia. They were particularly concerned about several dozen US citizens who had immigrated to Yemen to 'marry local women or after converting to Islam in American prisons'.[38] The committee noted that potential threats from Yemen and Somalia posed 'new challenges' for the homeland: 'The prospect that US citizens are being trained at Al Qaeda camps in both countries deepens our concern and emphasizes the need to understand the nature of the evolving dangers.'[39]

The committee's allegation that 'veteran fighters from Afghanistan and Iraq' were staffing training camps for Western students in Yemen were corroborated by journalist and film-maker Jamal Osman, who confirmed that it was possible for Western-born Muslims and converts to link up with recruiters inside Yemen's small network of Salafi madrassas and language schools. Osman had visited Sana'a in the last few months of 2009, where he interviewed a US citizen who claimed he had just returned from a training camp in Marib province. Osman also encountered Omar Farouq Abdulmutallab, the would-be Detroit plane bomber, although he did not learn about the Nigerian's impending suicide mission. Video footage later revealed that Abdulmutallab had also travelled to one of Yemen's desert camps around this time, where he practised target shooting and recorded his martyrdom statement, dressed in a white robe and skullcap.[40]

During the years before Detroit, Western—especially British—intelligence services had mostly focused on the radicalization of Western nationals in religious schools in Pakistan, but as Yemen rose up the list of foreign policy concerns during 2009, Western spooks began to pay closer attention. Towards the end of 2009, four British language students claimed they were tortured by Yemeni intelligence agents and interrogated about their contacts in London mosques, after they were dragged off a bus outside Sana'a.[41] In January 2010, masked men seized another language student, US citizen Sharif Mobley, when he went out to buy groceries in Sana'a. Mobley was injured in the ensuing struggle and transferred to a Sana'a hospital for medical treatment; he allegedly shot and killed a Yemeni guard during a subsequent escape attempt. The US media seized on the fact that Mobley had worked at five different nuclear power facilities in the States before he relocated to Yemen—a fact that was dismissed as 'fearmongering' by Mobley's lawyer.[42]

According to US officials, Mobley had left his New Jersey home to seek out the charismatic Yemeni-American preacher, New Mexico-born Anwar al-Awlaki.[43] Mobley's chosen mentor spent his childhood in the USA and his teenage years in Yemen, before returning to the USA to obtain an engineering degree in Colorado. He later preached in mosques in California and Virginia. Al-Awlaki's dual nationality and his ability to shift between 'perfect, idiomatic English and flawless Quranic Arabic'[44] placed him among a class of sheikhs who were speaking to 'a new generation'.[45]

Al-Awlaki's English-language lecture series, recorded from 2000 onwards and available as CD box sets, established his reputation as a 'powerful orator' among many mainstream English-speaking Muslims.[46] In one of these early lectures—available online as a free download from a range of internet sites—al-Awlaki offered guidance to Muslims living as a minority within the West.[47] (The emphasis and stress of al-Awlaki's English accent recalled the speech patterns of many other young Yemeni professionals who had lived, worked or studied in the US and were comfortable with US idioms.)

Despite al-Awlaki's populist colloquial approach, his apparent ease with US culture and the predominantly spiritual content of his early lectures, several US officials believed that al-Awlaki was the key link in a chain of radicalization that stretched back to the planning stages of 9/11. A decade earlier, the cleric had been linked to two of the 9/11 hijackers, Mecca boys Khaled al-Midhar and Nawaf al-Hazmi. Following their arrival in the States in 2000, the pair began praying with al-Awlaki at his San Diego mosque. When al-Awlaki transferred to a new preaching post in Virginia, Hazmi moved with him.

The FBI, whose agents interviewed al-Awlaki four times in the days after the 9/11 attacks, concluded that his contacts with the hijackers and other radicals were 'random, the inevitable consequence of living in the small world of Islam in America'.[48] However, *New York Times* reporter Scott Shane unearthed records from the 9/11 Commission showing that not all investigators agreed with this conclusion:

One detective, whose name has been redacted, told the commission he believed Mr Awlaki 'was at the center of the 9/11 story'. An FBI agent, also unidentified, said that 'if anyone had knowledge of the plot, it would have been' the cleric, since 'someone had to be in the US and keep the hijackers spiritually focused'. The 9/11 commission staff members had sharp arguments about him. 'Do I think he played a role in helping the hijackers here, knowing they were up to something?' said one staff member, who would speak only on condition of anonymity. 'Yes. Do I think he was sent here for that purpose? I have no evidence for it.'[49]

Ironically, in the weeks after 9/11, al-Awlaki's eloquent English, moderate outlook and the proximity of his Virginia mosque to Washington DC news bureaux made him a valuable 'go-to Muslim cleric for reporters scrambling to explain Islam' to a bewildered US public.[50] Al-Awlaki's public condemnations of the 9/11 attacks stood in sharp contrast to the 'Salafi-*takfiri*' position he would later adopt. At this stage, al-Awlaki was either concealing his private sympathy for *takfir* or his approval of violent measures was yet to develop, in response to what he saw as discriminatory measures. He had been critical of the 'anti-Muslim backlash' that followed 9/11, and was visibly disturbed by a series of federal raids on Muslim businesses and charities in Virginia, as part of Operation Green Quest's probe into terrorist financing.[51]

The Green Quest raids, which involved several people he knew, were a pivotal moment in al-Awlaki's transition towards a more hostile public position, argued journalist Scott Shane. In a speech following the raids, al-Awlaki's 'voice is shaking with rage [...] That's when he first uses the language that America is at war with Islam,' Shane observed.[52] Al-Awlaki's extremism came into increasingly sharp focus after the US-led invasion of Iraq in 2003. The following year he moved to London, where he continued to preach, and then, in 2006, he returned to Yemen. He told a friend he was considering running for parliament in Yemen, where his father—a former government minister—was still well connected.

But instead of getting elected, al-Awlaki ended up in jail, supposedly 'after he intervened in a tribal dispute'.[53] Al-Awlaki continued to study the Qur'an during eighteen months held in solitary confinement, and after his release from jail he used the internet to reach an ever-larger audience.[54] Al-Awlaki's original CDs were still widely available, and it was the spiritual content of these lectures and 'his ability as an orator and a compelling speaker' that accounted for much of his popularity.[55] However, listeners accessing al-Awlaki's later MP3 recordings were exposed to his increasingly extremist rhetoric, which was attracting self-confessed hardliners as well as young Muslims, who were 'curious about radical ideas but not yet committed'.[56]

Al-Awlaki's potent 'mix of scripture and vitriol' only began to generate substantial attention in the US media in November 2009 after a fatal shooting at Fort Hood in Texas, in which twelve US soldiers and a civilian were killed.[57] Al-Awlaki had been in email contact with the perpetrator, US army psychiatrist Nidal Malik Hasan, before the attack.[58] Al-Awlaki subsequently praised Nidal on his website as 'a hero', describing him as 'a man of conscience who could not bear living the contradiction of being a Muslim and serving in an army that is fighting against his own people'. Al-Awlaki added: 'The only way a Muslim could Islamically justify serving as a soldier in the US Army is if his intention is to follow the footsteps of men like Nidal.'[59]

By the closing weeks of 2009, al-Awlaki had gone to ground, and he was thought to be hiding out amid his tribe, the Awalak, in Shabwa. In a statement released by the Yemeni embassy in Washington DC after the Christmas Eve bombing raid in Shabwa, Yemeni officials said al-Awlaki was 'presumed to be at the site' of the strike.[60] This marked the first of several attempts to kill the US-born preacher, and the first of several false claims by the Yemeni authorities that they had assassinated him.

In the days that followed the attempted Christmas Day plane bombing in the skies over Detroit, when Abdulmutallab 'admitted to having been trained by AQAP in Yemen' and told FBI agents he was 'connected to the Qaeda affiliate [...] by a radical Yemeni cleric whom he contacted online', journalists and investigators swiftly began asking questions about al-Awlaki's radicalizing role.[61] The internet cleric subsequently admitted meeting the Nigerian, but denied that he had played any role in the attempted attack.[62] In a digital recording in the possession of Yemeni journalist Abdulelah Hider Sha'ea, al-Awlaki confirmed that Abdulmutallab was one of his students. 'I had communications with him,' the cleric said. 'I did not tell him to do this operation, but I support it.'[63]

As US media scrutiny increased in the early months of 2010, al-Awlaki's righteous anger seemed to escalate. Yemen's clerics had already issued an edict warning against further US interference in their country, but al-Awlaki called for the ulema to go further, and to approve the killing of American military or intelligence officials who assisted Yemen's counter-terrorism programme.[64] 'America as a whole has turned into a nation of evil,' al-Awlaki proclaimed in an internet sermon uploaded in March.[65] 'I eventually came to the conclusion that jihad against America is binding upon myself, just as it is binding on every other able Muslim.'[66] Al-Awlaki's brutal invocations were delivered in self-assured, sincere and steady tones. One local journalist who was working with a US news crew in Sana'a, claimed he received death threats a few weeks later, after poking around at al-Awlaki's former mosque.

In April, US officials confirmed the Obama administration had taken the 'extraordinary step' of authorizing al-Awlaki's targeted killing.[67] The National Security Council had approved Obama's 'rare, if not unprecedented' decision.[68] If Obama's initiative provoked a divided reaction among the US public, the initial outcry against the kill-order among Yemen's politicians was unanimous. The foreign minister, al-Qirbi, 'appeared to balk' at the news, and denied the government was actively hunting the USA's new 'number one' fugitive, while Prime Minister Ali Mohammed Megawar decried the notion of al-Awlaki's assassination as an unacceptable violation of sovereignty.[69] The Awalak tribe issued a statement saying they would 'not remain with arms crossed if a hair of [the preacher] is touched, or if anyone plots or spies against him'.[70] Dr al-Qirbi subsequently demanded hard evidence to support al-Awlaki's rearrest and trial in Yemen, on the basis of his active involvement in terrorism.

But Western diplomats were adamant that al-Awlaki had enabled AQAP to 'go global' by mentoring the Fort Hood gunman and the Detroit plane bomber.[71] US law enforcement officials said there was 'no doubt' that al-Awlaki 'decided to go from al-Qaeda propagandist to a full-fledged operative' in the final months of 2009.[72] US officials believed the cleric had played an 'important role in convincing Abdulmutallab to get on that plane'.[73] However, the 'slow trickle of information' emerging about al-Awlaki's case during 2010 did not add much evidence to support officials' claims that he had 'moved beyond preaching' and 'gone operational'.[74] The State Department's annual global terrorism survey stated only that Abdulmutallab had visited al-Awlaki 'at least twice in Yemen'.[75]

The charge against al-Awlaki hinged on crossing the line from 'calling for jihad to actively pursuing it'.[76] Many analysts agreed that the US-born cleric was acting as a powerful radicalizer. According to an unnamed US counterterrorism official cited in the *New York Times*, al-Awlaki performed the role of a 'talent spotter' who prepared the supply chain for AQAP by bringing in those already leaning towards *takfiri* ideology.[77] 'He's able to, in essence, fire them up,' argued one US terrorism expert.[78] He's able to 'bring thousands of people a step closer to joining the mujahideen, to going into a camp, to getting training. That's a tremendous asset.'[79] However, as a scholar, al-Awlaki lacked practical battlefield skills, such as bomb-making, and he had little experience of the 'tradecraft of terrorism', such as forming and managing cells.[80]

For Gregory D. Johnsen, it was not even clear that al-Awlaki was an AQAP member. 'Certainly there are suspicions, and his published statements and interviews clearly support Al Qaeda, but the organization has never acknowledged him,' he wrote in an op-ed for *Newsweek*.[81] Al-Awlaki's name had featured only once in twelve issues of *Sada al-Malahim* ('The Echo of Battles'), AQAP's Arabic journal newsletter, Johnsen claimed, and 'even that citation was hardly an endorsement: it merely disputed recent claims that al-Awlaki had been killed in a joint US-Yemeni airstrike. He has never written an article, released an audiotape, or starred in a video for the organization.' Johnsen added that 'others, like Adil al-Abab, a Yemeni religious figure, play a much larger role in attracting and recruiting would-be suicide bombers', concluding that al-Awlaki was 'at best, a midlevel functionary'.[82]

Whatever the precise nature of al-Awlaki's relationship with AQAP before the spring of 2010, the regional al-Qaeda affiliate was quick to capitalize on the fact that 'one of the most popular English-language jihadist shaikhs out on the circuit', and the target of an international manhunt, was alive and well and hanging out in their neighbourhood.[83]

In the weeks after the confirmation of the kill-order, AQAP's communications group, al-Malahim Media, released an exclusive video interview with al-Awlaki. [84] The video footage showed al-Awlaki seated opposite an anonymous inquisitor, who was positioned with his back to the camera, in the conventional style of a televised political interview. The inquisitor's head and left shoulder were just visible in the camera's frame, cloaked in a white robe and hood. The two men discussed the recent 'Western media hype' about al-Awlaki, referring to articles in the *Wall Street Journal* and the *Washington Post*, and citing a report from the Rand Corporation, a US research outfit.

The cleric, dressed in a Yemeni robe and *jambiya*, warned that the USA was trying to propagate a 'fake Islam' that was 'liberal, democratic, peaceful and civil'. Al-Awlaki condemned Obama as the 'current leader of the Christian Crusades' for stepping up airstrikes against Afghanistan and Pakistan, and for authorizing the new programme of airstrikes in Yemen. Al-Awlaki threw his head back and laughed out loud when his white-robed inquisitor referred to earlier media reports that the Yemeni security services had already killed him. 'The distinguishing feature of the Yemeni government is their lies,' al-Awlaki replied. 'People have lost all trust in this government [...] The rulers are corrupt. The only ones left who can guide the people properly are the scholars.'

In an open jibe to the Yemeni authorities, al-Awlaki claimed that he moved around freely with divine protection, as well as the support of his tribe and the Yemeni people 'who hate America'. Al-Awlaki maintained a calm and sober demeanour as he vowed that he would never turn himself over to 'this traitorous proxy government'. [85] He claimed that Obama could not afford to launch a third war in Yemen, after the occupation of Afghanistan and Iraq, because the 'American economy is reeling'. Instead, in a close approximation of the 2009 agreement struck between Brennan and Saleh, al-Awlaki claimed that the government of Yemen had told the Americans: 'you can have our air and our sea and we will provide you with Yemeni agents on land who will spy on the Muslims'. Al-Awlaki claimed that US kill-orders were processed with 'no evidence required', and 'then the Yemeni government hands over the bill, saying this is the price. The more they kill the more they profit.'

In July 2010, the US Treasury's Office of Foreign Assets Control listed Anwar al-Awlaki as a 'specially designated global terrorist', a move that automatically froze his assets and blocked his access to legal services.[86] The UN followed suit four days later by adding al-Awlaki's name to the 1267 Committee's list of terrorist suspects.[87] These two moves formed the first steps in a legal paper trail, initiated by al-Awlaki's father, who argued that the American authorities were attempting to circumvent normal judicial procedures. According to New York University law professor Sam Rascoff, the act of fast-tracking the cleric on to a global terrorist list was the same as 'going right to the death penalty phase of a case without ever bringing it to a jury'.[88] The following month, in August, the American Civil Liberties Union and the Center for Constitutional Rights secured a joint licence to represent al-Awlaki, and won permission to pursue 'litigation relating to the government's asserted authority to engage in targeted killings of American citizens without due process', acting on behalf of al-Awlaki's father.[89]

By summer 2010, al-Awlaki had already taken the next steps in his own global propaganda war, by penning articles for *Inspire*, AQAP's new English-language magazine. *Inspire*'s editor, Samir Khan, a US national with Pakistani heritage who was also based in Yemen, used his online publication to encourage 'small-scale, low-tech attacks in the West'.[90] *Inspire*'s potential to radicalize and recruit vulnerable Westerners, especially people who were not already 'on authorities' radar', was a growing concern for US counterterrorism officials.[91] Al-Awlaki's English-language output meant he was little known among Yemenis, but his physical presence in Yemen influenced the scope of US counterterrorism policy, which in turn influenced the Obama administration's attitude to change and risk in Yemeni politics.

* * *

In January 2010, US Secretary of State Hillary Clinton argued the time had come to elevate development as a central pillar of American foreign policy. In a speech to the Center for Global Development, she called for a holistic approach to 'strategically critical' places like Yemen, even though 'we are not guaranteed success'. She conceded: 'the odds are long. But the cost of doing nothing is potentially far greater.'[92] Clinton's rallying cry for a pragmatic balance between diplomacy, development and defence reflected a general shift towards a 'whole of government' approach to state-building within the Obama administration. This comprehensive approach also carried the day in London later in the same month, when the Friends of Yemen—a cluster of donor countries and international organizations—met to discuss Yemen's pressing need for political, economic and social reform.[93]

Despite Clinton's pronouncements, the Pentagon dominated government thinking about Yemen. In spring 2010, I asked an adviser to the US government who had the most influence on Yemen policy. 'General Petraeus' was the answer.[94] If the Pentagon had the loudest voice on Yemen, it also had more money to spend. US military aid rose to $150 million during 2010, and that sum was set to rise again, to $250 million in 2011.[95] By contrast, Washington's total annual aid budget for Yemen hovered at just over $100 million, which in turn was dwarfed by the administration's $10 billion aggregate commitment for the same fiscal year in Afghanistan, Iraq and Pakistan.[96]

The logic of Clinton's argument for a comprehensive approach to Yemen was supposedly underpinned by lessons learned in Iraq and Afghanistan,[97] but Saleh's Yemen had little in common with two countries where the West had installed fledging post-conflict governments and relied on troop deployments to help with state-building projects. Partly as a reaction against these 'long, costly wars' begun by the Bush administration,[98] Obama's Pentagon performed a quiet gearshift, and General Petraeus began promoting a global move towards 'small scale, preferably locally driven operations'.[99] In September 2009, Obama enshrined this new strategy in a 'seven-page secret order authorizing small teams of US special-ops forces to conduct clandestine operations' and use covert methods to 'penetrate, disrupt, defeat or destroy' al-Qaeda.[100]

By the end of 2009, the effects of Obama's new policy in Yemen were already becoming apparent, but information about the secret directive was not yet in the public domain. In the early days of 2010, General Petraeus followed Brennan's path to Yemen to firm up the terms of a new deal between the two countries. Petraeus promised to increase US military aid to Yemen, 'including a proposed $45 million to train and equip Yemen's CTU forces for aerial warfare against AQAP'.[101] In return, Saleh gave Petraeus authority to strike AQAP when 'actionable intelligence' was available. Using a cavalier turn of phrase that WikiLeaks would expose before the year was out, Saleh also agreed that Yemeni officials would 'continue saying the bombs are ours, not yours'. However, he refused Petraeus permission to enter the operations area, insisting that the Americans stay in the joint operations centre, but those present 'knew it was a collective lie they would all promote'.[102]

As the US military pushed ahead with a major buildup of intelligence and lethal assets in Yemen, unnamed US officials drip-fed information to selected journalists about their steadily expanding military footprint. In January 2010, the *Washington Post* revealed that US military teams and intelligence agencies were 'deeply involved in secret joint operations with Yemeni troops', helping them to 'plan missions, develop tactics and provide weapons and munitions'.[103] Members of Joint Special Operations Command (JSOC) were also passing 'highly sensitive intelligence' to the Yemenis, including electronic and video surveillance, as well as three-dimensional terrain maps and detailed analysis of the al-Qaeda network. JSOC advisers on the ground in Sana'a were 'acting as intermediaries between the Yemeni forces and hundreds of US military and intelligence officers'.[104]

In May, the *New York Times* broke the news about Obama's secret executive order authorizing General Petraeus to escalate clandestine military operations against al-Qaeda. That same month an ill-starred US missile strike in Yemen illustrated the perils of the new approach.[105] Rather than hitting AQAP's leadership in the Marib desert, as US officials intended, the strike killed the province's deputy governor, Sheikh Jaber al-Shabwani, 'who was a top mediator in the government effort to demilitarize members of AQAP'.[106] Al-Shabwani's tribe responded by throwing up roadblocks, rupturing oil pipelines and cutting electricity supplies to Sana'a.

The deceased sheikh's family reportedly accepted 200 Kalashnikovs and 5 million riyals in compensation from President Saleh, but such a generous payout was not enough to restore the Yemeni government's dented credibility, and Saleh went 'scrambling to prevent an anti-American backlash'.[107] In the days immediately after the attack, the capital was plagued with power cuts and Saleh's government took emergency measures by diverting power from the south. That decision had a knock-on impact elsewhere, inflaming the combustible situation in Aden, where Greek academic Thanos Petouris was living.

One night at the end of May, Petouris was reading a book at home in Aden's Crater district around midnight, when he heard gunshots, and he went to the window to look out. He recalled:

Crater is shaped like a bowl, boxed in by mountains, so any loud noises echo off the slopes of Jebel Shamsan. I saw a group of young men running through the alleyways beneath my apartment, chased by policemen firing tear gas. The riots lasted for most of the night and, the following morning, my neighbourhood was a wreck. Protestors had uprooted street railings, set fire to tyres in the street, and cut off the road to the airport.

For Petouris, the Crater riots illustrated the loosely woven but fragile fabric of Yemen's political order, where apparently unconnected events could set off an unpredictable chain reaction. 'At the time, no one in Aden linked the riots to al-Shabwani's death. People were simply rioting in response to the power shortage, and they blamed the government in Sana'a for corruption, mismanagement and theft of resources,' he said. Sana'a residents were no strangers to regular power cuts but Aden's summer temperatures peak above 40°C, and the southerners felt their loss of electricity more acutely than those in the temperate northern highlands.[108] 'When the air conditioning went off, I felt that I wanted to skin myself alive within ten minutes,' Petouris noted, adding that the thermometer in a friend's car registered 50°C during the week of the riots.

The Crater disturbances highlighted how America's encroaching security demands threatened to aggravate the relationship between the president and the tribes, stoking already raw political tensions. 'When the Americans killed Sheikh al-Shabwani, the tribes reacted by punishing the state and stopping the supply of electricity. The state responded by redistributing power and aggravating the situation in the south without really intending to do so,' Petouris argued.[109] US intervention had tipped the delicate internal balance of power and forced Saleh's hand in managing the allocation of domestic resources. It also exposed the government's general loss of legitimacy. 'Yemenis either thought "the government is incompetent and we've lost sovereignty to the Americans" or "our government is collaborating". Or both,' noted Petouris.

In August, the *New York Times* dubbed General Petraeus's escalating military action in Yemen as a 'shadow war',[110] noting that the Pentagon was seeking to 'break its dependence on the Central Intelligence Agency and other spy agencies' for information in countries like Yemen without a significant American troop presence.[111] Unlike covert actions carried out by the CIA, JSOC's 'hunter-killer teams'[112] did not require presidential approval or Congressional oversight for their missions, although Pentagon officials claimed that any 'significant ventures' would be cleared by the National Security Council.[113] *The Nation*'s Jeremy Scahill described Obama's secret directive as a 'permission slip' for special-ops teams to mount a sustained targeted killing campaign coordinated by JSOC, quoting a former defence intelligence analyst who described the 'evidentiary standard for actually killing people off' as 'frighteningly low'.[114] However, in November, the *Wall Street Journal* reported that there had been no reported US airstrikes in the country since Shabwani's accidental assassination six months earlier, and noted that the dearth of reliable intelligence sources on the ground had created 'a window of vulnerability' that the US government was working fast to address.[115]

The Americans turned to Saudi Arabia to help them 'fill the gap, melding American aerial surveillance with ground intelligence from Saudi informants'.[116] The Saudis had already concluded that Yemen's intelligence gathering was compromised, and were relying on their own 'web of electronic surveillance and spies', as well as hoping that traditional measures of tribal patronage would encourage Yemen's sheikhs 'to eject the extremists'.[117] In October 2010, the Saudis were able to forewarn the Americans about a plot to detonate PETN explosives packed inside printer cartridges, loaded on cargo planes bound for the Gulf, Europe and America.[118] The tip-off allegedly came from a Saudi national, former Guantanamo detainee and graduate of Mohammed bin Naif's rehabilitation centre, Jabir al-Fayfi, who had recently surrendered to the Saudi authorities (or was handed over to them after capture in Yemen), following a period spent embedded in Yemen's AQAP network.[119]

The fact that it was Saudi-sourced intelligence—not kinetic action in Yemen—that foiled the October printer cartridges plot should have given US military planners careful pause for thought. Despite a year of high-level security cooperation between the Pentagon and the Yemeni military, al-Awlaki was still at large, AQAP's leadership remained intact, and bomb-maker Ibrahim al-Asiri, the technician who supposedly manufactured the group's PETN devices, was still at work. However, US military commanders were apparently considering allocating up to $1.2 billion over five years for capacity building with

Yemen's security forces.[120] In doing so, the Pentagon was proposing to move even closer to President Saleh and his relatives, apparently confident that his family would retain control, while members of the regime elite in Sana'a were themselves divided and increasingly preoccupied by the prospect of a future confrontation.

At the same time, both the Houthi rebels in Saada and the southern hiraak were already in open revolt against the regime. Public discontent was also growing, as foreign exchange reserves hit a record low and the Yemeni riyal continued to fall in value against the dollar. Many Yemenis viewed the provision of US military aid to elite security and intelligence units under the command of President Saleh's relatives as artificially sustaining his family's ability to maintain control. CSF commander Yahya Saleh lived up to his reputation as a public relations disaster when he told ABC News, laughing: 'Every time things getting worse, we get support more.'[121] Yahya's tone-deaf statement played into the Yemeni perception that Saleh's family was manipulating the AQAP threat to stay in power.

The Obama administration was alert to this risk. In 2009, US Ambassador Stephen Seche attended Brennan's Sana'a meeting with Saleh, when the president offered to outsource Yemen's counterterrorism efforts to the Americans. In a classified cable, later published by WikiLeaks, Seche acknowledged that this arrangement would leave Saleh free to 'devote his limited security assets to the ongoing war against Houthi rebels in Sa'ada. The net effect [...] will be a clear message to the southern movement or any other party interested in generating political unrest in the country that a similar fate awaits them.'[122] Although the Obama administration was troubled by the prospect of further instability in Yemen, in partnering with Saleh and his family they were creating a dangerous paradox. 'The only way for Yemenis to remove Saleh now is through violence because external military support closes down the hope of peaceful renewal through the domestic political system,' said one European observer.[123]

9

SOUTHERN DISCOMFORT

BIRTH OF THE SOUTHERN SEPARATIST MOVEMENT(S)

Queen Elizabeth II, resplendent in crown and ceremonial jewels, smiled through pursed lips from the illuminated display screen on Lutfi Shatara's mobile phone, as he leaned against the counter of a central London sandwich shop:

> When the British had a presence in south Yemen, we learned some valuable lessons about running our country. But, in 1990, we made the terrible mistake of joining with the northerners, who have a totally different mentality. Now, the country is like Afghanistan, everyone in the south is suffering and we feel that we have gone back in time 500 years. When I compare the situation in south Yemen now with the way things were before unification, I feel like crying. I feel that I lost my country.[1]

Lutfi left Aden shortly after unification, in his mid-thirties, to move to Britain with his wife. The couple settled in a north-west London suburb in the same year that Prime Minister John Major extolled the enduring nature of traditional British values. In a speech to the Conservative Group for Europe, Major predicted: 'Fifty years on from now, Britain will still be the country of long shadows on cricket grounds, warm beer, invincible green suburbs, dog lovers and pools-fillers.' Major had been seeking to reassure British voters unnerved by integration with Europe and growing numbers of migrants, but in

155

Lutfi's eyes Britain defined itself by progress and self-renewal. 'Everything changes here. The British people have chosen several prime ministers since I came here, but in Yemen, the same man is still in power. You should be proud of your country,' he told me. 'British democracy is an example to everybody.'

When I protested that British colonial administrators had committed countless atrocities and messed up the withdrawal from Aden in 1967 during empire's last gasp, Lutfi waved his hand in the air:

> Leave the colonial politics out of it. I know my rights are protected here. In Yemen, the southern movement can't even hold a meeting without the Political Security Organisation interfering, but here I'm grateful for freedom of speech and for my dignity. Why do you think all the southern leaders are living in exile? They are better men than Saleh and they have more to offer the Yemeni people, but they are scared to go back home because, even in exile, they are receiving death threats.

Political violence in south Yemen had started two years earlier, in 2007, after retired officers from the disbanded southern army began to demand higher pension payments or reinstatement to army service.[2] General conditions in the south were 'ripe for unrest',[3] and the regime's heavy-handed response inflamed latent separatist sentiment, which spread throughout the south during the following months.[4] 'Instead of diffusing the initial problem by addressing the retirees' demands, Saleh allowed the movement to turn practical grievances into a political agenda. If your brother is shot and your neighbour is killed, it quickly creates a sense of solidarity,' said one political analyst in Sana'a.[5] Dozens died, hundreds were injured and thousands arrested in the ensuing years, in what turned into an 'escalating spiral of repression, protests, and more repression'.[6] Violence peaked in 2009, immediately after Saleh's decision to delay Yemen's scheduled parliamentary elections by two years. On one single day during the peak cycle of violence, security forces were forced to resort to hangars and even a sports stadium to hold all the detainees, because the prison system was unable to cope with the sheer numbers.[7] Human Rights Watch claimed the 'vast majority of large organized protests in southern Yemen, particularly those in urban centers such as Aden and Mukalla' did not involve armed protestors, although splits later developed between pacificists and advocates of violence.[8]

The southern movement (al-Hiraak al-Janoubi)—also known simply as the hiraak—was built around 'perceptions of southern marginalization'.[9] Southerners complained that Saleh had failed to implement the terms of the 1990 power-sharing agreement between the PDRY and the YAR, or to honour the terms of the ceasefire after the 1994 civil war. Grievances included land seizures, the forced retirement of southern security officials, the exclusion of southerners from northern patronage networks, corruption and economic mismanagement.[10] The hiraak started off as a 'rights-based movement requesting equality under the law', but, by late 2008, some protesters were openly calling for independence, indicating that discontent was shifting to the structure of the political system itself.[11]

If the southern movement was driven by popular frustration with the northern elite, its leadership—a coalition of tribal sheikhs, civic leaders and prematurely retired military officers allied to former Marxist politicians living in exile—was struggling 'to unite around a coherent agenda'.[12] For some, this indicated that the southern movement was a genuine grassroots phenomenon that stood beyond the reach of the traditional elite, and its strength lay in the fact that it could not be co-opted or divided by Saleh's patronage politics. 'Everyone wants to ride on the wave of the south and say that it's his wave but it belongs to no one. The street moved before the leaders came to incite it. You never hear a symphony playing in the south. Grassroots discontent is not orchestrated by any effective leadership,' said one Sana'a observer.[13]

By 2010, at least seven main groups were involved in the hiraak, creating 'deep divisions as the leadership of each group [tried] to impose its own agenda'.[14] Lutfi, however, had faith that the generation of politicians who fled Yemen after the 1994 civil war could eventually return home to help unite the disparate southern movement. Most prominent among them was former PDRY president, Ali Salim al-Beidh, who was also the strongest advocate of secession.[15] Speaking from exile in Europe in 2009, al-Beidh promised to 'lead a peaceful struggle' to reclaim 'the occupied south', but he denied he was seeking to revive the politics of the Cold War. 'I'm not in a party, and will not join any party, but after liberation I may like to be an advisor,' he said.[16]

Exiles Haidar al-Attas and Ali Nasser Mohammed, both former prime ministers and presidents in the PDRY and one-time rivals, were once again vying for a leadership role, but many southerners felt the Marxists were too discredited by their Socialist baggage. 'The Marxists destroyed South Yemen after independence. The British had established a functioning administrative structure but instead of building on their legacy, our leaders chose to fight among themselves,' said one Adeni friend.[17] 'Those guys are still busy trying to settle old scores and instead of coming up with a coherent strategy to improve the status quo, they're simply trying to create a new cult of personality that could replace support for Saleh,' argued another observer.[18]

Lutfi had once reported for a London-based Arabic daily newspaper, *Asharq Al-Awsat*, and he ran his own website, Adenpress, covering issues relating to the southern movement.[19] His skills as a journalist, his fluency in English and his personal media platform made him valuable to the exiled would-be leaders. They gradually drew him into their circle and flew him to their planning and strategy meetings in Cairo and Damascus. In Lutfi's eyes, Saleh had successfully hoodwinked the Western donors, by distracting their attention from the scale of the change that was really needed. 'This regime is like a cancer and Yemen is like a sick man. The country needs an operation to remove the malignant tumour,' Lutfi argued. He was dismayed by the lack of British support for the southern movement and frustrated by the donors' apparent refusal to consider alternatives to Saleh.

Western fears about the presence of AQAP in south Yemen were stoked when Tariq al-Fahdli, former mujahid and Saleh ally, apparently defected from the regime to join the southern movement. In pure political terms, Tariq's switch from the ranks of Saleh's patronage network to form an alliance with his former Socialist enemies marked a weathervane moment. The timing of his defection followed a shock first-quarter fall in government oil revenues—dropping 75 per cent on the same period in the previous year, in response to plummeting world oil prices—suggesting that Saleh's extensive patronage system was under strain and the logic underpinning the elite power nexus was in flux. Tariq's decision to break ranks was an explicit sign that Saleh's associates were looking ahead and starting to position themselves for the coming struggle within the elite.

Nevertheless, al-Fahdli's high-profile betrayal generated visible momentum for the separatist movement. He issued a press statement, shortly after his defection, stating that 'unity achieved nothing [...] Southern lands are confiscated and wealth stolen and the military officers of the north live in luxurious palaces.'[20] Tariq's criticism of the northern military elite was all the more significant given his sister's marriage to Ali Mohsin, but he was still regarded with suspicion by many southerners. 'One minute, he's flying the unity flag and the next minute he's aligned with the southern movement. He's after land and power, and he's playing his own game with local grievances,' said one Aden resident.[21]

Perhaps predictably, Tariq's defection prompted retaliation from Sana'a, and, in July 2009, fatal clashes broke out between Tariq's supporters and security forces during a 'festival' to support the hiraak, close to Tariq's family compound in Zinjibar, Abyan province. Human Rights Watch noted that video footage of the event portrayed a 'very different picture from footage and accounts of other non-violent protests viewed by the organization [...] Armed men are clearly visible among the crowd, including raising their weapons at times in support of the speakers on the podium.'[22] Tariq subsequently told Human Rights Watch: 'My brothers in the Southern Movement are not listening to me, but this regime doesn't understand what political dialogue is, they only understand force. I am in favor of [armed] resistance and instituting a military movement.'[23]

A photograph published in the New York Times, taken after Tariq's defection, portrayed a brooding, handsome man in middle life staring through a window, with a half-smoked cigarette drooping from his lips, and clasping a glass tumbler in his right hand.[24] His thinning beard was turning silver and the hair on his temples was flecked with pewter. Wearing a white short-sleeved shirt and apparently blessed with 'a taste for Scotch',[25] Tariq bore greater resemblance to a French existentialist than he did Osama bin Laden, but suspicions lingered about his ongoing sympathies for violent Salafi-style extremism. Concerns about Tariq's historical ties to al-Qaeda were enhanced when, shortly after his defection to join the southern movement, AQAP commander Nasser al-Wuhayshi called for Islamic rule in south Yemen and vowed to retaliate for civilian deaths in the recent unrest. 'Ali Abdullah Saleh is an infidel and an agent [...] and today he is using all forms of oppression under the pretext of preserving unity,' he said.[26] 'The time for the rule of Islam has come so that you could bask in the justice and toler-ance it brings.'[27]

In May 2009, I spoke to Tariq on the phone and followed up by email. Tariq dismissed concerns that he intended to create an Islamist state in south Yemen. 'That's not my intention,' he wrote. 'Far from it.' Tariq said he wanted to 'build a democratic south' where people were free to 'respect each other's speech and ideas' and create political parties. 'The people of the south will choose a governing party by fair elections through the ballot box and con-tinue the principle of peaceful exchange of power,' he wrote. 'We need the West to help us.' When I asked him what the Western donors could do to ease the suffering of the southern people, he replied: 'They should stop political and economic assistance to Saleh, because he uses it to crush the people of the south. There's no unity under the roar of tanks.' As for his personal history, he reminded me that jihad against the Soviets in Afghanistan 'was the consensus of the Western world', and told me not to forget that the people 'who trained us were mostly Westerners'.

Tariq's apologists claimed that he tried and failed to unite the hiraak leadership, but others were too suspicious of his motives to cooperate, or proved unwilling to follow through on earlier promises of solidarity and financial assistance.[28] However, if many hiraak supporters held the view that Tariq was exploiting their resistance struggle to pursue his own agenda, for Lutfi Shatara it was enough that Tariq had challenged Saleh. He complained: 'Saleh is trying to scare the international com-munity with the threat of al-Qaeda. He's a good propagandist and he knows how to push the donors' buttons, but the southern movement has nothing to do with al-Qaeda so why are they falling for it? The Americans are fools if they believe him.'

Lutfi argued that Saleh was drawing the Saudis and the Americans into Yemeni politics to 'make the problem bigger and stay afloat with their support, but he can only govern by force now. He has lost every-body's trust.' Despondent, Lufti saw foreign support as a negative development that would only prolong the problem:

> Everyone in Yemen is worried because there is no light at the end of the tunnel and aid money can't help. Aden could be like Dubai but no one in the region wants to invest money in Yemen until Saleh has gone. Democracy

is all about choices, right? Yemen is supposed to be a democracy, so why can't we have a genuine choice?

* * *

I flew to Aden one evening a year later, on a Yemenia flight from Sana'a. There was a storm in Sana'a that afternoon, and al-Sailah—the drainage channel that runs through the centre of the old city and doubles as a dual-lane carriageway—had filled to the rim with filthy rainwater, displacing the traffic. The plane took off in whipping, chilly winds and a sky that was hewn with lighting. The legs of my jeans were wet from chasing down a taxi in a waterlogged road. By contrast, even late at night, the heat and humidity in Aden were stifling, but the change in atmosphere was welcome.

The following morning, Captain Roy Facey, port development adviser to the Yemen Ports Authority, invited me to join him at his office for hot, spicy breakfast beans—known as *fassoulia*. A former merchant seaman with a deep tan, tidy white whiskers and gentle English courtesy, Roy had spent the best part of twenty years living in Aden. Early in the morning after the USS *Cole* attack in 2000, diligent US investigators had woken Roy in his bed to question him about any suspicious activity in the port before the suicide blast.[29] 'The attack on the *Cole* had virtually no impact on our cargo activity,' Roy told me, 'but it has dramatically changed the way in which naval ships all over the world have come to be protected.'

As we toured the port complex, Roy stopped to chat to workers wearing red armbands, a sign that they were preparing to go out on strike with the general labour union. In a room adjacent to his office, two of Roy's colleagues played with a baby while the baby's mother cooked our breakfast. 'This is one of the world's best natural deep water ports, but we're hardly doing any trade here. We handle just 350,000 units a year, compared to 11 million in Dubai,' Roy told me while we ate.[30] Since Dubai Ports World had taken over container operations in the port in 2008, as part of the regime's Gulf investment drive, the volume of trade had actually dropped from more than 500,000 units to around 370,000 units, and the rate of decline in throughput was accelerating as Aden continued to lose its transshipment business to other ports in the region.[31]

In the streets around the port, the government had rigged dozens of unity flags to the lamp posts but the security presence itself was not intrusive. People said that Saleh was trying to avoid provocation by keeping his forces out of sight in the run-up to the twentieth anniversary of unification on 22 May. Everywhere I went, though, I heard an outpouring of frustration and complaints about discrimination. I talked to professionals, politicians, receptionists and businessmen who were struggling to make an honest living. I spoke to one trader who told me that his food stocks had been stolen; he had been forced to pay the police to carry out an investigation. I heard countless stories of police corruption, and the military's involvement in smuggling and profiteering, running lucrative black markets in food, diesel, guns, drugs and migrants.

One afternoon I turned up at a police station and I heard a uniformed duty officer, sitting under a portrait of Saleh, denounce the president as a 'thief'. On another afternoon, I went to chew qat with the coastguard. We sat on a ragged, filthy carpet in a bedraggled-looking office where the paint was peeling off the walls. Coastguard officers were supposed to target maritime smugglers but there was no fuel, they told me, because of budget cuts, so they couldn't go out in their boats as often as they were supposed to.[32] Just around the corner, the 1930s-era Crescent Hotel, with its beautiful wooden latticework, stood derelict. The city reeked of neglect and missed opportunities. 'What are the British going to do to help? You must do something!' people implored me. 'If not, we will turn to Iran!' they warned.[33]

In a nearby office, I heard Khadija, a middle-class professional in her forties, speak fluently about her disappointment and unmet expectations after unification:[34]

In 1967, we won independence from the British and in 1990 we agreed to unification but we have not experienced development. Under communism, there was nothing to buy in the shops and our leaders imposed tough restrictions on every aspect of life. When unity came in 1990, we thought we would enjoy better conditions but we were wrong. Now we see plenty of goods for sale in the shops, but we can't afford to buy anything. Prices go up quickly but our salaries stay the same.

In Khadjia's eyes, the southerners had learned to respect law and order under British rule, but the northerners were venal, ignorant and uncouth. 'In Aden, we respect red lights at the crossroads, but northern sheikhs drive straight through the traffic junctions. They don't even respect the most basic rules in society,' Khadija said. For Khadjia, the intractable problem was cultural as much as political, but despite this, and despite the fact that she was 'desperate' for change, she was still cautious:[35]

> I want my children to have a better life than me but I am not calling for separation. Secession is not the same as ending a bad marriage, you can't just sign a paper and walk away. First, secession contains the potential for further violence. Secondly, people assume life in the south will be better after separation but who knows? It could be worse.

Khadjia had clear memories of the 1994 civil war, when Aden had been sacked, and she feared renewed street fighting.[36] 'We want change, and hope that Ali Abdullah Saleh awaits the same fate as Saddam Hussein, but we don't want the same treatment as the Iraqi people,' she told me. On the question of leadership and a potential replacement for Saleh, Khadija felt that Ali Salim al-Beidh was fatally compromised by his role in negotiating a ceasefire deal at the end of the 1994 civil war, and the rumoured personal fortune that he accepted in return for leaving Yemen. 'Why should I listen to Ali Salim al-Beidh?' she asked me. 'He sold us out to the north and then he left us here!'

Khadija's caution and her advocacy of peaceful change were fairly common among Aden's professional classes. 'The middle class has been the slowest to support secession as they are reluctant to lose their relative advantages and I know plenty of people here in Crater who want to avoid war at all costs,' said Thanos Petouris. He reminded me that Aden's geography, with the old colonial districts clustered around the base of Jebel Shamsan and linked to the mainland by a causeway, meant the historic centre of the city was extremely easy to close off. 'In 1994, the southerners still had their own army so they could at least fight back, but they don't even have that now.' Most of the demonstrations took place on the mainland in Sheikh Othman district, because it was the 'most impoverished and populated area in Aden'.

Petouris's Crater apartment was just a few minutes' walk away from the compound housing the offices of a popular newspaper, *Al-Ayyam* ('The Days'). It was here, on a quiet side street, that a man was killed when security services laid siege to *Al-Ayyam*'s compound during the peak of separatist violence in 2009.[37] When I turned up for an interview with a member of the newspaper's founding family a year later, the compound's 8 ft metal gate was still riddled with bullet holes, like a sketching exercise waiting to be completed in a child's dot-to-dot patterning book. Two dramatic bullseye hits—one in each vehicle— had shattered the windscreens of a Land Cruiser and a saloon car parked in the compound forecourt. Everywhere I looked the plaster-work was pocked and shattered by gunfire, and the brickwork sur-rounding a bedroom window on the first floor was still stained with blackened smoke from an RPG attack. I had arrived for the meeting almost half an hour early, but I was courteously shown to a cramped office at the back of the compound. General manager Bashraheel H. Bashraheel emerged a few moments later. 'Don't worry!' he reas-sured me, breezily, as he lit a cigarette and plonked himself in a chair behind his desk. He ordered his guard to bring me tea, and chain-smoked his way through our interview, brushing off allegations that his newspaper had played the role of agent provocateur during recent unrest. 'The government thinks that my family is inciting the southern movement, but I want them to show us the evidence!'

Bashraheel's family, originally Hadrami, had lived in Aden for six generations. Bashraheel's grandfather had launched a bilingual newspa-per during the 1950s that was split, a few years later, into *Al-Ayyam* and a now defunct English-language title. Both papers were closed down during the Socialist era, and *Al-Ayyam* didn't start rolling off the print-ing presses again until after unification, in November 1990. Throughout the 1990s, until its closure in May 2009, *Al-Ayyam* was a top-selling newspaper, claiming a hefty percentage of the national market share. After 1995, when the family imported a cheap second-hand printing press from India, *Al-Ayyam* became the only Yemeni newspaper pro-duced on a press that did not belong to the regime. Family members were proud of the paper's editorial independence and their willingness to take a controversial public stance. 'The day after 9/11, we published an op-ed condemning the attacks,' Bashraheel told me. 'The govern-ment didn't follow our lead until 12 days later.'

The Bashraheel family saw themselves as newspapermen in the old-fashioned mode, a fact that probably owes something to the imprint of British colonialism. Unlike many reporters working on northern news-papers, the Bashraheels had been schooled in the techniques of inves-tigative journalism, and Bashraheel appeared to cherish the role that a free press is supposed to play in a functioning democracy. Bashraheel told me that the family stored their documents in a secure offshore vault, and he claimed that they were sitting on extensive evidence of corruption, intimidation and crimes involving Yemeni officials. The perception that the Bashraheel family claimed to possess such incriminating material was perhaps their best protection and simultaneously posed the greatest threat to their security.

During a wave of press intimidation initiated by the Ministry of Information in May 2009, *Al-Ayyam*'s compound was raided and the paper was shuttered, along with seven other independent newspapers accused of harming national unity. (Foreign journalists were not exempt from the crackdown, and a team working for the Qatari satellite channel Al Jazeera reportedly received death threats for their coverage of the southern protests.)[38] Security services stormed *Al-Ayyam*'s Crater compound for a second time in January 2010, while a group of journalists and civil society activists was staging a sit-in to protest the newspaper's continued suspension.

The second raid—just like the first—looked like a simple assault on freedom of speech, and the International Committee to Protect Journalists dubbed *Al-Ayyam* as 'the premier target in the government's assault on free expression'.[39] However, the government's campaign of intimidation against *Al-Ayyam* was complicated by a land dispute, involving a contested property deal in Sana'a, and Aden's security chief claimed his riot police were attempting to enforce a court summons relating to the land case. Editor-in-chief Hisham Bashraheel was arrested with his son, Hani, the paper's managing editor. Another one of Hisham's sons, Mohammed, had been taken into custody a day earlier. Hisham, who had recently undergone heart surgery, was released a few months later, on health grounds.

In April 2010, at the time of my visit, the newspaper was still closed, Hani and Mohammed were still in custody and Bashraheel was effectively under house arrest. 'You'll have to come to me,' Bashraheel replied, when I sent him an SMS to fix the interview. Two senior British officials had recently been to tour the compound, but Bashraheel was scathing about the West's support for his family's plight:

I don't see any willingness from the West to address press freedom or corruption in Yemen. I thought freedom of speech was an inviolable principle for Western democracies, but I have been proved wrong. Journalists are on the front line in Yemen and nobody in the West gives a damn. Instead, the government has drafted a new press law that will introduce an extortionate licence fee for setting up website publications and will transfer judicial powers from the Ministry of Justice to the Ministry of Information to oversee the confiscation and closure of newspapers. If it gets passed, this new legislation will reverse all the progress we've made since the 1960s.

The day before our meeting, Bashraheel had made a rare authorized sortie from his Aden bunker for an audience with Saleh in Sana'a, in order to negotiate the release of his siblings. 'The president picked up the phone in front of me. He called the police commissioner and told him to cancel the charges against my brothers,' Bashraheel recounted. He was still waiting for his two brothers to be released, but he was pleased with this sign of progress.[40] 'I'm delighted that we've managed to overturn their detention orders but what about compensation for the newspaper's loss of earnings and all this property damage?'

While the approval of his brothers' release represented a welcome step forward for the family, Bashraheel was deeply pessimistic about the country's prospects:

People describe Yemen as a country that's about to fall off the edge of the cliff but I don't think that's an accurate analogy. No. Yemen is like a man who can't swim, who is bouncing up and down at the end of a high-diving board and as soon as he jumps off, the whole country will go into free fall. The West is trying to avoid the inevitable by continuing to support the president, but Saleh will eventually lose control completely and, at that point, the country will fragment.

When I asked Bashraheel if he thought it likely that Sana'a's increasingly restive and divided elite would ever confront each other militarily, he told me: 'They are equally matched. If they try to fight, they will destroy each other.'

Bashraheel predicted that after Saleh's departure, Yemen would divide into three subdivisions: a Sunni Shafai state, comprising several central governorates; a Zaydi state, north of Sana'a; and the south within the old PDRY borders. But the south itself was also geographically divided and in danger of fragmenting, as I learned over lunch at the Sheraton Gold Mohur Hotel, which was located just a few miles away from *Al-Ayyam*'s Crater office. At the hotel's main entrance, I walked through an airport-style body scanner and passed my bags through a metal detector. Two decades after the Aden-Abyan Islamic Army's attempted attack against US military personnel staying at the hotel, the building continued to be considered as a possible target for terrorism. Trade at the hotel was slow, reflecting the pitiful state of Yemen's tourism industry and the dearth of business travellers coming to Aden. A handful of glum-looking Gulf Arabs sat in the coffee bar, watching CNN on a flat-screen television.

If the atmosphere inside the hotel was forlorn, the exclusive scene on the hotel's beach was incongruous. A clutch of Western wives swam sedately in the opal waters of the Gulf of Aden, while bachelors and husbands lolled about on loungers, drinking beer and watching slow-moving tankers tracing the sea's horizon. A young Arab couple paddled out of sight behind an anchored fishing dhow for a hidden kiss before a zealous hotel attendant chased them out of the water. At prayer times, the tinny sounds of Western pop classics piping through speakers at the bar were drowned out by the *adhan*, broadcast from a petite pepper-pot mosque that overlooked the beach from a rocky outcrop.

At $6.50 for a day pass, the Gold Mohur's private beach was out of bounds to most locals, and a $20 meal in the hotel restaurant would cost a mid-level civil servant several days' wages. But I had been invited to have lunch in this expat ghetto with a humanitarian worker, called Frank.[41] While we ate our food, we dissected the demographics under-pinning the rolling wave of southern unrest that had started with retired generals' street protests and escalated ever since. 'The older generation were schooled in Cuba and Russia during the Cold War. They are much better qualified than their children,' he said. 'The younger generation are poorly educated and they can't find jobs. If someone organizes them, they quickly represent a threat.'

The focal points of discontent—Dhala, Abyan, Radfan and Lahj—lay beyond Aden's city limits, and it was becoming increasingly difficult for Westerners to negotiate a permit to travel to these areas. (Two American journalists were deported shortly after my visit for attempting to travel to the 'free south' disguised as Yemeni women.)[42] But Frank had recently visited Radfan and he told me what he'd seen. 'The souk was almost empty,' he said. 'There was nothing much on sale in the market, just a few wilting vegetables. I saw crowds of young guys standing around looking bored. Their university teachers were on strike because the government had stopped paying their salaries.'

Radfan's community leaders told Frank that, during the protests, army marksmen shot at the demonstrators from nearby hills rather than clashing at close proximity in the street. A new government-run hospital was empty because there was no money to sustain any services. A hospital in nearby Dhala was still operating but security services had recently detained several doctors for treating injured protestors. 'Access to health services is becoming increasingly politicized, because injured protestors are afraid they'll be arrested if they try to seek treatment in government-run hospitals,' Frank said. There was one private clinic in Aden associated with the southern movement, and 'if they go there, they know they'll be protected,' he added. Frank thought that links between grassroots activists in the four main centres of resistance were still fairly weak, despite recent efforts to synchronize demonstrations and strikes. 'I have the impression there's not much coordination or strong political leadership,' he said. Frank's view was shared by Thanos Petouris, who described a patchwork of diverse interests throughout the south, with local power brokers assembling a unique coalition of resistance at each focal point. He explained:

> Radfan and Dhala are on a different course from Abyan.[43] The protests in Dhala and Radfan are separatist and secular in character, and you see posters of Ali Salim al-Beidh all over the place, but agitation in Abyan displays distinctly Islamist overtones. When the trouble first started in Abyan in 2009, there were rumours that prostitutes and gay men were being murdered. It might have been because there was generally less security, but many people assumed that radical Islamists were responsible. Perhaps it was even a counter strategy by the regime to scare the Adeni middle classes about the prospect of al-Fahdli's dominance. And it did work![44]

Aden still retains a few faint traces of its liberal Marxist tradition and its historic cosmpolitian diversity, as the beach scene at the Gold Mohur had revealed. When my lunch meeting at the Gold Mohur finished, Frank's taxi driver, Ahmed, took Frank to his office and drove me to my next appointment. Ahmed wanted us to listen to a song by Akon, an American-Senegalese R&B star, who started pumping silky vocals from the car stereo.[45] 'When I see you, I run out of words to say,' ran the opening lines of 'Beautiful', Akon's signature track from his

2009 album, *Freedom*, as Ahmed's car sped through a tunnel in the volcanic rock of Aden's Jebel Shamsan. Back in daylight again, in Crater, we drove past an old man, hobbling along with a stick, and two slender veiled ladies following behind him. 'You're a symbol of what a beautiful woman should be,' Akon crooned. Ahmed caught my eye and gave me a shy smile in the rear-view mirror. Two weeks earlier, I had danced barefoot to the same song amid an all-girl crowd of northerners in a Sana'a wedding hall. My heart had been pounding from the thin oxygen at such high altitude, but my face was split in a wide grin. The women surrounding me were laughing with happiness, wiggling their sequinned shoulders and silk-clad booty. Akon may have been popular with young Yemenis, north and south alike, that summer, but my contacts in the hiraak movement had little apparent desire to frame their struggle in terms that might appeal to disgruntled Yemenis north of the pre-1990 border.

A young man's marriage prospects were directly related to his ability to pay a generous bride price, but youth unemployment was a national problem, affecting almost everyone except the sons and daughters of the wealthy and well connected (who were mostly northerners). Despite the country's distended youth bulge, young adults were poorly represented inside the hiraak, and many young southerners had no memories of the Socialist past that their parents now idealized.[46] 'Hiraak leaders knew from the beginning that they would not be able to forge a nation-wide coalition, even on the basis of common grievances like unemployment,' argued Thanos Petouris. Instead, they framed their supporters' resentment around the perception of a distinct southern history and identity, in part 'because of the way Saleh's regime had mishandled the issue of unity over the years'.[47] In doing so, the southern movement sought to retreat to a past that seemed a lost paradise. As Lutfi Shatara had previously told me in London: 'The northern opposition are fed up with Saleh and calling for change, but we are calling to re-establish our own *country* as the choice of the southerners.'

For hiraak supporters, the south was rich in fish, oil, minerals and pristine beaches, and had one of the world's best natural ports located on a busy international shipping route. The south, in fact, had all the country's best assets but they had no share of the profits. Instead, northern exploitation and corruption was cheating them of a viable economy, and thus four million southerners had fallen foul of the densely populated but resource-poor highlands where five-sixths of the country's population was currently dwelling. However, even within the south, assets were not equally shared. The country's most productive oil fields were located in the sparsely populated eastern desert province of Hadramaut, home to just 2 million people.[48]

For many hiraak supporters, Hadrami oil wealth was 'essential for the viability of a new independent Southern state', but very few Hadramis shared these aspirations. 'The Hadramis are not speaking about reviving the old north-south divide. They are more inclined to advocate devolution within a federal system, rather than secession,' said Thanos Petouris. He noted that Hadramis enjoyed close connections with the wealthy global Hadrami diaspora, but especially with business families of Hadrami origin in Saudi Arabia, 'including the Bukshan, bin Laden, Al-Amoodi and bin Mahfouz'.[49] Yemenis often speculated about Saudi Arabia's intention to annexe Hadramaut, creating a passage to the open sea, but the default option of creating a zone of soft power within a devolved or federated system seemed more plausible.[50]

Even the concept of federalism itself was understood differently throughout the south, with some people advocating multi-party federalism that would give four or five distinct regional groupings greater control over their own affairs. The more commonly held view of federalism involved splitting Yemen into two blocks along the pre-unification line, possibly followed by a referendum after four or five years to decide whether the south wanted to remain part of the federation or break away, along the lines of the Naivasha Agreement that gave birth to South Sudan.

The diversity of views within the hiraak and the absence of coherent leadership created the impression of multiple parallel movements without any clear goal. I found that southerners were happy to recite their grievances, but when I challenged them to outline a strategy to press their advantage in relation to the country's economic crisis and the impending power struggle within the regime in Sana'a, I got blank looks. When I asked where people stood in relation to the ongoing negotiations between the ruling party and the opposition over framework for the next round of parliamentary elections, they shook their heads. 'We've gone beyond faith in political reform,' they said.[51]

* * *

In spring 2010, in the run-up to the twentieth anniversary of unification, a Yemeni flag of colossal proportions flew over the centre of Sana'a. It was a gesture designed to symbolize the strength of national unity and glorify Saleh's achievements during the past two decades, but such a dramatic gesture only served to emphasize the fact that unity was rapidly fraying. Around this time, the government also ran an advertising campaign featuring slogans such as 'Yemen is in our hearts', showing young children with Yemeni flags painted on their cheeks.[52] When I interviewed Yassin Saeed Noman, secretary general of the YSP, at the party's Sana'a headquarters in April 2010, I remarked on the symbolism of the giant flag. 'The bigger the flag, the weaker the unity,' he said.

Noman, former PDRY prime minister, had a reputation for pragmatism and personal integrity, but the Socialist Party itself was seen as 'divided and weak, with limited popular appeal in the South'.[53] This stemmed from the fact that many in the party's leadership had played a prominent role in the PDRY era, as well as Saleh's policy of co-opting prominent opposition figures. While Noman favoured 'dialogue around a federal system in order to preserve national unity', more radical members of the party, who were also *hiraak* supporters, saw him as an apologist for unity.[54] Nevertheless, Noman tried to function as a 'bridge between extremists on both sides', and he was sometimes able to use his 'connections within Hiraak to communicate with and influence the movement'.[55]

Noman also used his stewardship of the party to build bridges to his colleagues in the opposition coalition in Sana'a, and he belonged to the group of negotiators who had tried and failed to broker a framework for the deferred 2009 parliamentary elections. Talks had broken down over the opposition's insistence on implementing electoral reforms recommended by EU election monitors after the last presidential ballot.[56] Noman blamed Yemen's Western donors for missing an opportunity to hold Saleh to account after his re-election in 2006:

> If the West had insisted on political reforms four years ago, we would be in a different situation now. Instead, they chose to focus on economic

reforms and now they are pressuring us to participate in parliamentary elections on unequal terms that almost guarantees our share of the vote will shrink. The stance of the international community is important, because Saleh uses their approval to consolidate his own legitimacy.

In 2009, Noman took part in a national grassroots consultation exercise to draw up an alternative vision for the future of the country, which was affiliated with the opposition and included consultation with 'parts of the Hiraak and the Southern leadership in exile'.[57] Islah benefactor Hamid al-Ahmar had supposedly sponsored this consultation exercise, and, throughout 2009 and 2010, he was building links to the southern exiles in a series of meetings in regional capitals, such as Cairo and Amman. The resulting national 'salvation plan' called for 'peaceful change' to relieve the country from 'despotism and corruption', and named the southern cause as 'the most serious hotspot of the national crisis'.[58]

Hamid had viewed 'his late father's support for Saleh with disdain',[59] and his political ambitions had only grown since his father's death at the end of 2007. In 2009, Hamid appeared on Al Jazeera to accuse Saleh of high treason, arguing that 'the president cares only about keeping power in his hands' and behaves as if Yemen is 'private property for the president and his sons'.[60] The extent of Hamid's political ambition was already clear, but 'Saleh misread the situation,' argued one Yemeni political analyst. 'Saleh still believed that Hamid was chiefly interested in money. When Hamid came back to Sana'a after the Doha interview, there was no punishment. Instead, Saleh allowed him to bid for a multi-million-dollar deal to build a power plant in Marib.'[61]

In August 2009, Hamid met a US official in Sana'a and revealed a secret plan to overthrow Saleh. He 'vowed to trigger the revolt if Saleh did not guarantee the fairness of parliamentary elections', and 'said he would organize massive demonstrations modelled on protests that toppled Indonesia's President Suharto a decade earlier. We cannot copy the Indonesians exactly, but the idea is controlled chaos,' Hamid said. He also revealed that his scheme would hinge on persuading General Mohsin 'to abandon the president and join the opposition'.[62] 'The Saudis will take a calculated risk if they can be convinced that we can make Saleh leave the scene peacefully,' he claimed.

Although the details of Hamid's conversation were not revealed until WikiLeaks published a classified account of the meeting in

November 2010, Yemen's political elite were aware of Hamid's ambition. By spring 2010, Sana'a was alive with plotting and speculation, and there was an awareness that tentative, pre-emptive new alliances were forming. Change was fermenting and yet the effects were not visible, especially to those excluded from the inner circles of Sana'a politics. Few Adenis had any premonition of the coming confrontation within the regime. 'The Adenis are outsiders,' said Thanos. 'Aden is a merchant-based, middle class society, and they grew up in a paternalistic colonial power structure, followed by another paternalistic system under the PDRY. They have no affinity with Sana'a's tribal politics.'

Increasingly, it seemed that Hamid was trying to use his power base inside the opposition coalition to weaken Ahmed Ali's prospects of succeeding his father, while also strengthening his own hand as a kingmaker, and perhaps even a future presidential candidate himself. Hamid had already stated that Yemen's next president should be a southerner, but General Nuba, a retiree who had organized the initial protests in the south, said he saw no difference between Hamid and Ahmed Ali as potential successors to Saleh, as both were northern tribesmen.[63] Deadlock over the deferred parliamentary elections was becoming, in part, a struggle between two northern tribal families, the Salehs and the al-Ahmars, to hold the balance of power in parliament in the run-up to the next presidential elections, scheduled for 2013. It contributed to a growing feeling that dynastic interests were distorting parliamentary politics and that both families were bringing the system to its knees by pushing for their own advantage—and, in doing so, making daily life harder and harder for ordinary Yemenis.[64]

10

BLACK BOX

HOUTHI-LED INSURGENCY IN THE NORTHERN PROVINCE
OF SAADA

'Saada is a black box. Nobody knows what's in it'
Ali Saif Hassan, Political Development Forum

Mobile phone footage on YouTube showed bombed-out houses. An Arab
woman sheathed in black moved through the ruins of a building. First a
kitchen, then a bathroom. Perhaps this was once her home, but it was no
longer habitable. She turned to the person filming her, and uttered a
keening sound, her voice pitched high with disbelief and sorrow.

Type 'Saada war' into YouTube in the closing years of Saleh's presidency and you could find grainy clips of a hidden civil war on the
doorstep of Saudi Arabia. From 2004 to 2010, the impoverished mountain province of Saada, butting up against Yemen's border with the
region's largest oil producer, played host to a bitter and brutal stop–
start war between government forces and local rebels. Amateur video
footage, smuggled through roadblocks and posted anonymously to the
internet, provided rare public evidence of the war's civilian carnage.

Human Rights Watch characterized the media blackout in Saada as the
strongest in the world. Foreign journalists were routinely barred from
entering the combat zone, and Yemeni journalists based in Sana'a were

often forced to rely on phone calls with local tribal contacts to report the conflict.[1] Claims and counterclaims were impossible to verify.

In 2007, with MiG jets screaming over Sana'a almost every day, I tried and failed to fix a meeting with Abdulkarim al-Khaiwani, a Yemeni journalist close to sources in Saada. Al-Khaiwani had previously been jailed for speculating about the succession dynamics inside Saleh's family, and his newspaper, *Al-Shura*, had been banned, then reopened with pro-government editors in charge—a common practice known as cloning. Such was the general paranoia about the authorities' intrusive interest in anyone discussing the Saada conflict, my Yemeni fixer flatly refused to call al-Khaiwani when I asked for his help to arrange an interview.

A year later, al-Khaiwani was arrested and jailed for six years for possessing video footage of the fighting in Saada and 'publishing information liable to undermine the morale of the military'. Al-Khaiwani's seven-year-old daughter recorded a video statement, posted to YouTube with the help of human rights groups, describing the night her father was beaten in front of her by security forces and dragged from their home. A few months later, al-Khaiwani accepted in absentia Amnesty International's prize for human rights journalism, from his prison cell.[2]

The lack of reliable information emerging from Saada helped to perpetuate this smouldering, multifaceted conflict.[3] There was neither a formal tally of casualties—nor an informal body count—but the combined number of dead soldiers, civilians and rebels supposedly numbered thousands. Claims for the war's causes encompassed Zaidi revivalism, accusations of *sayyid* supremacy, economic neglect, smuggling, profiteering, elite rivalry, regional interference and the relationship of the modern central state to semi-autonomous marginal communities, as well as calls for social justice. The rebels simply said they wanted their people released from prison, the withdrawal of the Yemeni army from Saada and freedom to worship according to their tradition.

Fighting first broke out in 2004, following an irregular wave-form pattern that built from skittish, nervy skirmishes to vicious combat, before ebbing to a precarious, gossamer-fine ceasefire. The war completed six cycles, but these neat divisions obscured the continuous, festering reality of the conflict, and ignored the regime's failure to resolve the various grievances that underpinned the war. Instead, each successive outburst of fighting grew more intense, and each fresh set of ceasefire violations compounded the anger and intransigence that fed an opportunist, warmongering mindset.

The first three periods of conflict ran from June to September 2004, March to April 2005 and July 2005 to February 2006. During the 'fourth' war, in 2007, the Qataris stepped in, waving a white flag. The Emir of Qatar was beginning to fashion a reputation for himself as a regional peacemaker, and he spotted a chance to position his emissaries as independent arbitrators in Saada.[4] Qatari engagement brought one heavy spasm of hostilities to a close in June 2007, but Qatar's mediation experience was said to be overplayed, and their involvement supposedly irritated the Saudis, who wanted a free hand in the border region. The next burst of fighting, in summer 2008, was the most intense yet.

Between May and July 2008, the conflict bled beyond Saada to neighbouring Amran province, and crept right to the outskirts of Sana'a. Just as Mohammed al-Badr's Royalist troops had brought the fight from their mountain base to the outskirts of the capital in the 1960s, now Saada's rebels were threatening Saleh's seat of power. Sana'a residents lay in bed at night, watching the glass rattling in their windowpanes and listening to the thump of shelling less than 20 miles away in the suburb of Bani Hushaish, populated by Houthi sympathizers.

The assault on Bani Hushaish lasted for more than a month. Army divisions supposedly tried to ring-fence the area and starve the population out, but there was deadlock between the rebels and the military. Artillery strikes were so heavy that dead bodies were reportedly left unburied in the streets.[5] In Sana'a, the intensive care unit at al-Thawra hospital was said to be closed to civilians because the number of soldiers needing treatment was overwhelming medical staff.[6] National security seemed to be hanging by a thread, and the qat-chew rumour-mill went into overdrive. Saleh was increasingly isolated and no one could get through to him, people said, so his abrupt declaration that the Saada war was 'over' came as a total shock.

Yemeni ministers were initially speechless during their bilateral meetings with Western embassy counterparts, apparently unable to explain Saleh's *coup de foudre*. One senior minister supposedly confessed to a European official that he knew nothing about the terms of the armistice.[7] Diplomats and humanitarian agency staff were disbelieving: they wanted more details before they were prepared to take Saleh's announcement at face value, and even then few were willing to believe that this year's ceasefire would succeed when previous efforts had failed. 'It's a seasonal war,' argued one sceptical source.[8] 'Both sides have probably run out of bullets and the fighting will start again when the rebels have managed to get their hands on fresh cash,'

A month later, state-run media reported that the rebels' leader had agreed to come down from the mountains and hand over his heavy weapons. The peace deal was supposedly based on a ten-point plan that mirrored Qatar's blueprint from the previous year, but the finer points were still obscure.[9] Throughout the 2008 conflict, Yemeni officials had closed the main trade routes into Saada, blocking the movement of fuel and food, but the roads were open once again and humanitarian agencies were also getting back to work.[10] As many as 130,000 people—more than one in every seven inhabitants in the province—had been internally displaced during the latest round of fighting, and roughly half had taken refuge in Saada city, the provincial capital.[11] Nearly fifty years after their initial mission to treat the wounded in Royalist Yemen, the ICRC was back on the ground in Saada, dealing with unfinished business dating back to the original Cold War conflict.

* * *

The birth of the modern republic in 1962 created an unprecedented schism in the north Yemeni polity. Members of the post-revolutionary elite continued to be drawn from the northern Zaydi families but few among them was *sayyid*.[12] This 'progressive' clique—including Saleh and Sheikh Abdullah al-Ahmar guarded their new privileges jealously, and their lingering resentment towards the ousted Imams extended to a generalized 'prejudice against *sayyids*'.[13] Almost overnight, the *sayyid* aristocracy perceived themselves to be marginalized and undermined. 'There's been a glass ceiling for *sayyids* in Yemen ever since the revolution,' grumbled one *sayyid* businessman, when we discussed the causes of the conflict during a meeting in 2007.[14]

The rebels in Saada were led by a charismatic *sayyid* family, the Houthis, who stood accused of wanting to turn back the clock by replacing Saleh's republic with the ancient Imamate. The Houthis denied the charge of a *sayyid* conspiracy, claiming instead that Saleh's regime was corrupt. Talking to Houthi supporters who downplayed the rebels' aggressive ambition to overturn the Republican order, I heard suggestions that Saleh was suffering from an arriviste insecurity complex. 'It's not the *sayyids* who are causing the problem. It's the government's fear of the *sayyids*,' said one Houthi apologist.[15] 'The regime is nervous,' said another. 'Even forty years after the revolution, they don't feel that they are ruling legitimately.'[16]

In 2005, before he was forced into hiding as a result of the conflict, Houthi patriarch Badr al-Din was quoted in the newspaper *Al-Wasat* as saying that the Imamate was the most preferable system of government for Yemen if the 'true and legitimate' Imam was present. 'Any just believer' could rule the country, he said, in the meantime. 'When asked whether he considered Salih a legitimate ruler, Badr al-Din declined to answer, telling the interviewer: 'Do not put me in a difficult position.'[17] In theory, Badr al-Din's *sayyid* descent set the Houthis a class apart from tribesmen in Saada. In practice, however, the Houthis were closely enmeshed with the local tribal system, including holding strong ties with the tribe of Marran.[18]

The Houthi family also enjoyed an enviable degree of legitimacy in the eyes of their supporters, which many believed that Saleh's family and associates were lacking. 'For years, local people have trusted the Houthi family to mediate in their inheritance disputes, formalize their marriages and provide charity to needy individuals. The Houthis are the super ego of the people,' argued one friend of the family. 'They perform many of the functions that are usually carried out by the criminal justice system or the welfare state, and that's directly linked to the weakness of Saleh's government. They are widely respected for their leadership and generosity, and not just because of their *sayyid* status.'[19]

The *sayyid* issue was just one problematic factor among many conundrums entangled within several competing narratives that attempted to define the conflict in Saada, an area that played a central role in Yemen's historical sense of self. Despite winning the war against the Royalists in these Zaydi heartlands, the Republican government had never fully extended its reach to the Imam's former stronghold. 'Saada was the last governorate to join the republic. The people of Saada have always been disloyal,' complained one Yemeni diplomat.[20] However,

Houthi supporters condemned the regime's punitive stance towards Saada as petty and short-sighted. 'It's a mistake to brand the people of Saada as royalists, when the last Imam is dead, and to continue to punish them for something that happened nearly five decades ago,' argued one supporter.[21] 'Saada has been deliberately neglected for years and there's hardly been any investment or infrastructure development in the area. How can the government in Sana'a build legitimacy in Saada when they don't offer anything to the people there?'

Although the arcane and convoluted discourse about the causes of the conflict could be extremely confusing, the Saada rebellion was a very modern war, provoked and sustained by 'war on terror' dynamics that heightened Yemen's internal tensions. Clashes between the rebels and the army began after Friday demonstrations outside the Great Mosque in Sana'a, a year after the US invasion of Iraq. Young Zaydi worshippers, fresh from midday prayers, hoisted banners and chanted: 'Allah is Great! Death to America! Death to Israel! Curse on the Jews! Victory to Islam!'[22] When the police corralled more than 600 protestors in Sana'a, and security forces tried to arrested ringleader Hussein al-Houthi in his family village, they sparked the first spell of fighting.

If these Friday demonstrations embarrassed Saleh, who was trying to bolster his newly improved relations with the Americans, they also gave him a chance to prove his worth to his new allies. He swiftly tried to brand the conflict as a local offshoot of the 'war on terror' by claiming the Houthis were in league with al-Qaeda.[23] For their part, the Houthis exploited widespread anti-American sentiment to broaden sympathy for their cause. 'Everyone in Yemen was against the invasion of Iraq, it wasn't just the Houthis,' said one observer.[24] 'I take the whole *sayyid* argument with a pinch of salt,' said another analyst. 'The Houthis would be happy to see anyone running Yemen who was morally legitimate in their eyes. They're calling for a ruler who respects Islam, but he should not be supporting a US president who backs Israel and invades Iraq.'[25]

The rebels' ringleader, Hussein al-Houthi, was a former MP who had served in Yemen's first parliament, representing al-Haqq, a small, predominantly Zaydi interest party.[26] Hussein justified his role in the unrest by telling friends that he wasn't breaching Yemen's constitution, but one source described him as a 'loose cannon with an inflated opinion of his own importance'.[27] Another source argued: 'Hussein probably enjoyed being provocative, but he was foolish not to get the message to stop when the regime began to crack down.'[28] When Hussein was invited to meet President Saleh, he procrastinated, supposedly worried about being assassinated en route to Sana'a.[29] If he had accepted, the war might not have escalated, one source speculated. 'The meeting could have eliminated Saleh's fears about Hussein's intentions,' argued one al-Haqq official.[30]

When Hussein's targeted killing in 2004 put an end to the first rebellion, the security services chose to display images of his corpse on massive poster boards inside Saada city as visible proof of his death, because hardly anyone living in Hussein's home district, who did not possess a private generator, had access to electricity or televisions.[31] Active leadership passed to his brother, Abdulmalik in 2006, and the Houthis' revolt against the regime's heavy-handed crackdown quickly snowballed, turning the border highlands into an angry hornets' nest. Thousands of suspected Houthi supporters were arrested or disappeared, along with official mediators, who were themselves sceptical about Saleh's commitment to reach a lasting, peaceful solution.[32]

In such circumstances, it was difficult for Houthi supporters freely to express their views. I spent one uneasy afternoon with a respected *sayyid*, a friend of the Houthi family. During our afternoon tea session, a visitor arrived with news of an incarcerated relative, and their collective anxiety settled on me like an itch. Conspiracy theories tend to flourish in such tense, unpredictable environments, and it was here that I heard a superlative example. 'Saada is a pre-emptive war,' my *sayyid* host told me, adding an entirely new twist to the intrigue swirling around the conflict. In my host's apocalyptic worldview, Saada would likely become the centre of future Islamic resurgence during the Messianic age, and both Jews and American Christians shared a common interest in trying to prevent this because it would lead to their subsequent demise.[33]

* * *

Jewish traders had first settled in south Arabia in the days of King Solomon, establishing one of the oldest diaspora communities in the world.[34] Pre-Islamic soothsayers were said to point in the direction of Yemen when asked to predict where the Jewish Messiah might come

from.[35] By the twelfth century, Yemen's Jewish community was suffering persecution, heresy and forced conversion, and they sought spiritual guidance from scholar and rabbi Maimonides. His letter to Yemen
counselled the Arabian Jews to hold their nerve and keep their sights
on the redemption of the coming Messianic age. 'Blessed be the Lord
that He has not imprisoned those who uphold the Torah and guard its
statutes in the most distant peninsulas,' he wrote. 'As he promised us
in his goodness and kindness through his servant Isaiah, you [the Jews
of Yemen] are the sign he was alluding to when he told us: "From the
corners of the earth have we heard songs."'

Seven centuries later, the partition of Palestine and the creation of
the new Israeli state provoked a series of bloody riots and brutal attacks
against Yemen's Jewish communities. Within three years, nearly all
Yemen's 50,000 Jews had been airlifted to safety in Israel, leaving a
rump population of a few hundred individuals clustered in small rural
communities north of Sana'a. It was in one of these small communities, the village of Salem, that gunmen—allegedly linked to the
Houthis—had threatened eight Jewish families with death when tensions in Saada began to escalate in 2007, a few weeks ahead of the
fourth round of fighting.

The Jews of Salem fled to nearby Saada city, where they spent two
weeks living in a hotel under the protection of the local governor. They
were subsequently evacuated to Sana'a, where I met them in spring
2007 at a residential compound opposite the American embassy, housing Russian contract workers and Arab businessmen. High walls con-
cealed neat rows of condominiums lined by dusty streets planted with
eucalyptus and oleander, along with a swimming pool, a health club
and a nightclub—one of very few places where foreigners could get
drunk in the capital.

In a meeting room in the director's reception suite, Yahya Yousef
Mousa explained to me how masked Houthi gunmen had hounded him
from his Salem home. Yahya's slight, wiry features were framed by *pe'ot*
sidelocks and a *yarmulke* skullcap. As he spoke, his eyes flickered to an
official observation panel that had assembled to monitor our interview.
There were nine of us in the room: Yahya, two of his neighbours from
Salem, me, my translator, two men from the Interior Ministry and two
taciturn Yemeni observers who did not bother to introduce themselves.
I assumed they were intelligence agents.

BLACK BOX

Yahya handed me a crumpled photocopy of a letter, handwritten in Arabic on a page torn from a lined notebook. The text complained that the Jews were spreading vice and corruption; it said they must leave the village or lose their lives. 'This is from the Houthis,' Yahya said. Is it true that you were brewing and selling wine? I asked. I had heard that your neighbours were offended that you weren't respecting local codes. His response was emphatic. '*La!*' he said. No! 'It's a lie.' Instead, he pulled some photos from the pockets in his robe and handed them to me, under the approving glance of the four government employees ranged around the table.

I thumbed through some shots of his adobe house, with traditional half-moon windows. A Toyota pick-up truck was parked outside and the *mafraj* was furnished in the usual low-slung style. So far, so Yemeni, I thought; but it was the large Yemeni flag hanging from the exterior wall of the house and the pro-government posters tacked to the interior walls of the living room that took me by surprise. I'd only seen such explicit political fervour during the presidential election campaign, which was now six months past, and I had never seen pro-government propaganda *inside* anyone's house. 'They attacked us because we are government supporters,' Yahya said.

For a minority group to make such a visible declaration of government support in an insurgency area, at any time, was highly provocative. Quite when Yahya had the presence of mind to take these photos and get them developed, I wasn't sure. Was it before, during or after the death threats and flight from the village, I wondered? But I zipped my lips and handed the snapshots back. All of us present in the meeting room that day knew that we were dancers in a tightly controlled and carefully choreographed performance, and these restrained dynamics told their own story.

I had already been told that someone powerful within Saleh's inner circle was footing the bill for the Salem Jews to stay in the tourist village, but I asked Yahya how he and his neighbours were making enough money to survive in Sana'a. There was some hesitation. 'Handicrafts,' he said, finally, 'but we would also like to find jobs.' Yahya bestowed frequent praise on Saleh for rescuing the Jews from the Houthis and improving their fortunes. 'Alhamdulillah,' he said, ringlets dangling as he nodded his head. Thanks to Allah.

As I left the boardroom, I passed a young Jewish boy bringing a tea tray to the Yemeni director of the compound. Yahya was holding hands with the two men from the Ministry of Interior, in their neatly pressed uniforms. Male arms were draped around male shoulders, in the local style. 'We are all Yemenis,' Yahya said, convivially. But, as I drove away from the 'tourist village', passing a heavy army presence at the main gates, my translator told me that Yahya was a liar. 'The Jews were forced to leave Salem because they were practising magic, making their Muslim neighbours sick and sending them crazy,' he said.

As with many things in Yemen, stories about the Jews were neither reliable nor consistent. At the start of the Saada war in 2004, while trying to garner public support for the campaign, Yemeni officials had accused the Jewish minority in Saada of *supporting* the rebellion.[36] Now, it seemed, officials were trying a different tack—highlighting the violation of Jewish minority rights in order to justify the crackdown in Saada. One Western observer alleged that Saleh was playing on Germany's history of the Holocaust in order to secure the extradition of Abdulmalik's brother, Yahya, from Germany to stand trial in Yemen on the basis of a 2007 Interpol arrest warrant.[37]

Yemen's Jews are formally protected under the constitution, and Yemeni Muslims are supposedly proud of their good community relations with the Jews, but in reality prejudice against the Jews was prevalent and unabashed. 'The Jews in Yemen used to kill our children and cook with their blood,' said one Yemeni friend, reviving the European medieval slander of the blood libel. In December 2008, a Jewish teacher was murdered in Raida, north of Sana'a, when he refused to convert to Islam. Mounting harassment led one international Jewish association to warn that a 'community dating back to Biblical times is on the brink of extinction'.[38] Shortly afterwards, an unwittingly ironic headline in the *Yemen Observer* trumpeted: 'Yemeni Jews to emigrate secretly', and a few months later, the *Wall Street Journal* revealed that US officials were facilitating the discreet evacuation of many of Yemen's remaining Jews, who were expected to settle in Brooklyn.[39]

* * *

Religious politics in the volatile crucible of Saada were stoked by the presence of the Salafis. Saada played host to a network of Salafi madras-

sas, sponsored in part by money from the Saudis, who established a
religious footprint throughout Yemen with Saleh's consent from the
1980s onwards.[40] Saudi-sponsored Salafism became a 'significant local
force, competing with traditional identities',[41] and many viewed 'the
spread of these schools as an attempt to weaken Zaidi social and political influence'. This, in turn, spurred the foundation of a Zaydi educational trust, called the Youthful Believers,[42] and disputes with the
authorities over the Youthful Believers' educational curriculum, cou-
pled with allegations that the government was replacing Zaydi imams
with Salafi preachers, contributed to the war's complex dynamics.[43]

The best-known of Saada's Salafi madrassas, Dammaj, was established by Sheikh Muqbil bin Haadi al-Wadi'i, a Saudi-educated cleric
who 'maintained ambiguous links with that country's rulers and religious elites until his death in 2001'.[44] The community he founded
formed a defensive pocket of a few thousand believers, living and wor-
shipping in the middle of the Zaydi highlands. Students at Dammaj
included local converts from low-status families attracted by the 'anti-
sayyid thrust of the movement' and Sunni Muslims from across the
world.[45] Volunteers formed a school militia to patrol the borders and
protect the madrassa from their Zaydi neighbours.[46]

In 2007, a French student was killed in Dammaj during clashes with
the Houthis. To find out more, I went to a mosque in an unmarked building on a busy Sana'a street, where I knew it was possible for foreigners
to arrange to travel to Dammaj. There were no signs alerting passers-by
to the presence of a Salafi madrassa, just a loudspeaker for the atthan
fixed to the roof of an adjacent furniture shop. Western men arriving for
classes walked with a slow, purposeful gait, dwarfing the passing Yemenis,
their solemn eyes seemingly fixed on a further horizon.

I wanted to know what the students here had heard about the death of
the French student in Dammaj, and whether they felt that the Salafi community in Saada was under attack. I stepped through a steel door into the
women's quarters, pushing past a dirty blue curtain into a dingy unlit
corridor. I slipped off my shoes and made my way up a short flight of
stairs in my bare feet, heading towards an open door on the mezzanine
level. Inside a room lit with a single fluorescent light and furnished only
with a broken whiteboard, I spotted an elderly woman, sheathed in black
and bent double in prayer, with her forehead resting on the grubby car-

pet. I went back to the hallway and sat in the gloom, waiting for something to happen. There was a cloying smell of Yemeni incense, and a dank, forgotten stink that reminded me of London garages. I heard a guttural exclamation—'Allahu Akbar'—from a microphone in the men's mosque on the first floor and the thud of a hundred pairs of knees hitting the floor above me in unison. After half an hour, the praying crone appeared at the top of the steps and wailed from the murk. I went to help her down the stairs. Her milky eyes, wet with age and sadness, peered at me through the slit in her veil. The shriveled fingers of one hand, stiff as talons, were carrying a plastic bag imprinted with large, glossy images of Saleh. Clutching my arm with the other hand and muttering 'maridha'—illness—as she pointed to her joints, we stepped along the corridor, through the door and out into the road, both of us suddenly overexposed in the lunchtime sunlight.

A few days later, I went back to the madrassa to attend a Qur'anic recitation class. In the prayer room at the top of the stairs, I took my place amid a group of foreign students, seated cross-legged on the floor. They came from Africa, Asia and Europe. Many of them had arrived in Yemen with their husbands, who were studying upstairs. We formed an attentive circle, absorbed in the task of imitating words as first spoken by the Prophet. Our teacher was fastidious, and the words were elegant, the rhythm captivating, the tones melodious and the sense eternal. We were reciting Sura Humazah, which warns against the wrong priorities in life. The text is sombre but there was laughter and warmth in our group, and children dozed in their mothers' arms, soothed by the poetic sound of our words. The mood in the room was respectful and sisterly, infused with a subtle sense of faith and solidarity. I had turned up intending to find out about the death in Dammaj but I left without even mentioning Saada. By the end of the class, I had lost the courage to ask.

* * *

Prohibited from travelling to Saada by official methods, and unwilling or unable to run the gauntlet by other routes, I went to drink tea with Dr Murtatha al-Mahatwary, founder and director of the al-Badr Centre for Islamic Studies in Sana'a. The mosque and charitable madrassa had been running for more than a decade, for the purpose of preserving Zaydi heritage and culture. The walls of the director's office were lined with wooden bookshelves, stuffed from floor to ceiling with Islamic texts. It was one of the few libraries that I ever saw in Yemen. With his blue waistcoat over his white robe, round glasses and shaved head, Dr al-Mahatwary conveyed eccentric passion and erudition. He wore a stiff little round and flat cotton hat, like the lid of a pillbox. He spoke with the fluency of a skilled preacher and a practised teacher, pulling me over to a book-case and jabbing his finger at an Arabic text. We began by talking about Qur'anic scholarship, but his attention was quickly diverted by the conflict. 'Saada is being destroyed. The condition of the people is terrible. Thousands are dead and whole families have been wiped out,' Dr al-Mahatwary lamented.

A clutch of the director's young students sat watching us while we talked. The next generation of Zaydi scholars were still pubescent boy-men with downy facial hair, lounging with bare feet on blankets and cushions arranged beneath a window in a far corner of the room. From among them, a silent teenager wearing long white thermal leggings under his *thoub* was nominated to present us with a tray of tea. The curvy little tea glasses were jam-packed with mint leaves and cardamom pods.

In this serene, cosy madrassa, the director's tape recorder positioned on the desk between us was the sole sign of the bitter war and persecution that was raging in Saada. While the Houthis and their supporters were Zaydis, not all Zaydis were Houthi supporters, and the tape recorder was Dr al-Mahatwary's insurance policy against misrepresentation in my published account of our interview. He had been imprisoned several times and his telephone was tapped, he said. His students were followed by the intelligence services and many had been detained. His personal assistant had recently been imprisoned for fifty days:

> Zaydis have always stood with poor and oppressed people against the tyrant, from the Ottoman Turks until the present day. For this reason, everybody tries to attack us. Even the Zaydi ruler doesn't provide good conditions for us now. Saleh is from a Zaydi family but, with respect to the president, he is trying to oppress us, because he knows he has avoided his responsibilities and he's afraid. Every ruler wants to sit on the seat of power for a long time.

The director stopped talking for a moment to wrap a fine, wizened hand around his little tea glass and lift it to his lips. 'He is angry and sad,' said my translator, leaning forward to speak in a half-whisper, 'because he sees corruption and deviation in Yemeni society. He says Yemen has taken the wrong direction.'

The director's tea glass was back on the desktop:

> If you want my personal view, I think the war has been fed by the belief that you must obey the ruler, even if he has deviated from the correct path. This perspective comes from teachings in Islam that we have to follow the ruler regardless of oppression and corruption. The ones who follow this Salafi thinking have told the president that we, the Zaydis, are the most dangerous, and now it has moved from thinking to bullets.

Dr al-Mahatwary was describing two starkly contrasting schools of thought regarding the right relationship to authority: the Salafi notion of loyalty at all costs, which stems from a desire to avoid *fitna*—or discord—in the political realm, and the Zaydis' defining *khuruj* tradition of overthrowing oppression. Despite Saleh's Zaydi background, the Houthis argued that he had cultivated a Salafi faction within his inner circle, whose members were said to exercise influence 'through secret advice given to the ruler'.[47] (Firebrand preacher al-Zindani was often described as belonging to this Salafi clique, despite his Muslim Brotherhood roots.) The story that al-Zindani's al-Iman university in Sana'a was built on *waqf* land confiscated from the last Imam's family, whether factually correct or not, illustrated the perceived degree of leverage that Saleh's Salafi allies enjoyed at the expense of the Zaydis.[48]

'The suffering of our people comes from these games by the authorities. The intelligence services have been penetrated by the Salafis, who are fierce and attacking like a crocodile. There is one high-ranking figure in the army who has Salafi thinking. He wants to bring Saada under his control,' said Dr al-Mahatwary. The director had one eye closed. His bony hands waved wildly, sleeves flapping, as he talked. Grey hairs peeped through the skin on his head, and several teeth were missing. He was relying on the comforts of the elderly, with a bed pillow propped behind him on his chair, but his voice was still loud and clear:

> I am against the authorities myself, but I believe in fighting oppression with peaceful means. When the authorities are wrong, we should advise them and point out their mistakes and pray so as they would act correctly. However, Hussein al-Houthi was here in this institute in 1996. He was so angry, complaining always about oppression and arguing that we must fight

against America and Israel. He was not patient and he had no time to read. But after all this fighting, have we killed America or Israel? No, we have only weakened ourselves.

Now Saleh is calling on support from the US to hit the Houthis, and he is asking for their support to fight terrorism but America is the godfather of terrorism! The Americans want their weapons factories to be working day and night, and our leaders are like Spanish oxen with two sharp horns. If you don't feed them with money, they will gore you!

As I left his office, Dr al-Mahatwary invited me to return to the madrassa and undertake a personal study programme with him. He rang me after the interview to repeat the offer: 'If you seek true Islam, I am at your service.'

* * *

When Dr al-Mahatwary singled out a high-ranking military figure with Salafi sympathies, he could only have meant Ali Mohsin. The commander of the First Armoured Division had prosecuted military operations in Saada since 2004, and the conflict was often referred to as 'Ali Mohsin's war'.[49] Ali Mohsin's Salafi sympathies and his Salafi power base within the security services contributed to Zaydi perceptions of discrimination. Zaydis believed he was using the war to strengthen his position and bolster the role of the Salafi nexus inside the power elite.[50] He was also rumoured to have recruited Salafi militiamen to support the war effort, drawing on his personal patronage links to the former mujahideen and wider *takfiri* networks. To mobilise Salafi recruitment, the conflict was framed as holy jihad and, echoing the terminology of sectarian violence in Iraq, the Zaydis were labelled as Shi'i 'refusers'.[51]

Where the Houthis saw Salafi elitism conspiring against the Zaydis, however, other observers saw a regime divided. 'As the war has escalated, different agendas have come into play. Saleh is now using the conflict to settle his own scores with Ali Mohsin,' argued one Sana'a analyst.[52] The hypothesis that the president was reluctant to allow his most powerful army commander to defeat the rebels went some way towards explaining the erratic cycle of the conflict.[53] Ali Mohsin was continually 'pressured to take the war to the rebels', but before he was able to crush the resistance, he was often 'outflanked by temporary ceasefires negotiated behind his back'.[54]

Rivalry between elite factions, which had underpinned the war since its outset, intensified during the fifth war. 'Saleh was trying to sap Ali Mohsin's resources and promote his son's chances of succession,' alleged one source, who claimed that Saleh made arrangements to supply the Houthis with US anti-tank missiles, which 'they dutifully used to annihilate Ali Mohsin's tanks'.[55] (Several people told me of this rumour, but none had actually seen the evidence.) Ali Mohsin was allegedly forced to capitulate before his tank division was completely destroyed, in a sudden move that brought the fifth war to an unexpected close in summer 2008. Saleh then used the opportunity created by Ali Mohsin's military humiliation to demote his allies in 'a series of carefully coordinated moves' that attempted to increase allegiance to his son, Ahmed Ali.[56]

Ahmed Ali's Republican Guard was also deployed in Saada, and Ahmed's rivalry with Ali Mohsin prevented the security services from acting as a coherent entity inside the combat zone. Several Yemeni sources even alleged that Ahmed and Ali Mohsin were taking advantage of chaotic battlefield conditions to prosecute a proxy war against one another, under cover of quashing the Houthis. 'The military command structure is totally opaque,' said one international aid worker, tasked with delivering humanitarian supplies and health services in Saada:[57]

> I have absolutely no idea how the security services function here, but it's clear that tensions within the regime are leading to clashes between different factions in the army. Different divisions fighting in Saada appear to be operating entirely independently of the Ministry of Interior and there's no real front line to speak of. Instead, there's a lot of freelancing going on, with shifting pockets and patches and spots controlled by either side.[58]

By all accounts, Saada was a messy war between tank brigades and troops who mostly moved in daylight, and insurgents who knew the territory intimately and often struck at night. As a *sayyid* family, the Houthis did not have a tribal identity, but they were strongly embedded within the tribal system and they recruited followers from sympathetic tribes to form their guerrilla army. In turn, different factions within the security services and key power brokers among Saleh's tribal allies allegedly paid stipends to mercenaries among rival tribes. The expedient manoeuvres of tribal mercenaries in the Saada conflict only added to the confusion surrounding the war. 'The tribes are pragmatic opportunists who are willing to switch sides, according to their calculations of relative advantage,' said one observer.[59]

The right to loot conquered territory was part of the bargain that Ali Mohsin and Ahmed Ali struck with mercenary tribes.[60] 'The regime is playing with fire,' said one observer. 'When they unleash tribal volunteers to loot from their own neighbours, the regime is laying down grievances that will remain in the memory for a generation. It doesn't make sense to arm the tribes and empower them like this when the state is so weak in the Saada area.'[61] International Crisis Group noted that the recruitment of militiamen also expanded the 'pool of potential war beneficiaries, increasing the incentive to prolong the fight' and gave 'rise to a war economy' that, in turn, also helped ensure the conflict's perpetuation.[62]

Yemen's arms dealers were among those who had 'an interest in the war's continuation'.[63] Several prominent sheikhs were said to supply the conflict, but perhaps the most notable feature of the war economy was the role of weapons trafficking inside the military.[64] Army leaders demanded additional weapons from their superiors to fight the insurgents, but diverted a 'significant proportion' to regional markets, including Somalia.[65] Illegal sales from army stockpiles played a role in driving down prices, because the army was selling 'so much stuff that the price of bullets falls to nothing'.[66] Paradoxically, many weapons then ended up in the hands of 'the rebels they were intended to combat'.[67]

Saada was also a regional smuggling hub where drug mules, arms smugglers and human traffickers plied their lucrative trade across the porous mountain frontier, shifting contraband goods from Yemen to Saudi.[68] Competition to control the border trade was another factor that was said to drive the conflict and lay among 'the war's unspoken stakes'.[69] Drugs that crossed the border included hash, opium and 'narcotic tablets', as well as qat.[70] Tribal relationships were the conduit linking traffickers on either side of the Yemeni-Saudi border. 'Cognitively, there's no demarcation between border communities. They are kith and kin, and they've been trading among themselves for centuries,' argued one researcher, who had conducted a study on cross-border migration. 'The border population is involved in smuggling, and it's all conducted in front of the eyes of the border protection units.'[71]

* * *

A year after my visit to Dr al-Mahatwary's madrassa, in July 2009, nine foreign aid workers were taken hostage in Saada. Yemeni shepherds found the bodies of three women shortly after the kidnapping. The corpses of a South Korean teacher and two German nurses had been mutilated and dumped on open ground. Residents of Saada city were so shocked that they marched in the streets to protest against such unprecedented violence. Yemeni tribes have a long history of kidnapping foreigners to extract concessions from the central government, but these 'bargaining chips' are almost always released unharmed. The calculated execution of captive hostages was previously unheard of.

Yemeni ministers immediately blamed the Houthis, who denied it outright. The Houthis had never taken Western hostages before, and the three murdered women were humanitarian workers providing services inside the conflict zone.[72] Local tribal leaders pointed the finger at al-Qaeda, but these horrific executions did not fit the organization's known pattern of violence in Yemen, and there was no subsequent media statement from the takfiri group claiming responsibility for the killings. The government announced a $250,000 reward for information and launched a search-and-rescue mission to find the six remaining hostages—a British engineer and a German family—who were still missing.[73]

The president's most recent ceasefire, abruptly announced in 2008, had already begun to deteriorate several months before the kidnapping took place. The inevitable build-up of military personnel that accompanied the search-and-rescue effort rapidly inflamed local tensions, and the frequency of checkpoint clashes began to intensify. 'By July 2009, we were wondering why the Yemeni media wasn't reporting that a new round of fighting had broken out. The only thing that was missing was aerial bombardments,' said one aid worker.[74] On 12 August 2009, President Saleh sent in the air force and announced the start of Operation Scorched Earth, marking the sixth bout of conflict.

Operation Scorched Earth was intended to deliver a short, sharp shock that would re-establish the credibility of the military. Having weakened Ali Mohsin during the previous round, Saleh now wanted to send a clear message to the rebels. 'He was trying to tell the Houthis: "You may have defeated Ali Mohsin but you have not defeated me,"' argued one source.[75] However, it quickly became clear that Saleh had overplayed his hand. 'The sixth round was much tougher than previous bouts. The

Houthis were fighting back from inside the old city of Saada, which meant the military no longer controlled their usual strategic stronghold,' said a source supplying food and medical equipment to the old city.[76]

During previous cycles of violence, the army stood accused of shelling mosques and houses, and these allegations continued throughout the sixth round.[77] In September, reports emerged of a fatal aerial strike against internally displaced refugees, killing more than eighty people and prompting calls for the UN to investigate possible war crimes.[78] Yemen's government said it had fired on artillery positions previously used by the Houthis, trying to portray this as a one-off accident, but, on the same day, viral video footage of a previous strike on civilian targets was circulating by email. Grainy low-resolution images appeared to show Yemenis pulling their dead neighbours and relatives from the rubble of their own homes. (I understood that the footage had been taken off YouTube on the grounds that it was too distressing for viewers.)

The number of internally displaced people swelled to half a million during the course of the sixth conflict, spread across four governorates, and humanitarian workers were struggling to reach the needy. Aid workers identified three main challenges to distributing aid: the degraded infrastructure in Saada, the lack of political will among Yemeni officials and the fact that no one within the aid community really knew how to navigate the power structure in order to negotiate access.[79] 'One day, you'll agree clearance to travel from A to B with an official, but an hour later, he's changed his mind, and the next day, someone else is in charge,' said one humanitarian source.[80]

After five years of obscurity, Arabia's hidden civil war was finally starting to hit the headlines, but Western media crews were restricted to filming refugees in camps in areas under government control. Rumours began circulating that Yemen's government had invited Sudanese advisers to help deal with growing numbers of humanitarian workers and journalists, on the basis of lessons learned in Darfur.[81] For their part, newly arrived reporters displayed a visible learning curve, struggling to get to grips with the elusive causes of the conflict. The BBC and Al Jazeera English both broadcast packages describing the rebellion as a Shi'i insurgency against a Sunni government, brutally simplifying Yemen's sectarian complexities in a way that made more seasoned observers wince.

This temporary spike in international media coverage also played a part in helping to propagate the notion that the Saada conflict was a product of Iranian expanisionism. Journalists recounted Saleh's long-standing allegations that Iran was supplying the Houthis with money, arms and military trainers. Western diplomats discreetly raised their eyebrows, arguing there was scarcely any evidence to support the charge of direct support by the Iranian state, and suggesting it was more plausible that money might change hands between regional Shi'i charities. Several analysts detected Saleh's attempt to discredit the Houthis by stoking the perception of Iranian power projection on the Arabian Peninsula and demonstrating common cause with Washington and Riyadh against Iranian regional influence.

However, many Yemenis professed to share the regime's allegation that Hussein al-Houthi had converted to Twelver Shi'ism during study visits to Iran, and accepted Saleh's assertion that the rebellion was financed with Iranian money. One commentator sourly noted that it was surprising how successfully Saleh managed to achieve this 'rebranding exercise', given the multiple homegrown causes of the conflict, the profusion of weapons available on the Yemeni market, and the wide gulf in doctrine and practice between Yemen's Zaydis and Iran's Twelver Shi'a.[82] Iranian officials denied all the charges outright, and offered to mediate in peace talks.[83]

The Houthis themselves had long argued that Saleh was guilty of pros-ecuting the war with foreign financing himself, by relying on money and material support from Riyadh.[84] During September and October, they began voicing new claims that Yemen was using Saudi airfields as back-bases for refuelling, and also allowing Saudi jets to bomb positions inside Yemeni territory. In early November, the Houthis dramatically raised the stakes by extending their insurgency into Saudi territory, taking control of strategic high ground, and killing a Saudi border guard. They justified their actions on the grounds that Riyadh's complicity with the Yemeni military rendered Saudi forces a legitimate target.[85]

Saudi Arabia responded by deploying ground and air forces, and initial statements from Riyadh suggested the Saudis might be planning to move deep inside Yemeni territory. One early news report raised the prospect of a joint ground operation to 'clean out' the rebel camps in coordination with the Yemeni authorities. Deputy Defence Minister

Prince Khaled Bin Sultan subsequently clarified the official position, stating that Saudi troops had 'purged the mountains on the Saudi side' of the border, but they 'did not cross and will not cross the Yemeni frontier'. However, he warned that Saudi artillery was creating a 10 km buffer zone at the border.[86]

The Saudis' unprecedented military deployment seemed calculated to send a clear signal that the border with Yemen was not a soft flank, and to increase their martial footprint in the border zone. As well as worrying about the potential spillover from Yemen's Zaydi uprising and its potential to incite their own Shi'i minority population, the Saudis were also concerned about the growing threat from AQAP, following the January merger between al-Qaeda affiliates on both sides of the boundary line. The Saudis' assessment of the mountain frontier as an area of increasing risk followed an October incident that saw a *takfiri* cell attempt to drive through a border checkpoint disguised in women's clothes, which ended in a shoot-out that left three people dead.[87]

However, as the winter weeks wore on, there was a growing danger that Saudi military intervention was sending precisely the opposite signal to the one that was intended—namely, that the region's best-equipped army could not defeat a fleet-footed bunch of Yemeni rebels. In mid-November, the Houthis uploaded several videos to YouTube, supposedly showing captured Saudi soldiers. In the early months of 2010, the Saudi body count—including 'many apparently from friendly fire'[88]—was running at well over a hundred fatalities, and Saudi Arabia's King Abdullah was reportedly angry that the military had failed to prove itself 'more capable'.[89] As Egypt's Nasser had learned to his cost during the 1960s, when the sandal was on the other foot and the Saudis were backing the *sayyids*, outsiders should think twice about attempting military action in the mountainous regions of north Yemen.

In February 2010, as a result of increased international pressure on all parties to bring an end of the conflict, the Houthis agreed to disarm, release captured soldiers, remove their roadblocks and withdraw from their strategic positions. In addition, the Houthis also pledged to end their offensive against Saudi targets. As Saada quietened down during 2010, the Saudis continued to resettle their population away from the border area, and proceeded with construction of a semi-permanent military complex close to the southern Saudi city of Najran, changing the material facts on the ground in the border area.[90] (It subsequently emerged that the regime had tried to assassinate Ali Mohsin by giving the Saudi Air Force coordinates of the General's base, supposedly as a recommended Houthi target.)[91]

* * *

Later that year, in deepest winter, I flew to Germany to visit rebel leader Abdulmalik's exiled half-brother, Yahya Houthi. The taxi from the airport to Yahya's house drove slowly through snow-streaked streets, passing provincial Mittel-European houses, with tiled, gabled roofs and Velux windows. Snow lay three inches thick on the roof of Yahya's house, and my cold toes were turning numb inside my boots as I waited with my translator, Léonie, for Yahya to greet us.

Yahya opened his front door wearing a white robe, with the top popper undone at the neck, and a brown Argyle jumper. His beard was closely trimmed in a thin, square band around his chin, and his black hair was neatly cropped. He stood, smiling in his socks, as Léonie and I hopped about like storks, removing our slush-stained boots in the hallway.

In a spotless newly fitted kitchen, Yahya asked us to help him serve soup, rice and chicken prepared in the northern Yemeni way. He had also made *bis bas*, a hot peppery sauce. I ladled soup into three small bowls, while Léonie heated rice in the microwave. Listening to Yahya's dialect, and touched by his thoughtful courtesy in offering us traditional Yemeni food, I felt the tendrils of his homesickness wrapping around our little trio. Out in the street, the slow whoosh of car wheels turning on tarmac and slush accentuated the loneliness of Yahya's banishment.

Yahya, a former MP for Saleh's ruling party, had acted as an intermediary between the family and the regime during the first year of the conflict. He had arrived in Germany in 2005 during a lull in the fighting in Saada, but he stayed on when the conflict resumed and applied for asylum, which was granted in 2006. The following year, Saleh's government stripped Yahya of his parliamentary immunity, and in 2008, it revoked his membership of parliament. Yahya was tried and convicted in absentia for spying and plotting to assassinate the American Ambassador in Yemen, which he denied, and sentenced to fifteen years' imprisonment.

Yahya had furnished his living room with a red and gold diwan in the Yemeni style. A flat-screen television showed the rolling news on BBC

Arabic. As we settled down to eat lunch, we watched English students rioting against rising university tuition fees in central London. The laptop that sat open on a low table was Yahya's lifeline to his family, his community and daily news from Saada. Unable to return home to Yemen, he had used the laptop to watch video footage of the funeral of his father, Badr al-Din, just a few weeks earlier.

The funeral procession showed a Toyota Land Cruiser, with no number plates, carrying Badr al-Din's body. A bunch of red silk roses had been taped to the Land Cruiser's front bumper, while bouquets of gold-peach silk flowers adorned the wing mirrors. A black and gold prayer rug covered the front bonnet and a photograph of Badr al-Din stood propped against the dashboard. On the front seat, barely visible through the wind-screen, four men sat shoulder to shoulder. Six crouching men held the coffin, draped in a green and gold prayer rug, in pride of place on the car roof.

The Land Cruiser drove slowly over the desert floor, listing as it tracked the unsteady ground. A convoy of flatbed pick-up trucks followed behind, horns peeping. All around the convoy, hundreds—if not thousands—of male mourners were chanting, shouting and stamping dust into the bright sky. They held hands, stretching like a dense shoal beyond the camera's frame and disappearing at the infinity point, framed by steep escarpments. Al-Qaeda claimed to have killed Badr al-Din in a suicide bomb attack timed to coincide with Eid al-Ghadeer, a Shi'i religious festival that commemorates Ali's succession as the fourth caliph.[92] But Yahya told us that his octogenarian father, who had been unable to seek hospital treatment because of restrictions on his movement, had died of natural causes. 'He was feeling weak and suffering from the cold weather in the days before his death, but he died peacefully,' he said. Yahya had already mourned the death of one of his own sons, and his three full brothers— Hussein, Abdelkader and Ahmed. Another half-brother, Ali, the full brother of Abdulmalik, had also died in the conflict. 'How can one family endure so much loss and suffering?' I asked. 'God gives us patience,' he replied.

Yahya believed the conflict sprang primarily from American disquiet about the Houthis' anti-American and anti-Israeli slogans, but he also blamed his sufferings on the Saudis: first, for giving Saleh billions of dollars to do their bidding; and second, for weakening Zaydi culture through their network of Salafi institutes. 'The Saudis would like to convert the Zaydis because they think they can't control Yemen as long as the Zaydi clerics and *sayyids* are there. Lots of tribes are happy to take money from the Saudis so if it wasn't for the Zaydis, Yemen would be just another part of Saudi.' Yahya also believed that Saleh's state was 'basically a Wahhabi institution. As a result, the state fails in all things except supporting Wahhabism and there is no progress in any other area.' He complained that all government ministries were distributing a pro-Saudi message, along with anti-Zaydi propaganda. 'Even in the army training camps, they are teaching Wahhabism,' he said.

Ten years earlier, Yahya and his brothers had gone to petition Saleh to stop supporting the Wahhabis. Saleh supposedly told them: 'It's all about money. You don't give us any money!' By contrast, Yahya said, Abdulmajid al-Zindani was empowered by Saudi money, which he claimed underwrote the running costs of al-Iman university as well as al-Zindani's role 'as imam to the Salafi movement'.

The battery on Yahya's mobile phone had died, and he plugged it into a wall socket to charge as we kept talking. 'Saudi is the centre of terrorism and America knows this. America wants to control the Saudis because they have oil, and the Saudis stir up trouble as a form of revenge, but at the same time, America uses the phenomenon of terrorism within certain limits to spread its military power. This is the game.' According to Yahya, the CIA and the Pentagon had even pushed Anwar al-Awlaki to centre stage. 'He was born in the USA and he grew up there. How can he come to Yemen and create an international problem without international support?' Yahya also believed that the Saudis had sent AQAP bomb-maker Ibrahim al-Asiri to Yemen to deflect attention from Riyadh. In order to help understand his meaning, Yahya told us a fable about a crafty fox that ate a lamb but left the bones in front of a sleeping bear. 'The evidence is right there for all to see, but the one who appears to be guilty is not the one who is actually responsible,' he said.

At the end of the day, Yahya offered to drive us to our hotel. In the driveway, he pushed thick-crust snow from the windows of his car with a long-handled broom, revealing a stuffed toy tiger staring out from the parcel shelf. He ignored the satnav's spoken instructions (because he didn't understand German) and followed the visual prompt of the moving arrow. When Léonie and I returned by taxi the following morning, the temperature was warmer and the air was soused with a fine mesh of rain. A pale glow broke through the joints in the bone-coloured clouds, which were parting close to the horizon.

Yahya ushered us into the living room to eat dates and drink coffee. The coffee pot, which had a long slender spout like the upturned tip of a genie's slipper, was warming on a raised tray fitted with a burning tea light. The situation in Saada had been mostly peaceful since the February ceasefire, and Qatar had resumed its mediation efforts. Yahya said the Houthis had now released all their Yemeni and Saudi prisoners, but Saleh was still backtracking.[93] 'Do the Qataris trust Saleh?' I asked. Yahya simply laughed.

Yahya told me the Houthis were controlling territory in three provinces: Saada, al-Jawf and Amran. They also had a limited presence in Hajjah, and claimed to have a 'hidden presence' among supporters in other governorates:

> We keep order in areas under our direct control and we provide electricity and water. We also provide some services for internally displaced people, such as medicines, food and shelter, as well as some limited education facilities for children but this is an exceptional situation. If and when the state is reformed we are willing to return to central control under a just government.

Yahya reminded us that although Saada's tribes were involved in the conflict, they were peripheral to the underlying dynamics:

> On the surface, this looks like a war between the tribes and the Houthis but the tribes are only acting as mercenaries. Tribal conflicts have their own rules and they don't occur on such a large scale. Saleh is trying to dress this up as tribalism, just as he sometimes tries to dress this up as sectarianism, but the real nature of the conflict is between the Houthis and the regime. Saleh is trying to deceive people by getting the Al-Ahmar family to fight with the tribes, but they are part of the regime too, and everyone understands this.

In the middle of the morning, a German heating technician arrived to service Yahya's central heating system. He stood 2 ft taller than Yahya, and I guessed that he weighed a third as much again. Still booted, he stood on the carpet in the middle of the living room, his height accentuated by our position, seated on the low-slung diwan cushions. He seemed bemused by the sight of me and Léonie in our socks, legs tucked up under our bodies on the diwan, surrounded by empty cups, date stones and mobile phones. Yahya offered him dates and coffee, but when the engineer asked which country he was from, Yahya was guarded. He answered: 'I am an Arab.' Yahya had only recently moved into the house, and the location was still secret.

Seven months earlier, Saudi intelligence agents had secured the release of two young German girls, aged three and five, who had been kidnapped with their parents and their baby brother in 2009.[94] When reunited with their German relatives, the two sisters had answered in Arabic when questions were posed in German and addressed each other using Arabic names, suggesting they had been separated from their parents for much of their confinement. Their parents and brother, and a British engineer, were still missing.[95] Some Western observers believed it was the regime—not the Houthis or al-Qaeda—who had ordered the 2009 kidnapping. Yahya agreed with this interpretation, arguing that Saleh had been looking for a pretext to restart the war, and adding that German nationals were deliberately targeted in order to pressure the German government to agree to his extradition.

Yahya wanted the international community to see through Saleh's games and hold him accountable for his conduct in the war, saying: 'I wish that Western powers were interested in the Yemeni people and not only Saleh's government.' He added: 'Shame on the West for supporting a strongman who has ruled for three decades when Western leaders are constantly being replaced. How many British prime ministers and American presidents have there been since 1978?' he asked me and Léonie, echoing the point made a year earlier by southerner Lutfi Shatara. 'Six in each country,' we answered, thinking it through.[96] 'If Western governments can't help to resolve things in Yemen, they should stop supporting Saleh and let us sort things out ourselves. Without support from the West, Saleh can't stay in power much longer because the people of Yemen don't want him any more.'

Yemen's popular awakening, prompted by the wave of regional uprisings dubbed the 'Arab Spring', was just over a month away, and Yahya voiced a palpable sense of impending disorder. 'If Saleh stays in power and the US continues to support him, we'll have no other choice. We'll have to do something. After all, thirty-two years is enough.' Yahya explained that he had initially held high hopes for reform, but Saleh was simply putting out 'media statements about reform and dialogue without taking any concrete steps. The regime is not interested in genuine democracy and we believe they are ready to falsify the next set of election results.'

Given widespread accusations that the Houthis were agitating to restore the Imamate, I asked Yahya if the Zaydi principle of *khuruj* (overthrowing oppression) could be applied within the system of parliamentary democracy. He told me:

> Revolution is one of the basic Zaydi principles, but it's also a universally accepted right for people to rise up against oppression. Rulers have always tried to eliminate this idea but the Zaydis have managed to maintain it. As long as there is a peaceful way to do things and the possibility of fair elections and a just government, that is what we want but, in the end, if there is no other solution, it will be necessary for the Houthis to march on Sana'a. If the regime does lose power, then the Houthis will be in a better position than all the other groups in Yemen.

As we finished, by discussing his own fate, Yahya grew increasingly irate. 'I haven't spoken directly to Saleh since 2004, when he asked me to negotiate. How can I be a criminal now when I was mediating just a few years earlier?' He threw his pen on the table in a gesture of frustration and pursed his lips shut, as he waited for Léonie to finish translating. 'This situation is so unjust!'

Yahya drove us back to the city centre, where we could find a taxi to take us to the airport. All three of us were pensive and quiet after the day's discussions. We passed Yahya's neighbourhood mosque just as the worshippers were leaving after Friday prayers. Yahya slowed the car as we approached the pedestrian crossing to let the men pass. On the road in front of us—some in jeans, some in Salafi-style robes—were Europeans, Arabs, Africans and Turks.

11

CHANGE SQUARE

YOUTH ACTIVISTS AND THE 2011 UPRISING

'A baby was just brought into the field hospital. Shot in the head'

@tomfinn2, 21 September 2011

A few weeks after visiting Yahya Houthi, I met a freelance British journalist, Tom Finn, outside an underground station in north London. It had been snowing steadily all day, and at 4 p.m. the sky had already dimmed and darkened. Christmas was just a few days away. Tom and I shook hands, and grinned at one another. Tom had graduated from university the previous summer and moved to Sana'a to work for the *Yemen Times*. We had been following each other on Twitter for a few months, and arranged to meet while he was back in Britain for the holidays.

We talked as we walked a mile to Hampstead Heath, a large expanse of grassland with views across London. At the perimeter fence we crossed into the park, climbing out of the evening rush hour and the glare of the street lamps as we trudged to the top of Parliament Hill. We stood at the crest, catching our breath and staring at the London skyline, spreading from east to west along the slack thread of the river Thames. The city was trapped under low cloud, spreading a snow-glow of refracted light.

203

Tom, fresh off a flight from Sana'a less than 24 hours earlier, had his hands jammed in the pockets of his coat. He was shivering, and the end of his nose was turning red in the cold air. His mind's eye was still crowded with memories of Sana'a: the smell of the souk in the old medina, the view of the mountain Jebel Nuqum from the roof of his house, the softening of the light in the hour before the '*magreb*' call to prayer. The rhythms of an entirely different city.

Tom admitted that, back home in London, he was surprised to find himself disoriented. He had grown used to striking up conversations with strangers on the Sana'a minibuses, and sharing hot pans of breakfast beans in Sana'a's shabby restaurants. These acts of kindness were rooted in a culture of generosity that thrived in spite of extensive poverty, and, by stark contrast, London's affluence seemed almost offensive. I knew the feeling well. Yemen had a way of leaving me feeling both enriched and wistful at the same time, and every homecoming provoked a subtle and temporary sense of loss.

A month later, when Tunisia's humiliated premier, Zine el Abidine Ben Ali, fled from crowds calling for his resignation, triggering the regional phenomenon of rolling street protests that became known as the 'Arab Spring', Tom had already returned to Yemen. I was in Riyadh with colleagues from Chatham House, researching Saudi policy towards Yemen. I rang my contacts in the Yemeni government and asked for permission to travel to Sana'a on a research visa, but I was told to go home and apply from the Yemeni embassy in London. In London, I discovered that Saleh's regime had issued a near-total ban on access for researchers and journalists. It was another six months before I was given permission to return to Sana'a.

Instead of witnessing events for myself during spring and summer, I had to make do with following the revolution from north London. I spent hours on Twitter, keeping track of Tom and others who were tweeting live updates from the Sana'a protests. Very few of the major international news networks had in-house expertise on Yemen; fewer still had correspondents on the ground. Coverage of Yemen's revolution was mostly left to a handful of young Western freelance journalists who were already living in Sana'a when the protests began.[1]

It was Yemeni journalist and activist Tawakkol Karman who was among those to ignite Yemen's own revolution.[2] On 15 January, a day after Ben Ali's departure from Tunis, Karman organized a small demonstration at Sana'a University in support of the Tunisians.[3] During the following week, more and more people—mostly students—came to join Karman's demonstration. She was arrested on 22 January, but the demonstrations kept going, with people draping themselves in pastel pink sashes to signal their peaceful intentions.[4] When Karman was released from jail a few days later, her brother Tariq received a phone call threatening Tawakkol with death if she continued her activism.[5] But she was adamant, and she was not the only person organizing the protests. Students were coming on to the streets in greater numbers and momentum was building, in Sana'a and in Taiz.[6] Karman lent her personal support to the biggest demonstration yet, dubbed the 'Day of Rage', planned for Thursday 3 February.

Fear of the potential impact on AQAP, combined with the assumption that Yemenis would quickly resort to violence, caused outright consternation in Washington, and US officials were said to be pressuring Saleh to make bold concessions in an attempt to placate the opposition and avoid the turmoil seen in Tunisia and Egypt.[7] On 1 February, Saleh gave a televised speech, promising to freeze a proposed constitutional amendment that would allow him to run again in the next presidential election, scheduled for 2013. In addition, he gave his word that his eldest son, Ahmed Ali, would not inherit the job of president.[8] He also offered to form a national coalition government and delay the next round of parliamentary elections (planned for April) until a bipartisan deal could be struck over the framework for the vote.

Schooled for decades in Yemen's dysfunctional politics, the opposition refused Saleh's offer to form a coalition government. Trust was too low and the memories of Saleh's reversal of his promise not to stand in the 2006 elections were still too fresh. Few opposition politicians believed that Saleh would be true to his word, and they themselves were unsure about how to press their new advantage. Many calculated that their best interest lay in holding out until the bitter end, rather than stepping in to save a discredited system. For others, their desire to see the system change was still tempered by their own fear of chaos, or the recognition that they themselves held a privileged position within the system, which tied them to the regime through family, common advantage and mutual business interests.

Saleh's offer also failed to deter Tawakkol and the other protestors, who planned to march from Sana'a University to the symbolic site of Liberation Square in central Sana'a on the 'Day of Rage'. However, when pro-Saleh tribesmen started to take up positions inside Liberation Square, the organizers called off the march, confining themselves to the streets in the area around the university. It was Mubarak's ignominious exit on 12 February that marked the moment when Yemen's street demonstrations really began to gain and sustain momentum. Violence broke out for the first time just two days after Mubarak's departure, when pro-Saleh supporters beat the Sana'a protestors with sticks,[9] and, a week later, two young protestors in Sana'a were shot dead by plain-clothes regime supporters, known as *baltegeya* or thugs.[10] By this time, demonstrations in Sana'a were pulling in around 2,000 people; protests in Taiz were even bigger.[11] Violence consolidated the drama and legitimacy of the movement, drawing ever-larger numbers to the streets in all Yemen's major cities. By Friday 25 February, one journalist estimated that 30,000 people were rallying in Sana'a, and that more than 100,000 protesters had taken to the streets across the country.[12]

Houthis in Saada were among those calling for the fall of the regime.[13] Southern separatists also began to change their secessionist tone, replacing their demands for independence with calls for Saleh to stand down.[14] Tribesmen, too, were also drawn to join the protests, complaining that even while Saleh was receiving growing amounts of US military assistance, the traditional streams of patronage had been drying up. 'The President has told the world that Marib is full of terrorists so he can get more military aid from America,' grumbled one Marib tribesman.[15] Another sheikh lamented: 'The government does nothing in my province [...] We have our own army. We even organize our own legal system. We ask, but the President gives us nothing.'[16] Tribal politics were, of course, intricately linked to elite dynamics, and the political geometry within the power elite was rapidly shifting. Both Saleh, and the al-Ahmar brothers, were rapidly trying to shore up support among the tribes, by distributing cash gifts and cars to loyalists in a bid to keep their key allies on side.[17]

By the end of February, the established opposition parties had formally put their weight behind the street protests, and on 1 March, Abdul-Majid al-Zindani—a member of Islah's Shoura Council—took

to a makeshift stage in the area outside Sana'a University. 'The caliphate is coming!' he cried. 'The caliphate is coming!'[18] Some believed
that al-Zindani had volunteered to speak at Saleh's behest, in order to
discredit the protest movement. (After all, he did not call for Saleh to
resign.)[19] Others saw it as a sign that Islah was gradually taking control
of the protest camp, by paying for food, supplying tents and genera-
tors, and controlling who was allowed to speak on the stage. Many
Yemenis assumed that Hamid al-Ahmar, who had bankrolled the opposition's recent national dialogue initiative, was under-writing the cost
to Islah of running the protest camp, now known as Change Square.

Tawakkol Karman—herself a member of Islah's Shoura Council—
had been opposed to al-Zindani speaking at Change Square, but she
'considered it absurd' that Westerners might worry about the role of
Islamists in the opposition movement. 'The real Islamists are in the
government,' she told Dexter Filkins from the *New Yorker*. 'Saleh and
Zindani are so close it is disgusting!' Karman saw the relationship
between the youth movement and Islah as symbiotic, arguing: 'Our
party needs the youth but the youth also need the parties to help them
organize. Neither will succeed in overthrowing this regime without the
other. We don't want the international community to label our revolution an Islamic one.'[20] However, not all the protesters in Change Square
belonged to Islah, and for many young independent activists, al-Zindani's appearance at Change Square was the galvanizing moment when
they realized they would have to start organizing if they wanted their
own voices to be heard.[21]

During February, Saleh had announced several waves of bread-and-
butter inducements, including public sector salary hikes and new jobs
for graduates, in an effort to reach out to the general public. In mid-
March, ten days after al-Zindani's controversial appearance at Change
Square, Saleh announced a new package of political concessions in
another bid to stay in power, offering to rewrite the country's constitution to give parliament a more powerful role in the country's affairs.
He also promised to devolve power to the regions and hold a referendum on the new system before stepping aside himself in 2013. These
constitutional changes were precisely the reforms that Saleh's opponents had long been calling for, and many believed they would form the
eventual basis of a future political settlement, but none now trusted
Saleh himself to deliver them.

Out on the streets, tension continued to rise, culminating in pitched street battles between the protestors and Yahya Saleh's CSF, who were stationed close to the perimeter of the protest camp in Sana'a. The first major crackdown took place on 12 March, when the CSF deployed water cannon and US-made CS gas canisters, which left many protesters with 'severe reactions [...] including seizures and foaming at the mouth'.[22] Yahya acknowledged that his troops were using imported tear gas canisters 'from countries that promote human rights', but he denied accusations that his troops were using excessive force against unarmed civilians.[23] 'We are not using live ammunition otherwise the death toll would be much higher,' he claimed.[24] In Aden, where at least twenty people had died in riots since January, Human Rights Watch described Yahya's CSF as the 'perpetrator of the worst incidents of violence'.[25]

During the following week, the number of new protesters coming to join Change Square swelled the size of the camp and expanded the perimeter. On at least one occasion, a CSF division found itself surrounded, leading to a tense stand-off between the isolated soldiers and the protesters. Meanwhile, in Taiz on Thursday 17 March, more than 100 people were injured when security forces tried to break up clashes between protestors and plain-clothes government supporters.[26] The following day, on Friday 18 March, tens of thousands of protestors gathered at Sana'a's Change Square to kneel in the streets for midday prayers, as they had done every Friday since the start of the uprising. More than fifty people were killed and one hundred injured when plain-clothes snipers opened fire on the worshippers from nearby rooftops.[27] Doctors said that snipers had shot the majority of corpses 'in the head or neck'.[28]

Saleh declared a thirty-day state of emergency in response to the violence, but he denied that his security forces were involved, claiming that local residents—fed up with the sprawling protest camp in the streets around their houses—had taken their anger out on the demonstrators.[29] However, protestors claimed that the houses where the snipers were positioned 'belonged to officials from Yemen's ruling party'.[30] Protesters also claimed that they had found 'military uniforms and Defense Ministry identification' in one of these houses.[31]

When prominent opposition leaders arrived at the protest site the following day to pay their condolences to the dead, blood still stained the ground where the shootings had taken place.[32] Yassin Saeed Noman, leader of the YSP, told the crowds: 'When the people come to the square of change, there is no voice louder than theirs [...] You are the generation that will bring the revolution to Yemen.'[33] Defections began swiftly after the shooting and on Sunday 20th, Saleh dismissed his entire cabinet.[34] The following day, Ali Mohsin appeared on television to declare his 'peaceful support for the youth revolution'. He promised to fulfil his 'complete duty in keeping the security and stability in the capital', but he warned that violence against protesters was 'pushing the country to the edge of civil war'.[35]

Suddenly, Sana'a—and the regime—was openly divided, and protestors at Change Square greeted defecting troops from Ali Mohsin's First Armoured Division as heroes.[36] This open split in the regime increased the speed of desertions from the ruling party, state-run media, government ministries and embassies.[37] Tribal leaders Sadek al-Ahmar of Hashid and Sinan Abu Lahoum of Bakil both confirmed their support for the people's revolution.[38] Abdulrahmin al-Iryani, the water minister, surrendered 'for fair accounting of any wrongs' he had committed, and pledged 'not to hold any public office in the future'. He denounced regime members who were 'now joining the revolution, when in fact they should surrender themselves to the revolution for trial for crimes that they committed against the people or looked the other way while these crimes were perpetrated'.

Yemenis feared a war or at least a coup, but Ali Mohsin appeared on television for a second time on 24 March to say that he had no interest in political power. 'Military rule in the Arab world is outdated,' he declared.[39] Saleh and Ali Mohsin had, in fact, met the night before at the house of the vice-president, Abdu Rabbu Mansour Hadi, and they had both agreed to step down and leave the country. The handover was scheduled for Saturday, but on Friday 25 March, competing rallies in Sana'a drew around 100,000 people each.[40] Saleh, in his own televised speech, said he was ready to yield power to 'safe hands' but not to 'malicious forces who conspire against the homeland'.[41]

When Saturday came, it was clear that Saleh believed he had survived his moment of greatest weakness. As negotiations over his exit continued, Saleh tried to protect the interests of his son and nephews, insisting that they retain their command roles in the elite counterterrorism units trained and financed by the US government.[42] At the start of March, one former US ambassador to Sana'a, Thomas C. Krajeski, admitted that Saleh was the 'main conduit' to everything the US administration was trying to achieve in Yemen, and he viewed the likely alternatives with consternation.[43] However, the violence on 18 March and Ali Mohsin's subsequent defection convinced serving US officials in Sana'a that Saleh himself was becoming more of a liability than an asset. Towards the end of March, the USA 'quietly shifted positions', concluding that Saleh had to be 'eased out of office'.[44] Even though US officials stopped short of calling publicly for Saleh to go—unlike in Egypt and Libya—they began to tell their allies that they viewed Saleh's hold on office as 'untenable'.[45] Discussions focused on persuading Saleh to hand power to a provisional government led by his vice-president until new elections could be held.[46]

These initial discussions evolved into a proposal brokered by the Gulf Cooperation Council, which would see Saleh stand down after thirty days, followed by elections after sixty days, in return for a guarantee of immunity, protecting him from prosecution. Opposition leaders accepted the proposal in principle in mid-April,[47] but offered the first in a series of conditions that bedevilled negotiations for the next six months.[48] They refused to join any power-sharing government until after Saleh's departure from power, and pointed out that they lacked any authority to force protesters to leave the streets, which was a key condition of the deal.[49] Saleh's supporters responded by taunting the opposition, claiming they were stalling on the deal because they were afraid of losing the eventual elections. Opposition leaders modified their position within a matter of days, agreeing to participate in a unity government during the initial transition phase but still insisting that they had no power to curb the street protests.[50]

Many Yemenis saw Saleh's flirtation with the GCC deal as a way of buying time, rather than 'a real attempt to calm the political turmoil'.[51] But towards the end of April, anticipation began to rise among diplomats who were exerting pressure on both sides to sign the agreement. On 1 May, GCC Secretary General Abdullatif al-Zayani flew to Sana'a to push for Saleh's signature. In Riyadh, GCC foreign ministers waited with the UK Ambassador to Yemen and the EU Ambassador to Yemen to receive the opposition delegation. By chance, I was also in Riyadh again at the beginning of May when Saleh scuppered the deal at the last moment, saying he would only sign the agreement in his role as leader of the ruling party and not as president.[52]

I was still in Riyadh the following day, on 2 May, when US Navy SEALs killed Osama bin Laden in a raid on his Abbottabad compound in Pakistan. Anwar al-Awlaki's name surfaced in the overnight media scramble to anoint bin Laden's successor as al-Qaeda's new mastermind, but documents seized during the Abbotabad raid revealed that bin Laden had not been in direct contact with al-Awlaki.[53] In fact, bin Laden had criticized *Inspire*, concerned that the magazine's promotion of 'indiscriminate slaughter' and 'bloodthirsty tone' could harm al-Qaeda's image among Muslims.[54] When Nasser al-Wuhayshi, AQAP's emir, had contacted bin Laden suggesting that he step down and name al-Awlaki as his replacement, bin Laden had rejected the idea.[55] Yemen counterterrorism specialist Gregory D. Johnsen cautioned that al-Wuhayshi and al-Raymi, along with Saudi bomb-maker Ibrahim al-Asiri, represented more of a threat than al-Awlaki ever had.

In Washington DC, where Defense Secretary Robert M. Gates viewed AQAP as the 'most dangerous of all of the franchises of Al Qaeda',[56] US officials supported a controlled transition that would 'enable the counterterrorism operation in Yemen to continue'.[57] Behind the scenes in Sana'a, US diplomats continued to push for a transition of power, but there was still no statement from Obama supporting the protesters and calling for Saleh to go. In mid May, the Civic Coalition of Revolutionary Youth published a letter pressing Obama to 'support our movement that seeks to build a new Yemen and prosperous society which can become a true partner in combating terrorism with the global community'. Wasim al-Qershi—who was emerging as a charismatic figure on the organizing committee in Change Square—published his own eloquent plea for international support. 'The youth of the revolution realize that once their civil state is born, it will form part of the wider world,' he argued. 'The more the revolution is supported today by the international community, the more that will motivate the youth to become a positive international partner when that day comes.'[58]

Despite the frustration of many youth activists, who were disillusioned by what they saw as the counter-revolutionary stance adopted by the international community, more seasoned political actors viewed the vibrant, articulate—albeit disparate—youth movement as a symptom of gradual social change as well as a catalyst.[59] The prominent role of women protesters led Tawakkol Karman to claim: 'This is not just a political revolution, it's a social revolution.'[60] The tribes were also part of that social change, with rural tribesmen leaving their guns at home and travelling to Sana'a to participate in the demonstrations as unarmed civilians. Many were unemployed, and disillusioned with a patronage system that had corrupted the values of traditional tribal justice. Some had even broken with their own sheikhs, who continued to show loyalty to Saleh, to attend the protests.

By the middle of May, the protest camp stretched for more than miles, and sustaining thriving businesses.[61] Numbers swelled every Friday, when supporters came to join the camp's permanent residents for midday prayers, and lines of worshippers knelt to pray on the nearby ring road. Many protestors saw the GCC deal as an elite stitch-up that betrayed their demands for an entirely new system. They rejected the proposed immunity deal for Saleh, and argued that the timetable was unrealistic. They wanted a six-month transitional phase under the leadership of an interim presidential council, composed of five members chosen for their 'expertise, honesty, and experience', who would draft a constitution for a 'modern democratic civil state based on equal citizenship, and an electoral system, with proportional representation', that would boost the role of parliament.[62]

Regardless of widespread opposition from protesters, diplomats continued to haggle over the GCC deal, and on 18 May, there were renewed reports that Saleh was—once again—ready to sign. However, when Brennan called Saleh and urged him to accept the deal, Saleh refused on the grounds that three of the five names put forward by the opposition coalition to sign the document were low-level figures who could not be held accountable.[63] On 21 May, opposition leaders went ahead unilaterally and signed the text of the GCC deal themselves, in what amounted to a form of clerical brinkmanship. (Saleh had supposedly invited the opposition to sign the deal at the palace but they had refused to accept). On 22 May, on the twenty-first anniversary of unification between North Yemen and the PDRY, Western diplomats and GCC officials gathered at the embassy of the United Arab Emirates in

Sana'a, hoping to witness Saleh sign the historic document. Instead, Saleh's armed supporters swarmed outside the building, trapping the diplomats inside, while Saleh continued to dally and confound expectations that he might close the deal.[64]

Saleh's default provoked an outbreak of violence in the Hasaba district of Sana'a, where forces loyal to Saleh clashed with tribal militia under the control of the Ahmar family. The two sides confronted each other with guns, tanks and rocket-propelled grenades, fighting for control of the Ministry of Industry and Trade, the Saba News building and the headquarters of the national airline, Yemenia, which was gutted by fire.[65] Mortars also blasted the headquarters of Hamid's television station, Suhail.[66] The next day, 'several prominent tribal sheiks came under fire as they arrived to help mediate the conflict, and at least two were reported killed'.[67] Sadek al-Ahmar refused any further mediation and sought to rally Yemen's tribes against Saleh, whom he branded a liar. 'We are firm. He will leave this country barefoot,' he said.[68]

The squabble in Hasaba lasted for nearly a fortnight, halting only when Saleh was injured in a bomb blast at the main palace mosque, during noon prayers on Friday 3 June. Assassins had placed their bomb in the wall behind a wooden lattice screen at the front of the mosque. When the screen splintered in the blast, it sent wooden shrapnel flying into the faces and torsos of the bowing congregation. Soon after the attack, witnesses reported seeing a fusillade of rocket-propelled grenades fired at the palace from the direction of Hadda.[69] In the confusion (and deliberate misinformation) that followed, the extent of Saleh's injuries were unclear. Government officials insisted that Saleh had suffered light injuries or 'scratches'.[70] A few days later, after his evacuation to Riyadh for medical treatment, it emerged that Saleh had severe burns, and although they were not life-threatening, he would 'require strong sedation for the pain and several months of convalescence'.[71]

Saleh's entourage fought hard to keep open the prospect of Saleh's return to Sana'a, in what turned into a protracted three-month propaganda war about the state of the president's health. In Saleh's absence, Vice-President Hadi assumed nominal control, but Saleh's son, Ahmed Ali, and his cousins were still running the family show. In their dialogue with Western diplomats, Saleh's faction began ramping up their argument that a transition of power would strengthen the Islamists. 'The Americans are making a mistake to support any change that will lead to the control of extremists and the Muslim Brotherhood,' warned Ahmed's cousin, Yahya. A full investigation was under way to find those responsible for the palace mosque attack, Yahya said, but the initial indications pointed to al-Qaeda, with involvement from members of the opposition.[72] As for the protesters, Yahya said: 'They should have some self-respect and go home. It's been five months now, and it's boring.'

After several months of living on the streets, the protesters themselves were beginning to admit that they were struggling to maintain their morale. In the first few jubilant days after Saleh's evacuation, protesters had expressed their elation by 'setting off fireworks and slaughtering cows'.[73] Borrowing a popular slogan from Egypt, the crowd chanted: 'The people, at last, defeated the regime!'[74] But their exuberance was premature. As June turned to July, protestors began to realize that their revolution was stalling and the political crisis had hit a stalemate. Morale fell further still after an attack on the country's main oil pipeline in Marib disrupted supplies of diesel. Prices of food, water and fuel sky-rocketed, and electricity supplies fell from poor to almost non-existent. Protest fatigue started setting in.

On 7 July, Saleh appeared on television in a pre-recorded broadcast that 'showed him speaking with difficulty' and seated stiffly. The skin on his face was darkened with burn tissue and his arms were bandaged. 'Terrorists and elements connected with terrorists targeted me,' he said, revealing that he had had multiple operations.[75] A month later, Saleh was discharged from hospital and he moved into a private residence. A brief video clip showed him walking, wearing medical gloves to protect his hands. According to a source who visited him in Riyadh at about that time, Saleh was also wearing a full-body surgical suit underneath his clothes to protect new skin grafts all over his body, and he was in considerable pain.[76] He privately admitted to his aides that he recognized he would have to stand down soon, on the grounds that his health would not fully recover for at least another year.[77]

Yemen's constitution allowed for a temporary transfer of power from the president to the vice-president in the event of emergency. The temporary period could last for up to sixty days, at which point elections must be held. Saleh had been evacuated to Riyadh at the start of June, and the sixty-day deadline came and went at the start of August, but Saleh continued to insist that he was still in charge. On 16 August, in another televised speech, Saleh promised his supporters that he would soon be coming home.[78]

However, with Saleh's consent, cross-party negotiators were already working on a detailed 'road map' to support a future transition of power.[79] Former Prime Minister Abdulkareem al-Iryani and Hadi were among those who met leaders of the opposition coalition to agree on the missing details that would enable them to implement the broad principles of the GCC deal. When Saleh publicly issued a decree on 12 September granting Hadi authority to negotiate an agreement that would lead to early presidential elections, the international community welcomed the move. The US government confidently voiced expectations that arrangements for a 'peaceful and orderly transition' would be agreed within a week.

However, during August and early September, while Saleh's mediators were quietly thrashing out the terms of this 'road map', elite rivals were busy stockpiling weapons, anticipating another cycle of violence. Mid-September saw renewed clashes in Sana'a between security forces under Saleh's control and the al-Ahmar brothers, provoked by the growing number of tribal fighters flooding into Sana'a at the al-Ahmars' behest.[80] On 18 September, in the middle of this volatile mix of suspicion and elite ambition, protesters in Change Square decided to take matters into their own hands by marching outside the southern boundary of their camp. They marched towards Zubayri Street, an arterial road running east–west across the city: Ali Mohsin controlled the area behind them, to the north, while Saleh's family controlled the area in front of them, to the south.

The protesters had decided to initiate the march because they were frustrated by the lack of progress, after months of political deadlock.[81] They marched directly 'into an area full of gun-toting pro-government thugs' and military police under the control of Yahya Saleh,[82] and they began to throw rocks.[83] Gunmen under Yahya's control opened fire, along with 'plainclothes proxies'[84] who were stationed on nearby rooftops, provoking immediate retaliation from Ali Mohsin's troops. The protesters got caught in the crossfire, and doctors working in the field hospital at Change Square said they were handling corpses that had been killed by 'live ammunition, mortar fire and heavy artillery'.[85]

The two military factions were fighting for control of a key intersection on Zubayri Street, which would bring Ali Mohsin's troops closer to the main presidential palace, central bank, Ministry of Defence and other government key institutions.[86] When Ali Mohsin's troops took over the junction on the first evening of the clashes, protesters 'erected tents in the intersection', but they quickly lost control again.[87] On 21 September, one of the heaviest days of violence, Tom Finn tweeted: 'A baby was just brought into the field hospital. Shot in the head.' His next tweet said: 'Can barely describe what I'm seeing. Dead people everywhere. Even children.' He added: 'Most of those being treated in here are defected soldiers. This is shifting from a crackdown on protesters to a military standoff.'

UN envoy Jamal Benomar and Abdullatif al-Zayani had flown into Yemen on the second day of the clashes. They came hoping to help cross-party mediators secure an agreement on the transition plan, but they found themselves in the middle of an urban battlefield, trying to negotiate a ceasefire between rival factions. For some observers, it was no coincidence that 'violence broke out just as negotiations were intensifying on a possible political settlement'.[88] To date, diplomatic negotiations had mostly been conducted with Saleh and ranking politicians, without much input from Saleh's elite rivals who also had a 'vested interest in the outcome'.[89] It was on 18 September that Ali Mohsin allowed the marchers to move outside the southern boundary of their camp for the first time.

Saleh's sudden return to Sana'a on 23 September after nearly a week of violence stunned partisans and opponents alike.[90] Clashes subsided within a matter of days, although few among Yemen's political class seemed able to agree on Saleh's likely intentions, and many still feared the prospect of full-blown civil war. John Brennan had stated earlier in September that counter-terrorism cooperation with Yemen was 'better than it's been in years', and on 30 September, Yemen shot back into the US headlines when CIA drones took off from a 'new, secret American base in the Arabian Peninsula' and 'unleashed a barrage of Hellfire missiles' at a car carrying Anwar al-Awlaki and *Inspire* editor Samir Khan, killing both men.[91] Obama described al-Awlaki's death as 'a major blow to Al Qaeda's most active operational affiliate',[92] and Saleh's faction moved swiftly to try and claim credit for the attack.

CHANGE SQUARE

Al-Awlaki's presence had played a significant role in determining Washington's priorities in Yemen, which, in turn, had influenced US officials' attitudes towards their options during the uprising. However, one US official warned that Saleh's departure 'remained a goal of American policy', and said that Yemen's government should be under no 'significant illusion' that the USA had 'changed its position' since al-Awlaki's death.[93] Yemenis were shocked and delighted a week later, when the Norwegian Nobel Committee awarded the 2011 Nobel Peace Prize to Tawakkol Karman, along with President Ellen Johnson Sirleaf of Liberia and the Liberian peace activist Leymah Gbowee, for their role in promoting women's rights. Karman heard the news surrounded by supporters in a worn blue tent in Change Square, where she had been living for the last nine months.[94] Her ensuing prominence in the mainstream global media as the face of Yemen's youth-led uprising briefly helped to overturn Western assumptions that Yemen was simply a harbinger of violence, poverty and terrorism.

12

SHEEP RUSTLERS

ELITE RIVALRY AND URBAN WARFARE

The road from Sana'a International Airport to the centre of the capital runs due south across a high mountain plateau, ringed with peaks. When I flew to Sana'a in mid-October 2011, during a brief lull in the spiralling cycle of urban violence, my journey from the airport terminal into the city was broken by makeshift roadblocks, manned by skinny teenagers clasping AK-47s. At one barricade, a group of boys in army uniforms watched my vehicle's progress from the back of a stationary gun truck. A few minutes later, their vehicle raced past me, with gleaming bullets the size of small carrots stacked in a heavy magazine, trailing from a mounted machine gun. The boys sitting in the back of the truck were grinning as if they hadn't had so much fun for years. The gun truck squealed to an abrupt halt a few hundred yards down the road, at a busy intersection marking the northern boundary of the suburb of Hasaba. The boys' driver parked outside the Interior Ministry, which was still scarred with damage from the fighting in May between Saleh's troops and tribal militias loyal to the sons of the late patriarch Sheikh Abdullah al-Ahmar. The building had suffered sustained shelling during the fighting and the ministry's brickwork was pocked with bullets. I could hardly see a square inch of the exterior walls that had not been hit by ordnance. The al-Ahmars' militiamen had briefly occupied the ministry in May, before handing it back to the government under the terms of a tremulous ceasefire.

A few hundred yards away, on the other side of the Hasaba intersection, I spotted the scorched headquarters of the national airline, Yemenia. My jaw dropped at the sight of this once gleaming multistorey office building now reduced to a towering concrete skeleton, gutted and blackened by fire. As my taxi crossed the road junction, I heard a loud crack […] it could have been a gunshot, or it might just have been a car backfiring. In any case, judging by the number of AK-47s that I had already spotted during my short journey from the airport, the ban on displaying weapons in the capital had clearly fallen by the wayside. Just beyond the torched Yemenia building, I stared slack-jawed (once again) at Sheikh Abdullah's bomb-damaged mansion, formerly a symbol of the family's phenomenal prestige.

Saleh's forces had deliberately avoided targeting the civilian population during their assault on the al-Ahmar family's compound, and none of the surrounding shops and houses showed any signs of damage. Rather, the Hasaba wars were a tit-for-tat struggle between two rival families who had shared power for more than three decades. The ruined buildings in Hasaba stood as a monument to a decaying political order that had already been coming under increasing strain in the years before the 2011 uprising. During spring and summer of that year, as the popular uprising morphed from a struggle between the regime and the street into a battle between competing factions inside the regime, the rival inheritors' sense of entitlement became visibly exposed.

Tension between Saleh's family and the al-Ahmars had grown increasingly apparent in the late 2000s, as Sheikh Abdullah sickened with cancer and Saleh tried to manipulate Ahmed Ali's own chances of succession. While he was still alive, Sheikh Abdullah had derived his exalted status—in part—from the social and political changes that followed the 1962 revolution, which displaced the *sayyid* aristocracy and gave the tribes 'unprecedented power'.[1] However, long before his death, and anticipating future turmoil, Sheikh Abdullah took steps to protect his dynastic interests by spreading his genetic bets. He masterminded a series of strategic appointments for the most able of his ten sons, securing a stake in the ruling party, the opposition coalition, the tribal aristocracy, the president's inner circle and the business elite.[2] As a result, Sheikh Abdullah's descendants were among the key beneficia-ries of the regime, even though they did not hold posts in the cabinet. Sheikh Abdullah had understood that access to commercial oppor-tunities within the newly liberalized economy provided a valuable source of influence and power, but it was his son Hamid who emerged as the family's most successful entrepreneur. Hamid chaired the family company, Al-Ahmar Group, a conglomerate of more than a dozen sub-sidiaries. Saba Islamic Bank, which Hamid helped to establish in the mid-1990s, was among these. Hamid also owned the satellite TV chan-nel Suhail, which championed the protesters' cause with its partisan coverage of the uprising,[3] as well as the mobile phone provider, Sabafon. In 2011, Saleh ordered the government to block calls from Sabafon numbers to landlines or international numbers, causing a rapid drop in the number of Sabafon subscribers.[4] A Sabafon spokesman claimed that the company's headquarters came under repeated attack by Saleh's forces because of Hamid's support for the protests, and more than 250 transmission towers were damaged by shelling.[5]

Hamid was said to be a 'hands-on billionaire', who kept a close watch on the dealings of Al-Ahmar Group.[6] His wealth was managed by PCP Capital Partners, a Dubai-based private equity company founded by Briton Amanda Staveley.[7] A *Financial Times* journalist who interviewed Staveley during 2011 noted that Yemen 'may offer one of the Arab uprising's most lucrative opportunities' in the region.[8] According to the *Financial Times*, Staveley was looking for acquisitions for Sabafon and confident that Hamid could 'emerge as a beneficiary of an eventual, and inevitable, political transition' in Yemen. 'He's a very, very religious man,' Staveley said. 'He's a very quiet, studied, educated, humble man. I read today a newspaper in Yemen saying we need a humble leader—that is him.' Staveley dismissed suggestions that Hamid was 'part of the same corrupt elite' who had mismanaged Yemen's economy for years. The problem, she said, was 'that the president's people are briefing against her client'.

Saleh was indeed furious, believing that Hamid was using his per-sonal wealth and his regional business connections to bankroll the protests. (Yemenis often mentioned Qatar in this context.)[9] At the end of March 2011, ten days after Ali Mohsin's defection, Hamid invited the BBC to film a television interview at one of his Sana'a houses. He told the BBC that Saleh and his family had 'no immediate future in Yemen' and 'they should leave the country for their own safety'. If Saleh stood down now, Hamid warned, he could 'still go with some dignity, but his time is running out'. He revealed that the opposition was planning to escalate anti-government protests, but he denied that Islah had any links to AQAP and signalled that he was looking for Western endorsement. He was already talking to the Americans, he said, and 'assuring them that any satisfactory plan to fight terror in Yemen will be respected by the country's new leadership'.[10]

Hamid briefly went to ground for several weeks after the attack on the palace mosque triggered a retaliatory assault on his own compound. However, at the end of June, he emerged from hiding to entertain a Western correspondent at his home in Sana'a, petting a baby goat that had the word 'leave' daubed on its forehead.[11] Hamid revealed he had recently met Hadi and Ali Mohsin, in order to 'clear the way' for Hadi to take power as an interim president. Hadi was 'the best person to lead Yemen at such a hard time. We will all back him and we will calm the tribes,' he said. He added: 'We want to rewrite the constitution, to build institutions [and] to turn Yemen into an effective member in the international community, not a source of trouble and a family-run rogue state.' Hamid pledged that once Saleh left office, he would himself 'stay out of politics for at least two years'.

Similarly, Hamid started a September interview with the *Washington Post* by trying to allay fears about his personal political ambitions. He explained he had stayed away from Change Square because he didn't 'want anyone to say that Hamid al-Ahmar is coming to take over the revolution, that he wants to make himself the leader of Yemen'. However, he went on to claim that the revolution owed at least some of its achievements to the work of experienced opposition leaders, like himself, and he ended the interview with a comment that raised fresh doubts about his own motivations. When the *Washington Post* correspondent asked his interviewee if he ever entertained the idea of becoming a future president, Hamid replied: 'If they would nominate me, and they think I am the right person [...] yes, why not?'[12]

Hamid's outright support for the revolution made him popular among many (although not all) Islah-affiliated protesters, but it was this interview that convinced some friends and allies that Hamid was guilty of hubris and misjudgement. According to one of Hamid's associates, who did not want to be named, Hamid made too many mistakes during the 2011 uprisings:

> He said things to the media that created enemies and the interview he gave to the *Washington Post* was one of the worst. I was angry after that interview because it showed Hamid was thinking in terms of personal gain when people were dying on the streets in the name of the revolution. While we were all trying to build a better future for our country, Hamid made it clear that he had a personal jealousy with Ahmed.[13]

Despite Sadek's seniority as the eldest of Sheikh Abdullah's sons and the paramount chief of Hashid, Hamid was still the strongest figure in the family, mainly because of his wealth, charisma, and involvement with Islah.[14] It was sometimes said that Sadek and Himyar—who had resigned from the ruling party but retained the post of deputy speaker of parliament—had doubts about Hamid's political tactics. Nevertheless, the brothers were united by common family interest, and after Saleh forces attacked the mediation meeting at Sheikh Abdullah's house in May, they agreed to stand together behind Hamid.[15] (In 2010, Sadek had accompanied Saleh to the UK, to attend the graduation of the president's son Khaled from the Royal Military Academy Sandhurst. It was less than a year before Sana'a was scarred by the families' violent rivalries.)

* * *

My visit to Sana'a coincided with the drafting of the UN Security Council's first resolution on Yemen. Leaked versions of the British-penned draft were circulating widely in Sana'a during that week, and both military men and politicians were preoccupied by the likely impact of the vote. All sides were posturing for attention in the run-up to the Security Council session in New York, and the tension was tangible. Youth activists had once again decided to escalate their protests, appealing to UN officials to distance themselves from the GCC's promised immunity guarantee for Saleh and his allies. For four days in a row, protesters broke out beyond the cordoned boundaries of Change Square, provoking sniper fire that led to multiple fatalities.

Shelling in Hasaba started again on 15 October, two days after I arrived—the boom of mortar fire echoing off the many cliffs and canyons that ring the capital—but it was most intense at night. Shelling was still a fixture several days later when I interviewed *Al-Sahwa* editor Rageh Badi in the lobby of a hotel in the centre of Sana'a. Rageh and I had first met five years before, when I had visited the newspaper's offices in Hasaba after the presidential elections. Now Rageh told me that shelling had completely destroyed *Al-Sahwa*'s office and the newspaper team was working out of a small apartment, still putting out a weekly edition and daily website updates.

In our first meeting, in 2006, Rageh had told me the Americans had more control over the president than the opposition. 'Do you still stand by that comment?' I asked him. Rageh nodded. 'Yes, I stand by that,' he said. 'We started a popular revolution here but Saleh hasn't left office because he feels he still has the support of the American government.' Rageh added: 'The opposition know that Saleh has no legitimacy in Yemeni eyes, but they recognize that Saleh and his family have an advantage that they can play against their rivals, because they still enjoy international support.' I challenged Rageh on this, referring to Obama's recent statement calling for Saleh to stand down, but Rageh laughed and dismissed my comments. Like many other opposition figures and youth activists in Yemen, he remained firmly convinced that Saleh was not yet on the receiving end of effective pressure to leave from the White House.

Rageh argued that the GCC deal was necessary, because Saleh could not be forced out of office without strong international pressure. However, Rageh felt the deal was weakened by its silence on the contentious issue of presidential succession that underpinned the current power struggle. At times, these rivalries seemed to separate the political class in Yemen in the way that mutual friends of a quarrelling couple feel obliged to apportion their loyalties at the end of a rancorous marriage. Speculation about the likely outcome of this struggle was often linked to guesswork about the preferences of the Americans and the Saudis, which were presumed to be decisive if either side was to gain the upper hand. Rageh said he had recently taken an American official to task on why there was no mention of these succession dynamics in the GCC proposal. 'The American told me that we'll have to find a solution to the succession problem ourselves once the initial transition has taken place.' However, Rageh believed the US administration was still preoccupied by the need to maintain continuity in their counterterrorism operations.

We discussed the violence that was dividing the city. Rageh and his family were living near Zubayri Street, in the crosshairs of the skirmishes between Ali Mohsin's First Armoured Division and Ahmed Ali's Republican Guard:

> My seven-year-old son wakes up at night, because he hears the sound of the shelling. He's afraid of the explosions, but myself, I'm afraid of what's coming next. Everything is mixed up now—the tribes, the military and personal rivalries. I don't want a military confrontation, I want a political solution, because if we fight, the battle will push us into a state of turmoil and we have no way of knowing when or how we will come out of it. On top of all that, the younger generation like Ahmed Ali and Yahya Saleh, don't have enough military experience. They've become commanders and leaders by virtue of their relationship to their fathers.

Journalist Tom Finn had arrived at the hotel lobby to join us, and he now began questioning Rageh about the role of Islam in the revolution. As a reporter, Tom was down at Change Square every day, counting the dead and injured at the field hospital, and interviewing the friends and relatives of the martyrs. 'A lot of the youth I meet are so fired up about the revolution that they really want to die for their cause. And the majority of ones who die at the marches are from Islah. Why?' Tom asked. 'It's because they're the majority in the square,' said Rageh. 'Change Square is 90 per cent Islah supporters, and only 10 per cent independent.' But Tom persisted: 'Do Yemenis want a more Islamic government?' 'No,' Rageh said. 'The Islamists can play a role in the future but they will not be the only ones.'

Tom's brow was furrowed as he pushed Rageh with further questions. He was struggling to understand why Rageh—the editor of Islah's mouthpiece newspaper—was downplaying the role of political Islam, and contradicting the views that Tom heard from the protesters' own mouths in Change Square. 'The protesters keep telling me that Saleh and his family have been neglecting Islam in the way they rule Yemen, and they don't respect the principles of Islam,' Tom told Rageh. 'Yes, that's true,' Rageh conceded. 'But that's not why we oppose Saleh. We oppose Saleh because he is corrupt, because he is a thief, because he doesn't apply justice and because he has failed to build a civic state.'

Tom was still not convinced. He told Rageh: 'I think observers in the West want to see the youth fighting for secular democracy in Yemen, and they're ignoring the presence of political Islam as a powerful component in the revolutionary movement.' Rageh stuck to his position. 'Youth activists initially went to join the protests in Change Square because they were angry about corruption and they felt that Saleh had no vision for this country. They didn't come on the streets first and foremost because Saleh's government is not Islamic.' Rageh also downplayed allegations that the revolution was fomenting divisions within Islah, and dismissed my question about the tensions between Muslim Brotherhood and Salafi tendencies inside the party. 'There are no Salafis inside Islah,' he said; but this comment may have revealed more about Islah's public relations strategy than it did about the party's politics.

Tom told Rageh that he had seen Ali Mohsin's soldiers carrying RPGs and machine guns and marching with the protestors. He had also seen First Armoured Division soldiers forcing their way into the field hospital at Change Square. 'Is that right?' Tom asked. Rageh answered: 'Ali Mohsin's soldiers should not be inside the square, only at the borders.' Tom replied that the protestors were too scared to tell the soldiers to leave, but Rageh responded:

> If the protestors disagree openly with Ali Mohsin, then Saleh's family will benefit. His defection was a huge step forward for the revolution, a strike to weaken Saleh's regime. Both Ali Mohsin and the youth want the overthrow of Saleh, so there are no big differences between the youth and Ali Mohsin right now. Our main goal is to win the revolution. If the revolution fails, then we will all be victims.

Rageh acknowledged there were concerns about Ali Mohsin's future role in Yemen, but he reminded us both that Ali Mohsin had promised to leave on the same aeroplane as Saleh if the president agreed to leave the country. 'Ali Mohsin is an old man and he has stated publicly that he doesn't seek any political role in Yemen's future. I heard him speak these words myself,' said Rageh. Tom looked at me across the coffee table and I briefly caught his gaze before lowering my eyes. I was not quite so convinced that these entrenched elite rivalries would be easily resolved. Tom's mobile phone started buzzing. 'I have to go,' he said. 'The protesters have started marching again.'

* * *

Early the following day, on 19 October, Abdulkader Helal—a member of the ceasefire negotiating committee[16]—sent a driver and an armed bodyguard to meet me. The air was morning-fresh and mountain-thin, and, like most mornings in Sana'a, the clear sunlight provoked a brief but giddying uplift. I settled comfortably on the back seat of Abdulkader's Land Cruiser, a spare Kalashnikov rifle lying on the floor of the car, close to my feet. My bodyguard—who also had a revolver tucked into his belt, discreetly covered by his blazer jacket—leaned over to grab the rifle with one hand and hoist it on to his lap in the front seat.

For the first time in several days, there had been no shelling overnight and the city was gearing up for another day of work. My driver pushed Abdulkader's Land Cruiser into the morning traffic, and we queued to pass the temporary checkpoints, stationed every few hundred yards on the main arterial roads. Behind us and in front of us, commuters filled the public mini-buses. One by one, we waited for a young soldier's cursory inspection. Many recruits—who were merely boys dressed in outsized uniforms[17]—glanced hesitantly through the car windows, seemingly uncertain of what they were looking for, before waving us through.

We endured the same tentative ritual as we passed from Saleh's territory into Ali Mohsin's quarter of the city, occupying the northwestern portion of Sana'a. The First Armoured Division's military base was situated on a small hill, overlooking Change Square. At the entrance to Ali Mohsin's headquarters, we waited a few minutes for clearance, with the car engine running. Staring unseen through our vehicle's charcoal-tinted windows, I watched a crowd of hopeful conscripts clustered beside us on the scrubland outside the camp gate. The rumoured monthly wage of $100 was enough to entice a significant amount of young men to join up, and the numbers of new recruits were rising.[18] When our clearance came through, it triggered an abrupt response. A soldier sprang on to our car's running board, shouting to colleagues to let us pass urgently, and rode with us, clinging to the car's roof, as we bumped along the dirt road into the camp.

My impression of the camp was fleeting, as we had only a three-minute journey to Ali Mohsin's office. We passed a troop of young conscripts, doing drills on the uneven ground of the training area, who looked as if they'd just been freshly recruited. 'They're students from al-Iman University,' my bodyguard told me. The camp had an air of sudden purpose, which seemed slightly overwhelming, as if the General was struggling to contain the current, frenetic activity inside the cramped confines of his city base.

We pulled up in a parking lot outside a squat two-storey building. It looked like a hangar, or an enclosed parade ground, but my bodyguard told me it was a sports hall. Inside, there were banks of tiered seats on both sides of an open floor. Someone had laid a large prayer rug on the ground, facing Mecca at an angle to the rectangular walls of the hall. They had also positioned one layer of breezeblocks around the rug to mimic the shape of a mosque, with a small protuberance to represent the mihrab—the curved niche in a mosque wall that the congregation faces to pray.

We raced past the makeshift mosque, moving quickly, and climbed a flight of stairs, passing countless men in uniforms, some clutching Kalashnikovs and some sporting beards. In a featureless office, where the blinds were drawn, Ali Mohsin stepped forward to greet me, with a friendly smile. I had been warned that he was charming. 'You'll like him. I'm sure of it,' my bodyguard had ventured during the car journey. Ali Mohsin conveyed a jolly, almost grandfatherly air—and yet there was also the slightest hint of a rogue about him. Indeed, it was only ten days since some of his men had kidnapped Saleh's personal translator, Mohammed Sudam, who had been detained inside this camp.[19] He was larger and physically more imposing than the president, but, perhaps uncertain of the protocol for meeting a younger foreign woman, he came across as mildly diffident.

I deliberately bowled him an innocuous opening question: 'What's more important, security or the economy?' His answer—'Security now, the economy later'—came as no surprise. The General was dressed in an army uniform, and he wore a maroon beret and rimless glasses. In the pause while my bodyguard translated my next question, about his motivation for joining the revolution, I noticed that Ali Mohsin's sideburns were turning grey, parallel with the arms of his spectacles, and the dark tufts of hair sprouting from his ears were clipped neat and short. 'The revolutionaries were a big force at the start, but they are weaker now. They do not have as much power and money as the regime,' he explained. 'In every protest square in the country, Saleh's soldiers were shooting the revolutionaries. That's why I went to protect them.'

Ali Mohsin's hands were clasped together on the desk in front of him, resting on a hardback atlas of satellite images of Yemen. To his left, I spotted what looked like a stack of large-scale high-resolution satellite images, printed out on vast sheets of technical-grade paper and folded up for storage. I told him that I'd heard people say the revolution had been corrupted, and hijacked by the regime's internal power struggle. His answer was pitch-perfect, and his cupped palms were open and facing skywards, presumably intended as a measure of his sincerity and benevolence:

> Saleh is trying to create the impression that this is an internal power struggle, but it's not. This is a struggle between the people and the regime, and the people are calling for an entirely new system. That's the wisdom of the revolution itself. The goal is a parliamentary system to replace the presidential system and, with that, all our problems will be solved.

> The revolution will continue until it reaches its goal, which is removing this regime from power. Tawakkol Karman's Nobel Peace prize recognized the peaceful nature of our revolution. The opposition parties have not stopped discussing with Saleh's mediators, in order to find a peaceful solution for the country. Even the Gulf countries, the EU and the USA want a peaceful solution for Yemen, but every time it seems that we are getting close to an agreement, the president changes his mind.

Ali Mohsin reminded me that he, too, was willing to hand over power as soon as the revolution reached its goal successfully. We discussed the March agreement, struck at Hadi's house, when Saleh agreed to leave office if Ali Mohsin went with him. Ali Mohsin also told me about a second deal, made in early April, when he once again agreed to stand down and leave the country. This time, the General insisted that Saleh's children and nephews had to go, too. In order to meet the expectation of balance—the principle of equal losses from both sides—Saleh supposedly accepted the proposed resignation of Mohammed Ali Mohsin, the General's close ally, who commanded the country's eastern military division. Ali Mohsin's own sons, who were businessmen rather than political players, were not included in this resignation package.

However, in order for the General and the president to safeguard against their tribal rivals emerging with an unfair advantage as a result of the mutual pact of sacrifice, the al-Ahmar family were also drawn into the resignation deal. Only three of the brothers—Sadek, Hamid and Hussein—were supposedly required to leave Yemen.[20] 'This agreement formed the basis of the GCC deal,' Ali Mohsin told me. I pointed out that the GCC deal didn't make any mention of Saleh's children. Ali Mohsin sighed, as if he agreed, but he avoided answering my question directly. 'Saleh doesn't want a deal. He wants to fight. No one believes what he says any more.'

I asked about his expectations of the imminent UN Security Council resolution, and he told me: 'At the beginning, we hoped to avoid a UN resolution because we were working towards a peaceful transfer of power, but unfortunately Saleh's behaviour caused the file to be sent to the UN.' I told him that, by all accounts, the first resolution was likely to be a weak one, but future resolutions were likely to be tougher. Did he think the threat of asset-freezing might alter Saleh's behaviour? He acknowledged that, ultimately, things might come to that, but the start of the UN process was 'the most important thing'. 'The protesters are depending on the UN to pressure Saleh to leave the country,' he added.

The General's notetaker, sitting directly to my left, wore a pistol strapped to his belt. He was a young man—younger than me, perhaps in his twenties—and his mobile phone rang incessantly during our meeting. At one point, he interrupted our conversation to pass his handset to the General, who talked for a few minutes before handing the phone back. The flow of our discussion had been broken, momentarily, and this was my chance to change tack in pursuit of more personal details. I told Ali Mohsin I was writing about Yemeni history, and I was curious to hear about his memories of the 1962 revolution.

'I was 15 years old when I first came to Sana'a from Sanhan. There were no roads outside Sana'a and Ahmed was the Imam. Ahmed's mind was like a stone. His level of education was very low and he was incredibly unpopular. Now, we have the same regime as the Imam and the president has the same mentality as the Imam.' Ali Mohsin explained that he had joined the army when he was 16 or 17, and fought for the Republicans. 'Before the 1962 revolution, the world didn't even know that Yemen existed, and our fight was a struggle to bring the country to a human condition. There is no difference between the 1962 revolution and this one. The first one was against an Imam; this one is a struggle against a republican imam.' He added, pointedly: 'In the 1960s, when the Imam was sent into exile, his children and his family had to go with him.'

I wanted to know more details about his childhood relationship with Saleh, and he told me: 'We grew up together and we were close friends. There was no school in our area but we tended sheep.' (Later, when I recounted this story to a mutual associate of both men, he laughed out loud. 'Oh!' he chuckled. 'The president told me that the two of them used to rustle other people's sheep!')[21] I asked Ali Mohsin how Saleh's character had changed over time. 'He likes himself too much now,' the General said. Then he quoted me a Yemeni proverb: 'Whoever likes himself too much will lose everything.' The implication was clear, but, as if to underscore this point, the General flicked the back of both his hands towards me in a gesture of dismissal.

I asked him if he thought that US military aid had created an unfair advantage for Saleh's family. His answer was studiously diplomatic: 'US military assistance is an agreement between two countries. We believe the US administration is doing an excellent job here in Yemen, but we are requesting US officials to consider the wishes of the Yemeni people.' On Saudi Arabia, he said: 'King Abdullah and Prince Naif have both advised the president to sign the GCC deal. Our relationship with Riyadh is very good. Whether it is direct or though a middleman, the lines between Sana'a and Riyadh are always open.' Ali Mohsin acknowledged that he had been talking to Saleh on the phone every day before the palace mosque attack in June, but 'we do not speak any more,' he confirmed.

My bodyguard signalled that our time was running out, and so I said a swift goodbye before hurrying to the parking lot. If my bodyguard had been in a rush to escort me to the car, my driver was even more impatient to get me out of the camp. I didn't ask why; I just did as he said. As we tore uphill towards the camp gate, we saw a brand-new all-black Land Cruiser with black-tinted windows, moving downhill towards us at haste. 'That's the political security chief, Ghalib al-Qamish,' said my bodyguard. 'He's a member of the ceasefire negotiating committee.' As we passed Qamish's vehicle, I turned to look behind me. We were cresting a small hill with a south-easterly view over Sana'a. The city suburbs spread several miles across the valley floor towards the presidential mosque, which stood gleaming in the morning sunshine like a recrimination or a survivor's taunt. Further to the south-east, in the far distance, lay the mountain crags of Sanhan, where the families of the two boy sheep rustlers were still living side by side.

My driver turned the Land Cruiser out of the camp gate, and went squealing on to the ring road. We were heading back in the direction that we had come earlier that morning, turning counterclockwise from the west of the city to south. Ali Mohsin's house perched high on a hill to our right. Also to our right, Hadi's house stood just a few yards back from the ring road, surrounded by security men and reinforced by tall steel panels, fixed to the compound's exterior brick wall. The property was perilously located just a few yards from the checkpoint that marked the boundary between Ali Mohsin's jurisdiction and Saleh's. 'Do you see the snipers?' asked my bodyguard, pointing to the roof of an unfinished office building that overlooked the vice-president's house. (I said that I did.)

A few minutes later, I knew we were back inside Saleh's territory, when—once again—we were driving past placards lashed to the lamp posts emblazoned with the slogan: 'Truth will reveal'. These placards bore photos of the late Abdul Aziz Abdul Ghani, an elderly politician and Saleh stalwart who had recently died of injuries from the June mosque bombing. Less than half an hour later we were parked outside the gates of the president's main palace compound, where Saleh was hosting a conference for the members of his ruling party. Once again, I watched through the car's tinted windows as we waited for clearance to enter. At the palace guards' feet, a flock of goats nibbled the bushes. A coterie of idle tribal bodyguards squatted in the shade, their sheikhs sequestered inside the palace complex.

Once inside the palace myself, I was ushered into an elaborate reception room, where Saleh sat on a raised podium, chairing a meeting of several hundred GPC delegates. He tapped the microphone on the table in front of him to bring the assembly to order, after a clamorous pause in the morning's lengthy proceedings. Following months of speculation about the state of his health, I was stunned to see him looking so lively and alert. I sat next to a presidential aide, level with the president's podium, and I spotted the foreign minister, Abu Bakr al-Qirbi, in the front row, reading a newspaper. I was the only foreigner in the room, and when the president caught sight of me, he looked to his aide for an explanation. The aide quickly left his seat, and went to the president's side. I presumed that he was explaining I had just come from Ali Mohsin's camp.

After a few more minutes, the president stood up and left the podium. He walked in front of me, heading to a side door that led to the cabinet room, and his aide beckoned me to follow. The president was dressed in a smart grey suit, but I noticed that his gait was a little uneven and his legs seemed stiff. Once inside the vast cabinet room, we were introduced. The first time we had met, in 2006, I had been wearing high heels and I had towered over him, but this time I was wearing flat sandals. Now, we stood almost eye to eye, studying each other, while aides and associates milled around us. The skin on the tips of the president's fingers was only just visible through the holes at the ends of his surgical gloves.

'I came to Yemen for the first time five years ago, before the elections,' I told him. I could see the healing network of fine scars on his face, where the skin was tinged with purple. 'Yes. I remember you,' he said. Saleh seemed weaker than my first recollection of him. It struck me suddenly that he was past his prime, and his energy was ebbing. 'So, what did Ali Mohsin say to you?' he asked me. 'Nothing new,' I replied, stalling and feeling a little awkward. This was no place for a detailed interview, and I knew that obvious questions would only provoke the obvious responses. Saleh held my gaze for a few more moments, then he dismissed me, and turned to deal with a clutch of other people who were clamouring for his attention.

As an aide escorted me back towards the palace gates, we met the president's nephew, Tariq, coming towards us. He planted his weight squarely on both feet, clad in black lace-up boots, as he stood to talk to us. He wore two Motorola radios strapped to his belt, along with a BlackBerry in a leather holster, a revolver and two spare cartridges. Tariq offered to show me round the bomb-damaged mosque, leading us past yellow 'crime scene' tape, labelled DANGER in English and Arabic. Shoes, glass shards and soldiers' berets were strewn across the entrance courtyard. Inside the mosque itself, someone had collected dozens of neglected mashaddas and heaped them together on one of the prayer rugs. Everything was coated in fine, pale dust.

Unlike the grandiose presidential mosque on the old airport road, the palace mosque was a simple, unpretentious structure. On the day of the blast, Tariq had been praying several rows behind Saleh. We stood in that spot now, a loose knot of three, and looked around us. The force of the blast had blown out each of the windows and left a hole in the exterior wall the size of a large paperback book. Black soot coated the walls and the supporting pillars, but otherwise I could see no structural damage.

As Tariq drove me back through the palace grounds, to the main entrance gate, we passed dozens of horses quartered in a stableyard and, among them, a single foal. I asked Tarek for his account of the three-way 'net losses' deal that Ali Mohsin had told me about. He answered: 'We all met together, all the members of our family, on the day before my uncle went to meet Hadi. My uncle told us, I am ready to hand over power and my cousin Ahmed replied: "Whatever you want, we are with you."' This was the official family narrative of loyalty and unity, emphasizing Ahmed's sense of duty to his father and obedience to Saleh's wishes. However, I heard from other sources that Ahmed was angry and reluctant to abandon the field to Hamid. The outcome of the next few weeks and months ahead had the potential to fester for a generation.

13

BREAKING THE BONES

POLITICS OF BALANCE AND THE 2012 TRANSITION

mizan pl. *mawazin* balance; scales; weight; measure; poetic measure; meter; rule; method; justice; equity; fairness; impartiality

Hans Wehr, Dictionary of Arabic

The Arabic word 'mizan' means weight or balance, but it also suggests the notion of order or regulation, according to principles of justice (or, indeed, to the intrinsic rhythm of poetry and the rules of grammar). In the Qur'an, the word 'balance' appears in the context of divine judgement on the day of resurrection, but it also conveys the expectation of good governance in earthly affairs. The sheer scale of corruption and its visible effects, combined with the sustained expression of public anger during the 2011 protests, left no doubt about the absence of fair government in Ali Abdullah Saleh's Yemen.

Many Yemenis—including those who invoked the holy standard of the Qur'an—hoped that the 2011 uprising would provide a chance to reform state institutions, pursue more equitable government and establish some discernible regulation in a country that appeared to exist in a permanent state of chaos. Yet the measure of relative strength and exercise of power within the Yemeni regime had long been governed by the principle of balance. In fact, Saleh had relied on a delicate equation of weight and counterweight to regulate political and eco-nomic advantage among Yemen's elite.

These patterns regulated concessions in the oil services sector, food imports, telecoms licenses, banking and military procurement; hardly any sector of the economy was untouched by this principle of weighted patronage. By the turn of the twenty-first century, eight or ten key groups and families controlled the 'commanding heights' of Yemen's economy.[1] Beneficiaries were married into both the Saleh family and the al-Ahmar family.

While Saleh increasingly tilted the balance in his own favour, it was sometimes said that he also tried to stir internal tensions between the al-Ahmar brothers, while playing each of them off against their own enemies. When he endorsed Himyar's appointment as deputy speaker of parliament in 2008, it was interpreted by one source as helping to stoke resentment towards Himyar among members of the ruling party, who were angry that yet another prestigious (albeit largely cer-emonial) appointment had gone to a member of the al-Ahmar family.[2] When Hamid called for Saleh to resign in 2009, Saleh encouraged Hamid to think about the balance between his own political and eco-nomic interests.

Sheikh Abdullah al-Ahmar had also played the balancing game in his turn. Before his death, he had secured the employment of two sons, first Himyar, then Hashem, in the president's personal protection unit, as a way of emphasizing his family's loyalty, yet also underscoring their stand-ing at the heart of the regime. Sheikh Abdullah used his tribal leadership role, including his position as the chosen dispenser of Saudi stipends to Yemen's tribes and his stewardship of Islah as a counterweight to Saleh's control of the state apparatus. (In doing so, Sheikh Abdullah gave the Saudis a chance to play their own balancing game, by maintaining an alternative centre of power that could keep Saleh in check.) Meanwhile, Saleh and Ali Mohsin—the two former sheep rustlers—both weighted Sheikh Abdullah's tribal dominance and his generous credit line in Riyadh against his family's lack of military patronage.

When Sheikh Abdullah died and authority passed to his sons, his fam-ily's power splintered and the mechanism for elite balance became more complicated. At the same time, the transition of power to the next gen-eration within the al-Ahmar family created a precarious asymmetry, which left Hamid free to pursue his own political ambitions while Saleh's son, Ahmed Ali, was still overshadowed by his father. During the 2011 protests, Hamid established a tactical alliance with Ali Mohsin, which balanced Saleh's family interests against his own. However, Ali Mohsin's defection also gave Sanhan a stake in the revolution, and prevented Hamid from claiming the uprising entirely as his own.

Throughout the protracted stalemate of 2011, Saleh and Ali Mohsin based their calculations on the implicit understanding that they each acted as effective counterweights to one another. 'They know the same tricks and they operate by the same code of conduct' one Yemeni official explained.[3] It was on this 'devil-you-know' basis that Saleh was said to be acting as a restraining influence on those who might have been tempted to escalate the battle with Ali Mohsin. Instead, Saleh authorized the Central Bank of Yemen to keep paying millions of riyals a month to feed and clothe Ali Mohsin's First Armoured Division, presumably to temper Ali Mohsin's hostile impulses and keep open the potential for reconciliation. In a twist of pure Yemeni irony, the cash was supposedly loaded into trucks at the Central Bank, under the watchful eyes of Ahmed Ali's Republican Guard, the First Armoured Division's adversaries.[4]

During autumn 2011, diplomacy hinged on persuading Saleh to relinquish power in a bid to avoid full-blown civil war, on the basis that the Republican Guard and the First Armoured Division were slinking towards a vicious confrontation. Yet neither Saleh nor Ali Mohsin was keen to cast himself as the aggressor, and both men knew they would be badly weakened if they ordered their armies to fight. Saleh controlled three-quarters of the capital and held the balance of conventional forces, as well as the air force, but this was not enough to ensure his victory. Instead, daily skirmishes in Sana'a took on the character of ritualized violence, as both sides sought to gain incremental advantage. In early November, a Yemeni official told me: 'They're still in the stage of breaking the bones. It's a concept from tribal law that means confrontation by degrees or tit-for-tat retaliation.'[5]

Ali Mohsin's tactic of sending his soldiers to accompany the protestors on their marches through the city, ostensibly as their protectors, helped to expand his physical sphere of influence.[6] It also turned the protesters into human shields, and led to the gradual militarization of what had started out as a civilian uprising.[7] When the two rival armies fired on one other during clashes at the protest marches, they could deflect blame on to the other side in a confusion that was not explicitly of their own making. In Hasaba, Saleh's forces targeted the al-Ahmar family property with striking precision, but the damage was confined to a small area. Elsewhere, the casualty rate from shelling was so low that it had the quality of a pantomime; people said that sound-bombs were being used instead of shells. Throughout 2011, the real conflict between Saleh and Ali Mohsin took place outside Sana'a and beyond the scrutiny of the international media, through proxies in Abyan, Arhab, Nihm and Taiz.

Neither Saleh nor Ali Mohsin appeared to have spotted sufficient incentives to strike a deal by 21 October, when the UN Security Council passed resolution 2014.[8] At times, it seemed as if they were squabbling like siblings who expected the Saudis to step in and take sides. The principle of balance between competing elite factions was inherent in the solution that Ali Mohsin had described to me during our October meeting, which would see equal losses on all sides, and King Abdullah was the only person thought capable of enforcing this deal. However, the Saudis seemed inclined to wait for the problem to resolve itself, and they had several reasons for dragging their heels— not least, a reluctance to lose all their key interlocutors in Yemen in a single diplomatic manoeuvre.

Saleh had already lost the trust of the Saudis, who were annoyed by his failure to eliminate the threat from AQAP, irritated that he had misled them about the extent of Iranian involvement in Saada and fed up that their cash payments 'tended to end up in Swiss banks'.[9] Yet even though Saudi princes viewed Saleh as a 'lying trickster',[10] they were unable to identify a preferred successor. The question of replacing Saleh was complicated by the fact that not one of the contenders was strong enough to assert himself outright, and the Saudis were unwilling to take sides when it was still unclear who would emerge as the eventual winner.[11] Despite Riyadh's formal sponsorship for a managed transition of power under the auspices of the GCC deal, King Abdullah held on to Saleh throughout the summer and early autumn while weighing options about who could replace him as the 'most effective strongman'.[12]

Riyadh's cautious stance prolonged the agony in Sana'a by creating a cycle of ambivalence that played directly into the stalemate, affecting the rivals' running calculations of the balance of power that lay between them. When the Saudis stepped forward to underwrite the Hasaba ceasefire deal in June 2011, they found themselves backing financially all three elite rivals—Saleh, Ali Mohsin and the al-Ahmars—to stop the fighting.[13] According to one Yemeni politician, King Abdullah telephoned Hadi in summer 2011 to plead with him to bring 'all three of our centres of investment together to make peace'.[14]

The Saudi struggle to respond strategically to the leadership crisis in Sana'a was inhibited by the nature of the decision-making process in Riyadh itself, where a small circle of ageing senior princes was grappling with widespread regional upheaval. King Abdullah had the final say on matters that he insisted on, yet he was only 'one player in a circle of powerful princes'.[15] His half-brothers, Interior Minister Prince Naif and Intelligence Chief Prince Muqrin, both played prominent roles in handling the Yemen file.[16] Foreign Minister Saud al-Faisal had a 'fairly limited voice', reflecting the Saudi view that Yemen was a matter of national security, involving 'intelligence, security, tribalism and informal contact' rather than foreign policy.[17]

The defence minister and crown prince, Sultan, had traditionally managed Riyadh's relations with Yemen, by overseeing payments to an extensive network of contacts through the Special Office for Yemen Affairs. The importance of these networks had begun to diminish after Abdullah's decisive role in securing the 2000 border agreement, and weakened further as both Sultan and Sheikh Abdullah began to age and sicken. At the start of 2011, Sultan still held formal responsibility for the Yemen portfolio, but the initiative was shifting to other actors within the House of Saud, and their approach was increasingly diffuse. Although senior princes acknowledged the lack of return on their spending in Yemen, they seemed reluctant to 'wean themselves off the old system', especially when they were under pressure.[18] These weaknesses in the Saudis' strategy were compounded by their preoccupation with their own dynastic problems, including the imminent succession from the eldest generation of princes—the sons of King Abdulaziz—to the next. When Sultan died in October 2011, his brother Naif, the interior minister, became crown prince. However, the Saudis had left many of their contacts to wither since the 2000 border agreement, and some of the leaders they traditionally dealt with had been replaced by younger, less familiar faces. There was 'less understanding of new and emerging actors' in Yemen.[19]

Underpinning the Saudis' own succession anxiety was a common trope that sons could not live up to the legacy of their fathers.[20] In Yemen, where they took a dim view of Sheikh Abdullah's sons, they saw these fears playing out in front of their eyes. Some Saudis had little faith in Hamid's political acuity, dismissing him as a businessman, rather than a politician—while others were enraged by what they saw as their betrayal by Hamid's brother, Hussein, who they believed had established ties with Libya's Muammar Gaddafi. (Gaddafi saw himself as the nemesis of the Saudis.) When the Hasaba conflict resumed in autumn 2011, there was a sense that Riyadh was content to see the al-Ahmar brothers temporarily taking a pasting, as a punishment for 'chewing qat in both cheeks'.[21]

In the end, the Saudis played a pivotal role in tipping the balance against Saleh, finally persuaded that perpetuating the status quo was doing no one any favours. However, they did not materially interfere in the process or the outcome of the final negotiations.[22] The UN Security Council had passed resolution 2014 in October, condemning the excessive use of force against peaceful protesters, demanding Saleh's compliance with the GCC proposal and calling for special envoy Jamal Benomar to deliver a progress report within 30 days.[23] (Russia had agreed to support the resolution as a trade-off for its obstinacy on Syria, where Moscow's interests were greater.)

In early November, Jamal Benomar returned to Sana'a, where he spent two weeks talking to all sides. Benomar was due to brief the UN Security Council on 21 November, in accordance with the deadline for the progress report. By mid-November, Saleh was effectively, and finally, cornered by the prospect that renewed Security Council activity would eventually lead to a travel ban and sanctions. Saleh agreed to face-to-face negotiations, enabling Benomar to stay on in Sana'a and broker a deal that formed the basis of the final transition agreement. By this stage, Ali Mohsin and Hamid were indirectly involved in the talks, aware that they, too, could be implicated in further Security Council action.[24]

On 23 November, Benomar travelled to Riyadh to witness Saleh ink the deal, with a delegation of Yemeni politicians and Western diplomats. (Saleh himself had flown to Riyadh overnight.) Saleh, smiling and seemingly in high spirits, signed a modified version of the original GCC deal, committing himself to hand power to Hadi during a three-month interim period and stand aside in February. King Abdullah's demeanour was grave, warning Yemenis that they would need patience and wisdom to deal with the challenges ahead. 'Don't let the past pull you into a maze of darkness,' he said. Although the Saudis were regarded as a 'leading force in the counterrevolution against the "Arab Spring"',[25] they found themselves acting as 'the midwives of change' in Yemen.[26]

* * *

Three months later, in February 2012, I stood on a marble-topped table in a vast reception room at the main presidential palace in Sana'a—in the same reception room where I had last seen Saleh in October. Peering over the heads of dozens of Yemeni journalists, foreign stringers and denim-clad cameramen, I had clear line of sight to a podium where Yemen's new president stood side by side with his long-serving predecessor. UN envoy, Jamal Benomar, watched from the front row of the audience, an inscrutable expression on his face. Sitting close by him was the US ambassador, Gerald M. Feierstein, who had earned the popular epithet 'Sheikh Feierstein' for the perception of his proprietorial attitude during the transition negotiations.

Yemen's electorate had collectively rubber-stamped Hadi's elevation from vice-president to two-year caretaker president one week earlier, on 21 February. Six million people, nearly a third of registered voters, had turned out for a nationwide mandate on the transition process: Hadi won 99 per cent of the vote.[27] Feierstein arranged for Saleh to visit the USA during the ballot, but the outgoing president flew home to Sana'a to attend his successor's inauguration in parliament on 25 February. (Saleh had no choice, as his diplomatic immunity expired on the date of the inauguration.) Now I watched as Saleh, still wearing his medical gloves, handed the Yemeni flag to Hadi in a symbolic transfer of power to 'safe hands', witnessed by generals and GPC loyalists.[28]

After the ceremony, departing male delegates laid their hands on platters of snack food displayed on trestle tables in the palace garden. Veiled women, wearing hijab and niqab, waited until the men grew bored with the food before scraping leftover pastries and bread rolls into their handbags. Food prices, which had spiked during the 2011 uprising, remained historically high, and the number of Yemenis struggling to feed themselves had nearly doubled during the previous years.[29] Despite these daily hardships, ordinary Sana'a citizens seemed cautiously optimistic about the transition process. There was a sense of collective relief that the electricity was back on again after nearly a year of severe power cuts, and everyone was glad that the shelling had stopped, along with the deadly protest marches. 'It's enough for now, and we hope that Hadi will do a good job,' people told me.

Saleh had already moved out of the presidential palace to a private house, supposedly to begin his retirement from daily political life. All across the city, new posters of Hadi's clean-shaven face, high-domed forehead and balding pate were replacing the familiar bewhiskered images of Saleh. Yemen's transition was hailed as the country's first democratic power-shift, but Saleh still retained his position as head of the GPC. In addition, he was now protected by a domestic immunity agreement, which parliament had passed in January in accordance with the GCC transition deal. 'Saleh has accepted. He may tinker, but he cannot spoil,' argued one of the former president's closest associates, despite widespread fears that Saleh would continue to meddle in Yemeni politics, with dangerous consequences.[30]

Saleh's room for manoeuvre was certainly growing more constrained, but the substructure of his patronage network remained in place. From the outset of the 2011 uprising, protestors had called for Saleh's relatives to quit military posts, but negotiators had deliberately deferred the issue of military restructuring, and thus the resolution of elite competition, until after February's milestone election. As a result, Sana'a was still a divided city. Ahmed Ali retained his command over the Republican Guard, which controlled most of the capital and ringed the empty presidential palace. On Zubayri Street, Yahya Saleh's military police tanks guarded the Ministry of Oil. Half a mile away, I watched a young girl wearing an abaya, sunglasses and a soldier's helmet, playing in the street next to sandbags marking the front line between the Republican Guard and the First Armoured Division. The infrastructure of the conflict of posture was still largely intact.

In early March, I returned to the First Armoured Division camp for a second interview with Ali Mohsin. I was escorted beyond the hangar-like building where I had first met the General towards the University of Science and Technology, which bordered Ali Mohsin's camp. An aide-de-camp confiscated both my phones before leading me deep into the bowels of the university building and showing me into a modest office with a single window that opened on to an airshaft, where Ali Mohsin greeted me with a perfunctory nod. Irritation replaced the avuncular tone of our previous encounter. He seemed edgy, if not nervous. He laid one hand flat on the desk, fingers splayed. He held a pen in his other hand, tapping the base of the pen on the desk in the space between each of his fingers. He repeated this sequence during every pause in our conversation, moving the pen from right to left. I noticed that his hair had recently been dyed, as the white tips of his sideburns were shorter than I had observed in October.

From my discussions with a close associate of both Ali Mohsin and Saleh, I knew that the two men had spoken on the phone at the start of the year.[31] Throughout the spring, Saleh continued to seek reconciliation, but Ali Mohsin wanted Saleh to leave Yemen, and he refused to participate in further talks—or so I was told.[32] (Saleh's response, allegedly, was to stockpile missiles in Sanhan.)[33] Yemen's political elite was divided over Ali Mohsin's intentions. Some believed that he was simply waiting until he could extract the highest concessions before standing aside, while others speculated that he wanted to retain enduring influence or play an even more decisive role. However, on this—and on all matters of contemporary importance—Ali Mohsin was tight-lipped. He refused to confirm or deny his ambition to stand for president in 2014. 'It's too early to talk about that,' he told me. On the matter of military restructuring, he simply said: 'I follow the new president. He has the right to ask for help, but he will decide.'

Yemen's new president had the unenviable task of reining in the two former sheep rustlers. Despite his explicit mandate to negotiate the demilitarization of the capital, under the terms of the GCC transition deal, Hadi barely controlled 20 per cent of the military. A ranking field marshal, originally from the southern province of Abyan, Hadi fled Aden with Ali Nasser Mohammed after the 1986 bloodbath in the Politburo. In return for their guarantee of sanctuary in Sana'a, Hadi had supported Saleh and Ali Mohsin in the 1994 battle to defeat al-Beidh. Saleh subsequently rewarded Hadi with the post of vice-president, which was largely a ceremonial role, and Hadi whiled away his fifties and most of his sixties keeping out of the political limelight.

The Arabic word 'hadi' is one of the 99 names of God, meaning one who guides the believer towards the right path; it also means calm. Many Yemenis suspected Hadi would have difficulty adjusting to his new role and moving beyond traditional balance-of-power politics to break the elite stand-off. However, in early April, Hadi made the first in a series of decisive moves against Saleh's faction, issuing a decree replacing Saleh's ally Mehdi Maqwalah, a northerner, with southerner Salem Qatan as southern regional army commander. A few weeks later, Hadi 'promoted' Saleh's half-brother, the air force commander Mohammed Saleh al-Ahmar, into a position of impotence, while he offered Tariq a new posting in the remote eastern desert province of Hadramaut.

Constitutionally, Hadi had the upper hand in his dealings with Saleh's family, but in reality he was constrained from moving too far and too fast. These early attempts to exercise his authority exposed the extent to which he was heavily dependent on the international community to enforce his decrees. Mohammed Saleh staged a temporary rebellion at Sana'a International Airport, while Tariq simply refused to deploy to Hadramaut. When Benomar returned to Sana'a in mid-April, he read the riot act to Saleh himself, warning him that no one could hold the new president to ransom. Benomar's high-profile intervention put renewed pressure on Saleh's family to comply—or, at least, to be seen to comply—with Hadi's orders. While Ahmed Ali appeared keen to create the impression that he deferred to Hadi's authority, few believed that he accepted the game was over. 'Ahmed is being publicly servile but privately insubordinate,' one Western diplomat surmised.[34]

During his mid-April meeting with Jamal Benomar, Saleh had complained that his own relatives were being disproportionately targeted in the military reshuffle, while Hadi was leaving Ali Mohsin's interests untouched. Hadi had, in fact, also dismissed one of Ali Mohsin's closest associates in April, eastern desert commander Mohammed Ali Mohsin, but there was still some truth in Saleh's complaint that his own allies were bearing the brunt of the changes. Hadi was no doubt aware of the need to placate public opinion, mindful that protesters had spent a year on the streets clamouring for Saleh and his relatives to leave power. By contrast, Ali Mohsin still enjoyed a degree of popular support as the 'protector of the revolution'. It was not yet clear, however, if Hadi was favourably predisposed towards Ali Mohsin, or simply cutting Saleh's faction down to size before embarking on more extensive restructuring measures.

Hadi's clear priority from the outset of his presidency was the escalating insurgency in his home province of Abyan, where an al-Qaeda off-shoot called Ansar al-Sharia (Partisans of Sharia) controlled several towns and was gaining momentum. Within days of Hadi's inauguration, Ansar al-Sharia ambushed an army division in Abyan, killing more than 150 government soldiers. Propaganda footage on YouTube showed Ansar al-Sharia building roads, restoring electricity supplies and delivering vigilante justice, including the execution of collaborators accused of supplying intelligence to the government. Yemeni troops were struggling to claim and hold ground against Ansar al-Sharia, yet Ahmed Ali and Ali Mohsin were allegedly reluctant to station their own men outside Sana'a unless deployments were consistent with the principle of balance. Hadi negotiated 'like-for-like' deployments from Sana'a to Abyan, while encouraging and supporting efforts to form a new grassroots militia, known as the 'popular committees', under local southern leadership.

Ansar al-Sharia's growing footprint in Abyan stoked US concerns that AQAP would be able to carve out greater room for manoeuvre. Although US officials were committed to working with 'institutions, not personalities', it seemed plausible that the CIA and SOCOM might want to keep their channels of communication open with Ammar and Yahya, while the State Department and the Pentagon focused on long-term institution-building. However, within a few weeks of his inauguration, it became clear that Hadi was successfully bypassing the Salehs and 'finding ways to do business without the old people'.[35] During the first six months of 2012, the number of US drone strikes in Yemen shot up to unprecedented levels.[36]

In early May, it became clear that Hadi was considering dismissing Ammar from his post. US officials insisted that Hadi issued presidential decrees without prior consultation, but it seemed unlikely that Hadi would initiate such a sensitive change without tacit consultation with the US embassy in Sana'a. On 16 May, President Obama signed an executive order authorizing sanctions against those 'obstructing the political process in Yemen'. Six days later, Hadi dismissed Ammar from his post at the NSB.[37] In June, the UN Security Council passed a second resolution on Yemen, signalling the prospect of sanctions against those who tried to undermine the transition, further circling the wagons.[38] (The second resolution followed two months of negotiations to allow Tariq's replacement as third brigade commander to gain access to the division base in Sana'a.)

The US administration's desertion of Saleh's nephews accompanied a parallel rethink on the need to shift away from reliance on boutique counterterrorism units and build a broader, more balanced alliance within the Yemeni military. US officials belatedly realized the folly of training and funding elite units under the command of Saleh's relatives on the grounds that this had accentuated the regime schism and over-looked the role of regular provincial forces that were currently struggling to hold their ground in Abyan.[39] In spring 2012, Pentagon officials began working with Hadi on a comprehensive plan to 'professionalize' the armed forces and bring them under a single, unified chain of command. Hadi was not yet strong enough to reorganize the First Armoured Division or the Republican Guard, or dismiss their commanders, but it seemed possible that he would try to move Ali Mohsin and Ahmed Ali sideways before the end of his two-year term as president.

Against this backdrop, Ahmed Ali's supporters tried to downplay the extent to which his rivalry with Ali Mohsin hinged solely on personal animosity, highlighting his role as a moderate secular counterweight to Ali Mohsin's Islamist sympathies. Western governments were certainly concerned about Ali Mohsin's ability to mobilize large numbers of loyal gunmen, regardless of Ahmed Ali's superior cache of tanks and artil-lery. However, if certain individuals within Western governments saw the logic of keeping Ahmed Ali in place as a temporary counterbalance to Ali Mohsin, senior Saudi princes were said to view Ali Mohsin as a useful tool to hold the remnants of Saleh's faction in check. While the Saudis signalled strong support for Hadi with a $3 billion aid pledge in May, they continued hedging on the future outcome of the transition.

Despite Riyadh's troubled relationship with the al-Ahmar family, the Saudis also continued to treat the brothers as important conduits to Hashid. One Yemeni politician told me that the Saudis should use these ties to ensure that the al-Ahmars adhered to the terms of the GCC initiative.[40] However, when I met Hamid at one of his mansions in

Sana'a's Soufan district in May 2012, he told me that the worst excesses of the patrician era of Saudi patronage were over. Hamid also claimed to be fostering a new, civic spirit among Yemen's tribes. 'Last year's revolution represented a historic step towards the formation of a civil state in Yemen,' he told me. 'We know what steps we need to take to achieve this, and we are serious in bringing the tribes towards this new mentality. We are working with the sheikhs to make sure that they can be part of it.'

Hamid denounced the Saleh family's disruptive influence over Hadi's fledgling government, claiming they were simultaneously supporting the Houthis, the hiraak and AQAP, as well as orchestrating attacks on electricity supplies and oil pipelines. 'These people are criminals, but we will not forget their crimes. The international community should freeze Saleh's assets immediately because it's dangerous to leave billions of dollars in the hands of this crazy family!' he exclaimed. Outside Hamid's mansion, tribal militia crawled through the streets of Soufan, the neighbourhood adjacent to Hasaba, where bomb damage from the previous year's fighting between the al-Ahmars and the Salehs was still not yet repaired. The Ministry of Trade and Industry stood unoccupied, every window blown to shards; at the Interior Ministry, breezeblocks and sandbags still filled the window cavities. (Both ministries were allocated to the JMP in the cabinet carve-up that accompanied the formation of Hadi's new unity government.)

If Hamid appeared to view Saleh's loss as his personal gain, perhaps he could not be blamed. His wealth gave him political scope, while the revolution gave him political cover. Far from dismantling the old regime, it seemed initially that the 2011 protests had simply shifted the political advantage from one elite faction to another. Hamid was said to be paying for coaching sessions to improve his communication skills, possibly anticipating a future presidential role.[41] If so, he had a hard task ahead to win over his critics, who caricatured him as arrogant, but he was also pitting himself against broader social trends. 'Hamid behaves like he's a prince but no one will accept that mentality any more. People are fed up with the old system, and the Arab Spring has given them an alternative vision,' argued one experienced Yemeni diplomat.[42] If Hamid's conduct during the revolution had damaged his own status and prestige, there was a sense that history might finally be turning its hand against his family's privileged status just as Hamid was getting his hands on the levers of power.

* * *

Hadi was the first southern-born president to hold power in Sana'a, and his prime minister, Mohammed Salim Basindwa, was also born in the south.[43] A former FLOSY activist, Basindwa had fled to Sana'a from Aden after the NLF seized power, and served as a minister under Hamdi, Ghashmi and Saleh.[44] At a qat chew in Sana'a in spring 2012, Basindwa—sitting barefoot on the *mafraj* cushions—dismissed my fears that elite competition remained unresolved and, as such, Hadi's government was inherently unstable. 'The revolution is a victory for the people!' he crowed. He reminded me that his judgement was underpinned by a political career spanning more than four decades, in which he had shifted from an early alliance with Saleh into active opposition, when he took on the role as secretary general for Hamid's national consultation exercise.

Basindwa, who was in his late seventies, portrayed his appointment as prime minister as a personal sacrifice. 'I'm an old man and the prime minister's burden is heavy. My life is in danger. When the British foreign secretary, William Hague, called to congratulate me on my appointment, I told him "just pray for me!" but, at this age, I don't really care what happens to me.' Basindwa's mobile phone rang and he made a gesture of apology. 'It's the president,' he told me. He raised himself slowly to his feet, his limbs shaking slightly with the exertion, and went to take Hadi's call in private. A few moments later he returned and settled back into his *mafraj* seat, rearranging the cushions and his pile of qat. 'I want to see a stable peaceful Yemen. The new unity government has already taken steps to improve the economy and the value of the riyal is rising again, but we should be emulating Indonesia, Malaysia and Turkey, and I want to make sure that we get on that track.'

As prime minister, Basindwa was tasked with setting and driving the cabinet's economic agenda, but his critics portrayed him as exceptionally weak and indecisive, and some people described him as too close to Hamid.[45] Just as Saleh's government had been paralysed by a tug of war between rival factions, so elite rivalry continued to affect cabinet dynamics in 2012. 'The government of national unity should be acting as a backbone for the country and leading changes in the national interest, but some ministers are still tied to their financial sponsors,' one politician complained.[46]

Since the formation of the national unity government, the distribution of formal power had shifted, but there was still a significant gap between formal power structures and informal networks of patronage. The political parties, which historically functioned as mechanisms for patronage distribution, were struggling to adapt to the need for renewal. Saleh's GPC still boasted a moderate 'secular'-style identity, but it had been weakened by mass desertions during 2011 and it was unclear what direction it could take under new leadership, or who would lead it. Islah enjoyed a large grassroots base, strong internal decision-making procedures and a large stake in the power-sharing agreement that underpinned the transition government. It also stood on the right side of the Islamist fervour sweeping the Arab region in the initial aftermath of the 'Arab Spring', but it still had to overcome internal divisions between moderates and extremists, as well as bottom-up pressure from its own youth activists and emerging leaders who were unhappy with the 'old guard' at the top.

During my encounters with senior Islah politicians and apparatchiks in spring 2012, I encountered widespread reluctance to discuss the specifics of the party's Islamist appeal. Without exception, Islahis emphasized the popularity of their anti-corruption stance, and spoke of their commitment to governing in a future coalition rather than seeking to win the next elections outright. Party chairman, Mohammed al-Yadoumi, who had taken over from Sheikh Abdullah in 2008, explained:

> Members of all parties go to the mosque, so the difference between the main parties is stylistic, not ideological—for example, how to provide services for the people. Until now, we have not been able to implement our ideas but now we have ministers in government, people can judge us by our actions. Our role in the coalition government shows that we want to cooperate. We do not want to dominate.

Not all Yemenis were willing to take such assurances at face value, and Islah's growing political dominance provoked a backlash from independent activists, the Houthis and the hiraak. On 24 November 2011, the day after Saleh signed the transition deal, activists stormed the stage in Change Square, pelting Islah speakers with rocks and starting fist fights. Resistance to Islah hinged on questions of religious identity, personal freedoms and the role of religion in public life. Two new 'centrist' parties had emerged in the creative energy of the uprising and its aftermath—Justice and Building, and the Homeland—espousing the idea that belief was a matter of individual conscience and Islam should not be used as a tool of political competition. Yet the same burst of political pluralism that encouraged their creation also accelerated the politicization process among activist Salafis, and gave birth to Yemen's first Salafi party, as well as the Houthis' political wing, Ansar Allah.[47]

Under the terms of the GCC transition deal and its implementing mechanism, the next parliamentary elections were scheduled to take place in February 2014 at the end of the two-year transition period. There had been no parliamentary ballot since 2003, and there was no reliable polling data to gauge Yemenis' voting intentions. The outcome would depend in part on the final form of the constitution as well as proposed revisions to the electoral laws, which could increase parliament's power and introduce proportional representation. These questions were due to be settled in a six-month nationwide consultation exercise, known as the national dialogue, preceding the redrafting of the constitution. The national dialogue would also address the future structure of the state, and consider the question of multi-party federalism or greater decentralization, in response to demands for regional autonomy from the Houthis and the hiraak.

Since spring 2011, when regime troops withdrew to Sana'a, the Houthis had been consolidating control over their own territory and learning how to run a local administration.[48] They had stumbled over their initial negotiations with international aid agencies, got drawn into clashes with Islah-aligned tribesmen in al-Jawf and briefly reignited their battle with the Salafis in Dammaj.[49] Otherwise, Saada was relatively stable and diplomats began to arrive on privately chartered flights for talks with Abdulmalik. 'The Houthis are now fully in control in Saada but at what price?' asked one Western diplomat, describing abject poverty and widespread property destruction. 'It's a sad basis for control.'[50] Yemeni critics continued to peddle the notion that the Houthis aspired to run the whole country, but diplomats suggested that Abdulmalik was angling for maximum regional autonomy.

In the south, the hiraak was still splintered, and it was unclear whether the secessionists were even willing to talk. When I met Yassin

Saeed Noman in Sana'a in spring 2012, he told me: 'The question of the future of the state is something to decide in the context of the national dialogue, with equal representation for north and south. All parties can come to the national dialogue and discuss their views, but they cannot insist on a position from outside the national dialogue.' Ali Nasser Mohammed and Haidar al-Attas had signalled their willingness to compromise, but al-Beidh—now based in Beirut—was still intransigent on the question of secession. Noman told me that the prominence of these three exiles was affecting the development of an indigenous leadership for the hiraak. He also reminded me that the traditional sultanates were more enduring structures than the PDRY, which only lasted for twenty-three years, and fragmentation within the south was highly likely, even temporarily. 'It's natural that the influence of these sultanates will resurge.'

Throughout 2012, there was a tangible sense of unfinished business. Saleh's resignation had created a rare 'open moment' to heal old wounds and resolve the quirks of previous power-shifts. Several among Yemen's political class, including Noman, saw the 2011 uprising as the latest stage in a series of progressive challenges to autocracy that had started during the Imamate and British rule, providing renewed impetus towards the formation of a modern, civil state. 'Previous revolutions in Sana'a and Aden were made by the military and political elites, but last year's uprising was created by the people,' said Noman. As such, it was the antithesis to military rule, and the army would no longer serve as a launching pad for a future president. 'The only political model that will work is a coalition government combined with genuine democratic government.'

According to Noman, even the northern tribal elite had finally reached the conclusion that the traditional patronage system was no longer viable. 'This is the key in the lock that we need in order to dismantle the establishment,' he said. Beneficiaries of the existing system stood to lose lucrative privileges in any future changes, but the revenues that underpinned their advantages were already rapidly dwindling. 'Peak oil' in 2002 had coincided with intensified elite competition, which ran in parallel with falling oil output, and the 2011 uprisings took place against the backdrop of a crisis in the patronage model. Anti-corruption campaigner Dr Saadaldeen Talib, who had left Yemen in protest at the failure of the reform agenda, was back in the country and sitting in the cabinet as minister for industry and trade. Dr Saad had once told me that corruption was so bad that Saleh and his associates were killing the chicken, not just stealing the eggs. 'The chicken is now on life support,' he told me in spring 2012.

'There has been tremendous change in the political system, but power did not go to the new forces yet. It's still the same players, to a large degree, but there will be new winners and new losers as political patronage diminishes,' argued Yemeni analyst Abdulghani al-Iryani. The breach that al-Iryani and Noman described entailed a historic shift in the national balance of power, empowering citizens in the populous and fertile lower highlands as well as the south.

However, political freedom alone would not be enough to achieve that change. It would also rely on the gradual implementation of an orthodox social contract: effective taxation, independent institutions and adequate rule of law. It further required a strategy for bridging the gap and managing the spoilers while Yemen's elite learned to play by a new set of rules. Without that, if the potential unleashed by the 2011 uprising was left unrealized, Yemenis looked set to get poorer, even hungrier and probably more violent. The gap between the quality of their lives and the lives of their GCC neighbours, where the average per capita GDP is forty times higher, would get even wider.

'If Ahmed Ali and Hamid are still in place in two years, it will mean that we've just extended the balance of power that's paralysed the country. It's a bleak scenario,' argued one Western diplomat.[51] However, for all their apparent differences, Ahmed Ali and Hamid had more in common with one another than they did with the majority of Yemenis. They both came of age in an era of globalization, which redefined the culture of the Sana'a elite. If the 1960s had introduced capitalism to Yemen, then the end of the Cold War exposed the country to the merry-go-round of neo-liberalism.[52] From the mid-1990s onwards, a gradual liberalization process—negotiated in partnership with the IMF, as part of a wider economic and administrative reform programme—opened up a raft of new domestic business opportunities, which grew more and more lucrative.[53]

Parallel deregulation in global financial markets ushered in unprecedented opportunities for capital flight, mostly to banking hubs in the Gulf states and Western secrecy jurisdictions. Global financial liberalization made it 'increasingly easy to transfer large financial assets abroad', and provided perverse incentives that undermined 'elite interests in building effective public authority'.[54] A new ruling cadre came to define Saleh's era, where competitors flaunted their wealth and conspicuous consumption as an indicator of their privilege and status. In the immediate wake of Saleh's resignation, there was little sign of change: the construction of new villas in Hadda continued apace, and these extravagant bolt-holes for the wealthy were getting bigger and bigger.

14

INTERREGNUM

HADI'S FAILURE AND THE RISE OF THE HOUTHIS

In spring 2012, in the aftermath of Hadi's February inauguration as president, I struggled to shake a subtle feeling of unease during my routine car journeys around Sana'a. Compared with six months earlier, at the height of the uprising and the zenith of factional violence, the city was calm. Shelling had stopped and there were far fewer roadblocks, but the security situation was niggling me. Carjacking was rising, and the new practice of contract kidnapping—where criminal gangs seized foreign hostages as commodities to raise lucrative ransoms—was threatening to replace the traditional system of tribal hostage-taking.[1]

The courts were on strike, and the police were hardly anywhere to be seen.[2] The rule of law seemed paper-thin. Once or twice, I caught sight of the UN special envoy, Jamal Benomar's convoy, flanked by gun trucks, speeding between meetings. At times, it seemed that Benomar's presence in Yemen, and the international community's collective insistence on the success of the transition, were the only things keeping the process on track—a vital but elaborate multilateral confidence trick. There was still a sense that large numbers of Yemenis themselves were crossing their fingers and hoping for the best.

The 2011 uprising and the 2012 transition had exposed and ruptured the underlying power-sharing agreement that held Saleh's regime together, for so long. There was no longer any certainty about how Yemen's competing interests would agree to hold themselves in a state of equilibrium. The national dialogue was supposed to provide an opportunity for all groups that perceived themselves to be politically and socially marginalized under the old order to press for renegotiation. Several prominent politicians espoused their vision of a power-sharing coalition within a stronger parliamentary system, effectively subjugating the principle of balance to the institutions of the state, albeit within a less centralized republic. But even if this could be agreed in principle, could it actually be implemented?

Yemenis often told me that they needed time to resolve their political differences and make slow progress towards the establishment of a civil state, but the grave condition of the economy did not allow for the luxury of time. It was unclear whether Hadi himself had sufficient political capital to steward the national dialogue and oversee subsequent constitutional revisions that would alter the structure of the state, while keeping Yemen's chaotic proclivities in check. During the early months of Hadi's presidency, there was a notable resurgence of atavistic identities that had been contained—more or less—under Saleh's leadership, and palpable anxiety that the state itself (or, rather, the regime) was no longer strong enough to arbitrate. Future patterns of confrontation seemed likely to involve localized clashes between competing non-state actors, such as the Houthis and Islah-aligned militias, or rival power centres in the south.

At the same time, these local tensions were complicated by renewed anxiety about external interference in Yemen. Just as Egypt's Nasser had positioned himself to benefit from the 1962 power-shift in Sana'a and the ensuing disquiet in Riyadh, Iran was now said to be taking advantage of Saleh's departure in order to stoke fears of a proxy conflict with Saudi Arabia. If concerns about Iranian involvement in Yemen had previously been overplayed, it was now a growing reality: Teheran was financing youth activists in Taiz and Aden, while the Houthis faced renewed allegations of Iranian support.[3] Speaking during a high-profile visit to Washington DC in September 2012, Hadi accused Iran of seeking a foothold in Yemen in order to undermine the transition process and create a 'climate of chaos and violence'. Initially, at least, Teheran's piecemeal pay-outs seemed to fall a long way short of a coherent agenda in Yemen but, nevertheless, Hadi's comments reassured his jittery backers in Riyadh.[4]

During the same speech in Washington, Hadi had praised the precision of US drone strikes, acknowledging that they formed an essential component of the campaign against AQAP.[5] The following month, White House counterterrorism adviser John Brennan revealed he had personally played a prominent role in crafting a 'joint US-Saudi policy' to bring a 'more cooperative government to power' in Yemen, by replacing Saleh with Hadi. Brennan acknowledged the 'upstream' problems of poverty and poor governance that led to 'downstream' radicalization, and argued that the USA should offer economic assistance to buttress its growing military and intelligence presence in Yemen.[6]

However, Yemeni public opinion was largely hostile to the US-targeted killing programme, and to some, it looked like the USA was backing Hadi in return for a free hand on drone strikes. Beneficiaries of the new power-sharing arrangement were reluctant to criticize US policy on drones and counterterrorism, and many civil society activists were starting to describe the transitional government as an international protectorate arrangement. Brennan seemed blind to the fact that lack of political legitimacy also created an 'upstream' problem, which would lead to wider political instability over the longer term. Testifying before a US Senate Judiciary subcommittee on the use of drones in 2013, Yemeni youth activist Farea al-Muslimi warned that every US 'tactical success is at the expense of creating more strategic problems'.[7]

If the US administration seemed poised to replicate its previous mistakes over counterterrorism cooperation, the wider governance agenda was also proving similarly problematic. The post-transition economy was still dominated by the same eight or ten key families, with current or former ties to Saleh. Western donors continued to call for governance reforms without fully allowing for the risk that they might inadvertently entrench one regime faction over another in the context of trying to sponsor reform, rather than successfully reframing the system altogether. Meanwhile, as direct political and economic competition between rival factions continued unabated, wealthy Yemenis carried on transferring their assets out of the country to safer havens. In summer 2012, one airline passenger spotted four suitcases strapped into business-class seats on a commercial flight leaving Sana'a, supposedly transporting hard cash to the Gulf.[8] It seemed that as long as the cabinet continued to flunk its economy scorecard, the private sector saw little incentive to invest in Yemen.

Public anger about elite corruption in Yemen mirrored broader regional discontent—about greedy leaders, inadequate livelihoods and the uneven benefits of neo-liberalism—that had underpinned the wider 'Arab Spring'. Yemen was the only 'least developed' country among Middle Eastern states to be affected during the 2011 uprisings.[9] However, a similar cocktail of inequality, capital flight and frustrated aspirations brought protestors on to the streets in countries spanning every income ranking: Egypt and Syria are classified as countries of 'medium human development'; Libya and Tunisia are 'highly developed' countries; while Bahrain is 'very highly' developed. The same issues—albeit presented in a different context—also galvanized the Western Occupy movement.

The geographical spread of the 2011 uprisings suggested a systemic problem rather than a series of localized flashpoints, highlighting the contentious relationship between states and markets in the wake of the global financial crisis. During the previous decade, the lack of international action to oversee financial regulation and constrain criminal activity in fragile states such as Yemen had created a situation in which unaccountable elites were able to exploit the resources of the countries they ruled with impunity. Tax havens (also known as secrecy jurisdictions) 'made it easier and cheaper to hide illicit incomes, and thus [...] increased incentives to earn them'.[10]

Fragile states were 'particularly vulnerable to the dynamics and risks involved in the process of globalisation because of their generally weak governance systems'; in short, they became 'risk dumps' for structural weaknesses in the international economic system.[11] In that sense, corruption, poverty and instability in Yemen were symptoms of a much broader problem. However, it would take collective international leadership at the level of the G20 to change this state of affairs, because financial globalisation had also outstripped the capacity of national governments— acting alone—to respond adequately to the challenge.

In 2011, as throughout the previous century, Yemen's latest power shock took place in parallel with larger, longer-term regional and global changes, demonstrating that contemporary domestic politics could be affected by international factors, such as food price spikes, media deregulation and the growth of mobile phone ownership, as well as the trend towards increased concentration of global poverty in fragile states.[12] Hadi's accession to the position of president in early 2012 was just the latest chapter in a much longer process of Yemeni leaders forging—and losing—authority as a result of this interplay between domestic, regional and international pressures. During the Cold War, revolution, decolonization and unification were the milestones of Yemen's political and historical development, followed by crony capitalism, organized crime and sham democracy in the post-Cold War, neo-liberal era.

As long as global financial structures remained unchanged, Yemen's future leaders would likely struggle to break the existing model of corruption, because the opportunities for personal enrichment through capital flight could prove too tempting. As a result, it seemed that Yemeni youth from their teens to their early thirties, who took to the streets in spring 2011 to protest against corruption—the catalyst for the subsequent wave of political upheaval—faced a lifelong struggle to hold their leaders to account. Veteran leaders of the established political parties continued to resist effective calls for reform from youth wings within their own parties, and youth activists across the board complained that despite creating the initial momentum behind the uprising, they were excluded from much of the deal-making that followed.

However, the street protests also represented a broader social and cultural shift in Yemeni society, beyond the regime's control.[13] They amounted to an assertion of rights by a generation that had 'different attitudes and aspirations' from their fathers and a rebellion against the traditional 'repressive, authoritarian' mind-set that had implications beyond the political sphere.[14] The 2011 uprising was a formative experience for an entire generation, spanning the social and political spectrum, but with the exception of several capable and well-educated technocrats who rose swiftly to prominence in the transitional government, youth activists were unlikely to find themselves in positions of power—as businessmen, civil society leaders, ministers and opposition politicians—for several decades.

Equally it was uncertain whether Saleh's departure from power would eventually signal the demise of the military republic, a model that had dominated regional politics for so long. Hadi's decision to increase military spending in his first budget, in 2013, suggested that— in the short term, at least—the new president was still playing by the same old rules as his former boss, even if he was rewarding new benefi- ciaries. (Hadi is only three years younger than Saleh, and served as his vice-president for two decades. They both belong to a generation that learned the political ropes during the 1960s and 1970s.)

During his first year in power, Hadi had shown himself to be acutely dependent on the support and reinforcement of the international com- munity. His grip on the military was partial and tenuous.[15] In spring 2013, he formally disbanded both the Republican Guard and the First Armoured Division, and he sent Ahmed Ali abroad as ambassador to the United Arab Emirates, while appointing Ali Mohsin as a presiden- tial advisor. In moving to clip the wings of his two rivals, Hadi attempted to bolster his own hand, promote his own allies and bring the military under the institutional control of the presidency and the ministry of defence.[16]

However, far from consolidating the ministry's authority, Hadi's mili- tary restructuring efforts led to further fragmentation in the real and effective chain of command. Ahmed Ali's private patronage networks survived many of these changes, and the International Crisis Group noted that Hadi risked sowing the seeds of a new conflict in the 'absence of an inclusive political pact'.[17] Briefing the UN Security Council in June 2013, Benomar warned that, despite participating in the political pro- cess, 'key political factions remain armed and appear to be amassing more weapons, creating the conditions for further violence and instabil- ity'.[18] At the behest of his international backers, Hadi's ambitious pro- gramme of security sector reform amounted to little more than unpick- ing the fiefdoms of the Saleh era and stoking intense competition among a growing number of veteran and aspiring warlords.

* * *

Sana'a's Movenpick hotel sits atop a prominent ridge overlooking the old city. Panoramic glass windows in the lobby coffee lounge offer spectacular views across the sprawling capital, facing west towards the mountain pass that marks the start of the road to Hodeidah and the Red Sea coast. In March 2013, Hadi chose the Movenpick to host the six-month national dialogue conference, in pursuit of a stable and enduring collective bargain intended to ease the way forward. In the event, the Movenpick's cavernous banqueting rooms played host to the dialogue for nearly a year. A series of working groups focused on Saada, the south and transitional justice, among other issues. More than 500 hundred delegates gathered from across the country to discuss the future structure of the state, under the de facto stewardship of Western diplomats and the United Nations.[19] Delegates received a generous stipend, at a time when increasing numbers of households were drifting towards breadline status, or falling further beneath the breadline.

In underwriting the national dialogue, Yemen's donors established their own patronage structure, competing with indigenous patronage structures in a contentious political environment where no paymaster had overall control. Nevertheless, the international community—notably the EU and the UN—went out on a limb to promote the inclusion of previously marginalized groups, including youth and women, and the dialogue amounted to the most diverse and accessible forum in Yemen's history. Hooria Mashoor, minister for justice and human rights, believed the conference 'voiced our national consensus because all political and social constituencies were represented in the talks.'[20]

Human rights activist Baraa Shiban, who became a prominent critic of the US drones programme, participated in the dialogue as a member of the transitional justice working group. During 2011, he had helped to run a media centre in Change Square and in 2012, he worked on a nationwide initiative to organise representation for the independent youth. Many of his revolutionary comrades were reluctant to join the dialogue, on the basis they had already rejected the GCC agreement, but Baraa had a pragmatic streak. 'I liked the idea of being an activist when the uprising started, but during the course of the national dialogue, I discovered how politics works. I learned that if you don't take part, someone else will make the decisions on your behalf. I also learned how to make trade-offs and build alliances.'[21]

For example. Baraa's transitional justice team struck a quid-pro-quo deal with the working group on the south. In return for the southerners' support for a recommendation that the new constitution contain a clause prohibiting anyone with a recent military career running for president (designed—in part—to prevent Ahmed Ali coming to power), the transitional justice working group agreed to support the southerners' demand to hold a referendum on the future of the south. However, the deal was struck even as the national dialogue was foundering over the question of who could negotiate on the southerners' behalf, as most *hirak* hardliners refused to engage or consider any measure short of independence.

According to Baraa, Hadi 'could have done more to get the right people from the south around the table'. Southerners who did attend the talks faced pressure to compromise in order to keep the political process moving, but they also bore the brunt of hostile criticism from their compatriots for making too many concessions. 'As time went by, they suspected that Hadi had made false promises to get them on board and that decisions regarding the future of the south were being kicked into the long grass. They concluded they were legitimising a process that was selling out their interests,' Bara'a said.

During the summer, some southern representatives withdrew from talks and threatened to boycott the rest of the dialogue, amid rolling protests in the south. In order to stave off the threat of secession, Hadi formed an emergency committee of sixteen members, with equal representation from north and south, and tasked them with negotiating a compromise solution. Committee members reached agreement on a commitment to a future federal state, but they were unable to resolve diverging views regarding division of resources, boundaries and the optimum number of federal regions.[22] (Among the options on the table, the committee considered and rejected a system of six regions.)

If federalism seemed like a tidy solution to the country's problem of gradual fragmentation in the eyes of international advisors who were drafted in to support the UN-led transition process, many Yemenis took a more cautious approach.[23] After all, the question of how to divide power and resources between Sana'a and Aden had led to civil war in 1994—and then, as now, southern politicians disagreed among themselves over the preferred constitutional formula, with those most amenable to Sana'a advocating federal reform rather than separation. Moreover, southerners were not the only ones with suspicious minds. In October, the Houthis confronted the Salafis in Dammaj, and began moving south towards Sana'a, where they clashed with militias aligned to Islah and the al-Ahmar family—and won.[24]

262

By the end of the year there was still no consensus on the future structure of the state among national dialogue delegates, even as the clock was counting down towards the end of the two-year transition period, in February 2014. The G10—a group of ten ambassadors in Sana'a, who were marshals of the transition process—was putting Hadi under pressure to bring the dialogue to a close.[25] However, in the hurry to conclude the talks, there was no time to harmonise the many recommendations produced by the various working groups, and make the necessary trade-offs that would be required to achieve a true corporate consensus.[26] As a result, one sceptical observer claimed that the dialogue had 'achieved everything, and nothing'.[27]

When Hadi oversaw the final plenary session of the national dialogue conference at the end of January 2014, the working groups presented him with nearly 1,800 recommendations.[28] With transition politics still in an open state of flux and military restructuring only partially underway, the conference agreed to extend Hadi's two-year caretaker presidency to allow for the outstanding elements of the GCC agreement—the drafting of a new constitution, a constitutional referendum, and elections—to be completed.[29] Diplomats were quick to pat themselves on the back and apply for promotion. There was only one problem: national dialogue delegates—and their diplomatic sponsors—assumed that the logic of institutional supremacy would prevail, but they had proved unable reconstitute a state inside a five-star hotel. Outside the Movenpick, Hadi had no monopoly over the use of force.

Since the start of Hadi's presidency, security conditions had gradually deteriorated, with an uptick in kidnappings and assassinations—a trend that would continue in the weeks and months after the conclusion of the talks.[30] Most of Yemen's armed groups had sent representatives or proxies to the Movenpick hotel, but they did not trust the dialogue process to protect their interests. While conference delegates debated the ideal structure of the future state, the warlords continued to settle scores. Local militias were exploiting the 'power vacuum created by the transition to gain territorial control before the new system of federal governance [was] implemented, allowing them to guide the process at a regional level'.[31]

In such a volatile environment, Hadi's next move was the political equivalent of lighting a cigarette at the scene of a fuel spill, and throwing the smouldering butt to the ground. Less than a month after the completion of the national dialogue, which had placed such great emphasis on inclusion and consensus, Hadi gave his approval to plans for a six-region federal system that were drawn up by a hand-picked special committee.[32] This new blueprint gave Sana'a and Aden self-governing status, while hiving off the country's oil and gas reserves into two separate southern regions, Hadramawt and Sheba.

Many southerners resisted splitting up the south, while Houthi leaders strongly objected to the inclusion of Saada in the new land-locked region of Azal. Azal also comprised the highland governorates of Amran, Sana'a and Dhamar, a formation that would deny the Houthis control over the Red Sea coast to west, cut them off from natural resources to the east, and fence them up against the Saudi border to the north. If the substance of Hadi's decision-making process was unacceptable, so was the timing. The Houthis were still mourning the death of Ahmed Sharif al-Din, who had been assassinated on his way to the Movenpick for the national dialogue's final plenary session.

The UN had engaged a number of technical advisors to support the process of drafting the new constitution but according to one international advisor, there were 'too many cooks in the kitchen.' In addition, poor translation of the national dialogue outcomes from Arabic to English created confusion among the technical experts. 'I was genuinely puzzled how the Houthis ended up in the same region as Dhamar, as everything would have suggested otherwise. If I was really interested in promoting stability, I would not have configured a new federal system in this way.' (He added, 'after many years working on these issues, I'm coming to understand that technical advice is always used to serve political interests.')[33]

Some blamed Hadi's personal failings, others thought he had no chance from the outset, as the requisite structures were not in place.[34] When the constitutional drafting committee eventually completed its work in January 2015, Yemen had the most progressive charter in the region but little means of implementing it.[35] External advisors had wrongly assumed there was a viable state to be reformed, rather than competing patronage networks operating under the camouflage of weak and illusory state institutions. One Western analyst noted: 'Diplomats, foreign advisers and Yemeni politicians devoted more energy to selling utopian long-term solutions than to addressing a deteriorating political, economic, security and humanitarian environment.'[36]

Since 2011, none of the key players had been certain of their real weight relative to the others, yet they understood they would have to keep testing each other until all sides were convinced of the new equilibrium. While the country's institutional parameters were still being debated, the warlords had no need to provoke a decisive confrontation. They could afford to meddle and wait, but as soon as Hadi showed his hand on the question of federalism, they were ready to move. As one veteran Yemeni politician, a stalwart of the Saleh era, told me: 'The biggest mistake the donors made was in thinking they could promote inclusive politics with the old regime players still in place.'[37]

* * *

In summer 2014, it was clear to almost everyone that the national dialogue's promise of political inclusion had been too good to be true, and the transition pact was crumbling. The atmosphere in the capital was increasingly edgy. In May, a French security contractor working for the EU was shot and killed in Sana'a, leading to the evacuation of EU diplomats and Brussels' decision to shut the EU delegation.[38] Street riots broke out in July, in response to the government's decision to cut fuel subsidies.[39] Diplomats were working hard to shore up Hadi's position, even as people complained that '[o]ne crony kleptocratic elite had made way for another.'[40] Yemenis wondered where all the donors' aid money was going, when they could see no results.

By this point, I had not been in the country for over a year but I continued to work on Yemen, as an independent consultant. I had been sceptical about the transition process from the outset, and I was preoccupied by the unravelling security conditions, including the spike in kidnappings.[41] I remained in contact with close friends and I heard from them how the situation was sliding out of control. In meetings with Western donors and diplomats, I repeatedly raised questions about 'risk mitigation' and 'contingency planning', but it seemed there was no plan B (or, at least, not one that ambassadors and desk officers would admit to). The arrogance and apparent lack of foresight among some senior decision makers, still riding on the success of negotiating the transition agreement and the completion of the national dialogue, was staggering.[42]

Over the course of previous months, the Houthis had been making gradual progress south from Saada, passing through the towns of Houth, Khamir and Raydah.[43] In July, they took Amran city, some 50 km north of Sanaa, where they seized the former CSF camp (renamed Special Security Forces by Hadi) and the headquarters of the 310th Armoured Brigade, and killed the brigade commander Hamid al-Qushaibi, an ally of Ali Mohsin.[44] Having negotiated a ceasefire agreement, which effectively consolidated the Houthis' gains, Hadi then turned up in Amran, 'and said all sides had agreed to allow the state to retake control'.[45] In August, having passed further south through Hamdan district, the Houthis set up camp on the outskirts of Sana'a—ostensibly, in protest against Hadi's removal of the fuel subsidy.[46]

During September 2014, the Houthis overran Sana'a city and Hadi found himself besieged. The Houthis did not overtly seize power but their presence in the capital triggered a political crisis that lead to the rapid negotiation of a new political charter, the Peace and National Partnership Agreement, which left Hadi in place as president. The formation of the new cabinet that followed this agreement—under the leadership of prime minister Khaled Bahah—was broadly inclusive, non-partisan and technocratic, allowing for greater participation by the Houthis and southerners.[47] However, ministers soon found that Houthi 'supervisors', deployed to monitor activities in every ministry, treated them with suspicion. 'You couldn't even walk into the building, let alone get the supervisor to rubber-stamp your official documents, if the Houthis didn't trust you,' one cabinet minister said.[48]

Until that point, Yemen's transition process had been celebrated in diplomatic circles as a regional success story—a rare positive outcome from the 'Arab Spring'—but in just a few days in September, the Houthis overturned many of these previous assumptions.[49] The Houthis' ambition to offer basic security, and their promise to safeguard the integrity of state institutions and restore the traditional status of the *sayyid* class came after decades in which the social authority of both *sayyids* and sheikhs had diminished—the former displaced by a previous revolution, and the latter coopted by Saleh's patronage system. As symbolic gestures of social justice, the Houthis also promised to put a stop to diesel smuggling and reverse the government's recent hike in diesel prices, claiming that the people should not suffer for the profiteering of a corrupt elite.

As populist measures, these were well conceived and there was some initial support for Houthis' reforms. Many people in the north declared support for the Houthis, especially those from *sayyid* families, but it was hard to escape the impression that the inclusive political space created by the youth-led uprising was becoming increasingly tenuous and precarious. In October, London-based conflict prevention NGO Saferworld released an online video showcasing their work with Yemeni youth activists. One activist, Muna, said: 'There is pessimism. It is a shock when someone's expectation levels have been raised and they realise that in reality they have not been given even a quarter of their goals.' She added: 'Somehow, society started blaming us (the youth) and saying that we are the cause of this current situation.'

Muna and others in the Yemeni-made video spoke openly of their depression and frustration. With the exception of a small cadre of young politicians and civil society representatives who had attended the national dialogue, the majority of young people who took to the streets in 2011 had no outlet for their political emotions, and little patience for the slow process of building capable institutions. Even many of those who had participated the national dialogue were losing faith in the political process. They feared that corruption, hardship, and high levels of youth unemployment would continue.

Perhaps these fears went some way to account for the anecdotal rise in drug use among young Yemenis since 2011. Friends in contact with Taizis and Adenis told me about the ready availability of pills, but couldn't tell me exactly what they were. A researcher who went to Taiz in 2014 to assess residents' perceptions of changing local security conditions revealed that young people had resorted to hiring their motorbikes as taxis, including to hit-men who needed wheels for drive-by assassinations (which were happening all-too frequently in Taiz, at that time), and they either received pills as payment in kind, or used their cash payments to buy pills, which they combined with qat, or took as a stand-alone drug.[50]

Amid all the uncertainty and political turmoil, those blessed with creative talent and sufficient resources were still able to capitalise on the opportunities that social media afforded for networking and self-expression. In December 2014, an independent media collective called Support Yemen released an emotive short film, *The Melody of our*

Alienation, which featured the hypnotic voice of a young woman activist reciting the words of contemporary Yemeni poet Abdel Aziz al-Maqaleh.[51] 'Has nonsense become common sense?' she asked. 'Has the non-rational overwhelmed the rational?'

Al-Maqaleh's poetry is a love song to old Sana'a, and a lament to the comfort and security that the city has historically offered to its visitors and residents. Sorrow and despair pervade the film, along with a menacing sense that darker times lie ahead. The mood is introspective, even as daily life continues amid the political troubles. A young man watches scenes from the battlefield on a flat-screen television. An elderly woman carries a shopping bag to her home. Children play in the market-gardens and streets of the city. Each face turning towards the camera seems to ask the same troubling question: 'In whom—or what—should I now place my trust and hope?'

Director Abdulrahman Hussein described his motivation in making the film to express the anxiety that so many Yemenis were feeling at that time. 'I had the sense that something was not as it seems. I was uncomfortable, and I was scared of the future. When I looked ahead, I saw a coming storm. I made the film because I didn't know what else to do. I'm not a writer or a politician. I wanted to represent those feelings.'

He added: 'To me, Sana'a is the most beautiful city in the world. For hundreds of years, people have walked through the same streets and alleyways, and just by entering the old city you become part of that ancient history. It's a place of kindness, generosity, and community. I was terrified of seeing all that destroyed. At the same time, the bricks of these old tower-houses still remain, like they are telling you that goodness can endure. I wanted to remind people of our Yemeni heritage, and the old city as a metaphor for our times.'

* * *

Four years earlier, when I had visited Yahya Houthi in Germany at the end of 2010, he had warned me that the Houthis would march on Sana'a if they lost confidence in the prospect of fair elections and a just government. He also predicted that the Houthis would emerge as Yemen's strongest armed group, if Saleh's regime eventually lost power. By the end of 2014, Yahya's prescient words appeared to be coming true. It seemed the Houthis had successfully consolidated their position as a dominant martial force, while political churn—and military restructuring—had weakened their former adversaries.

As soon as the Houthis arrived in Sana'a in September 2014, they set about making the most of their new-found advantages. They made a beeline for Ali Mohsin's former military headquarters, the site of the First Armoured Division base, and the neighbouring university, Al-Iman. They ransacked his private houses, revenging years of war in Saada, and opened them up for the public's amusement.[52] They drove Ali Mohsin out of home and country, who fled to Saudi Arabia, where he Tweeted photos of himself from the hajj. (In 1962, a republican general had ousted the ruling Imam, who escaped to Saada to mount a counter-offensive with Saudi support; half a century later, a Saada militia had marched on Sana'a to oust a prominent republican general.)

Hamid Al-Ahmar had already left the country before the Houthi advance on the capital, and Houthi militia swiftly occupied his palaces in Sana'a. Hamid's political powerbase had been successively weakened by Al-Saud's decision to brand the Muslim Brotherhood as a terrorist organisation a few months earlier, as part of their regional counter-move against political Islam, and also by his family's defeat at the hands of the Houthis in Amran. Once the seat of the al-Ahmar family's considerable prestige and power, the mighty Hashid tribal confederation had disintegrated as a result of internecine squabbles, in a matter of years—first between the al-Ahmars and the Salehs, and later between the al-Ahmars and Houthi supporters.

Ironically, Saleh worked behind the scenes to facilitate the Houthis' accession of Sana'a because their ascendancy also contributed to the rout of his own opponents. Despite having spent the best part of a decade on opposing sides in Saada's brutal civil war, Saleh and the Houthis appeared to have found common cause, in wanting to humiliate Hamid and Ali Mohsin. During 2014, as the Houthis progressed from Saada to Amran, and from Amran to Sana'a, Saleh's friends and tribal allies in these areas either put up no resistance, or provided material assistance.[53] Some even fought alongside the Houthis against Islah-aligned militias.[54] In October, Saleh's supporters were found to be manning 'Houthi' checkpoints in Sana'a.[55]

In November 2014, in what seemed to some observers as a panic measure that was both long overdue, and likely to backfire, the UN

Security Council and the US Treasury slapped sanctions on two senior Houthi commanders, Abdulkhaliq al-Houthi and Abdullah Yahya al-Hakim. Twitter joked that the only assets the two men owned was pay-as-you-go mobile phone credit. More serious, perhaps, was Saleh's inclusion on the blacklist, on the grounds that he had conspired to undermine the government, colluded with the Houthis, and used AQAP operatives to carry out targeted assassinations.[56] However, it was three years since diplomats had first threatened Saleh with the prospect of sanctions, which allowed for plenty of time to hide his assets.

Far from driving the final nail into his political coffin, sanctions boosted Saleh's popularity and gave him an excuse to visibly reactivate his powerbase. Saleh swiftly denounced Hadi as a traitor for succumbing to foreign interference by agreeing to sanctions, and expelled Hadi from the GPC—the political party that Saleh still controlled. On Friday 7 November, as if to demonstrate the extent of his enduring influence, Saleh addressed a crowd of passionate men and women from the balcony of his Sana'a home, speaking with a microphone to make himself heard above the roar of his chanting supporters.

Saleh is a natural showman, but, even as president, Hadi kept a low profile. In a political culture where leadership correlates with charisma, and power is forged through personal relationships, Hadi had no innate talent for the job.[57] Hadi was up against the maestro, and his personal failings drove many wavering supporters, particularly disgruntled northern sheikhs who found themselves displaced by the course of transition politics, to turn to Saleh or the Houthis instead.[58] Many northern tribes began to bet on a future Saleh-Houthi alliance, to reclaim what they rightfully saw as theirs.[59] As the Houthis consolidated their control over Sana'a and moved south of the capital, ostensibly in pursuit of AQAP, they were 'backed by military units loyal to the Saleh family'—notably, by former members of Ahmed Ali's Republican Guard.[60] In my conversations with people in Saleh's network, I thought I detected a tentative sense of optimism that their return to power might be imminent.[61]

Set against this voracious, well-armed alliance of sheikhs and warriors, Hadi's government of technocrats looked exceedingly vulnerable. At stake was the new constitution, which the drafting committee was trying to finalise with the support of international technical experts. During the national dialogue, the Houthis had agreed to the principle of a federal state but they refused to consent to the six-region model that Hadi subsequently championed. Unfamiliar with the niceties of diplomacy and suspicious of the interests of international actors in Yemen, the Houthis consistently felt themselves to be on the backfoot throughout the transition process.[62] They were repeatedly assured that their concerns would be addressed before the final stages, but they did not trust their political counterparts to play fair.[63]

Hadi had already failed to deliver on a number of substantive commitments agreed during the national dialogue, and the Houthis that feared this pattern would be repeated with the new constitution.[64] When the drafting committee completed its work in January 2015 and sent the resulting document to the president's office for ratification—complete with a clause stating 'the Federal Republic of Yemen consists of six regions', and provisions to establish the contentious new Azal region—the Houthis decided they were running out of options.[65] They abducted Hadi's chief of staff, Ahmed bin Mubarak, when he left his home to present the new constitution to Hadi. As an extra precaution, the Houthis then put Hadi, Bahah and several cabinet ministers under house arrest. The government promptly resigned.

This awkward sequence of events triggered a constitutional crisis, as there was no president to accept the cabinet's resignation, and the Houthis prevented parliament—which was last elected in 2003—from convening to accept the president's resignation.[66] In early February, the Houthis took advantage of the ensuing confusion to form a new executive body, the Supreme Revolutionary Committee, with Mohammed Ali al-Houthi at its head, and declare themselves in constitutional control of the government. Yahya Houthi, who was now back in Sana'a, told the BBC: 'This declaration will found a new era, an historic state, politically and economically, in the history of the Yemeni people. This state has been in the making for the last four years, and the beginning of all this is the declaration of the constitution.'[67]

Until this point, the Houthis had only limited experience of cooperating with international aid agencies in Saada, few diplomatic skills, and barely any experience of government. After ten years of war in Saada, their mind-set was paranoid and defensive. According to one well-placed Sana'a observer, the leadership likely intended to use bin

Mubarak's kidnapping as a traditional 'tactic to force Hadi into negotiations'.[68] According to the same source, Hadi and bin Mubarak were also likely willing to negotiate, but first they wanted to manipulate bureaucratic procedure as much as they could.[69] However, neither side accepted the rules of brinkmanship by which their opponents were playing and, on both sides, there was a chronic lack of trust. When Hadi escaped to Aden at the end of February, dressed as a woman, it was unclear whether history was repeating itself as tragedy or farce.

In Aden, Hadi immediately rescinded his resignation and declared Aden the temporary capital, calling his cabinet to return to work. Meanwhile, in Sana'a, the new Houthi administration was embarking on a zealous purification programme, designed to eliminate corruption. As the Houthis gradually consolidated their control over government ministries, they went on a hunt for records of state that they could use as evidence against their rivals. In a scene reminiscent of George de Carvalho's 1962 meeting with General Sallal during Yemen's previous revolution, Iraqi journalist Ghaith Abdul Ahad described an encounter with Mohammed Ali Houthi at the Supreme Revolutionary Committee headquarters:[70]

> A big man with a permanent infant-like smile, he crouched cross-legged behind a low table, sifting through documents. A Kalashnikov rested against the wall next to him. He opened a plastic shopping bag, pulled out a thick pile of papers and started throwing them on the floor in front of him, like a dealer cutting a new set of cards. Each sheet represented a corruption case that was draining Yemen's coffers and putting another burden on his shoulders.
>
> … Everything had been gathered in the one plastic bag and now lay on the floor at his feet. 'When we entered Sanaa, we never expected to be solving all these problems,' Mohammed Ali told me. 'There is an octopus of corruption in the ministries. It's trying to prevent us from working. But we have an intelligence network that sends us reports of corruption from inside the ministries themselves. People come to us with their problems. We don't charge anything: this is pure volunteer work. We want to solve problems quickly. Those who work in government want to delay in order to make money.'

Back in September, when the Houthis had taken control of Sana'a, several analysts and academics who had been following Yemen for many years—including me—assumed they were positioning for a longer-term deal and a controlling stake in government, rather than a front-of-house position. Even in January, many of us held to this position—with hindsight, perhaps naively. In February, one Houthi official in Sana'a told the *New York Times* that the group was 'eager to share power', and denied that they had carried out a coup.[71] He said: 'Ansar Allah does not want anything more than partnership, not control'.

Despite their ringing 'death to America' catchphrase, the Houthis also stressed that they wanted to normalise relations with the US administration.[72] The Houthis and the White House shared the same strategic objective of defeating AQAP, and the Houthis represented an effective fighting force that was motivated to tackle Sunni extremists for their own existential purposes, yet they objected to US drone strikes as a violation of Yemeni sovereignty; the Houthis wanted to take the fight to al-Qaeda themselves. However, in February, US diplomats pulled their embassy team out of the country, establishing temporary representation in Jeddah, and the Europeans followed suit.[73] The Houthis retaliated by seizing some US embassy vehicles.[74]

Why did things go so wrong? It's possible that the national dialogue gave the Houthis a taste for the national stage, after ten years of political exclusion. It's equally possible that Saleh stoked their hubris because he calculated their political style would make his family look reasonable by comparison. Saleh did not hold an outright military advantage and he also feared a backlash from the international community, if he tried to make a direct comeback. Rather than lead the fight himself, it suited him to exploit the Houthis because it fulfilled his personal goals and played to their own sense of purpose.[75]

A number of credible sources claimed that the Saleh-Houthi power-grab had been in the making for several years—with initial channels of communication between Saleh and Abdulmalik established through intermediaries, and direct cooperation occurring only after the Houthis took Amran.[76] Others suggested a gradual evolution of ties, with the Houthis only becoming aware of Saleh's role as a benefactor as late as summer 2014.[77] Maybe the Houthis had, indeed, been planning to act unilaterally since 2010, as Yahya had said. Either way, the government's decision to resign in January 2015, after failing to stabilise the economy and implement the national dialogue outcomes, gave the Houthis an excuse to take power. 'They were handed the country on a platter. They couldn't have asked for more', said one Yemeni businessman.[78]

As time went on, the Houthis gradually overreached themselves and misjudged the public mood. In doing so, they lost a significant amount of popular support. Fears of a Shia conspiracy appeared to be confirmed when an Iranian MP declared that Sana'a constituted the fourth Arab capital to have fallen into Tehran's hands, along with Beirut, Damascus, and Baghdad.[79] When the Houthis were slammed for backtracking on negotiated agreements, and enforcing oppressive social policies, including the arbitrary detention of Sunni Shafai and Salafi preachers, they persecuted their critics. They also retaliated by kidnapping increasing numbers of independent activists and journalists, accusing them of spying for the West.

Baraa Shiban, who was openly critical of the Houthis' human rights abuses, decided to leave the country for his own safety. During a London meeting in 2015, he told me: 'The Houthis have a fundamentalist mindset—it's "either you're with us or against us". There has never been any chance that they would act in good faith. Since they took Sana'a, the Houthis have instigated the same practices of kidnapping and torture that Saleh used but the Houthis' rules of detention aren't clear. In Saleh's time, I could go to a police station and negotiate to have detainees released; I knew how and when to interact with the authorities. Now, with the Houthis, no one understands how their system of repression operates.'

Baraa, like many independent youth activists, was dismayed by the Houthis' authoritarian shift, and the sectarian rhetoric with which they justified their assaults on the tribes in Sunni-majority governorates such as al-Bayda, by claiming that they were attacking al-Qaeda. In Sana'a itself, Houthi propaganda was rife. They plastered their slogans, and images of their martyred leader Hussein al-Houthi, on walls across the city. In this increasingly sectarian atmosphere, two pairs of suicide bombers targeted two Sana'a mosques—supposedly frequented by Houthis—during midday prayers on Friday 20 March, killing more than 130 people and wounded several hundred others. The Islamic State of Iraq and the Levant (ISIS) claimed responsibility.[80] Within a week, the Salehs and the Houthis had captured Aden, and Yemen was at war with its neighbours.

15

SALEH'S REVENGE

THE RETURN TO POWER

In the closing years of Saleh's presidency, there were times when I found myself in a Sana'a traffic jam staring through a taxi window, people-watching. A silent observer in an urban scene, I was surrounded by beggars, street vendors, and school children. Out on the streets, there was an evident pattern to daily life but, as a political analyst, I was already predicting that this order would fall apart. 'What makes me so sure that I'm right?' I would ask myself.

Sitting in the back of a Toyota Cressida, I would revisit my line of reasoning: that falling oil production, combined with weak institutions, endemic corruption, political stasis, chronic regional interference, and intensifying competition between elite factions were set to bring the country to its knees. All in all, I found the logic of my own argument too sound to abandon. So the next question I asked myself was: 'if things do fall apart, what will it look like?'

By the end of 2015, I had an answer to that question. Saudi-led air-strikes began in Sana'a in the early hours of March 26, in retaliation for the Salehs' and the Houthis' assault on Aden. Ballsy Sana'a residents adopted the Twitter hashtag #KefayaWar (Enough War) and posted real-time smartphone footage of Coalition airstrikes, standing on the roofs of their houses to film the bombardments.[1] On April 20, people in Sana'a circulated images on social media of a giant fireball billowing into the sky over Faj Attan district, following a Coalition airstrike that had apparently hit an underground munitions bunker.[2]

Hadi fled first to Oman and then to Riyadh in the final days of March, and the Saudis intervened in Yemen at his explicit request.[3] The Saudi-led Coalition included Bahrain, Egypt, Jordan, Kuwait, Morocco, Qatar, Sudan, and the UAE. Phase one—dubbed Operation Decisive Storm—was intended to eliminate fighter jets, anti-aircraft guns and ballistic missiles under the control of Sana'a's rogue authorities. The beginning of phase two commenced on 22 April, titled Operation Renewal of Hope,[4] which progressively destroyed the country's civilian infrastructure, including main roads, ports, and airports.[5] Only Yemen's oil and gas installations remained largely untouched.

After nine months of civil war and Coalition airstrikes, the poorest country in the region was significantly poorer still. Oil production had halted and exports fell to zero. The economy was in ruins, following a de facto port blockade that restricted food and fuel imports, and decimated commercial shipping.[6] The scarcity of fuel, combined with widespread damage to transport infrastructure made it extremely difficult to move people and goods to market. Hunger, always widespread, became increasingly prevalent. Thousands of schools were closed, while hospital workers were struggling to treat an influx of war casualties with fewer and fewer resources.

In December 2015, the UN estimated that more than 2,700 civilians had been killed and more than 5,000 wounded.[7] More than two million people had fled their homes in search of safety and security. Another 21 million people, or 82 per cent of the population, needed some form of humanitarian or protection assistance.[8] Trond Jensen, head of the UN's Office for the Coordination of Humanitarian Affairs in Yemen, noted that the longer the conflict went on, the more people's coping mechanisms were being tested.[9] However, the longer-term impact of rising rates of child malnutrition, psychological trauma, and the collapse of basic services, such as schooling and vaccinations, would still be felt in the next generation.[10]

At the start of Operation Decisive Storm, the UN had evacuated its staff, and restricted its in-country presence to life-saving missions only. UN envoy Jamal Benomar resigned in April, after four years in the role, and he was said to be privately furious that his efforts to mediate a political solution had been torpedoed. Benomar was replaced by Ismail Ould Cheikh Ahmed, a Mauritanian national with expertise in humanitarian affairs. Cheikh Ahmed had previously served in Yemen as the UN's resident coordinator, but he was heading an Ebola emergency response team when the call came requesting his services as a high-level political negotiator. His first attempt to mediate ceasefire talks, in Geneva in May, collapsed in disarray when representatives from Sana'a refused to meet face-to-face with Hadi's delegation.[11]

After the failure of Geneva, the Salehs and the Houthis resumed their task of laying waste to Aden. Together, they wreaked sweeping destruction on the historic colonial districts of Crater, Tawahi and Mualla, and the isthmus of Khormakser. As temperatures spiked during the summer months, residents of Aden suffered an outbreak of dengue fever.[12] Those with the means to leave the isthmus and its outcrop fled to the mainland, or paid traffickers' fees for a seat in a boat sailing to Djibouti.[13]

Resistance groups, including hiraki militias, fought back with Coalition support. In late July, Coalition troops, notably Emirati Special Forces,[14] enabled these resistance militias to 'liberate' Aden. The Salehs and the Houthis retreated north, first to al-Anad airbase in Lahj governorate, and then to the city of Taiz, where the frontline settled. In Taiz, Saleh's forces and the Houthis were able to restrict the supply of commercial goods and humanitarian supplies, because they controlled all the main access routes to the city.[15]

In both Aden and Taiz, Salafi fighters—including former students from Dammaj—played a prominent role in street battles with the Houthis. The radicalisation of formerly 'quietist', or apolitical, Salafis signalled the emergence of increasingly sectarian attitudes, which sharpened during the course of the war. In the south, some hiraki militias began to function as vigilantes in the aftermath of Aden's liberation but Hadi's lack of authority, which allowed for the open expression of separatist sentiment, also made it possible for extremist groups to flourish.

In Mukalla, AQAP had taken a stake in running the city council, occupied the headquarters of the 2nd regional military command, and seized the available weapons. In Abyan, Ansar al-Sharia had returned to Zinjibar and Jaar, after several years of giving ground to Hadi's forces. In Aden, ISIS was competing with AQAP to exploit the opportunities provided by the breakdown of the state—in October, they claimed responsibility for a suicide attack on the al-Qasr hotel, where Hadi's ministers and their Coalition minders were based, and in December, they killed the governor, Jaafar Mohammed Said, in a car bombing. Several sources doubted whether ISIS was really responsible for all the attacks carried out in its name.

Chaos in the south suited Saleh's objectives, because it undermined Hadi's credentials as the legitimate president and prevented his government from establishing effective control. Meanwhile, in Sana'a, Saleh was gradually consolidating his stopgap alliance with the Houthis by providing the personal contacts, patronage networks and know-how to run the remnants of the state. As a new hybrid group, Saleh-Houthi forces controlled the traditionally Zaydi areas of Al-Jawf, Amran, Bayda, Dhamar, Hodeida, Hajjah, Ibb, Sa'ada and Sana'a, which amounted to 'less than half of the Yemeni land mass, but includes most of the population'.[16] By contrast, Hadi managed to pay only a couple of fleeting visits to Aden, before retreating again to Riyadh.[17]

Hadi might have replaced Saleh as 'al rais', the president, but Saleh invoked a higher authority. His supporters began to call him 'al-za'im'—provider, guide, and guarantor. In May, after Coalition airstrikes targeted Saleh's residence in Sana'a, al-za'im filmed a characteristically unabashed stand-up television commentary from the street in front of his bombed-out home.[18] Saleh stressed that unlike battle-shy Hadi, who was living in safety and comfort in Riyadh, Saleh himself was proud to stand firm alongside the people of Sana'a in their daily sufferings. He rode a wave of popular anger that saw defiant phrases like 'death to al-Saud' spray-painted on the brickwork inside Sana'a city.

* * *

Rafat al-Akhali is among the most impressive and well-educated members of Yemen's 'Arab Spring' generation. With an MBA from Canada and a masters in public policy from Oxford University, he is a natural candidate for a future leadership role in public life. When he joined the transitional government as minister of youth and sports, following the Peace and National Partnership Agreement in September 2014, he became—at 31—the youngest member of a Yemeni cabinet since unification, in 1990.

During his brief stint in the post, before January's constitutional crisis triggered the cabinet's mass (but unofficial) resignation, he accompanied the national football squad to Saudi Arabia for the 2014 Gulf Cup. He witnessed their homecoming as national heroes, following an outstanding performance that united millions of Yemenis in a collective expression of popular sentiment for the first time since 2011. After the start of Coalition airstrikes, he declined an invitation to return to Riyadh with his cabinet colleagues as a government in exile, and Hadi appointed a new minister to his post in September 2015.

The following month, Rafat co-authored a comment piece for the *Guardian* with Farea Al-Muslimi, the youth activist who had previously told the US Senate Judiciary committee that every US 'tactical success' in Yemen risked 'creating more strategic problems'.[19] The pair reminded their readers that in 2011, 'Yemenis of all political stripes, including Houthis, flocked to the streets in hopes of a better future' but warned that now, 'the only beneficiaries from an extended conflict in Yemen and the consequent collapse of state institutions are extremist groups such as al-Qaida and Islamic State (ISIS)'.[20]

Rafat and Farea flagged the case of Moath Anwar, a young Adeni man in his early 20s, who had killed himself in the Qasr hotel suicide attacks, apparently orchestrated by ISIS. They wrote: 'The photos on his Facebook profile, where he goes by the alias "I'm a deadly crazy dude" written in colloquial Arabic, show him as a fashionable young man with well-groomed hair and clothing in the latest trends. Those who know him still cannot comprehend how he was recruited by ISIS. But we think the trend is clear: the starting point is always: "The future is lost. There is no hope."'

Prior to the 'Arab Spring', Rafat had helped to found Resonate! Yemen, a non-profit organisation that works to promote youth engagement in public policy. After the 2011 street protests, seeing how the established political parties had successfully drowned out independent voices, he co-founded a new party, Justice and Building, with the intention of creating a new platform for centrist ideals and civic principles. According to Rafat, the biggest lost opportunity of the transition period was the fact that the wider youth movement had not been able to organize itself after the uprising. For Rafat, if a single word could 'summarize everything the young Arab protestors were trying to express during the Arab Spring, the word would be Dignity'.[21]

However, the civil war and the Coalition air campaign were stripping the 'Arab Spring' generation of that last vestige of the uprising, their dignity. When we met in the UK in late 2015, he told me:

> Young people in Yemen have given up on the idea that they can make any change at a national level. People have real difficulty imagining what national-level participation might look like in this present situation, and the question of organizing is redundant. Now, the drivers are at the local level. People's sense of identity is changing, because everyone is affected by sectarian propaganda. Those of us who are lucky enough to survive this war will have different ideas about interaction with politics in the future.

Despite the malaise that Rafat described, many activists still bought into the achievements of the national dialogue and their commitment to many of the national dialogue outcomes had the potential to shape future peace-building efforts, explained Kate Nevens, manager of Saferworld's Middle East and North Africa programme, which was partnered with Resonate! Yemen. In a phone interview in 2015, she told me: 'Right now, Yemeni civil society and activist networks are less able to influence national political life but there is still an enormous willingness to engage. I get about 200 WhatsApp messages a day, which are posted to networks of which Saferworld is a part. These networks are being tested by the conflict but they are still intact and many of their members want to keep going, especially the youth and women's networks.'

Kate and I had worked together for several years at Chatham House, where we set up the Yemen Forum together. During 2011, we teamed up with organisations like Resonate! Yemen to facilitate youth activists' dialogue with international policymakers.[22] She added: 'Political participation has closed down phenomenally during the course of this year, so paradoxically the need for independent support is even higher than it was before. Part of the challenge is logistical. Our partner organisations can't move around the country to meet up and learn from each other, because of the daily violence. They focus on local issues instead because of the physical closure of space. Day to day, they are just trying to survive.'

Towards the end of 2015, I spoke to young activists on Whatsapp, in Sana'a and Taiz. I already knew that many of the young men and women who had participated in the 2011 uprising were struggling with depression and other mental health problems. Even before the war had started, they were mourning for the ideals that had brought them onto the streets. In addition, the untimely death of Ibrahim Mothana, a prominent young intellectual and progressive politician, in 2013, at the age of 24, had shaken his many supporters and peers. He had been an inspiration and support to his friends and they felt his absence profoundly.

Through my friendships with the members of Ibrahim's network, I became acutely aware of the collective trauma of the uprising and its aftermath. The war came as an assault on their personal emotional resources, as well as their intellectual architecture. One young activist in Sana'a spoke openly about his efforts to make sense emotionally of what was happening politically. 'I thought I was depressed a year ago, but things are so much worse now. I have nightmares and panic attacks. Looking back, it's hard to believe that the despair I was feeling then is nothing compared to what I am feeling now.'

When we spoke on WhatsApp in 2015, he asked not to be named, because he feared reprisals from the Houthis, as well as the Saudis. He told me: 'This country is everything I have. It's where my friends and family are. It's very ugly to imagine yourself as a refugee but I don't see any willingness for peace. People here have lost faith in the international community. Each time we see a small sign of hope, it gets shattered. It's like there's a higher power that does not want to stop the war. I am trying to come to terms with the idea that this is how it's going to be but how long can we cope in conditions like these, only focusing on survival?'

He went on: 'The international community spent millions, if not billions, on the national dialogue conference, but I don't know where this money went. I am just an activist. I don't know about policymaking, or how the UN works, but seeing where I am today tells me all I need to know. It doesn't make sense to me that the international community can't do anything to stop this madness but no one is speaking out about the airstrikes. Instead you hear that Saudi Arabia is becoming head of an influential committee at the UN human rights council.[23] This peace process has become a joke.'

* * *

In spring 2015, I signed an eleven-month contract to work as a home-based UN consultant, reporting to the sanctions committee in New

York. Resolution 2140 (2014) imposed a sanctions regime on Yemen and authorised the appointment of a panel of experts to monitor sanctions implementation, an annual mandate renewed in resolution 2204 (2015).[24] The panel appointed pursuant to resolution 2204 comprised a humanitarian expert, a finance expert, a regional expert, an arms expert, and an armed groups expert (me).[25] In the course of its work, the Panel visited Riyadh, Amman, London, Paris, Geneva, D.C., Moscow, Tehran, Abu Dhabi, Muscat, Cairo, and Djibouti.[26]

The Panel was tasked with gathering, examining and analysing information from Member States, UN bodies, regional organisations and 'other interested parties'. It had a mandate to report on individuals and entities threatening the 'peace, security or stability' of Yemen, violations of the targeted arms embargo established by resolution 2216 (2015), violations of international humanitarian law, and obstructions to the delivery or distribution of humanitarian assistance.[27] The Panel was also asked to report on sanctions measures, comprising an assets freeze and a travel ban, imposed on five designated individuals, which—from April 2015 onwards—included Abdulmalik al-Houthi and Ahmed Ali.

In early October 2015, the humanitarian expert, Lucy Mathieson, presented a confidential dossier to the sanctions committee on violations of international humanitarian law and human rights. Her report was subsequently leaked to Colum Lynch at the online magazine *Foreign Policy*, who revealed the Panel had found that all parties to the conflict had routinely violated international standards. Lynch wrote: 'The panel singled out the coalition for committing "grave violations" of civilians' rights, citing reports of indiscriminate airstrikes, as well as the targeting of markets, aid warehouses, and a camp for displaced Yemenis. It also raised concern that coalition forces may have intentionally obstructed the delivery of humanitarian aid to needy civilians.'[28]

Lynch further revealed that following Mathieson's presentation in New York, the US blocked a proposal to have the chair of the sanctions committee approach 'all relevant parties to the conflict and stress their responsibility to respect and uphold international humanitarian law and human rights law'. A month later, the US administration announced a $1.2bn deal to supply 'smart' bombs to Saudi Arabia, as a part of a much bigger transfer package.[29] Business was booming for British arms manufacturers, too. Between late March and the end of 2015, the government granted more than 150 new export licences for military goods to Riyadh, while during the course of that year, UK arms exports to Saudi Arabia—including 'combat aircraft and air-delivered bombs for the use of the Royal Saudi Air Force'—totalled over £2bn.[30]

The Coalition's air campaign in Yemen coincided with increasingly activist Saudi diplomacy in New York.[31] Although the United Kingdom was the designated penholder on Yemen, meaning that political officers in the permanent mission in New York were tasked with drafting the text of Security Council resolutions, following consultation with colleagues in London, British officials effectively surrendered the pen by allowing Coalition members to present an early draft of April's resolution 2216.[32] Furthermore, in September, it emerged that 'in the face of stiff resistance from Saudi Arabia', the UK, the US and France had backtracked on a proposal for the UN high commissioner for human rights, Zeid Ra'ad al-Hussein, to launch an inquiry into the conduct of all parties to the war in Yemen.[33] Instead, the UN human rights council adopted a weaker resolution supporting Hadi's appointment of a national commission of inquiry.

In late November, the *Independent* reported that Britain was at risk of being prosecuted for war crimes because of growing evidence that missiles sold to Saudi Arabia were being used against civilian targets in Yemen.[34] The following month, three London-based human rights lawyers published an independent legal opinion concluding that the government had 'misdirected itself in law and fact' in supplying arms to Saudi Arabia for use in Yemen, in breach of the UK's obligations under domestic, European and international law.[35] For British journalist Iona Craig, who had spent five months in Yemen during the course of the war, it was obvious that civilians were 'bearing the brunt of the conflict'.[36]

In mid December, human rights commissioner Zeid Ra'ad al-Hussein told the Security Council that a disproportionate number of civilian casualties in Yemen 'appeared to be the result of airstrikes carried out by coalition forces'.[37] The *New York Times* noted that the war in Yemen was 'turning into a political liability' and that 'cracks in the relationship between the United States and Saudi Arabia are beginning to show.'[38] US officials had invited Al-Hussein to brief the Council, and the US ambassador to the UN, Samantha Power, urged Saudi officials

to investigate strikes on civilian sites. Power also revealed that US officials 'had privately urged the Saudis to abide by international humanitarian law governing conflicts'.[39] However, there was still no sign that
the Obama administration intended to 'withdraw its support for the
Saudi-led operations, nor… that it would conduct its own investigations into military airstrikes that might amount to serious crimes'.[40]

The White House *omerta* regarding Saudi Arabia's conduct of the air
campaign in Yemen could not be decoupled from wider developments
in the region, including the timing of Obama's Iran deal. During 2015,
Iran had opted to normalise some aspects of its relations with the West
in return for curbs on its nuclear capabilities, after several decades of
diplomatic marginalisation. The Iran deal, agreed in June, placed considerable strain on Obama's relationship with the Al Sauds, who
objected to the prospect of their regional rival currying political favour
in Washington D.C.. Iran also stood to benefit economically from the
nuclear deal, which removed international sanctions and allowed
Teheran to sell oil on the global market.

The Saudis had taken the war to the Houthis in March 2015, in part
because they feared the expansion of Iranian influence in Yemen. Iran
was said to be shipping weapons to Saleh and the Houthis, and providing finance, training and intelligence. Almost everyone with an opinion
on the matter, including Western diplomats, agreed that Iran's projection of power in Yemen was certainly growing. Iran's perceived backing
for the new regime in Sana'a had also galvanised Sunni resistance
groups in the south, including AQAP, ISIS and the Salafis, to battle
against the Houthis and the Salehs. However, the precise extent of
Iranian involvement was hard to define and as a curious member of the
UN Panel, I found that hard evidence—as opposed to knowing speculation—proved hard to come by.[41]

In its final report to the Security Council, the Panel noted that in
February 2015 Ansar Allah had signed 'a memorandum of understanding on air transport cooperation with the Islamic Republic of Iran by
which the two countries would undertake direct flights between the
two countries for the first time'.[42] The Panel also reported one potential smuggling case involving anti-tank guided missiles, seized off the
coast of Oman, and allegedly destined for Yemen, which—on inspection—were found to display 'markings bearing the names of Iranian

industrial companies' and markings indicating that the missiles were 'likely to have been maintained or overhauled' in Iran.[43] While Iranian involvement in Yemen no doubt exceeded the Panel's modest investigative abilities, especially as the team was unable to travel to Yemen, the Panel did not present the Security Council with a smoking gun.[44]

In my personal view, Iran appeared to be trolling the Saudis, for apparently minimal capital investment. It also seemed plausible that there was a distinction to be made between the activities of Iranian officials who had negotiated the nuclear deal and were committed to its implementation, and other interests sitting within and alongside the Iranian state apparatus—but I had no means of substantiating this suspicion. In addition, as far as I could see from my spasmodic visits to New York, not one member state was willing to burn political capital on Yemen.[45] All told, it was hard for me to escape the impression that the US had 'given' Yemen to Riyadh as compensation for the Iran deal, and a real-time capacity building exercise for the Saudi air force. ('Yemen is the collateral damage of the Iran deal,' one UN official confided.)[46]

When the Panel's report was leaked to the media at the end of January 2016, several weeks prior to formal publication, British newspapers chose to focus on the finding that the Saudi-led Coalition had conducted "widespread and systematic" attacks on civilian targets in violation of international humanitarian law (IHL).[47] The Panel's report also highlighted systemic IHL violations and human rights abuses committed by Saleh-Houthi forces, the obstruction of humanitarian assistance, and use of starvation as a method of warfare. It further identified $48 million in assets belonging to Saleh and Ahmed Ali, and revealed two financial networks used to manage the family's wealth. One of these networks included nine companies, including the Pact Trust and the New World Trust Corporation, of which Ali Abdullah Saleh was the settlor and beneficiary. (The New World Trust Corporation had been registered in Canada in 1977, a year before Saleh took power.) These assets likely represented just a small proportion of Saleh's personal fortune, and in my view, his ability to draw on this offshore wealth contributed to his ability to sustain the conflict.

A year later, after I had stepped down from the Panel, my successors reported that Yemen was 'in danger of fracturing beyond the point of no return' and delivered their assessment that 'an outright military victory by any one side is no longer a realistic possibility in the near term'.[48] The Panel identified 'a tightening of the Houthi-Saleh political alliance', evident in their efforts to create a 'a functioning, de facto government that will be difficult to uproot'. The Panel also estimated that Central Bank reserves had fallen to zero and noted that the Salehs and the Houthis 'were relying on the shadow economy to support their war efforts'.[49] It added: 'The Panel has not seen sufficient evidence to confirm any direct large-scale supply of arms from the Government of the Islamic Republic of Iran, although there are indicators that anti-tank guided weapons being supplied to the Houthi or Saleh forces are of Iranian manufacture.'[50]

* * *

Amid all the sound and fury about Iran's influence in Yemen, it's worth noting one aspect of the animosity between the Houthis and the Saudis that gets overlooked in a simple sectarian framing: the Houthis are *sayyid* but Al-Saud are not. In addition, the Zaydi Shia notion of *khuruj*—which justifies confronting oppression—contrasts with the Sunni Salafi doctrine of absolute loyalty to the ruler underpining the construction of legitimate authority in Saudi Arabia. The Houthis also lay rhetorical claim to a 'greater Yemen', which pre-dates both the 1934 Treaty of Ta'if and the 2000 border agreement between Yemen and Saudi Arabia, stretching into the Saudi border provinces of Jizan, 'Asir and Najran, and the deeper history of Arabia.

By the start of 2016, video footage circulating on WhatsApp and YouTube purported to show Houthi crack teams, dressed in Yemeni army fatigues, making forays into towns on the Saudi side of the border.[51] Despite these acts of aggression, it was possible that the Houthis had previously been looking to reach some kind of accommodation with their northern neighbour, in return for a share of power in Sana'a. Several credible sources suggested that King Abdullah had been willing to countenance a more prominent role for the Houthis, as a counter-weight to Islah, as long as the Houthis were, in turn, constrained by opposing political forces.[52] Perhaps this ambivalence played a part in diplomats' laissez-faire attitude towards the incremental failure of the transition during summer 2014, and the Houthis' unopposed advance towards Sana'a. 'It was an open secret in Sana'a that there was going to be a coup,' one Western diplomat told me.[53]

It all came down to the theory of relativity. If King Abdullah had judged the Salehs and the Houthis to be the only indigenous actors capable of displacing Islah paymasters Hamid and Ali Mohsin, it followed that he had assessed their expedient alliance to pose less immediate and relative risk to Saudi interests than the prospect of Islah's consolidated revival in Yemen, in tandem with the Muslim Brotherhood as an empowered regional political force. It also seemed that Hadi might have had his own motives for encouraging—or tolerating—developments that would lead to the forced expulsion of Hamid and Ali Mohsin, as his powerful rivals. Evaluating the events of 2014, many of my sources speculated that Hadi had played a part in allowing the Houthis to enter Sana'a without much of a fight.[54]

However, once political forces are set in motion on this scale, it's hard to predict what direction they will take. On January 23 2015, King Abdullah died after an episode of pneumonia, aged 90—the third Saudi heavyweight to pass away since 2011. Abdullah was succeeded by his 79-year-old half-brother, Salman, who had reputedly played a part in financing the mujahideen in Afghanistan in the 1980s.[55] Salman's accession produced an unexpected shift in Saudi policy, which reversed Abdullah's previous position towards the Muslim Brotherhood. For Salman, the Houthis—and Iran—posed far greater risk to Saudi interests than Islah and the Muslim Brotherhood, and so in Yemen, Islah became 'the strongest element of the anti-Houthi coalition'.[56]

Salman's coronation represented formal continuity in the hereditary line of succession through the sons of the kingdom's founder, Abdulaziz. Until Salman's accession, crown prince and interior minister Mohammed bin Nayef ('MBN'), born in 1959, had been tipped as the first of Abdulaziz's grandsons eventually to inherit the monarch's title. However, with Salman's accession, the new king's son, Mohammed ('MBS'), began to gain unexpected political momentum. Salman appointed his Millennial son, born in 1985, to a portfolio of heavy-hitting posts: deputy crown prince, second deputy prime minister, minister of defence, chief of the royal court, and chairman of the council for economic and development affairs.[57]

Mohammed bin Salman's position as defence minister linked a successful outcome of the war in Yemen to the vagaries of court politics in Saudi Arabia and the respective political futures of 'MBS' and 'MBN'.

'MBS' had conceived Operation Decisive Storm as a quick war, with a quick win. The offensive was initially popular with the Saudi public, but as the war dragged on, the political and economic costs of the conflict began to mount. It provoked consternation about leadership-level decision-making among some members of the Saudi establishment, which took the form of a whispering campaign.[58] The war also coincided with a record budget deficit caused by low global oil prices, placing heavy pressure on state finances in the world's biggest oil exporter.[59]

At the same time, Yemen was also running out of money, and many Yemenis expected Saudi Arabia to foot the bill. During the humanitarian crisis provoked by the 2011 uprising and the bombing of the Marib pipeline, it was Saudi Arabia's emergency donation of several million barrels of crude oil that had kept Yemen's economy afloat. In 2012, Riyadh pledged $3 billion in formal development assistance to Yemen, including a billion-dollar loan to the Central Bank, signalling support for Hadi's transitional government.[60] In early 2014, Riyadh offered further billions to underpin the survival functions of the state and help make welfare payments to the country's poorest people.

The Saudis were understandably unwilling to bankroll a Houthi-led administration, which they believed had close ties with Teheran. Certainly, Saleh had his own relationship with the Iranians, dating back to his presidency, and he had visited Tehran several times as head of state.[61] In addition, he could rely on the services of several trusted interlocutors from key Zaydi families within his personal patronage network.[62] Several sources alleged that Ahmed Ali had travelled to Rome to meet the Iranians in 2014, while he was still serving as Hadi's ambassador to the UAE.[63] If Saleh had regarded Hadi's presidency as a hostile takeover of the family firm, in partnering with the Houthis, it seemed that he might have mounted a reverse takeover in return, with Iranian backing.

However, before Riyadh could install a more amenable regime in Sana'a, they first had to weaken the Saleh-Houthi alliance to such an extent that the culprits were willing to sue for peace—and by the start of 2016, that moment had not yet come. In January 2016, following the failure of another round of UN talks in Geneva, Saleh had announced that he would not negotiate with anyone other than the Saudis and as the year wore on, and yet more talks failed in Kuwait, it seemed unlikely that any UN-brokered solution was imminent.[64] Meanwhile, Ahmed Ali remained in the Emirates, where Hadi had posted him as ambassador before UN sanctions against him, including the travel ban, came into force in April 2015. The Emirati authorities—who regarded the Muslim Brothers as 'an existential threat not just to the UAE but to the region'[65]—appeared to be far from fully reconciled to Salman's new policy of supporting Islah.[66]

Amid this stasis, I spoke to an experienced Yemeni diplomat, who explained the dilemma as follows: 'When Salman came to power he changed the policy of King Abdullah by involving himself with Islah. Salman is trying to use Islah to achieve his goals in Yemen but the main concern for the Emiratis is a future Yemen controlled by the Muslim Brothers. So, the Saudis and the Emiratis are both on the same side, as partners in the Coalition, but they want different outcomes from this war.' He speculated that the Emiratis might want to use Ahmed Ali as a future card to play against the Saudi revival of Islah.

He added: 'Historically, no ruler has controlled Sana'a without the consent of the seven tribes of Sana'a, which are Hamdan, Bani Matar, Bani Hareth, Arhab, Bani Hushaish, Sanhan and Bilad al-Rous. Islah has some influence in Arhab but the remaining six are currently with Saleh and the Houthis. The only way to turn the seven tribes is with gold and money. Bani Hushaish and Hamdan will always resist Saudi bribes on ideological grounds but the others will eventually accept when they calculate that Saleh is running out of money. It's hard to know how much money he has. Enough to keep going for another few years, maybe?'

He went on: 'Saleh led the country in a very difficult time. He's the one who brought unity, democracy, and the multiparty system, even if it wasn't done in the best way. He also protected our sovereignty after a period of interference that followed the civil war in the 1960s, and he opened up some space for political parties, against our neighbours' wishes. Now he wants to make chaos after chaos, so that Ahmed Ali looks like a reasonable and respectable solution. That's the plan, but whether it will work—and whether Yemenis will accept it—is another question, because the Saleh family is associated with so much of this current bloodshed.'

Of course, bringing Ahmed Ali back to power was not what the youth-led uprising, or the transition, was meant to be about, but neither was the Houthi surge. I reminded my source of the three-way elite 'net losses' deal—in which Saleh, the al-Ahmars, and Ali Mohsin agreed to leave the country—and I asked if he thought this arrangement might provide the blueprint for a future exit deal, which could see Saleh leave Yemen as the quid pro quo for Ahmed Ali's return. He nodded. 'Yes. It's possible,' he said. 'But the future of the south is not yet clear, and the southerners will not accept control by Sana'a. Southern leaders also have their own history to come to terms with. You have to remember that Hadi was one of those involved in the civil war in 1986.'

We ended our meeting by discussing the prospects of Saleh's former rivals. In the view of my source, both Ali Mohsin and Hamid had been temporarily weakened by the Saleh-Houthi alliance, but they could yet return to Sana'a with Saudi support, depending how things played out.[67] 'Saleh capitalized on the animosity of the Hashid tribes towards the al-Ahmars, after they lost the conflict with the Houthis in Amran in 2014. For now, the tribal balance in the north is with Saleh but there's a danger that we'll get caught in another revenge cycle. The time will come when Hamid tries to get even with Saleh again.' He concluded: 'Hadi has no political future and no one is fighting for his return. The transitional government is divided among themselves. The only question people are asking about Hadi now is how to get him out?'

* * *

Diplomats and development types troubled by the latest cycle of bloodshed in Yemen might want to take a few moments to read the conclusion of Christopher Cramer's *Civil War Is Not A Stupid Thing*.[68] Cramer, a professor of political economy at the University of London's School of Oriental and African Studies, holds no illusions about the devastation of armed conflict, but he tries to steer a line between, on the one hand, the assumption that progressive social change can be achieved without violence and, on the other hand, a revolutionary vision of redemptive violence. He writes: 'War is not simply development in reverse. Rather, wars combine destruction with change; they provoke social, institutional and sometimes technical adjustments, some of which have the potential to contribute to longer-term accumulation.'

By the time civil war broke out in Yemen in 2015, the international community had spent three years investing considerable sums of political capital in a transition process that appeared to have hit a spectacular dead end. The Houthi surge to power may have temporarily eclipsed the achievements of the national dialogue conference and the constitutional drafting committee but these technical developments could yet pay political dividends for Yemen over the longer term. Indeed, as one former Yemeni official suggested, the war itself could turn out to be a more effective catalyst for restructuring the state and the armed forces than Hadi's previous top-down efforts. 'This is what they are fighting for in Taiz,' he told me. 'They're weighing the new balance and drawing the boundaries. We're moving towards the formation of regional micro-armies.'[69]

For those inclined to take a longer view, Yemen's Cold War history is worth reconsidering. In 1962, Egyptian-backed army commanders overthrew the ruling Imam, a Zaydi, who fled to the northern border region to mount a five-year fight-back with Saudi support, which ultimately failed. Political turbulence characterised the post-revolutionary period, with the siege of Sana'a by the tribes, multiple political plots, simultaneous assassinations, several wars, and plentiful accusations of external interference. On one occasion, in 1966, Yemen's entire presidential council found itself under de facto detention in Cairo. It was another decade before Saleh came to power in northern Yemen, in 1978, and even then, no one reasonably expected stability to follow.

The foundations of the modern republic were laid in the revolution of the 1960s, and reinforced with the introduction of democracy in the 1990s. Saleh himself must bear much of the blame for the corruption that ran Yemen's economy into the ground over the ensuing decades, leading to widespread loss of faith in the legitimacy of Yemen's political institutions by the end of the 2000s. The 'open moment' created by the 2011 uprising followed internal divisions within his own regime, and years of armed confrontation with non-state actors, including the Houthis. While the street protests of 2011 were initially peaceful, it was the prospect of brutal civil war between Saleh and his elite rivals that prompted the international community to intervene, but all they managed to do was delay the inevitable confrontation.

Now as in the 1960s, the outcome of this current power struggle will certainly be influenced—even if not conclusively determined—by the preferences of regional powers. Riyadh might wish to play the winning hand but the decisive cards could well be in the hands of the Emiratis. By deploying special forces to Aden in 2015 (and later, during 2016, in Mukalla), the Emiratis have already shaped the facts on the ground, and as a result of their outreach to grassroots groups across the south, they have also established significant ties with local power-brokers, including southern separatist groups.[70] Depending on the future stance taken by the Emiratis in relation to southern independence, Yemen's recent experiment in unification could yet turn out to be an aberration in the country's long and intricate history.

However, breaking the united republic apart would have significant implications for Yemen's already shattered economy, not least considering that much of Yemen's oil and gas wealth is concentrated inside the borders of the former PDRY. By the start of 2015, oil production had dropped to 50,000 barrels a day—nearly one tenth of the rate of production during 'peak oil' in 2002.[71] Most international oil companies declared *force majeure* shortly after the start of Operation Decisive Storm and shut down their operations. Future output will continue to fall, unless the reformed authorities can convince investors to explore for new finds.[72] If new investors prove hard to entice, or geology withholds, the end of Yemen's oil era will also mark the end of the resource curse.[73]

Tragically, more and more people living in this breadline economy will struggle to cope. At the end of this divestment process, the shape of the Yemeni state may look quite different but it (or they, if there is more than one jurisdiction) will still be heavily dependent on foreign aid and cash transfusions from the Gulf states—in the short-term, at least. Over the longer term, it's just about conceivable that it might be possible to assess the events of 2015, and the consequences, in a more positive light. Cramer writes: 'In retrospect, many changes that come to be seen as progressive have their origins in social conflicts that have taken a violent turn. This is the paradox of violence and war: violence destroys but is also associated with social creativity.'

Indeed, despite the many and varied indicators suggesting that Yemen's future lies on a crooked, downwards path, it's possible—just possible—that Cramer might indeed be right. It's also possible that the rest of the world will discover, in the fullness of time, that it has lessons to learn from Yemen's disruptive transition to a post-oil economy, not least in the abrupt and unexpected shift to use of a more sustainable energy source, solar power.[74] In November 2015, Siris Hartkorn, expatriate co-founder of Sana'a-based security advisory firm Safer Yemen, shared the following heartfelt message with her Facebook friends, and it is to her that I afford the ultimate words:

> Sana'a has been my home for almost five years and during these years the security situation, the public services, the economy, the infrastructure and almost everything else have only deteriorated and is now at a point where most other cities would have collapsed. Yet, Sana'a is still going strong despite the absence of government, the daily airstrikes, the frequent terrorist attacks, the spread of arms, the control by rebels who act without accountability and the complete breakdown of infrastructure…

> Sana'a hasn't seen even a glimpse of electricity since August, there is no city water available, the price of cooking gas has gone from about $7 up to sometimes $70 for a canister, the food prices have increased, the kilometer long queues outside the fuel stations have disappeared because whatever little fuel was there is now gone. Yet in this harsh reality people in Sana'a NEVER complain, because they know that in other parts of the country people are worse off. And in the midst of their harsh reality communities, neighbors and strangers gather to help each other.

> People with money buy water tanks and put in the streets, so that people with less money in the neighborhood can collect water in jerry cans. Each neighborhood coordinate cooking gas distributions and on every second street corner a guy is sitting on the back of his Hilux selling smuggled red petrol in jerry cans. The craters after airstrikes in the road are being filled up with garbage and becomes a little bump in the road, the supermarket shelves are filled with Saudi products being smuggled over the border breaking the import blockade, meanwhile shops cover their broken glass facades in plastic and turn on the solar when a customer enters.

> The entire city runs on solar energy and people charge their batteries (including truck batteries) at neighbors houses or the local solar-power-dealer meanwhile the dark nights lit up with stars so bright that you would think you were in the middle of the desert… Sana'a is a tough old lady who keeps going on, despite whatever hardship comes her way, and it's a city you can't help to love… There are 24 million reasons why this war will never destroy the #yemenispirit.[75]

NOTES

PREFACE

1. In 2009, Saudi armed forces arrested a sorcerer on the Yemeni border, who claimed that jinns had ordered him to cast magic spells in the conflict zone in Saada.
2. '#Yemen is so subtle and a word can mean many things that only some #Yemenis can decipher. I feel pity to stringers, analysts and the unwary.'—@alguneid—11 December 2011.
3. Ginny Hill, 'Yemen: fear of failure', Chatham House briefing paper, 2008. See http://www.chathamhouse.org/sites/default/files/public/Research/Middle%20East/bp1108yemen.pdf.
4. My work for the Panel was bound by contractual confidentiality requirements. In this book, I have quoted the Panel's final report, which is a public document, as well as media reports citing leaks. In addition, I have made generic comments about my experiences as a Panel member, as well as my personal views about political events during my period of service. However, I do not refer to ongoing aspects of the Panel's work.
5. I wrote the manuscript in progressive stages from 2009 onwards and, despite some minor revisions, I have largely left the text as I first drafted it, reflecting contemporary source material that was available to me at the time.
6. Diplomats wished to remain anonymous because they were not authorized to speak to the media. Journalists, academics and consultants working in Yemen on a regular basis were concerned that their visas would be revoked if they made any controversial statements. Yemeni sources were unwilling to compromise their personal safety or damage their patronage connections by speaking out against their paymasters.

INTRODUCTION

1. 'Death toll in Yemen conflict passes 10,000', Al Jazeera, 17 January 2017.
2. Yemen's ranking fell from 164 (2011) to 167 (2013) in the Transparency International Corruption Perceptions Index, out of 177 countries and territories. By 2016, Yemen was placed 170 out of 176, a joint position it shared with Libya and Sudan; only Syria, North Korea, South Sudan and Somalia were perceived as more corrupt. See www.transparency.org/cpi
3. https://docs.unocha.org/sites/dms/Documents/ERC_USG_Stephen_OBrien_remarks_to_the_media_Sana_2MAR2017.pdf

1. THE LAST IMAM: THE 1962 REVOLUTION IN THE YEMEN ARAB REPUBLIC

1. Paul Dresch, *A History of Modern Yemen* (Cambridge University Press, 2000), p. 11.
2. Sahih al-Bukhari, *Book of the Virtues of the Prophet and His Companions*, Hadeeth No. 4070.
3. Ibid., Hadeeth No. 3261.
4. Twelver Shi'as part company with Zaydis by recognizing Zayd's brother, Mohammed al-Baqir, as their fifth imam in a line of succession that ends with the twelfth imam, Mohammad al-Mahdi. Zaydis reject the Twelver Shi'a belief that the twelfth imam went into a state of occultation in 872 at the age of five while leading prayers at his father's funeral, and will reappear on earth as the saviour of mankind.
5. This principle is accepted by the dominant Zaydi school, the Hadawiyya.
6. Dresch, *A History of Modern Yemen*, p. 15.
7. Ibid., p. 5.
8. Ibid., p. 4 and n. 36 (referring to ch. 2, p. 229).
9. Ibid., pp. 4–5, 43.
10. The Ottomans established a presence in Yemen's interior during the sixteenth century but were pushed back to the Red Sea coast during the seventeenth century. They maintained intermittent control along the coast throughout the eighteenth and nineteenth centuries, and held Sana'a almost continuously between 1872 and 1918.
11. Dresch, *A History of Modern Yemen*, p. 5.
12. Ibid., p. 46.
13. Ibid., p. 9.
14. Ibid., p. 9.
15. Ibid., p. 51.
16. Ibid., pp. 27, 30.

17. Ibid., p. 30.
18. Michael Korda, *Hero: The Life and Legend of Lawrence of Arabia* (JR Books, 2010), pp. 516, 528.
19. Madawi al-Rasheed, *A History of Saudi Arabia* (Cambridge University Press, 2002) p. 101.
20. Said K. Aburish, *The Rise, Corruption and Coming Fall of the House of Saud* (Bloomsbury, 2005), p. 121.
21. Dresch, *A History of Modern Yemen*, p. 35.
22. Al-Rasheed, *A History of Saudi Arabia*, p. 101.
23. Ibid., p. 101.
24. Dresch, *A History of Modern Yemen*, p. 50.
25. Ibid., pp. 44, 46, 49.
26. Ibid., p. 47.
27. Ibid., p. 47.
28. Ibid., pp. 54, 105. Nu'man was a Shafai.
29. Dresch, *A History of Modern Yemen*, p. 53
30. Ibid., p. 54.
31. Ibid., p. 56.
32. Jane Fletcher Geniesse, *Passionate Nomad: The Life of Freya Stark* (Modern Library, 2001), p. 250. In 1926, Yahya signed a treaty with Italy's Benito Mussolini, who sold him an arms workshop and a machine for minting coins. See Dresch, *A History of Modern Yemen*, pp. 31–4.
33. Geniesse, *Passionate Nomad*, p. 250.
34. Ibid., p. 207.
35. Ibid., p. 172–3.
36. Ibid., p. 169.
37. Ibid., p. 247
38. Ibid., p. 249.
39. Ibid., p. 250.
40. Ibid., p. 251.
41. Ibid., p. 252.
42. 'Imam's coffee', *Time*, 15 Sept. 1941.
43. Geniesse, *Passionate Nomad*, p. 253.
44. 'Triangular round table', *Time*, 20 Feb. 1939.
45. 'Pan-Arab league', *Time*, 16 Oct. 1944.
46. 'Arab federation?', *Time*, 26 Feb. 1945; Dresch, *A History of Modern Yemen*, p. 56.
47. 'Around the ovals', *Time*, 6 Oct. 1947.
48. 'Just beginning', *Time*, 8 Dec. 1947.
49. Rachel Bronson, *Thicker than Oil: America's Uneasy Partnership with Saudi Arabia* (Oxford University Press, 2006), pp. 15, 19. Socal formed a wholly owned subsidiary, the Californian Arabian Standard Oil Company (Casoc), which merged with Texas Oil in 1936, and in 1944,

the two companies named their joint subsidiary the Arab American Company (Aramco).

50. Ibid., p. 20.
51. Ibid., p. 20. In fact, Ibn Saud had sent an envoy to London in 1932, to ask for a loan to support Saudi oil exploration, which a 'disdainful Foreign Office mandarin' refused. See 'The diplomat who said "No" to Saudi oil', BBC News, 8 Nov. 2014.
52. Ibid., p. 20.
53. Ibid., pp. 36–9.
54. Ibid., p. 42.
55. Ibid., pp. 46–7.
56. 'OIL: OIL new giant', Time, 1 Sept. 1947.
57. 'The chancelleries: the land of qat', Time, 4 March 1946.
58. 'OIL: OIL new giant', Time, 1 Sept. 1947.
59. Ibid.
60. 'Old Bedouin custom', Time, 22 March 1948.
61. 'Into the 19th century?', Time, 1 March 1948.
62. Dresch, A History of Modern Yemen, p. 56.
63. Ibid., pp. 62, 81.
64. Ibid., p. 64.
65. Ibid., p. 67.
66. 'After Ahmad the Devil', Time, 5 Oct. 1962.
67. Claude Fayein, Une française médecin au yémen (Juillard, 1955), referenced in Dresch, n. 24 on p. 67.
68. 'Revolt & revenge', Time, 25 April 1955.
69. 'Worn out', Time, 7 July 1961.
70. Dresch, A History of Modern Yemen, p. 64.
71. Ibid., pp. 65–6.
72. Ibid., p. 78.
73. Ibid., p. 77.
74. Ibid., p. 79.
75. Ibid., p. 80.
76. Ibid., p. 78.
77. Kevin Rosser, Education, Revolt and Reform in Yemen: The 'Famous Forty' Mission of 1947 (St Antony's College, 1998).
78. Dresch, A History of Modern Yemen, p. 78.
79. Bronson, Thicker than Oil, p. 45.
80. Ibid., p. 22.
81. Ibid., p. 45.
82. Ibid., p. 63.
83. Ibid., pp. 65, 67.
84. Lawrence Wright, The Looming Tower (Penguin, 2006), p. 64.

85. Steve Coll, *The Bin Ladens* (Penguin, 2008), p. 76; Wright, *The Looming Tower*, pp. 68, 84.
86. Bronson, *Thicker Than Oil*, p. 70.
87. Said K. Aburish, *Nasser: The Last Arab* (Duckworth, 2004), p. 89. Aburish argues that Nasser's early policy of 'positive neutralism' was an attempt to steer a middle course between the USA and the USSR. See also pp. 98, 132.
88. Wright, *The Looming Tower*, p. 30; Aburish, *Nasser*, p. 89; Bronson, *Thicker than Oil*, p. 70.
89. Aburish, *Nasser*, p. 107
90. Ibid., p. 121. Even Saudi Arabia felt compelled to support Egypt, establishing the first embargo on oil sales to Britain and France. See Bronson, *Thicker than Oil*, p. 71.
91. Aburish, *Nasser*, p. 147.
92. President Dwight D. Eisenhower announced the Eisenhower Doctrine in Jan. 1957, and Congress approved it in March of the same year. Under the Eisenhower Doctrine, a country could request American economic assistance and/or aid from US military forces if it was being threatened by armed aggression from another state. Eisenhower singled out the Soviet threat in his doctrine by authorizing the commitment of US forces 'to secure and protect the territorial integrity and political independence of such nations, requesting such aid against overt armed aggression from any nation controlled by international communism'—which was interpreted to mean Egypt. See Bronson, *Thicker than Oil*, p. 73.
93. 'Mission completed', *Time*, 13 May 1957.
94. Turkey, Iran, Iraq, Pakistan, Greece, Saudi Arabia, Lebanon, Libya, Ethiopia, Afghanistan, Israel. Jordan also implicitly subscribed to the doctrine in private.
95. 'The fleet withdraws', *New York Times*, 4 May 1957.
96. 'Mission completed', *Time*, 13 May 1957.
97. Dresch, *A History of Modern Yemen*, p. 82.
98. Ibid., p. 76.
99. Ibid.
100. Ibid., p. 86.
101. Ibid., p. 71
102. 'Turboprop strategy', *Time*, 25 Nov. 1957.
103. 'Arabia felix', *Time*, 26 Oct. 1962.
104. Dresch, *A History of Modern Yemen*, p. 81; see also Aburish, *Nasser*, pp. 83–4 and Bronson, *Thicker than Oil*, p. 71. 'On the go again', *Time*, 19 Aug. 1957.
105. 'The Imam's peace', *Time*, 14 Sept. 1959.

106. Dresch, *A History of Modern Yemen*, p. 86.
107. 'Koran v. Socialism', *Time*, 5 Jan. 1962.
108. Ibid. King Saud was implicated in a botched attempt to assassinate Nasser a few years before this speech. See Bronson, *Thicker Than Oil*, p. 75.
109. 'Arabia felix', *Time*, 26 Oct. 1962.
110. 'The big show', *Time*, 4 March 1957.
111. 'Arabia felix', *Time*, 26 Oct. 1962.
112. Fred Halliday, *Arabia Without Sultans* (Saqi, 2002) p. 101.
113. Ibid., p. 101.
114. Ibid.
115. Ibid.
116. Dresch, *A History of Modern Yemen*, p. 87. Ahmed died on 18 Sept.
117. Ibid., p. 87.
118. 'Arabia felix', *Time*, 26 Oct. 1962; 'Trouble for the sons of Saud', *Time*, 23 Nov. 1962.
119. 'Arabia felix', *Time*, 26 Oct. 1962.
120. Ibid.
121. Ibid.
122. Dresch, *A History of Modern Yemen*, pp. 89–90; 'Revolt within a war', *Time*, 17 Feb. 1967.
123. Dresch, *A History of Modern Yemen*, p. 91.
124. Bronson, *Thicker than Oil*, p. 85.
125. Dresch, *A History of Modern Yemen*, p. 90.
126. Ibid., p. 91.
127. Ibid., pp. 92–3.
128. Ibid., p. 96.
129. Ibid., p. 93.
130. Ibid., p. 91.
131. Ibid., p. 94.
132. Sallal came from a low-status blacksmith family in al-Jawf and rose to prominence in the army. Many tribesmen in the north joined the Royalists because they could not accept such a lowly person as their leader.
133. 'Trouble for the sons of Saud', *Time*, 23 Nov. 1962.
134. 'For Allah & the Imam', *Time*, 8 March 1963.
135. 'Obituary: Colonel Jim Johnson', *Daily Telegraph*, 13 Aug. 2008; Dresch, *A History of Modern Yemen*, p. 91; 'Diplomacy in the desert', *Time*, 7 Dec. 1962. David Smiley, another British cloak-and-dagger agent, made thirteen trips to Yemen between 1963 and 1968. See 'Obituary: Colonel David Smiley', *Daily Telegraph*, 9 Jan. 2009. Anthony Boyle, former aide-de-camp to the British High Commiss-

ioner in Aden, also acted as a Royalist military adviser. See 'The forgotten war', *Time*, 14 Aug. 1964.

136. Dresch, *A History of Modern Yemen*, p. 91.
137. See http://www.amazon.co.uk/War-That-Never-Was/dp/00995532
95/ref=sr_1_1?s=books&ie=UTF8&qid=136671827 7&sr=1–1.
138. Hashemites trace their ancestry to Hashim ibn Abd al-Manaf, the great-grandfather of Prophet Mohammed.
139. Bronson, *Thicker than Oil*, pp. 86–8.
140. 'Diplomacy in the desert', *Time*, 7 Dec. 1962.
141. Bronson, *Thicker than Oil*, p. 84. See also n. 27, ch. 4, p. 279.
142. Ibid., p. 84. See also n. 27, ch. 4, p. 279
143. 'A brace of kings', *Time*, 20 Nov. 1964; 'Revolution from the throne', *Time*, 24 June 1966.
144. Wright, *The Looming Tower*, p. 66. Wright notes that al Saud appropriated 30–40 per cent of the country's oil revenues as allowances (p. 87).
145. Bronson, *Thicker Than Oil*, p. 76. Faisal ibn Abdul Aziz al Saud was born in 1904 and became king of Saudi Arabia in 1964.
146. Ibid., p. 85.
147. Ibid., p. 85, see n. 34, p. 279. Fears that King Saud might be overthrown following Yemen's Egyptian-backed revolution were fuelled by the presence in Cairo of a disaffected reformist Saudi prince, Talal, and the defection to Cairo of several Saudi air force pilots. Bronson, *Thicker Than Oil*, p. 83.
148. Ibid., p. 77.
149. Ibid., p. 80.
150. Ibid.
151. Ibid., p. 86.
152. Ibid.
153. 'The U.S. intervenes on both sides', *Time*, 18 Jan. 1963.
154. Aburish, *Nasser*, p. 228; Arthur M. Schlesinger, *A Thousand Days: John F. Kennedy in the White House* (Mariner Books, 2002), p. 566.
155. 'For Allah & the Imam', *Time*, 8 March 1963.
156. Bronson, *Thicker Than Oil*, p. 86.
157. Aburish, *Nasser*, p. 232.
158. 'Poison gas on Arabia', *Daily Telegraph*, 8 July 1963.
159. 'The U.S. intervenes on both sides', *Time*, 18 Jan. 1963.
160. 'For Allah & the Imam', *Time*, 8 March 1963.
161. ICRC archives, B AG 251 225–001—Mission des Dr Jean-Maurice Rubli et Dr Guido Pidermann du 24 décembre 1962 au 8 janvier 1963, assistance aux victimes civiles et aux détenus en raison de la guerre entre républicains et royalistes 16/12/1962–14/01/1963.

162. ICRC archives, ACICR, B AG 251.225–002, Yémen (Yémen du Nord), Mission de Roger du Pasquier et Joseph Gasser du 15 janvier au 6 février 1963, assistance aux victimes civiles et aux détenus en raison de la guerre entre républicains et royalistes, 11.01.1963-12.02.1963.

163. ICRC archives, ACICR, B AG 251.225.003, Yémen (Yémen du Nord), Mission du Dr Jürg Baer du 29 mars au 31 mai 1963, assistance aux victimes civiles eet aux détenus en raison de la guerre entre républicains et royalistes, 25.03.1963–09.07.1963.

164. ICRC archives, ACICR, B AG 251.225.003—Letter no. 39—Sanaa Mai 19 1963—May 18 meeting with General Chebir.

165. ICRC archives, ACICR, B AG 251.225.003—Letter no. 43—23 Mai 1963—Dr Baer; Correspondance recu—Juin 5 1963.

166. ICRC archives, ACICR, B AG 251.225.003—Letter no. 44—Aden Mai 28 1963.

167. 'Nasser's planes use poison gas', *Daily Telegraph*, 8 July 1963.

168. Richard Beeston, London (2009).

169. 'Poison gas on Arabia', *Daily Telegraph*, 8 July 1963. The UN mission in Yemen, which had a mandate to create a 25-mile demilitarized strip along the Saudi–Yemeni frontier and supervise the withdrawal of Saudi and Egyptian troops, ended in Sept. 1964.

170. See Dresch, *A History of Modern Yemen*, p. 91, on the split between the Foreign Office and the Colonial Office over diplomatic recognition.

171. Al Kowma is presumably the same village as al-Kawma, which Beeston visited.

172. McLean's signed drawing is dated 30 June 1963

173. ICRC archives, see ACICR, B AG 202.225–001, Yémen (Yémen du Nord), Témoignages et plaintes concernant les bombardements de villages et d'hôpitaux et l'utilisation de bombes à napalm et de gaz toxiques, 30.11.1962–01.02.1965. ACICR, B AG 202.226–001, Yémen (République démocratique populaire du), Plaintes concernant l'utilisation de bombes miniatures, 04.11.1965–01.02.1965 [mission Marcoli in Jeddah—18 July 1963].

174. Hansard, YEMEN HC Deb 31 July 1963 vol. 682 cc92–3W. The statement was made by Edward Heath, MP for Bexley and Lord Privy Seal. He served as prime minister from 1970 to 1974. See also Hansard, YEMEN OPERATIONS (PROSCRIBED WEAPONS) HC Deb 15 July 1963 vol. 681 cc22–6.

175. The final three lines of a copy of McLean's report lodged in the ICRC public archives are redacted. See ACICR, B AG 202.225–001, Yémen (Yémen du Nord), Témoignages et plaintes concernant les bombardements de villages et d'hôpitaux et l'utilisation de bombes

à napalm et de gaz toxiques, 30.11.1962–01.02.1965. ACICR, B AG 202.226–001, Yémen (République démocratique populaire du), Plaintes concernant l'utilisation de bombes miniatures, 04.11.1965-01.02.1965.

176. See ACICR, B AG 202.225–001, Yémen (Yémen du Nord), Témoignages et plaintes concernant les bombardements de villages et d'hôpitaux et l'utilisation de bombes à napalm et de gaz toxiques, 30.11.1962–01.02.1965. ACICR, B AG 202.226–001, Yémen (République démocratique populaire du), Plaintes concernant l'utilisation de bombes miniatures, 04.11.1965–01.02.1965 [Note 186, 25 Jan. 1965, Marcel Boisard].

177. Ibid. This account is based on several days' research in the ICRC archives in Geneva; due to time constraints, it does not amount to an exhaustive survey of all potentially relevant documents in the ICRC archives, relating to the possible use of chemical weapons in Yemen.

178. See Text of the Red Cross Report on the Use of Poison Gas in Yemen, New York Times, 28 July 1967. See also Frederic Gonseth Productions, Humanitarian Citadel (2009), timecode 01:07:00.

2. VICTOR'S PEACE: THE END OF THE COLD WAR, UNIFICATION AND THE 1994 CIVIL WAR

1. Frederic Gonseth Productions, Humanitarian Citadel (2009).
2. Dresch, A History of Modern Yemen, p. 102.
3. Anthony H. Cordesman, The Military Balance and Arms Sales in Yemen and the Red Sea States: 1986–1992 (Center for Strategic and International Studies, 1993).
4. Frederic Gonseth Productions, Humanitarian Citadel (2009), timecode 00:32:36.
5. Aburish, Nasser, p. 228. David M. Witty, 'A regular army in counterinsurgency operations: Egypt in North Yemen, 1962–1967', Journal of Military History 65/2 (April 2001), p. 409.
6. Lt Cdr Youssef Aboul-Enein, The Egyptian-Yemen War (1962–1967): Egyptian Perspectives on Guerrilla Warfare (US Army Infantry School, 2004).
7. See Frederic Gonseth Productions, Humanitarian Citadel (2009) for the Royalists' treatment of the Egyptians.
8. 'Microcosm of a struggle', Time, 22 April 1966.
9. Witty, 'A regular army'.
10. 'The red bankroll', Time, 15 January 1965; Noel Brehony, Yemen Divided: The Story of a Failed State in South Arabia (I.B.Tauris, 2011), p. 13.

11. Dresch, *A History of Modern Yemen*, p. 105.
12. 'Back to the balcony', *Time*, 4 March 1966.
13. Dresch, *A History of Modern Yemen*, p. 105.
14. Ibid., p. 103.
15. Ibid., p. 105.
16. 'A call to Mecca', *Time*, 30 September 1966. Dresch, *A History of Modern Yemen*, p. 105.
17. Dresch, *A History of Modern Yemen*, p. 105.
18. 'Revolt within a war', *Time*, 17 February 1967; 'Desperation of a strongman', *Time*, 20 October 1967.
19. Aburish, *The Rise, Corruption and Coming Fall of the House of Saud*, p. 162.
20. Dresch, *A History of Modern Yemen*, p. 114. 'Desperation of a strongman', *Time*, 20 October 1967.
21. 'Faisal to resume help to Yemenis', *New York Times*, 28 February 1968.
22. Interview with Fred Halliday, London (2009). See also 'Faisal to resume help to Yemenis', *New York Times*, 28 February 1968.
23. Dresch, *A History of Modern Yemen*, pp. 114–15.
24. Cordesman, *The Military Balance*; 'Faisal to resume help to Yemenis', *New York Times*, 28 February 1968.
25. Cordesman, *The Military Balance*.
26. Bronson, *Thicker than Oil*, pp. 104, 154.
27. Source B2, London (2009).
28. Brehony, *Yemen Divided*, p. 11.
29. Dresch, *A History of Modern Yemen*, p. 91.
30. Halliday, *Arabia without Sultans*, p. 108.
31. Dresch, *A History of Modern Yemen*, p. 99. See also Brehony, *Yemen Divided*, p. 9 for the South Arabian Federation.
32. Dresch, *A History of Modern Yemen*, pp. 111, 97–9; see also Brehony, *Yemen Divided*, p. 12.
33. Dresch, *A History of Modern Yemen*, p. 99.
34. Ibid., p. 100.
35. 'Back to colonialism', *Time*, 8 October 1965.
36. Dresch, *A History of Modern Yemen*, p. 111
37. Ibid., p. 111.
38. Ibid., p. 114
39. The British had announced in 1966 that they would leave by 1968 (interpreted as 31 December 1967). The Foreign Secretary announced on 2 November 1967 that they would leave by the end of the month.
40. Frederic Gonseth Productions, *Humanitarian Citadel* (2009), timecode 00:59:00–01:05:15.
41. See www.britishpathe.com, film ID 2047.10 and 2047.21.

42. Dresch, *A History of Modern Yemen*, p. 113.
43. Frederic Gonseth Productions, *Humanitarian Citadel* (2009), timecode 00:59:00–01:05:15.
44. Sarah Phillips, *Yemen's Democracy Experiment in Regional Perspective: Patronage and Pluralized Authoritariansm* (Palgrave Macmillan, 2008), p. 46.
45. Dresch, *A History of Modern Yemen*, p. 121. According to Noel Brehony, tribalism remained alive in a different guise. People talked in tribal terms but used different expressions for it; for example, the NLF secretary, in effect, became the tribal sheikh. Tribalism revived in the late 1970s and became a major influence again in the 1990s after unity.
46. Ibid., pp. 11, 89.
47. Ibid., p. 117.
48. Bronson, *Thicker than Oil*, p. 103.
49. Ibid., p. 92. Saud did not go without trouble: he tried to mount a coup, harangued his brother from Cairo on Voice of the Arabs, and travelled to Yemen to support the Egyptian-backed Republicans against the Saudi-backed Royalists. See also Aburish, *Nasser*, pp. 256, 268.
50. Madawi al-Rasheed (ed.), *Kingdom without Borders: Saudi Arabia's Political, Religious and Media Frontiers* (Hurst, 2008).
51. Bronson, *Thicker than Oil*, p. 100
52. Ibid., p. 89.
53. Ibid., p. 97.
54. Ibid., p. 90.
55. Ibid., p. 94.
56. Ibid., pp. 94–6.
57. Ibid., p. 94; n. 66 cites: 'From Ambassador Hart to Secretary of State,' 31 October 1963, Folder: 9/63–11/63, Box 157A, Countries: Saudi Arabia, National Security Files, Presidential Papers of John F. Kennedy, JFKL.
58. Dresch, *A History of Modern Yemen*, pp. 120, 147.
59. 'Army and Cabinet purges bolster Yemeni chief', *New York Times*, 20 September 1968.
60. Dresch, *A History of Modern Yemen*, p. 103.
61. Ibid., pp. 123–4; see also Gabriele vom Bruck, *Islam, Memory, and Morality in Yemen: Ruling Families in Transition* (Palgrave Macmillan, 2005), pp. 55, 60.
62. Isa Blumi, *Chaos in Yemen: Societal Collapse and the New Authoritarianism* (Routledge, 2011), p. 80.
63. Dresch, *A History of Modern Yemen*, p. 124.
64. Ibid., p. 126.
65. Ibid., p. 124.

66. Victoria Clark, *Yemen: Dancing on the Heads of Snakes* (Yale University Press, 2010), p. 104.
67. Dresch, *A History of Modern Yemen*, p. 130.
68. Ibid., pp. 128, 130.
69. Phillips, *Yemen's Democracy Experiment*, p. 44.
70. Clark, *Yemen*, pp. 104, 107; Dresch, *A History of Modern Yemen*, p. 130.
71. Dresch, *A History of Modern Yemen*, p. 130.
72. Ibid., p. 130.
73. Phillips, *Yemen's Democracy Experiment*, p. 46.
74. Brehony, *Yemen Divided*, p. 31.
75. 'Aden takes over foreign concerns', *New York Times*, 28 November 1969.
76. Phillips, *Yemen's Democracy Experiment*, p. 46.
77. 'South Yemen plans trials of officials under British', *New York Times*, 8 February 1968.
78. Brehony, *Yemen Divided*, p. 31.
79. Lisa Wedeen, *Peripheral Visions: Publics, Power, and Performance in Yemen* (University of Chicago Press, 2008), p. 52.
80. Brehony, *Yemen Divided*, p. 132.
81. Ibid., p. 53.
82. Dresch, *A History of Modern Yemen*, p. 128.
83. See 'US putting off bid to southern Yemen', *New York Times*, 6 August 1978, for the Carter administration's view of Salmayn's pragmatism.
84. Dresch, *A History of Modern Yemen*, pp. 135, 147.
85. Clark, *Yemen*, pp. 109, 110.
86. Dresch, *A History of Modern Yemen*, p. 147.
87. 'South Yemen chief reported slain but pro-Red group stays in power', *New York Times*, 26 June 1978; 'Aden opens battle site of coup for reporters', *New York Times*, 16 July 1978.
88. 'South Yemen chief reported slain but pro-Red group stays in power', *New York Times*, 26 June 1978.
89. Brehony, *Yemen Divided*, pp. 97–101.
90. Dresch, *A History of Modern Yemen*, pp. 128, 148. Saleh 'commanded the post at al-Mafraq on the whisky road from Mukha' to Ta'izz'.
91. Source Q2, Sana'a (2006).
92. Blumi, *Chaos in Yemen*, p. 120.
93. Ahmed Saif, 'The Yemeni politics of survival 1978–2003', paper presented at Fifth Mediterranean Social and Political Research Meeting, European University Institute, Florence, 24–8 March 2004, p. 5.
94. Blumi, *Chaos in Yemen*, p. 79.
95. Brehony, *Yemen Divided*, p. 112.
96. Phillips, *Yemen's Democracy Experiment*, p. 46.

97. Cordesman, *The Military Balance*.
98. Blumi, *Chaos in Yemen*, p. 79; Wedeen, *Peripheral Visions*, p. 16.
99. Dresch, *A History of Modern Yemen*, p. 150.
100. Blumi, *Chaos in Yemen*, p. 79.
101. Dresch, *A History of Modern Yemen*, p. 150; Cordesman, *The Military Balance*.
102. Initially, the shah and his wife fled to Egypt, but later, US President Jimmy Carter admitted Mohammed Reza to the USA for medical treatment.
103. Yemenis were among the insurgents. Wright, *The Looming Tower*, p. 90.
104. 'Yemen invites role for US in economy', *New York Times*, 18 February 1979.
105. 'Saleh in our alley', *New York Times*, 3 December 1979.
106. 'US plans to send advisers to Yemen', *New York Times*, 13 March 1979.
107. Dresch, *A History of Modern Yemen*, p. 150. He notes that most of the anti-tank missiles 'in fact stayed in Saudi hands'.
108. 'In Yemen, chance of peace seems slim', *New York Times*, 28 March 1979.
109. 'Yemen invites role for US in economy', *New York Times*, 18 February 1979.
110. Blumi, *Chaos in Yemen*, p. 79.
111. 'Saudis are said to induce Yemenis to end Soviet arms advisers' role', *New York Times*, 19 March 1980.
112. 'Saleh in our alley', *New York Times*, 3 December 1979.
113. Blumi, *Chaos in Yemen*, p. 80.
114. Ibid. Blumi notes that Saddam Hussein 'initiated a long-term relationship with Salih's government. In time Baghdad sent upwards of $300 million to shore up the regime's position as a bulwark against Saudi pretensions of hegemony in the region as well as give it additional leverage over South Yemen.'
115. 'In Yemen, the east and west do meet', *New York Times*, 7 May 1980.
116. Bronson, *Thicker than Oil*, p. 127.
117. Ibid., p. 143.
118. Ibid., p. 162.
119. Brehony, *Yemen Divided*, p. 132.
120. 'US putting off bid to southern Yemen', *New York Times*, 6 August 1978.
121. Brehony, *Yemen Divided*, p. 109; see also 'Moscow and Aden', *New York Times*, 22 January 1986
122. Brehony, *Yemen Divided*, p. 110.
123. Ibid., pp. 110, 117.
124. Ibid., p. 110.

125. Ibid., p. 120.
126. Ibid., p. 122.
127. Ibid.
128. Ibid., p. 122 and Dresch, *A History of Modern Yemen*, p. 169.
129. 'Moscow and Aden', *New York Times*, 22 January 1986. 'Massacre with tea: southern Yemen at war', *New York Times*, 9 February 1986.
130. Phillips, *Yemen's Democracy Experiment*, p. 46.
131. Ibid. Ismail's criticisms were used by Ali Nasser's opponents to undermine Ali Nasser.
132. Dresch, *A History of Modern Yemen*, pp. 151 or 169.
133. Brehony, *Yemen Divided*, pp. 131–2.
134. Ibid., p. 155.
135. 'Battle for southern Yemen: how the fury began', *New York Times*, 30 January 1986.
136. Phillips, *Yemen's Democracy Experiment*, p. 46. Brehony, *Yemen Divided*, p. 122. Ismail's body was never found.
137. 'Battle for southern Yemen: how the fury began', *New York Times*, 30 January 1986.
138. 'Moscow and Aden', *New York Times*, 22 January 1986. Al-Attas later claimed that he decided to go to Moscow as the place that might have information on, and influence the situation in, Aden.
139. 'Battle for southern Yemen: how the fury began', *New York Times*, 30 January 1986.
140. Dresch, *A History of Modern Yemen*, p. 179.
141. Ibid. Al-Beidh had fled the Politburo meeting room when Ali Nasser's guards opened fire. Al-Attas was visiting India on the day of the slaughter.
142. Ibid.
143. Brehony, *Yemen Divided*, p. 157.
144. Phillips, *Yemen's Democracy Experiment*, p. 46.
145. Dresch, *A History of Modern Yemen*, p. 172.
146. Brehony, *Yemen Divided*, p. 169.
147. Dresch, *A History of Modern Yemen*, p. 172.
148. Ibid., p. 182; Brehony, *Yemen Divided*, p. 168.
149. Interview with Thanos Petouris by email (2011).
150. Brehony, *Yemen Divided*, p. 161.
151. Dresch, *A History of Modern Yemen*, p. 181.
152. Ibid., pp. 181–2.
153. Wedeen, *Peripheral Visions*, p. 19.
154. Brehony, *Yemen Divided*, p. 183.
155. Ibid., p. 178.
156. Dresch, *A History of Modern Yemen*, p. 194. Phillips, *Yemen's Democracy Experiment*, p. 47.

157. Brehony, *Yemen Divided*, p. 182, Dresch, *A History of Modern Yemen*, p. 191. Ali Nasser Mohammed was forced to leave Yemen as a condition of unification, imposed by the YSP.
158. Brehony, *Yemen Divided*, p. 179. Blumi, *Chaos in Yemen*, p. 129.
159. Wedeen, *Peripheral Visions*, p. 17. Dresch, *A History of Modern Yemen*, p. 186.
160. Dresch, *A History of Modern Yemen*, p. 185.
161. 'Mideast tensions; Yemen's chief assails Saudis on Gulf Crisis', *New York Times*, 26 October 1990.
162. 'The World; how Yemen is coming undone', *New York Times*, 29 May 1994.
163. Brehony, *Yemen Divided*, p. 192; Blumi, *Chaos in Yemen*, p. 130.
164. Phillips, *Yemen's Democracy Experiment*, pp. 48–9; Dresch, *A History of Modern Yemen*, p. 161.
165. Dresch, *A History of Modern Yemen*, pp. 181, 193–4; Phillips, *Yemen's Democracy Experiment*, pp. 48–9. See Phillips and Blumi for suggestions that YAR withheld information from the PDRY on the extent of South Yemen's oil and gas reserves, before unification. See also Brehony, *Yemen Divided*, pp. 164, 174.
166. Dresch, *A History of Modern Yemen*, pp. 193–4.
167. Ibid., pp. 186, 189.
168. Ibid., p. 186. Phillips, *Yemen's Democracy Experiment*, pp. 43, 54. Sheikh Abdullah's father and brother had been executed by Imam Ahmed in 1960, which had prompted him to join the Republican cause.
169. Brehony, *Yemen Divided*, p. 183; Dresch, *A History of Modern Yemen*, p. 187.
170. Brehony, *Yemen Divided*, p. 192; Dresch, *A History of Modern Yemen*, p. 187.
171. Dresch, *A History of Modern Yemen*, p. 191.
172. Ibid., p. 193. Phillips, *Yemen's Democracy Experiment*, p. 48.
173. Dresch, *A History of Modern Yemen*, p. 194.
174. Sheikh Abdullah replaced Yassin Saeed Noman. See Brehony, *Yemen Divided*, p. 192.
175. Ibid., p. 193.
176. Ibid., p. 193–4.
177. Blumi, *Chaos in Yemen*, p. 134.
178. Brehony, *Yemen Divided*, p. 194.
179. 'Secessionists in southern Yemen name heads of new government', *New York Times*, 23 May 1994.
180. Brehony, *Yemen Divided*, pp. 196–8.
181. Dresch, *A History of Modern Yemen*, pp. 196–7.
182. Phillips, *Yemen's Democracy Experiment*, p. 58.

183. 'U.N. opens Yemen talks', *New York Times*, 28 July 1994.
184. Blumi, *Chaos in Yemen*, pp. 119–22.
185. Brehony, *Yemen Divided*, p. 198.
186. Dresch, *A History of Modern Yemen*, pp. 197–8.
187. www.presidentsaleh.gov.ye (accessed 2009).
188. 'A poverty plan', *New York Times*, 3 June 2009. Arab Human Development Report, p. 116.
189. Global Hunger Index, The Challenge of Hunger, 2008.
190. The Global Gender Gap Report, World Economic Forum, 2008.

3. AN ILLUSORY STATE: PARLIAMENTARY POLITICS AND PRESIDENTIAL PATRONAGE

1. 'YEMEN: when cultural norms underpin gun ownership', IRIN, 21 May 2006. See http://www.irinnews.org/InDepthMain.aspx?InDepthId=8&ReportId=41050
2. Derek B. Miller, *Demand, Stockpiles, and Social Controls: Small Arms in Yemen* (Small Arms Survey, 2003).
3. 'YEMEN, when cultural norms underpin gun ownership', IRIN, 21 May 2006.
4. US AID Yemen Corruption Assessment, 2006. See http://yemen.usembassy.gov/root/pdfs/reports/yemen-corruption-assessment.pdf.
5. Phillips, *Yemen's Democracy Experiment*, p. 47.
6. Sheila Carapico, 'Elections and mass politics in Yemen', *Middle East Report*, Middle East Research and Information Project 185 (November–December 1993). See http://www.merip.org/mer/mer185/elections-mass-politics-yemen.
7. US AID Yemen Corruption Assessment, 2006.
8. Source Q1, London (2009).
9. Source K1, Sana'a (2009).
10. Franz Gerner and Silvana Tordo, *Republic of Yemen: A Natural Gas Incentive Framework* (Formal Report 327/07. Energy Sector Management Assistance Program, World Bank, 2008).
11. Yemen's oil production reached its peak in 2002, with an average production rate of 457,000 barrels a day. By 2010, this had fallen to 264,000. See: BP Statistical Review of World Energy, June 2011.
12. Arab Human Development Report 2009, p. 116.
13. Transparency International Corruption Perceptions Index 2008 ranked Yemen 141 of 180, falling to 164 in the 2011 Index.
14. Source A1, via Skype (2009).
15. Arab Human Development Report 2009.
16. Source F1, London (2009).
17. Source Z1, Sana'a (2008).

18. Source M1, Sana'a (2007).
19. Sarah Phillips, 'Evaluating political reform in Yemen', *Democracy and Rule of Law Program*, Carnegie Papers Middle East Series 80 (February 2007). Phillips describes Yemen's political system as pluralized authoritarianism. Sarah Phillips, 'Politics in a vacuum: the Yemeni opposition's dilemma', *Viewpoints: Discerning Yemen's Political Future* (The Middle East Institute, June 2009).
20. Phillips, *Yemen's Democracy Experiment*, p. 9.
21. Source F1, London (2009).
22. Source G1, London (2009).
23. Phillips, *Yemen's Democracy Experiment*, p. 168.
24. Ibid.
25. Gregory D. Johnsen, 'Salih's road to reelection', *Middle East Report*, Middle East Research and Information Project 267 (13 January 2006). See http://www.merip.org/mero/mero011306.
26. Saleh was elected president of the presidential council in 1993, after the first parliamentary election in Yemen. He was directly elected president in 1999, but he stood against a candidate from his own party and won with 96 per cent of the vote.
27. During the four-week campaign, seven people were killed in election-related violence, forty people died in a stadium stampede, four French tourists were kidnapped and al-Qaeda Yemen attempted the first simultaneous car bomb attacks on two major oil installations. On the eve of polling, Saleh announced the arrest of bin Shamlan's bodyguard, who was accused of plotting the foiled suicide bombings.
28. Better this devil—*Al-Ahram Weekly* online 812 (14–20 September).
29. Source C1, Sana'a (2006).
30. Source N3, London (2009). See also Phillips, *Yemen's Democracy Experiment*, p. 162.
31. In 2006, 20 riyals were equivalent to 5p or 10c.
32. The president's translator was Mohammed Sudam.
33. Saleh later removed himself from the Supreme Judicial Council and introduced elections for provincial governors.
34. Phillips, *Yemen's Democracy Experiment*, p. 54.
35. Islah formed the junior partner in a coalition government with the GPC between 1993 and 1997, inhibiting the immediate sense of its role as an effective opposition force, and in the presidential elections in 1999, Islah nominated Saleh as its own candidate. See Phillips, *Yemen's Democracy Experiment*, p. 142.
36. *2003 Parliamentary Elections in Yemen: Final Report* (National Democratic Institute).
37. Paul Dresch and Bernard Haykel, 'Stereotypes and political styles:

Islamists and tribesfolk in Yemen', *International Journal of Middle East Studies* 27/4 (November 1995), pp. 405–31.

38. *2003 Parliamentary Elections in Yemen: Final Report* (National Democratic Institute). *Yemen: Coping with Terrorism and Violence in a Fragile State* (International Crisis Group, January 2003).

39. Profile of Sheikh Abd al-Majid al-Zindani—Terrorism Monitor Volume: 4 Issue: 7, 6 April 2006, Jamestown Foundation, Gregory D. Johnsen.

40. Ibid.

41. See Brehony, *Yemen Divided*, p. 180, and Wedeen, *Peripheral Vision*, p. 17, on Zindani's role in unification. See also Laurent Bonnefoy, *Salafism in Yemen: Transnationalism and Religious Identity* (Hurst, 2011), p. 24. In 1993, after Yemen's first multi-party elections, Zindani became one of the five members of the new presidential council, representing Islah.

42. Phillips, *Yemen's Democracy Experiment*, pp. 54, 138, 150.

43. Ibid., p. 138.

44. Ibid., p. 55.

45. 'Hashid tribe expresses allegiance to Sadeq Al-Ahmar as new leader', *Yemen Times*, 26 January 2008.

46. 'Largest Yemeni opposition party appoints new chief', *Gulf News*, 7 January 2008.

47. Sarah Phillips, 'Foreboding about the future in Yemen', *Middle East Report*, Middle East Research and Information Project 267 (3 April 2006). See http://www.merip.org/mero/mero040306.

4. GIRAFFE ARMY: AK-47S, ARMS-DEALERS AND WARLORDS

1. 'The AK-47: the world's favorite killing machine' (Control Arms Campaign, June 2006).

2. Miller, *Demand, Stockpiles, and Social Controls*. 'The category of small arms includes revolvers and self-loading pistols, rifles and carbines, assault rifles, sub-machine guns, and light machine guns. Light weapons include heavy machine guns, hand-held under-barrel and mounted grenade launchers, portable anti-aircraft and anti-tank guns, recoilless rifles, portable launchers of anti-tank missile and rocket systems, portable launchers of anti-aircraft missile systems, and mortars of calibres of less than 100 mm.'

3. 'The information: world gun ownership', *FT Weekend* 26/7 (April 2008).

4. 'The AK-47: the world's favorite killing machine' (Control Arms Campaign, June 2006).

5. 'Yemen's six to nine million guns "far fewer than previously claimed"', *Small Arms Survey*, 7 August 2003.

6. 'The AK-47: the world's favorite killing machine' (Control Arms Campaign, June 2006).

7. Phillip Killicoat, *Weaponomics: The Global Market For Assault Rifles*. World Bank Policy Research Working Paper 4202, April 2007.
8. Ibid.
9. Miller, *Demand, Stockpiles, and Social Controls.*
10. Ibid.
11. 'Armes louées, hospitalité assurée', *Courrier International*, 1 February 2007: 'Comptez 10 riyals pour un poignard, 20 riyals par jour pour une kalachnikov, 15 riyals pour un pistolet (munitions utilisées en sus), et munissez-vous de vos papiers d'identité. Attention: les prix doublent les jours de fête.'
12. Source P1, London (2009).
13. Saudi men also 'rent' temporary Yemeni wives. See 'Tourism marriage drives Yemeni girls to prostitution', *Yemen Observer*, 13 August 2009.
14. Ahmed al-Haj, 'Yemen, Saudis join to stem weapons trade', Associated Press, 17 October 2003.
15. Since I visited Dhamar in 2007, the price of ammunition has risen.
16. 'One man leads often dangerous quest to quell violence in Yemen', *New York Times*, 8 October 2006. Despite the dramatic nature of global media reports about tribal violence in Yemen, the estimated number of fatalities—at roughly 2,000 deaths every year—is closely matched by the high incidence of fatal traffic accidents on Yemen's roads.
17. Miller, *Demand, Stockpiles, and Social Controls.*
18. International Crisis Group, 'Yemen: coping with terrorism and violence in a fragile state', Middle East Report 8 (January 2003): 'Tribal clashes also often have a political dimension, as tribalism is used to serve broader political objectives. Indeed, many Yemenis are persuaded that the government either ignores the problem of tribal conflicts or actually fuels it by pitting one tribe against another, keeping tribal areas in a state of permanent unrest in order to deflect potential tribal challenges to central authority.'
19. Source A1, Sana'a (2008).
20. Miller, *Demand, Stockpiles, and Social Controls.*
21. Source A1, Sana'a (2008).
22. Source C1, Sana'a (2007).
23. 'US embassy cables: who will succeed Saleh in Yemen?', the *Guardian*, Monday 21 March 2011. Cable dated 17 September 2005: 'SUBJECT: WILL SALEH'S SUCCESSOR PLEASE STAND UP?'.
24. Dresch, *A History of Modern Yemen*, p. 148.
25. Ibid., p. 149.
26. Source A1, Sana'a (2007).
27. 'US embassy cables: who will succeed Saleh in Yemen?', the *Guardian*, Monday 21 March 2011. Cable dated 17 September 2005: 'SUBJECT: WILL SALEH'S SUCCESSOR PLEASE STAND UP?'

28. 'Salih and the Yemeni succession', *Jane's Intelligence Digest*, August 2008.

29. Ibid.; also International Crisis Group, 'Yemen: defusing the Saada time bomb', *Middle East Report* 86 (May 2009); see http://www.crisisgroup. org/~/media/Files/Middle%20East%20North%20Africa/Iran%20Gulf/Yemen/086%20Yemen%20Defusing%20the%20Saada%20Time%20Bomb.pdf

30. 'Yemeni women sign up to fight terror', BBC News, 2 April 2007.

31. The National Security Bureau was established after the USS *Cole* attack, with Ali Muhammed al-Anisi as chairman and Ammar Saleh as deputy director.

32. Source E1, London (2009).

33. Buck is not his real name

34. Center for Defense Information 2007 briefing on Yemen.

35. Cordesman, *The Military Balance*.

36. Center for Defense Information 2007 briefing on Yemen.

37. Jeremy M. Sharp, 'Yemen: background and US relations' (Congressional Research Service, 22 March 2011). See http://fpc.state.gov/documents/organization/159782.pdf.

38. Dresch, *A History of Modern Yemen*, p. 30.

39. Cordesman, *The Military Balance*.

40. Ibid.

41. *Jane's World Armies*, issue 21 (2007).

42. Source B3, date and location withheld.

43. Figures based on conversations with friends in Sana'a. $240 per calendar month was estimated as a teacher's basic salary in mid-2009.

44. Source T1, location withheld (2009).

45. US AID Yemen Corruption Assessment 2006.

46. Source A1, Sana'a (2007).

47. US AID Yemen Corruption Assessment 2006.

48. Shaun Overton, 'The Yemeni arms trade: still a concern for terrorism and regional security', *Jamestown Foundation Terrorism Monitor* 3/9 (6 May 2005).

49. Miller, *Demand, Stockpiles, and Social Controls*. 'Landslide causes Yemen military depot blasts', Reuters, 31 May 2007.

50. YECO was formerly known as the Military Economic Corporation (MECO).

51. Dresch, *A History of Modern Yemen*, p. 159.

52. Ibid., p. 208.

53. Ibid., p. 163.

54. US AID Yemen Corruption Assessment, 2006. See http://yemen.usembassy.gov/root/pdfs/reports/yemen-corruption-assessment.pdf.

55. Source A1, Sana'a (2008).

56. Misha Glenny, *McMafia* (Vintage, 2009), pp. 2–7.

57. Ibid., p. 7
58. http://www.sipri.org/databases/armstransfers/armstransfers
59. Source J3, location and date withheld.
60. Sasha Lezhnev, *Crafting Peace: Strategies to Deal with Warlords in Collapsing States* (Lexington Books, 2006), p. 2.
61. Source A1, by Skype (2009).
62. Robert Cooper, *The Breaking of Nations: Order and Chaos in the Twenty-First Century* (Atlantic Books, 2004), p. 147.

5. ACROSS THE GULF: PIRACY AND PEOPLE-SMUGGLING FROM THE HORN OF AFRICA

1. Haroun is not his real name.
2. Paul Dresch and Bernard Haykel, 'Stereotypes and political styles: Islamists and tribesfolk in Yemen', *International Journal of Middle East Studies* 27/4 (November 1995), pp. 405–31.
3. Bonnefoy, *Salafism in Yemen: Transnationalism and Religious Identity*, p. 44.
4. Source C1, Sana'a (2006).
5. Lucine Taminian, 'Rimbaud's house in Aden, Yemen: giving voice(s) to the silent poet', *Cultural Anthropology* 13/4 (November 1998), pp. 464–90.
6. 'Rimbaud in Yemen', *Al-Ahram Weekly* online 5469–15 (August 2001). 'Arthur Rimbaud, coffee trader', *Saudi Aramco World* 52/5 (September/October 2001). See also Charles Nicholl, *Somebody Else: Arthur Rimbaud in Africa, 1880–91* (University of Chicago Press, 1999).
7. T.E. Lawrence to Colonel C.E. Wilson, 8 January 1917
8. Michael Scheuer, *Through Our Enemies' Eyes* (Potomac Books, 2002), pp. 137–8.
9. The Soviets dropped the Somalis in favour of Ethiopia during the 1977–1978 Ogaden war but after that, the Somalis received significant support from the US until the end of the 1980s. Losing American support probably was more significant in the end, according to Somalia analyst Roger Middleton.
10. UN Security Council Resolution 733 (1992).
11. United Nations Press Release SC/7957, dated 16.12.2003, regarding UN Security Council Resolution 1519.
12. United Nations Security Council 25 March 2003 (S/2003/223)—see para. 74.
13. UN Security Council S/2005/625 (2005). See http://www.poa-iss.org/CASAUpload/ELibrary/S-2005–625.pdf.
14. 'From Somalia to Yemen', Channel 4 News, October 2006. See http://www.channel4.com/news/articles/world/africa/from%20somalia%20to%20yemen/171290.

15. Interviews conducted on the beaches in Shabwa, October 2006.
16. 'U.S. used base in Ethiopia to hunt al-Qaeda', *New York Times*, 23 February 2007; 'Pentagon sees covert move in Somalia as blueprint', *New York Times*, 13 January 2007.
17. Interview With Meles Zenawi, *Washington Post*, 14 December 2006.
18. Source S1, Washington DC, by phone (2007).
19. United Nations Security Council Report (July 2007).
20. UN S/2008/274 (April 2008). See http://www.fas.org/programs/ssp/asmp/issueareas/manpads/S2008274.pdf
21. UN S/2008/769 (December 2008). See http://www.securitycouncilreport.org/atf/cf/%7B65BFCF9B-6D27-4E9C-8CD3-CF6E4FF96FF9%7D/Somalia%20S2008%20769.pdf
22. UN S/2005/625 (2005). See http://www.poa-iss.org/CASAUpload/ELibrary/S-2005-625.pdf
23. http://www.daallo.com
24. 'Dubai World buys African carrier', *Gulf News*, 13 November 2007.
25. A total of 1,704 passengers flew in or out of Bosaso airport in 2004. Also see Bosaso—First Steps Towards Strategic Urban Planning (UN Habitat, 2009). See http://www.unhabitat.org/pmss/listItemDetails.aspx?publicationID=2730. In 2011, 69 million people passed through Heathrow.
26. A new terminal building and runway was planned for Bosaso airport.
27. 'Somali gunmen "besieged" after seizing women medics', *The Times*, 27 December 2007. See also 'Colin Freeman: the moment My Somali kidnap hell began', *Daily Telegraph*, 5 January 2009.
28. *Bosaso—First Steps Towards Strategic Urban Planning* (UN Habitat, 2009).
29. Ibid. In 2005, official figures record the export of 1.5 million sheep and goats, 90,500 head of cattle, 7,800 camels and 18,760 tonnes of incense.
30. UN S/2005/625 (2005). See http://www.poa-iss.org/CASAUpload/ELibrary/S-2005-625.pdf
31. Source A1, Sana'a (2008).
32. In 1998, the northern region of Puntland declared itself a semi-autonomous state.
33. Yemen is one of the few countries in the region to have signed the 1951 Convention relating to the Status of Refugees.
34. Mousa and Mohammed are not their real names.
35. Freya Stark, *Winter in Arabia*, ch. XVI: The site of Cana.
36. Ibid., p. 4.
37. See France 3's 'Les martyrs du Golfe d'Aden'.
38. Towards the end of the 2000s, the proportion of Ethiopian boat passengers was rising, even though Ethiopians did not receive automatic

refugee status and they were regarded as illegal migrants. See Sally Healy and Ginny Hill, 'Yemen and Somalia: terrorism, shadow networks and the limitations of state-building', Chatham House briefing paper, 2010. See http://www.chathamhouse.org/sites/default/files/public/Research/Africa/bp1010_yemensomalia.pdf

39. Source Q1, Sana'a (2007).
40. UN, December 2008. See http://www.securitycouncilreport.org/atf/cf/%7B65BFCF9B-6D27–4E9C-8CD3-CF6E4FF96FF9%7D/Somalia%20S2008%20769.pdf
41. Source R1, London (2009).
42. 'Yemen economic update', World Bank, Summer 2008. See http://www-wds.worldbank.org/external/default/WDSContentServer/WDSP/IB/2009/06/24/000333038_200906 24235850/Rendered/PDF/491010NEWS0YM010Box338941B01P UBLIC1.pdf
43. In 2008, Sarah Phillips found that around 50 per cent of subsidized diesel, which cost the state \$3.5bn—or 12 per cent of that year's GDP—went to smuggling rings within Yemen. See Sarah Phillips, 'Al-Qaeda and the struggle for Yemen', *Survival* 53/1 (February–March 2011), pp. 95–120.
44. In 2007, Yemen ranked 15th and accounted for 0.4 per cent of the global seizures of cannabis resin, with 4,663 kg—Spain was highest with 50 per cent, followed by Morocco with 9 per cent.
45. Source A2, Sana'a (2009). The 2009 World Drug Report only lists Captagon use in Saudi Arabia.
46. Sally Healy and Ginny Hill, 'Yemen and Somalia: terrorism, shadow networks and the limitations of state-building', Chatham House briefing paper, 2010. See http://www. chathamhouse.org/sites/default/files/public/Research/Africa/bp1010_yemensomalia.pdf
47. 'Somalia's pirates flourish in a lawless nation', *New York Times*, 31 October 2008.
48. UN, April 2008. See http://www.fas.org/programs/ssp/asmp/issueareas/manpads/S2008274.pdf
49. UN, December 2008. See http://www.securitycouncilreport. org/atf/cf/%7B65BFCF9B-6D27–4E9C-8CD3-CF6E4FF96FF9%7D/Somalia%20S2008%20769.pdf
50. Source R1, London (2009). See also UN, December 2008.
51. 'The privateers of Yemen', *Foreign Policy*, 17 November 2010.

6. THE CHICKEN AND THE EGG: ELITE COMPETITION, CORRUPTION AND REFORM

1. www.thesecret.tv

2. The observations in this section are based on the author's extensive formal and informal discussions with Jalal and his associates, and with Western officials, from 2006 onwards. They represent the author's personal opinions.
3. 'Millions In Aid Linked To Yemeni Reform', *Christian Science Monitor*, 27 February 2007.
4. Source I1, Sana'a (2008).
5. Source I4, location and date withheld.
6. Source I1, Sana'a (2008).
7. The ten-point plan identified the following priorities: merit-based recruitment for senior civil service jobs, GCC labour market access, reduced diesel subsidies, fast-track oil exploration, land reform, increased presidential oversight of the reform process, Aden action plan, strengthened rule of law, development of a water road map and improvement to Yemen's branding. See 'As nations meet, Clinton urges Yemen to prove itself worthy of aid', *New York Times*, 27 January 2010.
8. 'Speaking in 2012, one of Ahmed Ali's associates reflected: "He gave us authority when we needed his help to push things through government. He supported our moderate challenges, but he backed off when it came to anything really difficult. He was a balancer, like his father, and he wasn't willing to pay any real political cost. Why should he lose?"'—See Ginny Hill, Peter Salisbury, Léonie Northedge and Jane Kinninmont, 'Yemen: Corruption, Capital Flight and Global Drivers of Conflict', Chatham House Report, September 2013.
9. Peter Salisbury, 'Yemen's economy: oil, imports and elites', Chatham House, 2010. See http://www.chathamhouse.org/sites/default/files/1011pp_yemeneconomy.pdf
10. Source G1, London (2009).
11. 'Yemen to open up for foreign investment', Reuters, 23 April 2007. The announcement coincided with the appointment of a new prime minister, Ali Mohammed Mujawar, after sustained donor pressure to remove his predecessor, Abdul Qader Bajammal. See 'Yemen swears in government, targets corruption', Agence France-Presse, 7 April 2007.
12. 'Doing business 2009', World Bank/IFC. Yemen was awarded the top reform slot in the 'starting a business' category—for reducing to zero the second largest minimum capital requirement in the world, per capita.
13. Source J1, Sana'a (2008).
14. 'Saad Sabrah CEO-Chairman for Shibam Holdings', *Yemen Post*, 10 April 2010.
15. 'Saad Sabrah CEO-Chairman for Shibam Holdings', *Yemen Post*, 10 April 2010.
16. Parliament passed a law in September 2009 allowing foreign compa-

nies to buy land wholesale from the government for the first time, and the General Investment Authority was given authority to sell land in Yemen to international developers. Source J3, by email (2011).

17. Source K3, Sana'a (2010).
18. 'Yemen confronts plight of child brides', *Christian Science Monitor*, 22 August 2008.
19. The definition of food subsistence was 2,200 calories.
20. Skype interview with Adam (2009).
21. 'SIAC wins Sana'a mosque contract', MEED (www.meed.com), 19 January 2001; 'Big mosque for president puzzles Yemen's poor', Associated Press, 23 November 2008.
22. Source U1, Sana'a (2008).
23. Michael Gilsenan, 'Out of the Hadhramaut', *London Review of Books*, 20 March 2003.
24. Alice encounters the blue caterpillar smoking a hookah pipe in Lewis Carroll's *Alice in Wonderland*.
25. Dr Saad's grandfather left Hadramaut in the middle of the nineteenth century for Indonesia and Singapore, returning to Yemen in the 1930s, where he died. Dr Saad's father, a Singapore-born Hadrami, spent nearly 35 years in Singapore before returning home to marry a Yemeni woman and father his second child, Saad. Dr Saad was born in 1959 and raised in Aden, before moving to Singapore and Egypt, where he graduated from university in Cairo with a medical degree and a post-graduate qualification in surgery.
26. 'Shifting Light in the Qamariyya: The reinvention of patronage networks in contemporary Yemen', unpublished PhD, April Longley Alley (2008).
27. I interviewed Dr Saad in 2008. The following year, Dr Saad emailed me to say that he had resigned from SNACC and left the country. 'I'm now living in self-imposed exile in Singapore,' he wrote. 'This may be an important fact to include in your book, if you want your readers to understand the failed reform process in Yemen.'

7. LAYLA AND THE MADMAN: YEMEN'S ROLE IN THE ORIGINS OF AL-QAEDA

1. My 2008 encounter with Nasser al-Bahri was arranged and translated by Yemeni journalist Nasser Arrabyee, who wrote his own account of this meeting: see 'Jihad think-tank to be established in Yemen', *Yemen Observer*, 13 September 2008.
2. Jonathan Mahler, *The Challenge: Hamdan v Rumsfeld and the Fight over Presidential Power* (Farrar, Straus & Giroux, 2008), pp. 5–6. See also

'Detainee Assessment Brief ICO Guantanamo Detainee ISN US9YM-000149DP (S)', US Department of Defence, 4 September 2008.

3. Wright, *The Looming Tower*, p. 97.
4. Source B2, London (2009).
5. Wright, *The Looming Tower*, p. 61. Osama's mother is Syrian.
6. Ibid., p. 97.
7. Ibid., p. 137.
8. Ibid., pp. 104, 138.
9. Ibid., p. 145.
10. Ibid., pp. 132–3.
11. Ibid., p. 150–1.
12. Ibid., p. 234.
13. Ibid., p. 222.
14. Ibid., p. 309.
15. See National Commission on Terrorist Attacks upon the United States, *The 9/11 Commission Report* (W. W. Norton & Co., 2004),p. 59 for details of the Aden bombs; *The 9/11 Commission Report*, pp. 108–9 for Osama bin Laden's links to the bomb plot; p. 218 for Mihdhar's links to the Aden Abyan Islamic Army; and Mary Quin, *Kidnapped in Yemen: One Woman's Amazing Escape from Terrorist Captivity* (Mainstream Publishing, 2006), p. 98 and pp. 216–17 on Abu Hassan.
16. Wright, *The Looming Tower*, p. 310; *The 9/11 Commission Report*, pp. 151 and 155. Khallad is also known as Tawfiq bin Attash, Waleed bin Attash or Walid bin Attash.
17. 'The reeducation of Abu Jandal', *Newsweek*, 8 June 2009. Wright, *The Looming Tower*, p. 248.
18. Ibid., p. 248.
19. Mahler, *The Challenge*, p. 7.
20. Wright, *The Looming Tower*, pp. 5–6.
21. Ibid., p. 273.
22. Ibid., pp. 277–8.
23. Ibid., pp. 275–8.
24. Ibid., p. 271.
25. Ibid., p. 277.
26. Ibid., pp. 283–5, 296. Casualty numbers at Khost were disputed by the Pakistani military, US officials, the Taliban and al-Qaeda—the latter claimed that only three Yemenis and three other men were killed.
27. Ibid., pp. 284–5.
28. Ibid., pp. 289–90.
29. Mahler, *The Challenge*, p. 7.
30. Ibid., p. 9; Wright, *The Looming Tower*, p. 363.
31. 'The reeducation of Abu Jandal', *Newsweek*, 8 June 2009.

32. Wright, *The Looming Tower*, pp. 307–10; *The 9/11 Commission Report*, p. 160.
33. *The 9/11 Commission Report*, pp. 161, 225.
34. Ibid., p. 156.
35. Ibid., p. 232. 'KSM estimates that in any given camp, 70 per cent of the mujahideen were Saudi, 20 per cent were Yemeni, and 10 per cent were from elsewhere. Although Saudi and Yemeni trainees were most often willing to volunteer for suicide operations, before 9/11 it was easier for Saudi operatives to get into the United States.
36. Ibid., p. 181.
37. Wright, *The Looming Tower*, p. 309; *The 9/11 Commission Report*, p. 155.
38. Wright, *The Looming Tower*, p. 310.
39. *The 9/11 Commission Report*, p. 181.
40. Wright, *The Looming Tower*, p. 309. See also *The 9/11 Commission Report*, p. 158. Khallad, Abu Bara and Hazmi travelled to Kuala Lumpur from Karachi, where KSM had schooled them in basic English and coded communications. They were taught how to make travel reservations and read flight schedules, and they watched films featuring hijackings. Mihdhar joined them from Yemen.
41. *The 9/11 Commission Report*, p. 155. Nashiri had fought with the Taliban in Afghanistan before joining al-Qaeda, and his cousin had been a suicide bomber in the 1998 Nairobi attack.
42. Ibid., pp. 151–2. For the authors of *The 9/11 Commission Report*, it was al-Nashiri who managed the operation in Yemen with Khallad's help. For Lawrence Wright, Nashiri was the 'local supervisor' but Khallad was the mastermind: see *The Looming Tower*, p. 318. The *New York Times* website notes: '[Khallad] claims to have been involved in the attack on the United States Navy destroyer *Cole*. In statements made in a Combatants Status Review Tribunal, released by the Defense Department, Mr Attash said he bought the boat, recruited operatives and brought explosives for the October 2000 attack on the ship.' See http://topics.nytimes.com/topics/reference/timestopics/people/a/walid_bin_attash/index.html
43. *The 9/11 Commission Report*, p. 155. 'Khaled was driving the car of another conspirator in the ship-bombing plot who was wanted by the Yemeni authorities.'
44. Ibid.
45. Ibid.
46. Wright, *The Looming Tower*, pp. 299–300.
47. Mahler, *The Challenge*, pp. 8–9; Wright, *The Looming Tower*, p. 338. Abu Jandal's nuptials were arranged and paid for by bin Laden.
48. 'The reeducation of Abu Jandal', *Newsweek*, 8 June 2009.

49. Ibid.
50. *The 9/11 Commission Report*, pp. 156, 191. The two suicide bombers were Hassan al-Khamri and Ibrahim al-Thawar, also known as Nibras.
51. Ibid., p. 191; Wright, *The Looming Tower*, p. 320.
52. Ibid., p. 191.
53. Ibid.
54. Ibid.; Wright, *The Looming Tower*, p. 331.
55. Wright, *The Looming Tower*, p. 318.
56. Ibid., p. 320.
57. *The 9/11 Commission Report*, p. 192.
58. Ibid.
59. Wright, *The Looming Tower*, p. 329.
60. Ibid.
61. *The 9/11 Commission Report*, p. 193. In 2004, when the 9/11 Commission released its public report, the authors described the USS *Cole* attack as a 'full-fledged al Qaeda operation, supervised directly by Bin Laden. He chose the target and location of the attack, selected the suicide operatives and provided the money needed to purchase explosives and equipment' (p. 190).
62. Wright, *The Looming Tower*, p. 330.
63. Ibid., p. 325.
64. Ibid., p. 323.
65. *The 9/11 Commission Report*, p. 192. Wright, *The Looming Tower*, p. 328.
66. Wright, *The Looming Tower*, p. 330. 'It now seems evident that the money was used to purchase first-class air tickets for the 9/11 hijackers Mihdhar and Hazmi and support them when they first arrived in Los Angeles a few days later, which would have been obvious if the CIA had told the bureau about the two AQ operatives.'
67. Ibid., pp. 329–30; *The 9/11 Commission Report*, p. 494.
68. See *The 9/11 Commission Report*, p. 159 on the sequencing of Khallad's two meetings in Bangkok and Kuala Lumpur.
69. Wright, *The Looming Tower*, pp. 310–11.
70. *The 9/11 Commission Report*, p. 354.
71. Wright, *The Looming Tower*, p. 314.
72. Ibid., pp. 309, 314; *The 9/11 Commission Report*, pp. 266–7.
73. Wright, *The Looming Tower*, pp. 330–1.
74. *The 9/11 Commission Report*, p. 272.
75. Wright, *The Looming Tower*, pp. 340–3; *The 9/11 Commission Report*, p. 268.
76. Wright, *The Looming Tower*, pp. 342–3.
77. *The 9/11 Commission Report*, pp. 267–9.
78. Wright, *The Looming Tower*, pp. 341, 352–4; *The 9/11 Commission Report*, p. 270.

79. *The 9/11 Commission Report*, p. 314.
80. Wright, *The Looming Tower*, p. 362.
81. *The 9/11 Commission Report*, p. 267.
82. Wright, *The Looming Tower*, p. 362.
83. Ibid.
84. Ibid., p. 363.
85. Ibid., pp. 363–4.
86. Ibid., p. 365.
87. Ibid., pp. 366–7.
88. Ibid., p. 366.
89. Testimony of Ali Soufan', US Senate Committee on the Judiciary, 13 May 2009.
90. *The 9/11 Commission Report*, p. 336.
91. 'Yemen tries to salvage image', *Christian Science Monitor*, 25 September 2001. See also Human Rights Watch, Disappearances and Arbitrary Arrests in the Armed Conflict with Huthi Rebels in Yemen (Human Rights Watch, October 2008). See http://www.hrw.org/sites/default/files/reports/yemen1008web.pdf. 'Since siding with the United States in its counter-terrorism efforts after September 11, 2001, Yemen's gains in respect for the rule of law and civil rights have eroded.'
92. International Crisis Group, 'Yemen: coping with terrorism and violence in a fragile state', *Middle East Report* 8 (January 2003). The US citizen was Ahmed Hijazi, aka Kamal Derwish. 'After the attack, US officials publicly tied Hijazi to a group in Buffalo that came to be known as the Lackawanna Six. Hijazi had been named as an unindicted co-conspirator in the alleged plot of six Yemeni-Americans to provide material support to Al Qaeda.' See 'The dangerous US game in Yemen', *The Nation*, 30 March 2011.
93. 'The dangerous US game in Yemen', *The Nation*, 30 March 2011.
94. Brian Fishman and Joseph Felter, *Al-Qaida's Foreign Fighters in Iraq—A First Look at the Sinjar Records* (Harmony Project, Combating Terrorism Center at West Point, 2007). See http://www.ctc.usma.edu/wp-content/uploads/2010/06/aqs-foreign-fighters-in-iraq.pdf. This study covers the period between August 2006 and August 2007. The majority of Yemenis travelled to Iraq through Syria—and all Yemeni volunteers crossed the Syrian border, but some came to Syria via Egypt, Jordan, Malaysia and Saudi Arabia.
95. 'Yemen's new anti-terror strategy', BBC News, 16 December 2003.
96. 'A loophole emerges in Yemeni campaign against extremists', *Wall Street Journal*, 14 August 2006.
97. 'The reeducation of Abu Jandal', *Newsweek*, 8 June 2009.
98. Wright, *The Looming Tower*, pp. 364–5.

99. 'USS *Cole* plotter freed by Yemen', BBC News, 27 October 2007.
100. 'Yemen's fight against resurgent Al Qaeda', *Christian Science Monitor*, 29 August 2008.
101. In March 2007, al-Qaeda members assassinated the chief criminal investigator in Marib, Ali Mahmud al-Qasaylah, for his alleged role in the 2002 drone strike that killed Harithi. See 'The dangerous US game in Yemen', *The Nation*, 30 March 2011.
102. 'Yemen's fight against resurgent Al Qaeda', *Christian Science Monitor*, 29 August 2008.
103. Gregory Johnsen, 'Wednesday papers or when al-'Awfi went to Yemen', *Big Think*, 18 February 2009.
104. 'Al Qaeda's most dangerous franchise', *Wall Street Journal*, 10 May 2012.

8. SHADOW WAR: US CRUISE MISSILES AND DRONES

1. The Battle of Marib, Al-Malahim Media, Sha'ban 9, 1430 AH. See http://www.dailymotion.com/video/xbzdmp_battle-of-marib-august-1430-english_travel.
2. Al-Raymi's comments invoked al-Bukhari's hadeeth. See Chapter 1.
3. Sarah Phillips, 'What comes next in Yemen? Al-Qaeda, the tribes, and state-building', Carnegie Endowment for International Peace, Middle East Program no. 107 (March 2010).
4. General Petraeus served as CENTCOM commander from 13 October 2008, to 30 June 2010.
5. The Battle of Marib, Al-Malahim Media, Sha'ban 9, 1430 AH. See http://www.dailymotion.com/video/xbzdmp_battle-of-marib-august-1430-english_travel.
6. http://bigthink.com/ideas/25711: Battle of Marib video, 8 September 2009. Johnsen later joined Buzzfeed and, in 2012, he published his first book: *The Last Refuge: Yemen, Al-Qaeda, and America's War in Arabia*, W.W. Norton & Company.
7. Ibid.
8. 'An act of futility', *Newsweek*, 13 April 2010.
9. http://bigthink.com/ideas/25711: Battle of Marib video, 8 September 2009.
10. Phillips, 'What comes next in Yemen?'.
11. Ibid.
12. The Battle of Marib, Al-Malahim Media, Sha'ban 9, 1430 AH. See http://www.dailymotion.com/video/xbzdmp_battle-of-marib-august-1430-english_travel.
13. Source Q1, Washington DC, March 2010.
14. Phillips, 'What comes next in Yemen?'.

15. Ibid.
16. 'Fears over "internal" terror bomb', BBC News, 26 September 2009.
17. 'People & power: Riyab in Riyadh', Al Jazeera English, 2009.
18. http://www.youtube.com/watch?v=7Vf7hcME0RI. Mohammed al-'Awfi surrended to the Saudi authorities on 17 February 2009. Source: 'Al Qaeda figure surrenders to Saudi authorities', Reuters, 17 February 2009.
19. Human Rights Watch, *No Direction Home: Returns from Guantánamo to Yemen* (Human Rights Watch, 2009). See http://www.hrw.org/sites/default/files/reports/ct0309web.pdf
20. Ginny Hill, 'Yemen: the weakest link', Open Democracy, 31 March 2009. See http://www.opendemocracy.net/article/yemen-the-weakest-link
21. Daniel Benjamin's April 2010 speech to the Jamestown Foundation.
22. 'US military teams, intelligence deeply involved in aiding Yemen on strikes, *Washington Post*, 27 January 2010.
23. See http://wikileaks.org/cable/2009/09/09SANAA1669.html:'Brennan-Saleh meeting', 6 September 2009
24. 'The dangerous US game in Yemen', *The Nation*, 30 March 2011.
25. Ibid.
26. Ibid.
27. Ibid.
28. Gregory Johnsen, 'Week(s) in review: former Guantanamo Bay detainee reportedly killed', *Big Think*, 28 December 2009. See http://bigthink.com/ideas/26050. See 'The dangerous US game in Yemen', *The Nation*, 30 March 2011, for the role of the CTU.
29. Gregory Johnsen claimed the missiles on 24 December hit the farm of Fahd al-Quso—'the cameraman that fell asleep and missed the USS *Cole* strike'. Quso was released from prison in 2007. See: http://bigthink.com/ideas/26050
30. 'Yemen says it attacked a meeting of Al Qaeda', *New York Times*, 24 December 2009.
31. Gregory Johnsen on 'Is the US fighting a secret war in Yemen?' (audio), The Takeaway, 23 December 2009. See http://www.thetakeaway.org/2009/dec/23/us-fighting-secret-war-yemen/
32. 'Officials point to suspect's claim of Qaeda ties in Yemen', *New York Times*, 26 December 2009.
33. Source Q1, London (2009).
34. 'Obama plays down military role in Yemen', *New York Times*, 20 January 2010; 'The dangerous US game in Yemen', *The Nation*, 30 March 2011.
35. 'The dangerous US game in Yemen', *The Nation*, 30 March 2011.
36. 'Should the US engage in Yemen offensive', Fox News, at www.foxnews.com, 3 January 2010.

37. 'Al Qaeda in Yemen and Somalia: a ticking time bomb', US Committee on Foreign Relations, 21 January 2010.
38. Ibid.
39. Ibid.
40. 'Militant video said to show Abdulmutallab in Yemen before failed jet bombing', *New York Times*, 27 April 2010.
41. 'British Muslims detained in Yemen claim they were tortured in prison', the *Guardian*, 11 January 2010.
42. Cori Crider, by email (2011).
43. 'Purported al-Awlaki message calls for jihad against US', CNN, 18 March 2010.
44. 'The new face of al Qaeda?', *Foreign Policy*, 18 May 2011.
45. http://jarretbrachman.net/?p=1398
46. 'Imam's path from condemning terror to preaching jihad', *New York Times*, 8 May 2010.
47. Anwar al-Awlaki, 'Lessons from the companions living as a minority', JIMAS Conference, 2002.
48. 'Imam's path from condemning terror to preaching jihad', *New York Times*, 8 May 2010. Al-Awlaki's phone number was also found in the Hamburg apartment of Ramzi Binalshibh. See 'For lack of hard evidence, a terrorist evaded capture', *Washington Post*, 26 March 2010.
49. 'Imam's path from condemning terror to preaching jihad', *New York Times*, 8 May 2010.
50. Ibid.
51. Ibid.
52. 'The rise of Anwar al-Awlaki', Carnegie Endowment of International Peace, Washington, 1 June 2010.
53. 'Imam's path from condemning terror to preaching jihad', *New York Times*, 8 May 2010. The Yemenis notified US director of national intelligence John Negroponte that they were holding a US citizen. Negroponte supposedly gave a green light to keep holding al-Awlaki without charge. Al-Awlaki was questioned by FBI officials but eventually released, with the consent of US officials. See 'The rise of Anwar al-Awlaki', Carnegie Endowment of International Peace, Washington, 1 June 2010.
54. 'Imam's path from condemning terror to preaching jihad', *New York Times*, 8 May 2010.
55. 'The rise of Anwar al-Awlaki', Carnegie Endowment of International Peace, Washington, 1 June 2010.
56. 'US knew of suspect's tie to radical cleric', *New York Times*, 9 November 2009.
57. 'Imam's path from condemning terror to preaching jihad', *New York Times*, 8 May 2010.

58. 'Death Penalty for Rampage at Fort Hood', *New York Times*, 28 August 2013.
59. 'US knew of suspect's tie to radical cleric', *New York Times*, 9 November 2009.
60. 'Yemen says it attacked a meeting of al Qaeda', *New York Times*, 25 December 2009.
61. 'Country reports on terrorism 2009', US Department of State, Office of the Coordinator for Counterterrorism, August 2010. See http://www.state.gov/j/ct/rls/crt/2009/index.htm. See also 'Officials point to suspect's claim of Qaeda ties in Yemen', *New York Times*, 26 December 2009. However, this report states: 'The cleric is not believed to be Anwar al-Awlaki.'
62. 'Cleric in Yemen admits meeting airliner plot suspect, journalist says', *New York Times*, 31 January 2010.
63. Ibid. Abdulelah Hider Sha'ea was kidnapped in Sana'a six months later. He claimed he was interrogated by the security services, and then released. In January 2011, Sha'ea was rearrested and sentenced to five years in prison on terrorism charges. He was alleged to have provided information about targets to al-Qaeda members while reporting on the group. See 'Yemen sentences American-born cleric in absentia', *New York Times*, 18 January 2011.
64. 'Cleric in Yemen admits meeting airliner plot suspect, journalist says', *New York Times*, 31 January 2010.
65. ABC News, 30 September 2010. See http://abcnews.go.com/blogs/politics/2011/09/the-us-case-against-awlaki/
66. 'Imam's path from condemning terror to preaching jihad', *New York Times*, 8 May 2010.
67. 'US approves targeted killing of American cleric', *New York Times*, 6 April 2010. Confirmation from the White House emerged three months after the *Washington Post* first quoted anonymous military officials as saying that al-Awlaki had 'been added to a shortlist of US citizens specifically targeted for killing or capture' by the Joint Special Operations Command. See 'US military teams, intelligence deeply involved in aiding Yemen on strikes', *Washington Post*, 27 January 2010.
68. 'US approves targeted killing of American cleric', *New York Times*, 6 April 2010.
69. 'Yemen balks at possible US strike on cleric Anwar al-Awlaki', *Christian Science Monitor*, 12 April 2010. 'The LWOT: US confirms Awlaki on CIA hit list; Gitmo military trial begins', *Foreign Policy*, 8 April 2010. 'Any US attempt to kill Awlaki in Yemen unacceptable, Reuters, 31 May 2010.
70. 'Yemen balks at possible US strike on Cleric Anwar al-Awlaki', *Christian Science Monitor*, 12 April 2010.

71. Source Z2, London (2010).
72. 'US turns up heat on internet Imam Awlaki', National Public Radio, 29 July 2010. 'For lack of hard evidence, a terrorist evaded capture', *Washington Post*, 26 March 2010.
73. 'The rise of Anwar al-Awlaki', Carnegie Endowment of International Peace, Washington, 1 June, 2010
74. 'Incomplete picture on justification for killing American citizen', *The Atlantic*, 7 April 2010. 'US turns up heat on internet Imam Awlaki', National Public Radio, 29 July 2010.
75. 'Country reports on terrorism 2009'. US Department of State, Office of the Coordinator for Counterterrorism, August 2010. In 2017, the FBI released 200 pages of redacted interview summaries to The New York Times, following a two-year legal battle under the Freedom of Information Act, which suggested 'that the Obama administration had ample firsthand testimony from Mr. Abdulmutallab that the cleric oversaw his training and conceived the plot.' See 'Inside Al Qaeda's Plot to Blow Up an American Airliner', *New York Times*, 22 February 2017. See also Scott Shane, *Objective Troy: A Terrorist, a President, and the Rise of the Drone* (Tim Duggan Books, 2016).
76. 'Incomplete picture on justification for killing American citizen', *The Atlantic*, 7 April 2010
77. 'Focus on internet Imams as al Qaeda recruiters', *New York Times*, 1 January 2010.
78. 'The rise of Anwar al-Awlaki', Carnegie Endowment for International Peace, Washington, 1 June 2010.
79. Ibid.
80. Ibid.
81. 'An act of futility', *Newsweek*, 13 April 2010.
82. Ibid.
83. 'Blogging Imam who counseled Fort Hood gunman and 9/11 hijacker goes silent', *New York Times*, 13 November 2009. See also http://jarretbrachman.net
84. An English translation of al-Malahem's video release: 'A premiere and exclusive interview with the Islamic preacher, Sheikh Anwar al-Awlaqi', The Global Islamic Media Front, Jumada al-Thani 43, May 2010. See http://publicintelligence.net/anwar-al-awlaki-may-2010-interview-video/
85. Ibid.
86. 'Yemen will be Obama's Afghanistan, warns al-Qaeda cleric', *Daily Telegraph*, 20 July 2010; 'ACLU sues to represent suspected terrorist in Yemen', *Los Angeles Times*, 4 August 2010.
87. UN 1267 Committee's Sanctions List. See http://www.un.org/sc/committees/1267/pdf/AQList.pdf

88. 'US turns up heat on internet Imam Awlaki', National Public Radio, 29 July 2010.

89. 'Civil liberties groups win approval to sue US over terror target list', Bloomberg, 5 August 2010. See http://www.bloomberg.com/news/2010–08–05/u-s-terrorist-hit-list-may-face-legal-challenge-by-civil-liberties-groups.html

90. Ginny Hill and Gerd Nonneman, 'Yemen, Saudi Arabia and the Gulf states: elite politics, street protests and Regional Diplomacy', Chatham House briefing paper, May 2011. See http://www.chathamhouse.org/sites/default/files/19237_0511yemen_gulfbp.pdf. In the UK, Awlaki was linked to Roshonara Choudhry's attempt to murder British MP Stephen Timms and Rajib Karim's plot to attack British Airways flights. See also 'The new face of al Qaeda?', Foreign Policy, 18 May 2011.

91. 'The new face of al Qaeda?', Foreign Policy, 18 May 2011.

92. 'Development in the 21st century', Center for Global Development, 6 January 2010.

93. 'High-level meeting on Yemen: chairman's statement', 27 January 2010. See http://reliefweb.int/report/yemen/high-level-meeting-yemen-chairmans-statement

94. Source Y2, USA (2010).

95. 'US drones on hunt in Yemen', Washington Post, 7 November 2010; 'US pursues wider role in Yemen', Wall Street Journal, 16 November 2010. For more information on US military aid to Yemen, see Jeremy Sharp, 'Yemen: Background and US Relations', Congressional Research Service, 6 October 2011. See http://www.fas.org/sgp/crs/mideast/RL34170.pdf

96. Ginny Hill, 'What is happening in Yemen?', Survival: Global Politics and Strategy 52/2 (April–May 2010), pp. 83–104.

97. Ibid.

98. 'Secret assault on terrorism widens on two continents', New York Times, 14 August 2010.

99. Ibid.

100. 'US is said to expand secret actions in mideast', New York Times, 24 May 2010.

101. See http://wikileaks.org/cable/2010/01/10SANAA4.html: 'General Petraeus' meeting with Saleh on security', 4 January 2010.

102. 'The dangerous US game in Yemen', The Nation, 30 March 2011.

103. It was this report that first quoted anonymous military officials as saying that al-Awlaki was one of three Americans who had 'been added to a shortlist of US citizens specifically targeted for killing or capture' by the Joint Special Operations Command (JSOC). See 'US

military teams, intelligence deeply involved in aiding Yemen on strikes', *Washington Post*, 27 January 2010.

104. Ibid.

105. 'Tribes: government must surrender air strike maestro, or else', *Yemen Times*, 26 May 2010.

106. Scahill notes that Shabwani was in a key position to negotiate, given that his brother, Ayad, was the local AQAP leader. See 'The dangerous US game in Yemen', *The Nation*, 30 March 2011.

107. 'Secret assault on terrorism widens on two continents', *New York Times*, 14 August 2010.

108. 'A hot summer of discontent', *The National*, 12 June 2009.

109. Aden had been plagued by power cuts in summer 2009, but Thanos Petouris believed that by summer 2010, Saleh was trying to avoid giving a pretext to southerners for unrest.

110. 'Secret assault on terrorism widens on two continents', *New York Times*, 14 August 2010.

111. 'US is said to expand secret actions in mideast', *New York Times*, 24 May 2010.

112. 'Yemen covert role pushed', *Wall Street Journal*, 1 November 2010.

113. 'US is said to expand secret actions in mideast', *New York Times*, 24 May 2010.

114. 'The dangerous US game in Yemen', *The Nation*, 30 March 2011.

115. 'US pursues wider role in Yemen', *Wall Street Journal*, 16 November 2010. See also 'U.S. doubts intelligence that led to Yemen strike', *Wall Street Journal*, 29 December 2011.

116. 'US sees complexity of bombs as link to al Qaeda', *New York Times*, 30 October 2010.

117. Ibid. See also 'Saudi dominate Yemen security help', Reuters, 18 January 2010. See http://wikileaks.org/cable/2009/05/09 RIYADH670.html, 'Special Advisor Holbrooke's meeting with Saudi Assistant Interior Minister Prince Mohammed bin Nayef', 16 May 2009.

118. Abdullah al-Asiri's brother Ibrahim was suspected of manufacturing the PETN explosive devices used in the attack on Prince Mohammed bin Naif, the Detroit plane bomb and the ink cartridges plot.

119. 'Bombs tip-off "came from former al-Qaeda member"', BBC News, 1 November 2010. Gregory Johnsen, 'Saudi disinformation?', 18 October 2010. See http://bigthink.com/ideas/26148. US analyst and blogger Gregory Johnsen disputed this claim, arguing 'that al-Fayfi couldn't have been the intelligence link that led to the discovery of the bombs as AQAP knew he was "captured" or "arrested" [...] and AQAP should have known that any information he had was

compromised'. See 'Initial notes on AQAP's statements', 5 November 2010, http://bigthink.com/ideas/26242

120. 'US looks at bolstering funding for Yemeni military', Agence France-Presse, 2 September 2010.

121. 'Front row seat with Yemeni forces', ABC News, 5 January 2010.

122. See http://wikileaks.org/cable/2009/09/09SANAA1669.html: 'Brennan-Saleh meeting', 6 September 2009.

123. Source H1, location withheld (2010).

9. SOUTHERN DISCOMFORT: BIRTH OF THE SOUTHERN SEPARATIST MOVEMENT(S)

1. The International Crisis Group noted that Britain's 'colonial history in South Yemen places the UK in a unique position. It is common to hear Southerners, especially Adenis, speaking fondly of the British period, selectively ignoring the bitterness of occupation, strongly felt at the time' and claiming that British rule was 'more tolerable' than subsequent northern dominance. See International Crisis Group, 'Breaking point? Yemen's southern question', *Middle East Report* 114, 20 October 2011, p. 22. See http://www.crisisgroup.org/~/media/Files/Middle%20East%20North%20Africa/Iran%20Gulf/Yemen/114%20Breaking%20Point%20—%20Yemens%20Southern%20Question.pdf.

2. Ibid.

3. Ibid.

4. The first fatalities occurred in Habilayn—the same city where the independence struggle took off against British rule in 1963. 'The symbolic impact of the Habilayn shooting on 13 October 2007 galvanised protests, and soon thousands joined the pensioners in a much broader movement'. See International Crisis Group, 'Breaking point? Yemen's southern question', *Middle East Report* 114 (20 October 2011).

5. Source M1, Sana'a (2010). In fact, the government did reinstate a number of retired officers and/or increase pension payments but these, and other, concessions 'were inadequate, came too late and were never part of a strategic vision for sustained development in, and political inclusion of the South'. See Nicole Stracke and Mohammed Saif Haidar, 'The southern movement in Yemen', Gulf Research Center and Sheba Centre for Strategic Studies, April 2010, www.grc.net/data/contents/uploads/The_Southern_Movement_in_Yemen_4796.pdf; (also International Crisis Group, 'Breaking point? Yemen's southern question', *Middle East Report* 114 (20 October 2011).

6. Human Rights Watch, *In the Name of Unity: The Yemeni Government's Brutal Response to Southern Movement Protests*, (Human Rights Watch, 2009). See

http://www.hrw.org/sites/default/files/reports/southyemen1209web-wcover.pdf

7. Ibid.

8. Ibid. See also International Crisis Group, 'Breaking point? Yemen's southern question', *Middle East Report* 114 (20 October 2011).

9. 'Yemen: economic crisis underpins southern separatism', *Arab Reform Bulletin*, 2 June 2009 (Carnegie Endowment for International Peace).

10. Ibid.

11. International Crisis Group, 'Breaking point? Yemen's southern question', *Middle East Report* 114 (20 October 2011).

12. 'Yemen: economic crisis underpins southern separatism', Arab Reform Bulletin, 2 June 2009 (Carnegie Endowment for International Peace). By October 2011, five main groups represented the hiraak inside Yemen. The largest and most influential appeared to be the Council of the Peaceful Movement to Liberate the South, under President Hassan Baoum. Two UK-based organizations, the Democratic Forum for South Yemen (TAJ) and the National Forum for Supporting the Southern Movement, represented the hiraak overseas. See International Crisis Group, 'Breaking point? Yemen's southern question', *Middle East Report 114* (20 October 2011).

13. Source M1, Sana'a (2010).

14. See Nicole Stracke and Mohammed Saif Haidar, 'The southern movement in Yemen', Gulf Research Center and Sheba Centre for Strategic Studies, April 2010.

15. International Crisis Group, 'Breaking point? Yemen's southern question', *Middle East Report* 114 (20 October 2011).

16. 'Yemen: economic crisis underpins southern separatism', Arab Reform Bulletin, 2 June 2009 (Carnegie Endowment for International Peace). The Gulf states are formally committed to Yemeni unity. Al-Beidh had been living in Oman since 1994, but in May 2009, the Omani government withdrew his residency rights and he moved to Europe. See Nicole Stracke and Mohammed Saif Haidar, 'The southern movement in Yemen', Gulf Research Center and Sheba Centre for Strategic Studies, April 2010.

17. Source T1, location withheld (2009).

18. Source R2, by email (2009).

19. *Al-Sharq Al-Awsat* is published by the Saudi Research and Marketing Group.

20. Tariq al-Fahdli's press statement was issued on 2 April 2009.

21. Source W1, Aden (2010). 'Before joining the Hiraak in March 2009, Fadli was a member of the ruling party's highest executive body, the General Committee. His base of support is the Fadli tribe in Zinjibar,

and he has a mercurial relationship with other Hiraak leaders, at times cooperating with them and at others publicly attacking former socialist leaders. He is a pragmatic opportunist, known for quick shifts in allegiances—from the regime to the Hiraak, away from the Hiraak, back to the Hiraak, etc.—yet he retains support from tribesmen and mujahidin networks.' See International Crisis Group, 'Breaking point? Yemen's southern question', *Middle East Report* 114 (20 October 2011).

22. Human Rights Watch, *In the Name of Unity: The Yemeni Government's Brutal Response to Southern Movement Protests*, (Human Rights Watch, 2009).
23. Ibid.
24. 'Ex-jihadist defies Yemen's leader, and easy labels' *New York Times*, 26 February 2010. Al-Fahdli's age was given as 42 in this article.
25. Ibid.
26. 'Al Qaeda call for Islamic state in southern Yemen', *Asharq Al-Awsat*, 14 May 2009. 'Al Qaeda calls for Islamic rule after Yemen violence', Reuters, 13 May 2009.
27. 'Yemen: economic crisis underpins southern separatism', *Arab Reform Bulletin*, 2 June 2009 (Carnegie Endowment for International Peace).
28. Source J4, date and location withheld.
29. The explosion dislodged some of the shutters on a former British garrison church, located more than 2 km away from the *Cole*. The church held a service to mark the tenth anniversary of the attack on 12 October 2010.
30. Container portation is measured in 20 ft equivalent units (TEUs).
31. By 2011, the volume of container trade had fallen further still to 170,000 TEUs, as Aden lost its transshipment business, and Aden handled only 'base load' cargo (that is, cargo that is specifically shipped to or from Aden). However, the 2011 volume was nearly twenty times the volume of container trade—9,000 TEUs—handled at Aden in 1995.
32. Sally Healy and Ginny Hill, 'Yemen and Somalia: terrorism, shadow networks and the limitations of state-building', Chatham House briefing paper, 2010.
33. Southerners made claims to future Iranian support on the basis that the PDRY had supported Teheran during the Iran–Iraq War in the 1980s. Sources L3 and M3, Aden (2010), Source D4, location withheld (2011).
34. Khadija is not her real name.
35. For a more detailed discussion of Adeni culture and identity, see International Crisis Group, 'Breaking point? Yemen's southern question', *Middle East Report* 114 (20 October 2011).

36. Dresch, *A History of Modern Yemen*, p. 197.

37. 'Yemeni security forces fire on newspaper offices', Committee to Protect Journalists, New York, 13 May 2009. http://www. refworld. org/cgi-bin/texis/vtx/rwmain?page=country&catego ry=&publisher =CPJ&type=&coi=YEM&rid=&docid=4a1d5d78c &skip=0

38. Death threats against Al Jazeera staff came from a phone number registered in Saudi Arabia. A number of Yemeni bloggers living in Saudi Arabia were also detained or rendered to Yemen. See Human Rights Watch, *In the Name of Unity*.

39. 'In Yemen, press freedom worst in 20 years', Committee to Protect Journalists blog, 16 July 2010.

40. Hani and Mohammed were released on 8 May 2010, and all charges against *Al-Ayyam* and the Bashraheels were dropped on 21 May 2010, following a presidential pardon.

41. Frank is not his real name.

42. 'How I got detained and permanently banned from Yemen', Voice of America, 21 May 2010.

43. The hiraak had its core support in southern Dhala and Lahj governorates, where the movement started and where demands for separation appeared to be strongest. The International Crisis Group noted that these areas 'provided the bulk of the PDRY's army. After the 1994 civil war, these areas suffered most from forced retirement.' The International Crisis Group also noted that the hiraak's armed wing, Haraka Taqreer al-Maseer (The Movement for Self-Determination), was most active in Dhala and Radfan, and 'by most estimates has a maximum of several hundred fighters'. See International Crisis Group, 'Breaking point? Yemen's southern question', *Middle East Report* 114 (20 October 2011).

44. The ICG noted that 'support for the Hiraak appears less ubiquitous in Abyan and Shebwa, where leaders arguably have benefited more from unity, given their alliance with the Saleh regime. Reflecting the population and its social and political preferences, the Hiraak there tends to be less secular and more deeply enmeshed in tribal loyalties.' It also notes that divisions between the Zumra (primarily from Abyan and Shabwa) and the Tughma (mostly from Dhala and Lahj) have their roots in the politics of the 1980s. See International Crisis Group, 'Breaking point? Yemen's southern question', *Middle East Report* 114 (20 October 2011).

45. http://www.myspace.com/akon

46. The Union of the Southern Youth under the leadership of Fadi Hasan Ba'aum was the only group that provided a platform for the youth. Fadi was sentenced by a court in Yemen to five years' imprisonment

on 29 March 2010. Fadi's father, Hasan Ba'aum, led the Higher National Council for the Liberation of the South. See Nicole Stracke and Mohammed Saif Haidar, 'The southern movement in Yemen', Gulf Research Center and Sheba Centre for Strategic Studies, April 2010.

47. Interview with Thanos Petouris, 2011.

48. Hadramaut is Yemen's 'largest governorate, covering approximately 37 per cent of the country's total land mass, but is home to only 5 per cent of the population.' See International Crisis Group, 'Breaking point? Yemen's southern question', *Middle East Report* 114 (20 October 2011).

49. Ibid.

50. 'Southerners seeking independence tend to downplay Hadramawt's uniqueness, while those supporting unity often invoke the threat of Hadrami secession as an argument against opening the Pandora's Box of federalism.' See ibid.

51. Sources L3 and M3, Aden (2010).

52. Interview with Thanos Petouris, by email (2011).

53. International Crisis Group, 'Breaking point? Yemen's southern question', *Middle East Report* 114 (20 October 2011).

54. Ibid.

55. Ibid.

56. 'Democracy on hold in Yemen', *Arab Reform Bulletin*, 13 July 2010 (Carnegie Endowment for International Peace).

57. The JMP's initiative was known as the Preparatory Committee for National Dialogue. See International Crisis Group, 'Breaking point? Yemen's southern question', *Middle East Report* 114 (20 October 2011).

58. http://yemenvision.wordpress.com/

59. See http://wikileaks.org/cable/2009/08/09SANAA1617.html: 'Yemen: Hamid Al-Ahmar sees Saleh as weak and isolated, plans next steps', 31 August 2009.

60. 'Without Borders' talk show Al Jazeera, 5 August 2009.

61. Source A1.

62. 'US was told of Yemen leader's vulnerability', *Washington Post*, 8 April 2010.

63. Nuba was 'considered one of the Southern protest movement's founders but his influence has lessened over time'. See International Crisis Group, 'Breaking point? Yemen's southern question', *Middle East Report* 114 (20 October 2011).

64. 'Democracy on hold in Yemen', *Arab Reform Bulletin*, 13 July 2010 (Carnegie Endowment for International Peace).

10. BLACK BOX: HOUTHI-LED INSURGENCY IN THE NORTHERN PROVINCE OF SAADA

1. For a Yemeni journalist's report based on government-approved access to Saada and published in a pro-government English-language newspaper, see 'Media finally allowed into Sa'ada, to report on life there after war', *Yemen Observer*, 26 June 2007.
2. www.amnesty.org.uk/alkhaiwani
3. Maysaa Shuja al-Deen, 'Media absent from Yemen's forgotten war', *Arab Media & Society* 8 (spring 2009).
4. 'Qatar, playing all sides, is a nonstop mediator', *New York Times*, 9 July 2008.
5. 'Yemen northern rebels move near capital', Associated Press, 5 May 2008. http://usatoday30.usatoday.com/news/world/2008–05–31–3913491873_x.htm
6. Source K2, Sana'a (2008).
7. Source L2, Sana'a (2008).
8. Source V1, Sana'a (2008).
9. 'War is over, Al Houthi says in letter to president', Gulf News, 7 August 2008.
10. Human Rights Watch, *Invisible Civilians: The Challenge of Humanitarian Access in Yemen's Forgotten War* (Human Rights Watch, November 2008). See http://www.hrw.org/sites/default/files/reports/yemen1108web-wcover.pdf
11. Human Rights Watch, *Disappearances and Arbitrary Arrests in the Armed Conflict with Huthi Rebels in Yemen* (Human Rights Watch, October 2008).
12. There were exceptions, such as Yahya Mutawakkil, who was interior minister in the 1970s.
13. Dresch, *A History of Modern Yemen*, p, 123.
14. Source E2, Sana'a (2007).
15. Source F2, Sana'a (2007).
16. Source H2, Sana'a (2007).
17. Sarah Phillips, 'Cracks in the Yemeni system', *Middle East Report* (Middle East Research and Information Project, 28 July 2005). See http://www.merip.org/mero/mero072805. Several leading Zaydi ulama since distanced themselves in writing from the Zaydi principle that the ruler must be a *sayyid*, according to Source H1 (2012).
18. Source H1, location withheld (2012).
19. Source H1, location withheld (2009).
20. Source I2, location withheld (2009).
21. Source H1, location withheld (2009). Mohammed al-Badr died in the London suburb of Bromley in 2004.

22. Human Rights Watch, *Invisible Civilians*. The Houthi rallying cry is known as al Sarkha.
23. Saleh also accused the Houthis of accepting support from Libya, Iran, Hizbollah, Iraq's Sadrists and the Yemeni Jews.
24. Source H1, location withheld (2009).
25. Source O1, location withheld (2008).
26. Al-Haqq was dismantled after the rebellion got under way.
27. Source M2, by phone (2008).
28. Source H1, location withheld (2009).
29. Source H1, by email (2012).
30. 'The conflict in Saada governorate—analysis', IRIN, 24 July 2008. See http://www.irinnews.org/Report/79410/YEMEN-The-conflict-in-Saada-Governorate-analysis
31. Source H1, location withheld (2009).
32. Human Rights Watch, *Disappearances and Arbitrary Arrests*.
33. Source F2, Sana'a (2007).
34. 'Secret mission rescues Yemen's Jews', *Wall Street Journal*, 31 October 2009.
35. Martin Lings, *Muhammad: His Life Based on the Earliest Sources* (The Islamic Texts Society, 1983; audiobook timecode 1:15).
36. 'Mediators try to persuade Yemeni dissident scholar to surrender', Agence France-Presse, 27 June 2004.
37. Source H1, location withheld (2009). See 'Interpol agrees to extradite al-Houthi, government says', *Yemen Observer*, 14 April 2007.
38. 'The tragedy of the Yemeni Jews', *The Guardian*, June 2009.
39. 'Yemeni Jews to emigrate secretly', *Yemen Observer* 20 May 2009; 'Secret mission rescues Yemen's Jews', *Wall Street Journal* 31 October 2009. See also 'Hackney: the Promised Land for Yemen's Jews', the *Independent*, 25 March 2010.
40. 'Yemeni republican elites, although only rarely being Salafis themselves, appeared to tolerate this movement if not support its rise since the 1980s because of its antagonism with Zaydi royalists and revivalists and due to its appeal for automatic loyalty to government.' See Bonnefoy, *Salafism in Yemen: Transnationalism and Religious Identity*, p. 147.
41. 'Salafism in Yemen: a "Saudisation"?', in Madawi al-Rasheed (ed.), *Kingdom without Borders* (Hurst, 2008), pp. 245–62.
42. Saleh initially supported the Zaydi revival movement, but he later backtracked and started shutting down Zaidi revivalist madrassas. See Human Rights Watch, *Invisible Civilians*.
43. Human Rights Watch, *Invisible Civilians*.
44. Laurent Bonnefoy, 'Varieties of Islamism in Yemen: the logic of integration under pressure', *The Middle East Review of International Affairs* 13/1 (March 2009).

45. Shelagh Weir, 'A clash of fundamentalisms: Wahhabism in Yemen', Middle East Report, Middle East Research and Information Project 204 (July–September 1997). See http://www.merip.org/mer/mer204/clash-fundamentalisms
46. Source T2, Sana'a (2008).
47. Laurent Bonnefoy, 'Varieties of Islamism in Yemen: the logic of integration under pressure', Middle East Review of International Affairs 13/1 (March 2009).
48. Source A1 (2010).
49. 'Salih and the Yemeni succession', Jane's Intelligence Digest, 18 August 2008.
50. International Crisis Group, 'Yemen: defusing the Saada time bomb', Middle East Report 86 (27 May 2009) p. 15.
51. Source T2, Sana'a (2008).
52. Source A1 (2010).
53. 'Salih and the Yemeni succession', Jane's Intelligence Digest, 18 August 2008.
54. Ibid.
55. Source A1 (2008).
56. 'Salih and the Yemeni succession', Jane's Intelligence Digest, 18 August 2008.
57. Source Z1, Sana'a (2008).
58. Ibid.
59. Ibid.
60. Government soldiers and Huthi forces were also accused of looting. Human Rights Watch, Invisible Civilians.
61. Source Z1, Sana'a (2008).
62. International Crisis Group, 'Yemen: defusing the Saada time bomb', Middle East Report 86 (27 May 2009) pp. 15–16.
63. Ibid., p. 16.
64. Ibid.
65. Ibid.
66. Source E1, by email (2009).
67. International Crisis Group, 'Yemen: defusing the Saada time bomb', Middle East Report 86 (27 May 2009) p. 16.
68. 'Saudi-Yemen talks set on cross-border smuggling', Arab News, 31 January 2007.
69. International Crisis Group, 'Yemen: defusing the Saada time bomb', Middle East Report 86 (27 May 2009) p. 16.
70. In a single year, Saudi border guards stopped 344, 781 intruders and 2,894 smugglers and confiscated 12,000 kg of hashish, 32 kg of opium, 10,000 narcotic tablets and more than five million kg of qat.

See 'Saudi-Yemen talks set on cross-border smuggling', *Arab News*, 31 January 2007.

71. Source V2, Sana'a (2010).
72. Several hostages were working for the Christian charity Worldwide Services, which gave rise to allegations that they had been killed for proselytizing.
73. The reward sum was a hundred times higher than a good annual salary in Yemen.
74. Source U2, Sana'a (2010).
75. Source A1 (2010).
76. Source U2, Sana'a (2010).
77. For 2008, see 'In pictures: aftermath of Yemeni strikes in Sa'ada', *The Long War Journal*, http://www.longwarjournal.org/multimedia/Yemen-Saada/index.html. For earlier rounds, see witness testimony published in 2005 on www.armiesof liberation.com
78. 'War crimes in Yemen?', the *Guardian*, 18 September 2009.
79. In 2009, Médecins Sans Frontières (MSF) decided to include Saada in its annual 'top 10 humanitarian crises'. Yemen's response was to suspend authorization for all MSF activities throughout the country and to offer a deal: MSF could resume operations but only if it agreed to deny that the Yemeni government was restricting access and that there was a health-care crisis. MSF reluctantly agreed, issuing a letter acknowledging that its report might have appeared biased. See http://www.guardian.co.uk/global-development/2011/nov/20/medecins-sans-frontieres-book?newsfeed=true
80. Source N2, location and date withheld.
81. Ibid.
82. Source X2, by email (2010).
83. 'Does Iran play role in Yemen conflict?', *Christian Science Monitor*, 11 November 2009.
84. 'Huthi field commander interviewed on Yemen hostilities, contacts with Iran', *Al-Sharq Al-Awsat*, 20 September 2009.
85. See http://wikileaks.ch/cable/2009/12/09RIYADH1687. html. Houthis claim they had pushed the Yemeni army from Jabal Dukhan, a strategic mountain on the border, and agreed with the Saudis that the Yemeni army would not be allowed to take up positions there again. As the army returned, so did the Houthis; Saudi border posts opened fire, killing one or two. For a timeline of the military conflict, see AEI Critical Threats, 'Tracker: Saudi Arabia's military operations along Yemeni border', 7 January 2010: http://www.criticalthreats.org/yemen/tracker-saudi-arabia%E2%80%99s-military-operations-along-yemeni-border

86. 'Tracker: Saudi Arabia's Military Operations Along Yemeni Border', criticalthreats.org, 4 January 2010. See also Hill and Nonneman, 'Yemen, Saudi Arabia and the Gulf states: elite politics, street protests and regional diplomacy', Chatham House briefing paper, 2011. France and the United States provided the Saudis with satellite imagery to improve precision bombing, ostensibly to avoid civilian casualties; the US also supplied 'stocks of ammunition'. Also see http://wikileaks. ch/cable/2009/12/09RIYADH1687. html

87. 'Yemen conflict creates Saudi problems', UPI, 14 October 2009.

88. See http://wikileaks.ch/cable/2009/12/09RIYADH1687.html

89. Ibid.

90. Ginny Hill and Gerd Nonneman, 'Yemen, Saudi Arabia and the Gulf states: elite politics, street protests and regional diplomacy', Chatham House briefing paper, 2011.

91. 10RIYADH159, released 7 December 2010, subject: (S) Saudi Arabia: Renewed Assurances on Satellite Imagery.

92. In 2010, Eid al-Ghadeer was celebrated on 24 November, the same day as the Houthis announced the death of Badr al-Deen.

93. Hundreds of Houthi prisoners had been released, but reconstruction efforts were hampered by Saleh's reluctance to authorize large flows of funds to the region, and to grant humanitarian agencies access to Houthi-controlled areas. See Ginny Hill and Gerd Nonneman, 'Yemen, Saudi Arabia and the Gulf states: elite politics, street protests and regional diplomacy', Chatham House briefing paper, 2011.

94. 'Saudi forces rescue German girls held hostage in Yemen', *The Guardian*, 18 May 2010.

95. 'UK is "doing too little to free British hostage in Yemen"', *The Independent*, 23 May 2010.

96. Carter 1977–81, Reagan 1981–9, Bush 1989–93, Clinton 1993–2001, Bush 2001–9, Obama 2009–13. Callaghan 1976–9, Thatcher 1979–90, Major 1990–7, Blair 1997–2007, Brown 2007–9, Cameron 2010–15.

11. CHANGE SQUARE: YOUTH ACTIVISTS AND THE 2011 UPRISING

1. *Times* stringer Iona Craig and *New York Times* stringer Laura Kasinof both produced outstanding reports throughout the uprising.

2. Tawakkol Karman founded an advocacy group in 2005 called Women Journalists without Chains. In 2007, she began staging sit-ins in front of Yemen's parliament and cabinet buildings, demanding greater press freedoms and more humane treatment for marginalized groups. See 'Among 3 women awarded Nobel Peace Prize, a nod to the Arab Spring', *New York Times*, 7 October 2011.

3. 'Letter from Yemen: after the uprising', *New Yorker*, 11 April 2011.
4. 'Yemen's opposition goes to code pink', *New York Times*, 27 January 2011.
5. 'Letter from Yemen: after the uprising', *New Yorker*, 11 April 2011.
6. 'Waves of unrest spread to Yemen, shaking a region', *New York Times*, 27 January 2011. See also 'In Taiz, Yemen Protest Movement Grows', *New York Times*, 25 February 2011.
7. Source D3, by telephone (2011).
8. The proposal had been circulated for discussion in early January, and was sure to be endorsed by parliament, where the GPC held a super-majority.
9. 'Violence erupts on fourth day of protests in Yemen', *New York Times*, 14 February 2011.
10. 'Clashes over Yemen's government leave 2 protesters dead', *New York Times*, 22 February 2011.
11. 'Letter from Yemen: after the uprising', *New Yorker*, 11 April 2011. 'Clashes over Yemen's government leave 2 protesters dead', *New York Times*, 22 February 2011.
12. 'Yemen's big protests: Saleh's opponents get critical mass', *Time*, 25 February 2011.
13. Ibid.
14. Ibid.
15. Ibid.
16. Ibid.
17. Gregory Johnsen, 'The tribal element of the protests: a battle between the two Bayt al-Ahmars (updated)', *Big Think*, 17 February 2010. See http://bigthink.com/waq-al-waq/the-tribal-element-of-the-protests-a-battle-between-the-two-bayt-al-ahmars-updated.
18. 'Letter from Yemen: after the uprising', *New Yorker*, 11 April 2011.
19. Ibid.
20. 'Tawakul Karman, Yemeni activist, and thorn in the side of Saleh', the *Guardian*, 26 March 2011.
21. Interview with Rafat al-Akhali, by telephone (2011).
22. http://ionacraig.tumblr.com/post/4771214027/march12-clashes-sanaa-yemen. See also 'Yemen police and protesters clash as deal is sought to end political crisis', *New York Times* 19 April 2011.
23. 'Yemen police and protesters clash as deal is sought to end political crisis', *New York Times*, 19 April 2011.
24. http://bit.ly/g5PRvu
25. Human Rights Watch, *Days of Bloodshed in Aden* (Human Rights Watch, 9 March 2011). See http://www.hrw.org/sites/default/files/reports/yemen0311webwcover.pdf

26. 'Dozens injured in clashes in Yemen', *New York Times*, 17 March 2011.

27. 'Dozens of protesters are killed in Yemen', *New York Times*, 18 March 2011. See also karamahasnowalls.com

28. Ibid.

29. Ibid.

30. 'In Yemen, opposition encourages protesters', *New York Times*, 19 March 2011. See also http://ionacraig.tumblr.com/post/4088293825/sanaasnipersyemen

31. 'Dozens of protesters are killed in Yemen', *New York Times*, 18 March 2011.

32. 'In Yemen, opposition encourages protesters', *New York Times*, 19 March 2011.

33. Ibid.

34. 'Key supporters are forsaking Yemen leader', *New York Times*, 21 March 2011.

35. Ibid.

36. Ibid.

37. 'In Yemen, opposition encourages protesters', *New York Times*, 19 March 2011.

38. 'Yemen's leader in talks on exit but still defiant', *New York Times*, 24 March 2011.

39. Ibid.

40. 'Yemeni leader would yield power only to "safe hands"', *New York Times*, 25 March 2011.

41. Ibid.

42. 'Yemen talks stall', *Wall Street Journal*, 28 March 2011.

43. 'Yemen protests have US worried about ally's future', Agence France-Presse, 2 March 2011.

44. US shifts to seek removal of Yemen's leader, an ally', *New York Times*, 3 April 2011.

45. Ibid.

46. Ibid.

47. 'Yemeni opposition sets meeting with Gulf bloc', *New York Times*, 17 April 2011.

48. 'Yemeni opposition conditionally welcomes Gulf plan', Reuters, 23 April 2011.

49. 'President of Yemen offers to leave, with conditions', *New York Times*, 23 April 2011.

50. 'Yemen's opposition accepts deal for transfer of power', *New York Times*, 25 April 2011.

51. 'President of Yemen offers to leave, with conditions', *New York Times*, 23 April 2011.

52. 'Deal to end Yemen crisis is faltering as talks bog', *New York Times*, 1 May 2011.

53. 'Bin Laden's preoccupation with US said to be source of friction with followers', *Washington Post*, 12 May 2011.

54. Sebastian Rotella, 'New details in the bin Laden docs: portrait of a fugitive micro-manager', ProPublica, 11 May 2011. See http://www.propublica.org/article/bin-laden-documents-portrait-of-a-fugitive-micro-manager

55. Ibid.

56. See http://articles.cnn.com/2011–03–23/world/yemen. protests_1_president-ali-abdullah-saleh-abyan-province-jmp/2?_s=PM:WORLD

57. 'US shifts to seek removal of Yemen's leader, an ally', *New York Times*, 3 April 2011.

58. 'The youth will win in Yemen', the *Guardian*, 12 May 2011.

59. http://www.youtube.com/watch?v=HpkN-hPTeg0&feature=share

60. Tawakul Karman, Yemeni activist, and thorn in the side of Saleh', the *Guardian*, 26 March 2011.

61. 'In Yemen, sit-in against the government yields business opportunities', *New York Times*, 30 March 2011.

62. See 'Draft document: demands of the youth revolution, April 2011': https://www.facebook.com/CCYRC

63. 'Yemeni leader refuses deal', *New York Times*, 18 May 2011.

64. 'Yemeni leader's allies blockade embassy as he refuses peace deal', *New York Times*, 22 May 2011.

65. 'After talks collapse, violence flares in Yemen', *New York Times*, 23 May 2011.

66. 'Clashes in Yemen spread to tribes beyond capital', *New York Times*, 26 May 2011.

67. 'Fighting intensifies in Yemen as the government battles tribal groups', *New York Times*, 24 May 2011.

68. 'Clashes in Yemen spread to tribes beyond capital', *New York Times*, 26 May 2011.

69. 'Yemeni president wounded in palace attack', *New York Times*, 3 June 2011.

70. 'Citing medical needs, Yemeni leader goes to Saudi Arabia', *New York Times*, 4 June 2011.

71. 'Yemen uncertainty grows; leader's burns called severe', *New York Times*, 7 June 2011.

72. 'President's health adds to uncertainty in Yemen', *New York Times*, 2 July 2011.

73. 'Protesters in Yemen rejoice as leader goes to Saudi Arabia', *New York Times*, 5 June 2011.

74. Ibid.

75. 'Yemen president speaks on TV for first time since injury', *New York Times*, 7 July 2011.
76. Source C3, location withheld (2011).
77. Ibid.
78. 'Yemen's leader vows to return soon and defies calls for his ouster', *New York Times*, 16 August 2011.
79. Source C3, location withheld (2011).
80. 'Clashes erupt in Yemen, and a sit-in is attacked New York Times, 17 September 2011.
81. '8 months after first protests, Yemen enters dangerous new phase', *New York Times*, 21 September 2011.
82. Ibid.
83. Ibid.
84. Ibid.
85. 'Mortars fall on Yemeni capital as battles continue', *New York Times*, 20 September 2011.
86. '"Stop this massacre," Yemeni doctor begs', *Toronto Star*, 20 September 2011.
87. 'Clashes erupt for 2nd day in Yemeni capital, as troops fight defectors', *New York Times*, 19 September 2011.
88. Ibid.
89. Ibid.
90. 'Violence surges in Yemen despite call for cease-fire', *New York Times*, 24 September 2011.
91. 'Two-year manhunt led to killing of Awlaki in Yemen', *New York Times*, 30 September 2011. See also 'Inside America's dirty wars', *The Nation*, 24 April 2013.
92. 'Two-year manhunt led to killing of Awlaki in Yemen', *New York Times*, 30 September 2011.
93. 'Yemen notes its own role in US attack on militant', *New York Times*, 1 October 2011.
94. 'Among 3 women awarded Nobel Peace Prize, a nod to the Arab Spring', *New York Times*, 7 October 2011.

12. SHEEP RUSTLERS: ELITE RIVALRY AND URBAN WARFARE

1. Sarah Phillips, 'Cracks in the Yemeni system', *Middle East Report*, Middle East Research and Information Project (28 July 2005).
2. See www.alahmar.net for a photo of Sheikh Abdullah with his ten sons.
3. 'Suhail TV, la lucarne de la révolution yéménite', *Le Monde*, 8 October 2011.
4. 'Yemeni military battles opponents on two fronts', *New York Times*, 30 May 2011.

5. 'Yemen mobile firm Sabafon alleges govt vendetta', Reuters, 20 December 2011.
6. See http://wikileaks.org/cable/2009/08/09SANAA1617.html: 'Yemen: Hamid Al-Ahmar sees Saleh as weak and isolated, plans next steps', 31 August 2009.
7. Lunch with the FT: Amanda Staveley', Financial Times, 5 August 2011
8. Ibid.
9. In mid-May, Qatar withdrew from the GCC deal. See 'Huge protests in Yemen as talks drag on', New York Times, 13 May 2011.
10. 'Yemen's Hamid al-Ahmar urges President Saleh to leave', BBC News, 31 March 2011.
11. 'Hopes rise for Yemen breakthrough', Financial Times, 21 June 2011.
12. In Yemen's struggles, signs of tribal clout', Washington Post, 3 September 2011.
13. Source A3, Sana'a (2011).
14. Ibid.
15. Ibid.
16. Abdulkader Helal was a member of Sanhan, and former governor of Hadramaut and Ibb. He was killed in a Coalition airstrike in Sana'a in 2016. See 'Saudi-Led Airstrikes Blamed for Massacre at Funeral in Yemen', New York Times, 8 October 2016.
17. 'YEMEN: conflict generating more child soldiers', IRIN, 20 July 2011. See http://www.irinnews.org/Report/93281/YEMEN-Conflict-generating-more-child-soldiers. The Republican Guards, Central Security and the First Armoured Division all stand accused of enlisting child soldiers.
18. Ibid.
19. 'Yemen defected army abducts Reuters correspondent', Yemen Observer, 9 October 2011. Sudam was released a few days later, as part of a prisoner exchange for officers from the First Armoured Division.
20. Ali Mohsin said that PSO chief Ghalib al-Qamish, Dr Abdulkareem al-Iryani and Abdulkader Helal were all present at this meeting.
21. Source C3, location withheld (2011).

13. BREAKING THE BONES: POLITICS OF BALANCE AND THE 2012 TRANSITION

1. Daniel Yergin and Joseph Stanislaw, The Commanding Heights: The Battle for the World Economy (Free Press, 1998). For further information on Yemen's political economy, see 'Yemen: Corruption, Capital Flight and Global Drivers of Conflict', Chatham House Report, Ginny Hill, Peter Salisbury, Léonie Northedge and Jane Kinninmont, September 2013.

2. Source A3, Sana'a (2011).
3. Source B3, location withheld (2011).
4. Source E4, Sana'a (2012).
5. Source B3, location withheld (2011).
6. 'Dance of the daggers', *Foreign Policy*, October 2011. See http://www.foreignpolicy.com/articles/2011/10/24/the_dance_of_ daggers
7. Ibid.
8. See http://www.un.org/News/Press/docs/2011/sc10418.doc. htm
9. Source F3, location withheld (2011). Also see http://wikileaks. org/cable/2009/05/09RIYADH670.html: 'Special Advisor Holbrooke's meeting with Saudi Assistant Interior Minister', 17 May 2009.
10. Bernard Haykel, 'Saudi Arabia's Yemen dilemma', *Foreign Affairs*, 14 June 2011. See http://www.foreignaffairs.com/articles/67892/bernard-haykel/saudi-arabias-yemen-dilemma
11. Source F3, location withheld (2011).
12. 'Analysis: Saudi policy on Yemen and Syria seen floundering', Reuters, 13 July 2011.
13. Source F3, location withheld (2011).
14. Source C3, location withheld (2011).
15. Al-Rasheed, *Kingdom without Borders*.
16. Ginny Hill and Gerd Nonneman, 'Yemen, Saudi Arabia and the Gulf states: elite politics, street protests and regional diplomacy', Chatham House briefing paper, May 2011.
17. Ibid.
18. Source C3, location withheld (2011).
19. Ginny Hill and Gerd Nonneman, 'Yemen, Saudi Arabia and the Gulf states: elite politics, street protests and regional diplomacy', Chatham House briefing paper, May 2011.
20. Ibid.
21. Source H3, by email (2011); also Source Q3, location withheld (2011).
22. Source information withheld.
23. https://www.un.org/News/Press/docs/2011/sc10418.doc.htm
24. Source information withheld.
25. Bernard Haykel, 'Saudi Arabia's Yemen dilemma', *Foreign Affairs*, 14 June 2011.
26. 'Citing medical needs, Yemeni leader goes to Saudi Arabia', *New York Times*, 4 June 2011.
27. Yemen's electoral rolls were out of date. In 2006, there were 10.2 million voters on the list, but by 2012, the number of eligible voters was around 12.2 million. Hadi won 50 per cent of the real vote, around 60 per cent of the electoral roll, and 99 per cent of those who voted.

28. 'A new president and an "American sheikh" deal with post-Saleh Yemen', *Time*, 29 February 2012.
29. See http://www.un-foodsecurity.org/node/1307
30. Source C3, location withheld (2012).
31. Source S3, Sana'a (2012).
32. Ibid.
33. Source V3, Sana'a (2012).
34. Source U3, Sana'a (2012).
35. Source U3, Sana'a (2012).
36. See http://www.thebureauinvestigates.com/2012/07/02/yemen-strikes-visualised/
37. Hadi's decree followed a suicide bomb attack at a military parade ground in Sana'a, which killed more than 90 people.
38. UNSCR Resolution 2051.
39. Source details withheld (2012).
40. Source X3, Sana'a (2012).
41. Source A3, Sana'a (2012).
42. Source Y3, location withheld (2012).
43. Abdulrahmin al-Iryani was the first sunni to hold power in Sana'a.
44. Brehony, *Yemen Divided*, p. 114.
45. Source B4, Sana'a (2012).
46. Source X3, Sana'a (2012).
47. 'Yemen's Islamists and the revolution', *Foreign Policy*, 9 February 2009. See http://mideast.foreignpolicy.com/posts/2012/02/09/yemens_islamists_and_the_revolution; also 'Interview: Abdulwahab Al-Homaiqani, Secretary-General of the Yemeni Rashad Union', *Yemen Times*, 2 July 2012.
48. Source G4, Sana'a (2012).
49. Source G4, Sana'a (2012).
50. Source A4, Sana'a (2012).
51. Source F4, Sana'a (2012).
52. Halliday, *Arabia without Sultans*.
53. Dresch, *A History of Modern Yemen*, p. 198. See also 'Yemen: Corruption, Capital Flight and Global Drivers of Conflict', Chatham House Report, Ginny Hill, Peter Salisbury, Léonie Northedge and Jane Kinninmont, September 2013.
54. 'An upside down view of governance', Institute of Development Studies, 2010. See http://www.ids.ac.uk/go/news/an-upside-down-view-of-governance

14. INTERREGNUM: HADI'S FAILURE AND RISE OF THE HOUTHIS

1. Between the start of the 2011 and spring 2012, more than seventy

foreigners were taken hostage in Yemen, and more than 30 attempted or realized kidnaps occurred in Sana'a.—*Changing Tactics & Motives Kidnapping of Foreigners in Yemen 2010–2014*—A study conducted by Safer Yemen—May 2014

2. See Justice in Transition in Yemen—*A Mapping of Local Justice Functioning in Ten Governorates in Yemen*—United States Institute of Peace, 17 September, 2014.
3. 'With arms for Yemen rebels, Iran seeks wider mideast role', *New York Times*, 15 March 2012.
4. Source H3, Riyadh (2012).
5. 'Yemeni president: I love drones', *Foreign Policy*, 28 September 2012. See http://blog.foreignpolicy.com/posts/2012/09/28/yemens_president_warns_iran_endorses_us_drone_policy_0
6. 'A CIA veteran transforms US counterterrorism policy', *Washington Post*, 25 October 2012.
7. See also 'Drone strikes turn allies into enemies, Yemeni says', *New York Times*, 23 April 2013.
8. Source H4, location withheld (2012).
9. http://en.wikipedia.org/wiki/List_of_countries_by_Human_Development_Index
10. Mick Moore, 'Globalisation and power in weak states', *Third World Quarterly*.
11. 'Think global, act global: confronting global factors that influence conflict and fragility', OECD consultation paper, September 2012. http://www.oecd.org/officialdocuments/publicdisplaydocumentpdf/?cote=DCD/DAC(2012)36&docLanguage=En
12. Fragile States 2013: Resource Flows and Trends in a Shifting World (Paris, OECD).
13. Brian Whitaker, 'Arabs and the long revolution', 18 May 2011. See http://www.al-bab.com/arab/articles/text/arabs_and_the_ long_revolution.htm
14. Ibid.
15. Reforming Yemen's military, *Foreign Policy*—22 March, 2012. Yemen's presidential gambit, Foreign Policy—16 May 2012.
16. International Crisis Group, 'Yemen's military-security reform: seeds of new conflict?', International Crisis Group, *Middle East Report* 139 (4 April 2013).
17. Ibid.
18. Report of the secretary-general pursuant to Security Council Resolutions 2014 (2011) and 2051 (2012), June 2013.
19. The nine-member NDC Presidency consisted of: President Hadi (Chairman), Abdulkareem Al-Iryani (GPC), Yassen Saeed No'man

(YSP), Sultan Al-Atwani (Nasserites), Yassin Makkawi (Peaceful Southern Movement), Saleh bin Habra (Houthis), Abdul-Wahab Al-Ansi (Islah), Nadia Al-Saqqaf, and Abdullah Lamlas.

20. Hooria Mashoor served as minister for human rights from December 2011 to November 2014. By email, 2015.
21. London, 2015.
22. 'Process Lessons Learned in Yemen's National Dialogue', February 2014, United States Institute of Peace, Erica Gaston.
23. 'Federalism, conflict and fragmentation in Yemen', –Saferworld–October 2015.
24. 'Government Sits Idle As Dammaj Conflict Widens', Yemen Times, 26 December 2013.
25. The G10 constituted the permanent five members of the UN Security Council (US, UK, France, Russia, China), four Gulf countries (Saudi Arabia, UAE, Bahrain, Kuwait) and EU.
26. 'Federalism, conflict and fragmentation in Yemen', –Saferworld–October 2015.
27. Source A1, by Skype (2014).
28. http://www.ndc.ye/ndcdoc/NDC_Final_Communique.pdf
29. 'Process Lessons Learned in Yemen's National Dialogue', op. cit.
30. 'Changing Tactics & Motives Kidnapping of Foreigners in Yemen, 2010–2014'—A study conducted by Safer Yemen, May 2014.
31. 'Federalism, conflict and fragmentation in Yemen', –Saferworld–October 2015.
32. For a critique of Hadi's handling of the constitutional drafting process, see Yemen's Fraught Constitution Drafting Committee, Carnegie Endowment for International Peace, May 2 2014.
33. Source Z4, location withheld (2015).
34. Sources T4 and N4, location withheld (2015).
35. Source Z4, location withheld (2015).
36. 'Federalism, conflict and fragmentation in Yemen', –Saferworld–October 2015.
37. Source X3, location withheld (2014).
38. French security contractor shot dead in Sana'a as violence against foreigners rises, Financial Times, 5 May 2014.
39. Army breaks up protests as Yemen raises fuel prices, Reuters, July 30 2014.
40. Diary, London Review of Books, May 21 2005; Ghaith Abdul-Ahad, 'Yemen's Astonishing Financial Meltdown', Foreign Policy, 11 December 2014.
41. See Gregory D. Johnsen's account of his attempted kidnapping in Sana'a, 'My Last Day In Yemen', Buzzfeed News, 16 November 2014.

AQAP hostage Luke Somers, a joint British-American national, died during a rescue attempt by US special forces in December 2014.

42. Multiple interviews with diplomatic sources, June–September 2014
43. The al-Ahmar family have historic ties to Khamir. Khamir was also the site of tribal conferences in 1965 and 1975; the first to seek a truce in the civil war, and the second to challenge President al-Hamdi. See Robert D. Burrowes, *Historical Dictionary of Yemen* (Metuchen, NJ: Scarecrow Press, 2009), pp. 215–216.
44. 'Houthis Take Control Of Amran City', *Yemen Times*, 10 July 2014.
45. 'Yemen president says Houthis agree to return town to state control', Reuters, July 23 2014
46. 'Tens of thousands of Yemeni Houthis protest against fuel reform, government', Reuters, 18 August 2014.
47. Stacey Philbrick Yadav and Sheila Carapico, 'The Breakdown of the GCC Initiative', *Middle East Report*, MERIP, 273 (Winter 2014). 'Houthis on the Rise in Yemen', Carnegie Endowment for International Peace, 31 October, 2014.
48. Date and location withheld.
49. The special envoy's office had alerted the Security Council to the threat posed by the Houthis, as early as October 2013. After the Houthis took Amran in 2014, the Security Council held an emergency meeting on Yemen. According to one UN source: 'The special envoy wanted the Council to act before it was too late but the permanent five, in particular the US and the UK, had no interest in sanctioning the Houthis at that stage. Even after the Houthis had entered Sana'a and taken it over, the Security Council pushed back on calling it a coup. They were not interested in hearing that word, and they asked for the evidence that a coup had been carried out.'
50. Source B5, by email (2016).
51. http://supportyemen.org/.
52. 'Ali Mohsen's House: A Museum With Houthi Tour Guides', *Yemen Times*, 4 November 2014.
53. Sources L4, M4, N4, T4 and J3 (2015). In a leaked audio recording circulated on social media in February 2016, Saleh admitted helping the Houthis to reach Sana'a.
54. Source J3, by email (2016).
55. 'The Trouble With Yemen', 29 October 2014, Bloomberg Businessweek
56. Security Council 2140 Sanctions Committee Designates Three Individuals as Subject to Assets Freeze, Travel Ban—7 NOVEMBER 2014—SC/11636, http://www.un.org/press/en/2014/sc11636.doc.htm

57. Sources L4, N4, J3 (2015).
58. Sources L4, M4, J3 (2015).
59. Source M4, location withheld (2015).
60. 'Federalism, conflict and fragmentation in Yemen',–*Saferworld*–October 2015.
61. Source information withheld.
62. Source L4, location withheld (2015).
63. Source L4, location withheld (2015).
64. Hadi's failure to deliver on substantive commitments agreed by national dialogue delegates, set out in the Guarantees Document, http://ndc.ye/ndc_document.pdf (p287 onwards), included: failure to appoint a new government, following the conclusion of the national dialogue, in order to allow all political parties that participated in the talks to be partners in implementing the outcomes (ie. extending political representation beyond the signatories to the GCC agreement); failure to restructure the shoura council, as above; failure to restructure the Supreme Council for Elections and Referenda, to oversee new voter register; and failure to establish a national body to monitor implementation of national dialogue outcomes in compliance with the terms set out in the guarantees document (see above link), including irregularities in the appointments process, and the fulfilment of its mandate (specifically, in relation to the timing of the drafting of the constitution, see Yemen's Fraught Constitution Drafting Committee, Carnegie Endowment for International Peace, May 2 2014). Hadi's additional oversights included: failure to define the precise nature of dispute resolution mechanisms in the context of decision making by consensus, which was stipulated as the basis of all transition milestones; failure to implement agreed confidence-building measures promised to the southerners and the Houthis, with the exception of the cabinet's apology to the people of the south and Saada for previous wars; and failure to establish a special committee to inquire into violations committed during against protestors during the 2011 uprising. For their part, the Houthis violated their PNPA commitments to disarm, and cede control of territory to the state; on the contrary, they expanded south of Sana'a.
65. http://www.constitutionnet.org/files/yemen-draft_constitution-15jan2015-_english.pdf
66. If parliament had convened and accepted Hadi's resignation, power would have been transferred to the speaker, Yahya al-Ra'ii, a GPC politician who was close to Saleh. Although the Houthis were allied with Saleh, they were careful not to give him the upper hand.
67. 'Yemen crisis: UN warns rebels after they seize power', 7 February 2015, BBC News

68. Source L4, location withheld (2015).
69. Source L4, location withheld (2015).
70. Diary, *London Review of Books*, May 21 2015, Ghaith Abdul-Ahad. www.lrb.co.uk
71. 'U.S. Embassy Shuts in Yemen, Even as Militant Leader Reaches Out', *New York Times*, 10 February, 2015
72. Ibid.
73. In Yemen, Militants Are Increasingly Isolated, *New York Times*, 11 February, 2015
74. Yemen rebels seize US embassy equipment, *Financial Times*, 11 February 2015
75. Source L4, location withheld (2015).
76. Sources M4, J3, U1 (2015).
77. Sources J3 and I4 (2016).
78. Source I4, location withheld (2016).
79. 'Yemen crisis: Who are the Houthi rebels?', *Daily Telegraph*, 19 Jan 2015.
80. 'Yemen crisis: Islamic State claims Sanaa mosque attacks', BBC Online—21 March 2015.

15. SALEH'S REVENGE: THE RETURN TO POWER

1. 'Tired of War, Yemeni Bloggers Say, "Enough"', *New York Times*, 31 March, 2015
2. 'At Least 25 Die as Airstrike Sets Off Huge Blast in Yemen', *New York Times*, 20 April, 2015
3. On 19 March, fighter planes targeted the presidential palace in Aden, where Hadi was in residence. The Salehs and the Houthis had already secured the main access roads to the city, and they tried to seize Aden airport. On 24 March, Hadi requested that the GCC and the Arab League 'immediately provide support, by all necessary means and measures, including military intervention, to protect Yemen and its people from the continuing aggression by the Houthis'. The following day, with Saleh-Houthi forces advancing towards the presidential palace, Hadi fled to Oman.
4. http://www.operationrenewalofhope.com/
5. Paragraphs 137, 170 and 180. 'Letter dated 22 January 2016 from the Panel of Experts on Yemen established pursuant to Security Council resolution 2140 (2014) addressed to the President of the Security Council' (S/2016/73) http://www.un.org/ga/search/view_doc.asp?symbol=S/2016/73.
6. See OCHA's Yemen: Snapshot on Shipping and Food Imports

(a11 November 2015) http://reliefweb.int/sites/reliefweb.int/files/resources/ocha_yemen_shipment_snapshot_11112015.pdf

7. See OCHA's 4 facts on Yemen after 9 months of war (December 31 2015) http://reliefweb.int/report/yemen/4-facts-yemen-after-9-months-war and Press briefing notes on Yemen, Spokesperson for the UN High Commissioner for Human Rights, 5 January 2016 http://www.ohchr.org/EN/NewsEvents/Pages/DisplayNews.aspx?NewsID=16923&LangID=E#sthash.hbZEQGWe.dpuf

8. See OCHA's Yemen: Humanitarian Snapshot (29 December 2015) http://reliefweb.int/report/yemen/yemen-humanitarian-snapshot-29-december-2015

9. Comments made at a Chatham House workshop in London, November 2015, held under the Chatham House rule; cited following clearance with both the speaker, and the event organisers.

10. My thanks to Helen Lackner for these points, as above.

11. Paragraph 35. 'Letter dated 22 January 2016 from the Panel of Experts on Yemen established pursuant to Security Council resolution 2140 (2014) addressed to the President of the Security Council' (S/2016/73) http://www.un.org/ga/search/view_doc.asp?symbol=S/2016/73. For an alternative account of UN diplomacy, see www.innercitypress.com/ and search for articles on Yemen.

12. Relief Web, 'Yemen: Dengue Outbreak', June 2015

13. 'Postcard from Djibouti: Inshallah', *Harper's Magazine*, 4 June, 2015

14. 'Foreign Ground Troops Join Yemen Fight', *New York Times*, 3 August 2015 and 'UAE flexes military muscle alongside Saudis in Yemen', *Financial Times*, 11 August 2015.

15. 'Life under siege: inside Taiz, the Yemeni city being slowly strangled', *The Guardian*, 28 December 2015.

16. Paragraph 49. 'Letter dated 22 January 2016 from the Panel of Experts on Yemen established pursuant to Security Council resolution 2140 (2014) addressed to the President of the Security Council' (S/2016/73) http://www.un.org/ga/search/view_doc.asp?symbol=S/2016/73.

17. See 'Yemen crisis: President Hadi returns to Aden from exile', BBC Online, 22 September 2015; 'Yemen conflict: Exiled President Hadi returns to Aden', BBC Online, 17 November 2015

18. http://www.yementodaytv.net/

19. In 2014, Farea was ranked first in *The Guardian's* survey of global leaders under thirty in digital media. See 'The top 30 young people in digital media: Nos 10–1', *The Guardian*, 17 March 2014.

20. Yemen is shattered and peace seems a long way off. The world can't just watch on, '*The Guardian*, 22 October 2015.

21. See https://blogs.bsg.ox.ac.uk/2015/12/03/overcoming-failure-restoring-dignity/

22. See 'Where Next for Yemen? Perspectives on the Youth Movement', Chatham House event transcript July 2011 and The Role of Youth Activists in Yemen's Transition Process, Chatham House Workshop Summary, May 2012.

23. In September, UN Watch revealed that Saudi Arabia, a member of the UN Human Rights Council, had been selected to oversee the council's consultative group, an advisory committee that selects experts working on specific human rights issues. See www.unwatch.org

24. See S/RES/2140 (2014) and S/RES/2204 (2015)

25. I was initially appointed as the Panel's Coordinator, as well as armed groups expert. I served as Coordinator for just over three months, before I was replaced following the Panel's mid-term update to the sanctions committee in August.

26. For further information on the Panel's mandate and working methods, see 'Letter dated 22 January 2016 from the Panel of Experts on Yemen established pursuant to Security Council resolution 2140 (2014) addressed to the President of the Security Council' (S/2016/73) http://www.un.org/ga/search/view_doc.asp?symbol=S/2016/73. See also https://www.un.org/sc/suborg/en/sanctions/2140/panel-of-experts/work-and-mandate.

27. See S/RES/2216 (2015).

28. 'U.S. Support for Saudi Strikes in Yemen Raises War Crime Concerns', *Foreign Policy*, 15 October 2015.

29. 'The Government of Saudi Arabia: Air-to-Ground Munitions', Defense Security Cooperation Agency News Release, November 16 2015. See also 'A Saudi-American Reset', *New York Times*, 21 September 2015.

30. See letter from Stephen Twigg MP to Justine Greening MP, Secretary of State for International Development, February 2 2016, http://www.parliament.uk/business/committees/committees-a-z/commons-select/international-development-committee/. See also Press release: 'UK Government breaking the law supplying arms to Saudi say leading lawyers', Saferworld, 16 December 2015. The spike in arms sales came amid revelations that the UK government had identified Saudi Arabia as a 'priority market' for contracts in health, security, defence and justice. See 'Revealed: how UK targets Saudis for top contracts', *The Guardian*, 18 October 2015.

31. Source K4, New York (2015)

32. See http://www.securitycouncilreport.org/monthly-forecast/2015-08/yemen_17.php: "The UK, the penholder on Yemen, essentially ceded the role to Jordan and the GCC, which drafted the initial texts of res-

olution 2201 adopted in February, a 22 March presidential statement and the 14 April resolution 2216." This account of the drafting of 2216 is corroborated by source K4.

33. 'Saudi Objections Halt U.N. Inquiry of Yemen War', *New York Times*, 30 September, 2015. It subsequently came to light that Britain had conducted 'secret vote-trading deals' with Saudi Arabia to ensure that both states were successfully elected to the UN human rights council in 2013, for a two-year period (2014–2016). See UK and Saudi Arabia 'in secret deal' over human rights council place, *The Guardian*, 29 September 2015.

34. 'UK could be prosecuted for war crimes over missiles sold to Saudi Arabia that were used to kill civilians in Yemen', *Independent*, 28 November 2015.

35. See http://www.saferworld.org.uk/resources/view-resource/1023-the-lawfulness-of-the-authorisation-by-the-united-kingdom-of-weapons-and-related-items-for-export-to-saudi-arabia-in-the-context-of-saudi-arabias-military-intervention-in-yemen. In February, Campaign Against the Arms Trade challenged the UK government in the High Court on the legality of licensing arms exports for Saudi Arabia. See www.caat.org.uk/campaigns/stop-arming-saudi

36. 'Britain: Saudi Arabia's silent partner in Yemen's civil war', *The Independent*, 19 December 2015

37. 'Saudi-Led War in Yemen Frays Ties With the U.S.', *New York Times*, 22 December 2015.

38. Ibid.

39. Ibid.

40. Ibid.

41. In August 2015, Obama told reporters at a press briefing to discuss the nuclear deal that Iran had tried to discourage the Houthis from marching on Sana'a in 2014. He said: 'When the Houthis started moving, that wasn't on orders from [Iran]… That was an expression of the traditional Houthi antagonism towards Sanaa, and some of the machinations of the former president, [Ali Abdullah] Saleh, who was making common cause out of expediency with the Houthis… We watched as this proceeded. There were moments where Iran was actually urging potential restraint… Now, once the Houthis march in…. are [the Iranians] interested in getting arms to the Houthis and causing problems for the Saudis? Yes. But they weren't proceeding on the basis of, come hell or high water, we're moving on a holy war here.' He added: 'What we've seen, at least since 1979, is Iran making constant, calculated decisions that allow it to preserve the regime, to expand their influence where they can, to be opportunistic, to create

what they view as hedges against potential Israeli attack, in the form of Hezbollah and other proxies, in the region. I think what Iran has been doing in Yemen is a perfect illustration of this.' See 'Iran Tried To Stop Houthi Rebels In Yemen, Obama Says', *Huffington Post*, 6 August 2015.

42. Paragraph 24. 'Letter dated 22 January 2016 from the Panel of Experts on Yemen established pursuant to Security Council resolution 2140 (2014) addressed to the President of the Security Council' (S/2016/ 73) http://www.un.org/ga/search/view_doc.asp?symbol=S/2016/ 73.

43. Paragraphs 78–82. 'Letter dated 22 January 2016 from the Panel of Experts on Yemen established pursuant to Security Council resolution 2140 (2014) addressed to the President of the Security Council' (S/2016/73) http://www.un.org/ga/search/view_doc.asp?symbol= S/2016/73.

44. Ibid. See paragraph 15 for an account of the Panel's attempt to travel to Yemen.

45. Russia's position on Yemen was tempered by Moscow's decision to sign a series of lucrative cooperation agreements with Riyadh in June 2015, including nuclear technology sharing. Meanwhile, Russia had more pressing priorities in Syria.

46. Source Y4, location withheld (2015). See also 'Quiet Support for Saudis Entangles U.S. in Yemen', *New York Times*, 13 March, 2016.

47. See UN report into Saudi-led strikes in Yemen raises questions over UK role, *The Guardian*, Wednesday 27 January.

48. 'Letter dated 27 January 2017 from the Panel of Experts on Yemen addressed to the President of the Security Council' (S/2017/81) http://www.un.org/ga/search/view_doc.asp?symbol=S/2017/81

49. Ibid. Paragraph 95.

50. Ibid. Paragraph 62.

51. For examples of Houthi claims of responsibility for artillery strikes and cross-border raids targeting Saudi military installations in Asir and Jizan, see Yemen News Agency statements on June 2, June 7, June 15, July 2, July 22, August 10, August 17, August 24, August 30, September 5, September 7, September 13, September 16, September 19, September 22, September 29, October 19, October 22, and October 24 2015. www.sabanews.net/en/

52. Source information withheld. However, there are conflicting views on this issue: that Riyadh was encouraging Saleh, Hadi and Ali Mohsin to reach an agreement with each other in order to unite against the Houthis, as late as July 2014 (source U1); that the Saudi leadership was preoccupied with impending succession issues, following from

King Abdullah's gradual decline in good health, and unable to devote sufficient attention to the impending crisis in Yemen (source Q4); that the Houthis reached out to the Saudis but Riyadh refused to talk (sources K4 and Q4); that Western embassies in Sana'a were under-staffed and unable to maintain a wide contact base in Yemen (source R4); that Western embassies relied on tried-and-tested contacts who often told officials what they wanted hear and confirmed their analy-sis, in order to preserve their own privileged status as interlocutors (source K4); that Western capitals ignored warning reports from their Sana'a embassies, partly because senior officials in London, Paris, D.C. and New York already had their hands full with crises in Syria and Libya (source P4); and that, in general, Western diplomats, in post and in capital, underestimated the Houthis (sources R4 and K4). As source M4 told me: 'Everyone knew the Houthis would come to Sana'a but they deliberately closed their eyes.'

53. Source P4, location withheld (2015); corroborated by source K4, loca-tion withheld (2016).

54. Sources U1, B3, K4, L4, M4, N4 (2015), and others.

55. 'The Next King of the Saudis: Salman, the Family Sheriff', *The Daily Beast*, 23 January 2015, and King Salman's Shady History, *Foreign Policy*, 27 January 2015.

56. Source information withheld (2015).

57. In May 2015, Saudi Arabia created a 10-member supreme council for Saudi Aramco, headed by Mohammed bin Salman. See Analysis: 'King Salman Consolidates Family Grip On Saudi Power And Aramco', *Platts*, 6 May 2015.

58. 'Saudi royal calls for regime change in Riyadh', *The Guardian*, 28 September 2015.

59. 'No more new cars or furniture, says king as oil slump forces cuts on Saudi Arabia', *The Guardian*, 8 October 2015.

60. *Yemen: Corruption, Capital Flight and Global Drivers of Conflict*, Chatham House Report, Ginny Hill, Peter Salisbury, Léonie Northedge and Jane Kinninmont, September 2013.

61. Relations between Sana'a and Teheran were strained during Saleh's alli-ance with Saddam Hussein in the Iran-Iraq war, and later by the Saada wars.

62. Source information withheld.

63. Source information withheld.

64. Saudi Arabia rejected Saleh's proposal. See Asiri: 'Saudi Arabia Will Not Negotiate with Saleh', *Asharq al-Awsat*, 10 January 2016.

65. 'UAE told UK: crack down on Muslim Brotherhood or lose arms deals', *The Guardian*, 6 November 2105.

66. The Emiratis appeared to hold to these reservations, perhaps with ambivalence, in spite of a ballistic missile strike by Saleh-Houthi forces that killed more than forty Emirati troops stationed in Marib in September 2016.

67. Christopher Cramer, *Civil War Is Not A Stupid Thing*, London: Hurst, 2006, pp. 279–289.

68. Hadi appointed Ali Mohsin as his vice president in April 2016.

69. Source B3, location withheld (2015).

70. 'Yemen: A battle for the future', Remote Control Project, Ginny Hill and Baraa Shiban, October 2016.

71. 480,000 b/d, 2002; 145,000 b/d 2014; 50,000 b/d 2015. See BP Statistical Review of World Energy, 2015.

72. Source O3, by Skype (2015).

73. See 'The Republic of Yemen: Unlocking the Potential for Economic Growth, A Country Economic Memorandum', October 2015, World Bank, Middle East and North Africa Region Macroeconomics and Fiscal Management Global Practice.

74. Yemen demand for solar energy skyrockets, Middle East Eye, 15 May 2015.

75. With the author's permission. The latest World Bank estimate of Yemen's population is 26.8 million. See http://data.worldbank.org/indicator/SP.POP.TOTL?locations=YE&view=chart

INDEX

al-Abab, Adil, 146
Abbottabad, Pakistan, 211
ABC News, 153
Abdul Ahad, Ghaith, 272
Abdulaziz 'Ibn Saud', King of Saudi
  Arabia, 12, 15, 16, 18, 19, 21,
  239, 287
Abdul Ghani, Abdul Aziz, 232
Abdul Hamid II, Ottoman Sultan,
  119
Abdullah bin Abdulaziz, King of
  Saudi Arabia, 195, 231, 238,
  239, 241, 286, 287, 289
Abdullah bin Hassan, 26
Abdullah bin Yahya, 16
Abdullah II, King of Jordan, 78
Abdulmutallab, Omar Farouq, 139,
  141, 144–6
Abu Bara, 123
Abu Hassan, 121
Abu Jandal, 122–3, 124–5, 128–34
Abyan, Yemen, 45, 120, 138, 159,
  167–8, 238, 243, 245, 277
Abyssinia, see Ethiopia
Aden, Yemen, 3, 156, 159, 160–73,
  256, 272
  British colonial era, 11, 13, 14,
    16, 18, 20, 23, 34, 36–8, 40,
    42, 89, 114, 155–6, 158, 163

Arab Spring uprising (2011),
  208
al-Ayyam, 163–6
Civil War (1994), 47, 49, 163,
  262
Civil War (2015–), 8, 274, 275,
  277–8, 292
Dubai Ports World, 108, 161
federalism, 47, 264
PDRY era (1967–90), 44–6, 71,
  120, 248
al-Qasr hotel bombing (2015),
  278, 279
refugee camp, 100
riots (2010), 150–51
smuggling, 90, 98, 267
southern movement protests
  (2009), 156, 163
USS Cole bombing (2000), 94,
  108, 121, 124–6, 128, 139,
  161
Aden-Abyan Islamic Army, 121,
  130, 167
Adenpress, 158
Afghanistan, 155
aid, 149
heroin trade, 102
al-Qaeda, 120–25, 129–30,
  133–34

359

INDEX

INDEX

INDEX

and patronage, 2, 39, 45, 52–67, 107, 136, 157
in police force, 162
Saleh, xii, 1, 3, 4, 45, 54, 56, 64, 83–4, 105–17, 157, 179, 252, 291
and southern movement, 162, 165, 170
Yemen Parliamentarians Against Corruption, 116, 117
counter-terrorism unit (CTU), 79–83, 138–9, 149, 209–10, 216
Craig, Iona, xii, 283
Cramer, Christopher, 290, 292
Crater district, Aden, 150–1, 163, 165, 166, 169, 277
Crescent Hotel, Aden, 162
Cuba, 35, 82, 167
Cuban Missile Crisis (1962), 24
cult of personality, 77, 158
Cultural Revolution (1966–76), 40
Czech Republic, 112
Czechoslovakia, 29

Daallo Airlines, 94
Daily Telegraph, 26, 29–30, 31
Dammaj, Sa'ada, 185–6, 250, 262, 277
Dar al-Salaam, 72–75
Dar es Salaam, Tanzania, 122, 123, 126
'Demands of the People, The', 18
democracy, 1, 4
Arab Spring (2011), 212, 225, 229
and corruption, 113–17
elections, *see under* elections
and freedom of speech, 165–6
and Houthis, 201, 268
and southern movement, 156, 160–61, 170–71

and unification (1990), 48–50, 52
Democratic Republic of Yemen (1994), 49
dengue fever, 277
Destiny's Child, 96
Dhahran Air Field Agreement (1945), 16
Dhala, Yemen, 167, 168
Dhamar, Yemen, 73, 109, 264, 278
Dharan, Saudi Arabia, 19
diesel, 5, 101, 117, 162, 214, 265, 266
Djibouti, 94, 277
Document of Pledge and Accord (1994), 49
Dome of the Rock, al-Aqsa Mosque, 74
Dresch, Paul, 10, 17, 37
drones, 130, 135, 216, 245, 257, 261, 273
droughts, 18, 95
Drug Enforcement Agency, US, x
drugs, *see* narcotics
Dubai, United Arab Emirates, 94, 96, 114, 127
Dubai Ports World, 108, 161
Dubai World, 94
PCP Capital Partners, 221

East Germany (1949–90), 46
Eastern Province, Saudi Arabia, 37
economies of scale, 84
Eddy, William, 16
Edgware Road, London, x
Egypt, 13, 15
1925 Geneva Protocol for the Prohibition of Poisonous Gases, 29–30
1944 Alexandria Protocol, 15
1945 Cairo conference on pan-Arab constitution, 15

INDEX

INDEX

INDEX

INDEX

INDEX

INDEX

192–3; Hamid al-Ahmar meets with US official, 172; Saleh meets with Brennan, 138, 147, 153; Houthi incursion into Saudi Arabia, 194–5; US Tomahawk missile strike in al-Ma'jalah, 138; US missile strikes in Shabwa, 139, 144; Northwest Airlines bomb plot, 5, 139–41, 144–6

2010 Mobley detained, 142; Houthis agree ceasefire, 195, 199; German hostages released from Sa'ada, 200; Saleh strikes deal with Petraeus, 6, 149; raid on *al-Ayyam*, 165; twentieth anniversary of unification, 171; al-Shabwani killed in US missile strike, 150; Aden riots, 150–51; death of Badr al-Din al-Houthi, 197

2011 Arab spring protests, xii, 1, 2, 3, 4, 55, 56, 77, 200, 204–5, 279–80; Saleh offers concessions, 205; protests intensify, 206; al-Zindani calls for caliphate, 206–7; Saleh offers further concessions, 207; CSF crackdown on protesters, 208; snipers fire on protesters in Sana'a, 6, 208–9; Ali Mohsin declares support for uprising, 6, 209, 221, 237; Saleh and Ali Mohsin agree to step down, 209, 229, 234, 290; Saleh negotiates transition, x, 1, 3, 7, 209–12, 229–30; Saleh defers transition deal; violent clashes in Sana'a, 7, 213, 219–20, 222, 238; Saleh injured in bomb blast, 7, 213; Saudis broker ceasefire

in Hasaba, 239; Saleh evacuated to Saudi Arabia, 213–15; Saleh grants Hadi negotiation powers, 215; violent clashes resume in Sana'a, 215–16, 240; arrival of UN envoy, 216; return of Saleh, 216; al-Awlaki killed in US missile strike, 216–17; Karman awarded Nobel Peace Prize, 217, 229; shelling resumes in Hasaba, 223; return of Benomar, 240; Saleh signs transition deal, 240–41; Islah attacked in Change Square, 249–50; Basindwa becomes prime minister, 248

2012 domestic immunity agreement, 242; Hadi becomes president, x, 3, 7, 241, 242, 255; Ansar al-Sharia attack in Abyan, 245; Hadi demotes Saleh allies, 244; return of Benomar, 244; US escalates drone strikes, 245; Ammar dismissed from NSB, 245–6; Hadi works with Pentagon on military professionalization, 246; Hadi's Washington speech, 256–7

2013 military spending increased, 260; Republican Guard and First Armoured Division disbanded, 260; Ahmed Ali appointed UAE ambassador, 260, 288; Ali Mohsin appointed presidential advisor, 260; launch of national dialogue conference, 260–62; death of Mothana, 281; Houthis advance towards Sana'a, 262